REVOLT AGAINST DESTINY

Paul A. Carter

REVOLT
AGAINST DESTINY

An Intellectual History
of the United States

Columbia University Press
NEW YORK

Small portions of this book were previously published in:

"Out West" and "The Golden West," In Karen J. Dahood editor, *Out West: The Literature of Action* and *Golden West: The Literature of Comprehension* (Tucson, Arizona: Arizona Historical Society, Co-sponsor, with the Tucson Public Library, of "Writers of the Purple Sage," a project funded in part by the National Endowment for the Humanities, 1983).

"And Adam Gave Names . . . To Every Beast of the Field," *Antioch Review* (Summer 1985) vol. 43, no. 3.

The author is grateful for permission to reprint these extracts here.

COLUMBIA UNIVERSITY PRESS
New York   Oxford
Copyright © 1989 Paul A. Carter

Library of Congress Cataloging-in-Publication Data

Carter, Paul Allan
Revolt against destiny/Paul A. Carter.
   p.   cm.
Bibliography: p.
Includes index.
ISBN 0-231-06616-3 (alk. paper)
1. United States—Intellectual life.
2. United States—Politics and government.
I. Title.
E169.1.C286   1989
973—dc20

89-7054
CIP

Book design by Jennifer Dossin

Casebound editions of Columbia University Press books are Smyth-sewn and printed on permanent and durable acid-free paper

Printed in the United States of America

10 9 8 7 6 5 4 3 2 1

This Book Is For Brian Carter

Let him not quit his belief that a popgun is a popgun, though the ancient and honorable of the earth affirm it to be the crack of doom.

Ralph Waldo Emerson

CONTENTS

Contents

REVOLT AGAINST DESTINY

The freedom then of man, and liberty of acting according to his own will, is grounded on his having reason.

John Locke

Truth, in the great practical concerns of life, is so much a question of the reconciling and combining of opposites, that . . . it has to be made by the rough process of a struggle between combatants fighting under hostile banners.

John Stuart Mill

ONE

The Dream of the West

Early in the modern age a new people emerged, to take their place in the world alongside long-existent others: Greeks and Africans, Russians and Mongols, Polynesians and Japanese. Who were these new folk, these Americans? asked a Frenchman, Hector St. John de Crèvecoeur, in 1782. Other foreign observers, and the Americans themselves, have continued to ask that question. This book will ask it once more, and propose a few answers of its own.

While asking *who* the Americans were and are, one must also ask *where*. As one of their own poets has written, "The land was ours before we were the land's." Inhabitants of a surprising place that lacked the signposts abundant in the old country, shaped as much by a heritage of attitudes about "the West" that they brought over from abroad as by the uncharted land itself, Americans confronted "nature"—a word they loaded with special meanings—in a way that would not have been possible in the older, more homogeneous and hierarchical settled cultures they had left behind. Science would in due course demythologize their Romantically conceived natural locale—but never completely. Even in present-day high-tech urban milieus where Nature can (for a time) be ignored, the remembrance of it continues inescapably to haunt Americans' dreams.

1. Imagined America

In the beginning was the land; and the land was clean. Along one rocky shore, to the east, the lobsters scuttled at low tide; off another, to the west, the sea lions mated and fought and cried. The skies darkened behind clouds of passenger pigeons; the earth shuddered beneath armies of buffalo. Shaggy trees marched all down the length of Manhattan and crowded the shores of Lake Michigan; clear, smogless air shimmered in heat-haze over sagebrush hills in California or blew in hurricane violence across empty beaches in Florida. An orbiting satellite, as it passed over other parts of the planet, might have picked out the handiwork of human beings: a great wall winding over the north Chinese hills, or the triangle-faced tombs crumbling in the Egyptian desert—but not here.

Far to the south, in the Valley of Mexico, that spying eye might have picked out the smoke of many fires, gardens, temples; here in the North American wilderness it could have discerned only the momentary gleam of a paddle silently dipped and raised, or at night the flickering of a campfire. This was not yet a "New World," named in contrast to an "Old." To its own inhabitants it was simply *the* world; there was no other. To the inhabitants of that other hemisphere, this was at most a mass of rolling, uncharted water, if indeed it existed at all.

Europe, Asia, Africa; for centuries they had been the solid content of western geography. Old maps show them over and over again: Europe on the left, Asia on the right, Africa on the bottom; the coasts of Greece and Italy and the Crimea tolerably well known and drawn; the silklands of China and the philosophic borders of India vaguely sketched in. Mapmakers arranged the three great continents on a flat disk, bordered neatly by the ring of Ocean, and beyond that only the world's edge. By Pythagoras's time (sixth century B.C.) the flat disk was swelling into a ball; and orderly Greek minds began to break out of the Europe-Africa-Asia triad. To balance the great mass of land in the northern hemisphere, some reasoned, there must be a corresponding unknown landmass to the south; a *terra australis incognita*, lying beneath unseen southern stars—*antarktikos*, literally "opposite to the bear" whose hindquarters point the way to the Pole. For generations a vast "Antarctica" would lurk at the lower edge of the world-mass, as would a murky "Hyperborea" at its upper border. Neither, however, had much to do with the perceived scientific reality: Europe, Asia, Africa. So rationally balanced a microcosmos held no room for as wild and disruptive a concept as America.

The inquisitive community of librarians and tinkerers who gathered at Alexandria in the third century B.C. greatly expanded their circumscribed world's outer limits. Eratosthenes of Cyrene, working in Alexandria's great library, had access to vast amounts of information, as any librarian does; no mere bibliographic drudge, this Athenian-trained savant had also the wit to put some of it together. Five hundred miles south of Alexandria at the First Cataract of the Nile, he knew, the sun at noon on June 21st stood exactly at the zenith, striking all the way down into a deep well. In Alexandria on the same day at the same time, an obelisk under the same sun cast a shadow—a discrepancy of 7 1/2 degrees, or 1/48 of a 360-degree circle. Therefore, the distance between Alexandria and the First Cataract must be 1/48 of the distance around the Earth, which works out to 24,000 miles—a remarkably educated guess.

The Christian centuries that followed did not simply drive all such knowledge into outer darkness, as is often assumed. Pundits whose piety outran their common sense might indeed draw maps of a flat earth neatly quartered by inscribing an "O" around a "T" (the initials for *Orbis Terrae*, the circle of the earth), with Europe, Africa, and Asia drawn into the spaces thus bounded; in the eleventh century it was common to assert that the intersection of those lines lay at Jerusalem. But the best minds of late antiquity, and even of the so-called "Dark Ages," knew better. In the invasions of barbarians and the plunderings of emperors they lost much, but they never really forgot the sphericity of the Earth. Dante's imagined world is unmistakably Catholic-Christian—on the unknown far side of the planet, directly opposite Jerusalem, stands the Mount of Purgatory—but it is just as unmistakably rational and Greek. Faced, for example, with the problem of the Antipodes—the realm, on the opposite side of the earth from ourselves, where if people existed they would have to walk about with their heads downward—the author of the *Divine Comedy* gave his round Earth a center of gravity, toward which the Antipodeans' feet point, even as ours do. At the end of the *Inferno*, after the narrator and his guide, Virgil, have descended all the way to the bottom of hell's pit, they "pass the point to which all gravities from every part are drawn," the center of the Earth—out of which they must climb laboriously upward to the other side, to behold again the stars.

It was not lack of knowledge that held back the Europeans from exploring the New World in the Middle Ages, any more than it was lack of knowledge that more recently has held back some of us, their heirs, from exploring outer space. Yes, they knew they could sail to the Antipodes, as we knew we could fly to Mars, but why bother? St. Augustine thought it "utterly absurd" to dream of voyaging "across the immense tract of the ocean" to the planet's far

3

side. For Dante, eight centuries later, it was not absurd to dream of such a voyage, but it would still be an act of impiety. In Canto 26 of the *Inferno* he made Odysseus set forth on one last journey, telling his trusty shipmates in true Greek-scientific fashion as they passed through the portals of the Mediterranean and headed Westward that they "were not formed to live like brutes, but to follow virtue and knowledge." And so they sailed on, and "saw the other pole with all its stars," and foundered in a downdraft from the Mount of Purgatory, and so Odysseus ended up among the Evil Counsellors in the Eighth Circle of Hell.

Beyond the neatly drawn logical boundaries of Greek speculation and the vigorous "thou-shalt-nots" of churchly apologists, however, at the disorderly fringe between consciousness and dream, the idea of a West beyond the Pillars of Hercules continued to cast its subversive spell. Homer sang of "the Elysian plain at the world's end," where "day after day the West Wind's tuneful breeze comes in from the Ocean;" Hesiod wrote of "the Hesperian nymphs who guard the beautiful golden apples and the trees which bear that fruit on the further shore of the great Ocean"; Plato wrote of an island in the Atlantic Ocean, "larger than Libya and Asia put together," called Atlantis. Christian bards picked up such themes also, and sang of blessed St. Brendan's Isle somewhere west of Ireland. Long before America came into focus as a known place on an unambiguous map, it existed in the imagination of the Old World as a powerful mythic idea.

2. Explorers Into Reality

"America is, above all, about ideas and dreams," T. H. White has written of the America of 1980, and some of those dreams far antedate the America of 1776, or even of 1492. A thousand years ago the Icelandic *Saga of Eric the Red* was already, in a sense, an American story:

> Leif put to sea when his ship was ready for the voyage. For a long time he was tossed upon the ocean, and came upon lands of which he had previously no knowledge. There were self-sown wheat fields and vines growing there. . . . Leif found men upon a wreck, and took them home with him . . . and procured quarters for them all during the winter. In this wise he showed his nobleness and goodness, since he introduced Christianity into the

country, and saved the men from the wreck; and he was called Leif the Lucky ever after.

"Already present in this medieval account," comments the church historian Sydney Ahlstrom, "are the major themes of the American saga: a religiously oriented sense of mission, an abundant land, a noble hero, and a favoring Providence. Even the vital ingredient of luck was there."

Four centuries later, as European explorers actually did begin in large numbers to cross the seas and climb the mountains of what they named the New World, they brought the inherited America of the imagination with them in their baggage, and imposed it upon the actual America that they found. They made, and lost, fortunes, energized by their assurance of the endless bounty of nature. They built plantations in the river valleys and cities on the coastal hills, reassured against storms and smallpox and Indian raids by the belief that here in the new West happiness, or at least the free pursuit of it, was certain. They strewed their bones on sea bottoms and among the trees and in swampy muck, for not even Americans could in truth banish death; but they left on the raw new shores their progeny, whose children's children would invoke for each new American generation a mystique of eternal youth.

Yet ideas and dreams cannot grow too much out of touch with reality; else life would become, in Thorstein Veblen's words, "insufferably grotesque." To cross the seas and climb the mountains and build their towns the new Americans perforce brought with them in their boats the Old World skills of carpentry and blacksmithing, codfishing and cattle driving, navigation and statecraft. The *Niña*, *Pinta*, and *Santa Maria*, as they drove on in the late summer of 1492 toward the unknown West, were crewed not by jailbirds, as folklore has it, but by competent, experienced sailors.

The old tale of Columbus's crewmen cowering in terror lest they sail off the world's edge, and raising a mutiny to compel their obsessed commander to turn back, is one of many such stories which no amount of historical debunking seems able to put down. The boy Columbus of schoolbook fantasy, learning on the Genoa docks as if for the first time that a ship sailing out of sight goes hull-down over the horizon, is likewise a modern schoolteacher's invention; *any* experienced sailor knew as much. Those crewmen of 1492 did indeed mutiny, as the legend has it, but from a perfectly rational motive; their commander had by that time been sailing

5

downwind before the uninterrupted Northeast Trades for thirty days, and if the wind never was going to shift, how in God's name were they going to get back? Twice they had made false landfalls, and after the longest oceanic voyage thus far in history they were still charging blindly on into the unknown. Imagine "a modern chart with America blotted out," suggests Samuel Eliot Morison, and it becomes easier to understand those sailors' state of mind. They had long since passed the point at which their skipper had predicted they would find an Asian shore. Autocratic, visionary, pigheaded, and single-minded, Christopher Columbus may have cast himself in the role of a Christian knight crusading *in partibus infidelium,* but to the men up on the forecastle he must have seemed at times more like Captain Ahab.

Two days after the mutiny, which the commander apparently quelled by promising to turn back if nothing were sighted in the next two or three days, the three small ships made landfall in the New World. The flat, unspectacular island that rose out of the west in the small hours of October 12, 1492 was not, of course, a new world to those who already lived there. Its inhabitants called it *Guanahaní,* after the iguanas that crawled over its sands; but Columbus, unfurling Ferdinand's and Isabella's banners, named it *San Salvador.* Both the island's reptiles and its people have vanished; the conqueror's idea of what the West should be came crashing down on the West's local reality.

For the moment the mythic West, the west of Plato and St. Brendan, dropped from sight. In its place, the exploring admiral substituted the farther East, a region which—after a fashion—he already knew. In the reports Columbus wrote his King and Queen back home he frantically seized upon ways that native American societies, coastlines, or place-names plausibly resembled the geographic hearsay and garbled map-lore of the Old World. Cuba, he declared, must be Japan. No; it was a province of China, and so the expedition's official interpreter must march off to the interior of the island with a Latin passport and letters of introduction from Ferdinand and Isabella to the Great Khan. Three more voyages failed to break the Admiral's obsession; a sketch map drawn by his brother after their journeyings were over still showed a range behind the Honduran coast that Don Diego Columbus labeled the "Chinese Mountains." Similarly, the chili peppers found along the Costa Rican coast seemed evidence that the Spaniards had come to the spicelands of the East Indies. From Panama—or the Malayan Peninsula, as he supposed—Columbus wrote of peoples nearby who were said to possess mounted cavalry and warships equipped with cannon; and from South America he came back with the tallest tale of all: he had been sailing, he affirmed, very near to the Terrestrial Paradise.

Even in so credulous an age that was a bit much; "there is no indication," Morison wryly acknowledges, "that even the pious Isabella was impressed with the notion that the Garden of Eden had been annexed to her empire." What did impress the Admiral's royal sovereigns, and kept them underwriting his and other madmen's expeditions to the New World, was gold. Those simple people the invaders first encountered set no great store by it, save as ornament; but they quickly learned that these mad Europeans would kill or enslave them for it. On his first Christmas in the New World Columbus wrote that the gold and spices his men were finding would enable his King and Queen within three years "to go and conquer the Holy Sepulchre." Like other Christian sovereigns before them, Ferdinand and Isabella got nowhere near Jerusalem; but closer to home their heirs' New World wealth flowed out and became Old World power. Spanish historians continued into modern times to describe the years of Spain's European hegemony after the time of Columbus as *el siglo de oro*—"the century of gold." Without that gold, Morison argues, Spain's sovereigns might well have written off the Columbus expeditions as a bad investment; and would modern America's sovereign people in the 1970s have been quite so quick to write off manned expeditions into space had Neil Armstrong found similar treasure on the moon?

The native Americans in the path of the greedy newcomers quickly learned to humor them: tell the strangers what they want to hear; this will get them temporarily away from our previously untroubled villages. Yes, the gold or the Great Khan or the Fountain of Youth is just down the road a little way. And so the *conquistadores* went on questing into the unknown. Some fared badly, some fared well; on the mainland up in the Valley of Mexico, it turned out, there was a lootable empire, but further on into North America, near the Grand Canyon, where legend located the Seven Cities of Cibolá, reality turned out to be a handful of modest, dusty pueblos. Still further north were tall prairie grass; black oak and shagbark hickory; spruce and hackmatack and white pine. And no gold.

Save for Montezuma's domain the New World really was *new*;

and the visitors from the other side of the planet had to incorporate its newness into their centuries-old fantasies of the Atlantic West. America was not another Europe, Africa, or Asia. It was the wilderness; the Great American Desert; the virgin land. And that rawness in turn had an impact upon the Old World's perception of its own past; for "in the beginning," John Locke would write two centuries after Columbus's landfall, "all the world was America." Societies and governments begin not with mythic law-givers but in a state of nature, and one can make of them what one will.

Even America, however, was not "America," in quite the sense Locke was talking about. It was certainly in no "state of nature," for it already had a society—many societies, in fact; as diverse— and, in some cases, as mutually antagonistic—as Briton and Frenchman, or Christian and Turk. A bewildering variety of languages, cultural forms, works of art, social organizations, religions covered a world which, on its own terms, was not "New" at all. Typically, a native American tribal group's name for itself translated simply as "The People," as though there were no other. From the invading Europeans' standpoint, on the other hand, these various new found peoples ought not to have been there at all. To the extent that they fitted into Europe's own traditions in any way, they played the role of the Canaanites who stood in the path of the people of ancient Israel as they entered the Promised Land. We do not have ready access to the Canaanite version of Joshua's invasion; but we do know what happened to the American Indians.

3. Wilderness or Paradise?

Early accounts treated the new found lands with a terrible ambivalence. From the beginning the European experience in the New World was an encounter, writes Howard Mumford Jones, with "the unpredictable, the abnormal, the inhuman, the cruel, the savage, and the strange"; the uncorrupted natural garden trembled on the verge of mutation into an untamed and horrible jungle, "a land of the incredible, the immeasurable, the unpredictable, and the horrifying," where "the extreme thing seemed to happen more often than not."

The age of exploration generated back home in Europe a sensational literature based upon these new, extreme expectations. It ranged from the thoroughly plausible to the entirely outrageous.

8

Alongside the factual narratives of judicious Jesuit missionaries and the commonsensical journals of Captain Cook, far more fanciful accounts mirrored the discovery and exploration of the New World: travel tales of fantastic voyages to problematical places where one might encounter creatures as other-wordly as any imagined later on in outer space, or human societies, some of them wondrously utopian (the very word "utopia" dates from this period) and others afflicted with problems—subject to satiric exaggeration—not unlike one's own.

What were they really looking for, those perennial romantics who went wandering off to find something lost behind the Ranges? Gold and glory; the spread of the religion of the Cross; the might of empire—but also, the sheer wonder of a world dramatically different from their own. In a way the transgressing Europeans' own religious tradition prepared them to encounter the extreme thing. The Promised Land of milk and honey, in Judaeo-Christian lore, alternates with (and easily shifts into) the Wilderness, where the children of Israel wandered for forty years and where Christ fasted and was tempted for forty days.

Sometimes a voice spoke for the rational, Greco-Roman moderate side of the European synthesis. Thomas Haricot, a voyager to Sir Walter Raleigh's ill-fated Virginia colony, returned home to regale his fellow Britons in 1588 with *A Brief and True Report of the New Found Land of Virginia*, praising the "fine grasse as good as ever we saw any in England"; "the excellent temperature of the ayre there at all seasons, much warmer than in England, and never so violently hot as sometimes is under & between the Tropikes, or nere them"; and the fertile soil in which "our kinde of fruits, rootes, and hearbes may bee there planted and sowed, as some have ben alreadie, and prove wel." But not all accounts of the New World were thus suffused with a realtor's optimism. In 1579, notes historian Benjamin Keen, an atlas of New Spain compiled by the Flemish mapmaker Abraham Ortelius gave Old World readers a far more ominous image of the New than they could have gleaned from the enthusiastic promotional pages of Haricot: a nude allegorical figure representing America, "gorged with human flesh," reclining on the ground and holding a severed human head.

Paradise or Wilderness; horn of plenty or Earthly purgatory; nodding grain or severed heads—which was the real America? "In a sense," writes Leo Marx, "America was *both* Eden and a howling desert; the actual conditions of life in the New World did lend plausibility to both images." It seemed a land where all things were possible, both for good and for ill. Perhaps, Europeans hoped, they could come storming into the new lands and find or make a middle ground, free from both the ancient corruptions of Old World civilization and the destructive menace of the New World wasteland. Shakespeare's play *The Tempest* (*ca.* 1611), in which "redemption is made póssible by a journey away from Europe into the wilderness," Professor Marx argues, is in essence an "American" story, despite its poetic vagueness of locale. Yet the cast of characters on Shakespeare's imaginary island includes both Ariel, the free, music-making child of nature, and the lumpish and bestial Caliban, equally a child of nature. Could the migrants from the Old World to the New expect to renew themselves and release their creative energies in this unspoiled land? Or could they expect only to be barbarized?

They could not wait too long to resolve such hesitations. Competition for empire was drawing them into America, and they would have to take their chances on barbarization. Besides, the quest for new spheres of action overseas might be of indirect benefit back at home. "Truthe it is that throughe our long peace and seldome sicknes . . . wee are growen more populous than ever before," Richard Hakluyt summed up England's social condition in 1584. "Nowe there are of every arte and science so many, that they can hardly lyve one by another, nay rather they are readie to eate upp one another." Why not solve the domestic population crisis and the threat from European rivals at one stroke? "The frye of the wandringe beggars of England, that grow upp ydly, and hurtfull and burdenous to this realme," transported from the Old World to the New, Hakluyt argued, might be transformed from a liability into an asset. The erstwhile vagabonds will be a benefit to themselves, as they "people waste contries . . . to their owne more happy state," and also to the realm of England; for "this enterprise may staye the Spanish Kinge from flowinge over all the face of that waste firme of America." Whether any waste firm be an Eden or a desert, from an imperialist's view of the matter, is a secondary question. Nobody argued whether the destination aimed at was Wilderness or Paradise when the Russians and Americans in the 1960s were racing for the moon.

The wandering beggars themselves might pardonably have assumed that any change from their wretched situation at home was bound to be an improvement. Historian Richard Hofstadter reminds us, however, that we must not overpraise early America as a land of opportunity. Most migrants arrived not as free individuals but as indentured servants, he points out, and "the sadness that is natural to life was overwhelmed in the condition of servitude by the stark miseries that seem all too natural to the history of the poor." But *they* did not know, beforehand, whether stark misery or glorious opportunity was to be their lot; and once landed on the New World's shores they could at the very least bet on the future of their children.

Though the new land showed to its first settlers "a wild and savage heiw," wrote Plymouth's governor William Bradford, and though "they had now no friends to wellcome them, nor inns to entertaine or refresh their weather-beaten bodys; no houses or much less townes to repair too, to seek for succoure," yet the very wildness of the land constituted part of its lure. America might be in large part a "countrie full of woods and thickets" behind which lurked hostile inhabitants "readier to fill their sides full of arrows than other wise"; but there was savage murder in the streets of London also. Europe's burgeoning throngs, with their inherited feuds and injustices, were constrained by the burden of their history toward certain courses of action and foreclosed from others. The fearful and hopeful truth about the unknown West that swam out of Greek and Judaic legend into practical reality was that it was (or seemed), by comparison with Europe and Asia, empty; and that initial emptiness may have been the most important single fact in American history. Politically, the new immigrants were free to fill it with anything.

4. The Concept of a Frontier

Four hundred years down the road from Columbus's landfall in America, replicas of those first three ships were towed or sailed over the Atlantic, to an America which was no longer the great unknown. A World's Columbian Exposition, swiftly built during the winter of 1892–93 on lakeshore dunes at the heart of the continent, appropriately celebrated the First Voyage's anniversary. In July 1893, the American Historical Association held a special meeting in conjunction with that Chicago extravaganza, and a youngish historian named Frederick Jackson Turner read to his fellow historians a bold conjecture as to what the breakout from Europe,

Asia, and Africa had really meant. His essay was titled *The Significance of the Frontier in American History*.

Turner lived in an age whose perception of reality was, as Veblen noted, "peculiarly matter-of-fact." History, like much else in the 1890s, had to present itself as "scientific" in order to be credible. The wonder concealed in the Atlantic's misty vastness must shrivel, under the dry light of science, into a quantifiable statistic. The Isles of the Blest and the abode of the dead, together with the Biblical garden and wilderness, vanished from sight and were replaced by a textbook-like assertion about the *physical* New World: "The existence of an area of free land," Turner declared, "its continuous recession, and the advance of American settlement westward, explain American development."

The pleasure-principle, Freud might have said, has here given way to the reality principle; the romantic crusade into an imagined West has been diluted into a long, continent-spanning series of land grabs. But the overtones of romance in the American story were not so easily gotten rid of. The geographic determinism Turner proposed was oddly diluted with the older idea that the Wilderness was a place where one went, for forty years or forty days, to restore one's soul. "The Wilderness masters the colonist," Turner wrote in an often-quoted passage:

> It finds him a European in dress, industries, tools, modes of travel, and thought. . . . It strips off the garment of civilization and arrays him in the hunting shirt and the moccasin. . . . In short, at the frontier the environment is at first too strong for the man. . . . Little by little he transforms the wilderness, but the outcome is not the old Europe. . . . The fact is, that here is a new product that is American

—and this new product, purged and regenerated by the wilderness experience, Turner implied, was clearly better than the old.

Early observers of the process of settlement in North America would have agreed with Turner that the wilderness first mastered and then transformed the colonist. Some of them—the eighteenth-century writer on agriculture Arthur Young for example—added that this transformation began even before the settlers arrived, in the pre-selection of the kinds of people who would become migrants in the first place: "Men who emigrate are, from the nature of the circumstances, the most active, hardy, daring, bold and resolute spirits, and probably the most mischievous also." The implications of that adjective "mischievous," Richard Hofstadter comments, are profound: "Young was suggesting that the most venturesome or visionary, the most impatient and restive under authority, the most easily alienated, the most desperate and cranky, were the most ready to leave, giving at least the initial population of the American colonies a strong bias toward dislike of authority."

Are we to infer from such testimonials, however, that the *women* who emigrated to North America's shores in the beginning and re-emigrated to successive Western frontiers were mischievous, alienated, rebellious against authority, and all the rest of that behavioral catalogue? Perhaps so, perhaps not; but to mention them at all is to shake male historians' generalizations about them. Were they, as Karen Anderson has argued, dragged along to the frontier in the wake of their men, "draftees in a male enterprise," regardless of what their own preferences or personality traits may have been? Turner's description of the "striking characteristics" that were formed by the frontier into "the American intellect"—"that coarseness and strength combined with acuteness and inquisitiveness; that practical, inventive turn of mind, quick to find expedients; that masterful grasp of material things, lacking in the artistic but powerful to effect great ends; that restless, nervous energy; that dominant individualism, working for good and for evil, and withal that buoyancy and exuberance which comes with freedom"—sounds, in overtone at least, distressingly male-macho. What would become of this inventory of frontier traits if one associated them with the pronoun "she"?

The charge that gender chauvinism lurks under every line of Turner's descriptions of "the pioneer" is but a recent instance of the adverse criticism that has dogged Turner's frontier hypothesis since its inception. Marxists, for example, have accused him of the heresy of "American exceptionalism"—the belief that America is somehow exempt from the tragic burdens all other inhabitants of an industrializing, urbanizing planet must bear. Certainly the very concept of a "frontier" as a line between settled and unsettled territory betrays insensitivity toward the inhabitants on the "unsettled" side of the line. The archaic term *marches* favored by Arnold Toynbee (e.g., the Roman Empire's Rhine and Danube and Scottish borderlands, or the British Empire's Afghan frontier) may be a more accurate word, in its recognition that frontier zones have been places where people marched against each other, again and again, from the disaster that befell Varus's legions in the Teutoburg Forest in 9 A.D. right down to Custer's Last Stand.

Other critics, more mildly, have noted that the new, supposedly "non-European" civilization that arose out of the American wilderness owed much to its pre-New World memories. On their maps along with garbled Indian names the new Americans set down lengthy lists of Spanish saints; English seaports or country towns (Salisbury and Shrewsbury, Bangor and Belfast, Worcester and Leicester, Chatham and Chelmsford); French descriptive terms (Fond du Lac, Prairie du Chien); and even names imported from the Asia-Europe-Africa triangle: Ithaca and Troy, Syracuse and Athens, Antioch and Alexandria, Carthage and Rome. They filled the New World not only with the Old World's laws, languages, religions, and races, but also, as Alfred Crosby shows in his book *Ecological Imperialism* (1986), with its bugs and weeds. "Perhaps European humans have triumphed because of their superiority in arms, organization, and fanaticism," Crosby comments, "but what in heaven's name is the reason that the sun never sets on the empire of the dandelion?"

The cogency of these and other objections to Turner's free-land theory can not be casually set aside. On the other hand there has been among many historians of late something of a reaction in Turner's favor; a sense that anything as massive as the American frontier must have had *some* kind of impact on subsequent history. In any event, the "truth" or "untruth" in any myth—that of free land in America or any other—may have little to do with its power to motivate action.

5. When the Frontier Ends

Not only did the frontier break down the old European culture and replace it with something fresh and new, Turner argued, but the process also repeated itself all the way across the continent: "Moving westward, the frontier became more and more American." To study this recurring destructive/creative process, Turner insisted, "is to study the really American part of our history." Even as unmistakably "Eastern" an American intellectual as Henry David Thoreau—Harvard graduate and suburban Bostonian—could testify that anyone who wished, as he did, to "speak a word for nature, for absolute freedom and wildness," would need to turn toward the West: "Eastward I go only by force, but Westward I go free," Thoreau wrote in his essay *Walking* (1862). "I must walk toward Oregon, and not toward Europe." Thoreau also sensed that this impulse "to go to a West as distant and fair as that into which the sun goes down" was not triggered simply by the existence of a great deal of undeveloped real estate; that, on the contrary, it drew upon deep and venerable unconscious yearnings: "The island of Atlantis and the islands and gardens of the Hesperides . . . appear to have been the Great West of the ancients, enveloped in mystery and poetry."

As Americans walked—or rode, or floated, or drove—on toward Oregon, were they approaching at last that western El Dorado that had haunted their ancestors' imaginations since Homer's time? Or were they moving toward a realm of life-destroying barrenness? A New Englander, abandoning a hillside farm whose buried boulders bent and broke his plow, or a Southerner, in flight from soil that was going back to scrub pine because his ancestors had exhausted it by growing tobacco with never a care for renewal, might well have believed themselves approaching the Terrestrial Paradise as they entered the Mississippi Valley, with its fantastic black dirt that veritably oozes vitamins when one picks up a clod. It was not just farmland (which Turner was moved to focus upon because of his own agrarian political biases) that was abundant; it was *everything*: hydroelectric power, timber, coal, iron, oil. "The very essence of the frontier," commented historian David Potter, "was its supply of unappropriated wealth." *People of Plenty*, Professor Potter called the Americans, and that plenitude, he argued, has shaped their national character even more sweepingly than Turner imagined, influencing even such intimate matters as the way they rear their children.

But as the westering Americans moved on toward the land of little rain, the dialectic between the Wilderness and the Promised Land began to resolve in favor of the desert. First the forests fell behind them; then the buffalo grass. They made the natural shortages worse by their own heedlessness; in another century a third of that rich topsoil would have washed down into the sea. And then, as people came to settle the High Plains, they learned to their dismay that shortly there wasn't going to be enough water. "One

15

year with another," the scientist-adventurer J. W. Powell prophetically warned North Dakotans in 1889, "you need a little more than you get."

Science and technology might postpone this Martian doom, but at the cost of putting the new inhabitants of that wilderness into a fragile self-created environment at one far end of a skinny water pipe. And the arid, "desert" West only showed more vividly what was also true of the "garden" West (e.g., California): *it was finite.* Turner knew this, and the conclusion of *The Significance of the Frontier in American History* should not be taken as a hymn of national self-congratulation—as some of Turner's critics mistakenly read it—but rather as a cry of alarm: "And now, four centuries from the discovery of America, at the end of a hundred years of life under the Constitution, *the frontier has gone,* and with its going has closed the first period of American history."

Walter Prescott Webb, Turner's greatest disciple, saw implications in that concluding peroration which most commentators on Turner, advocates and detractors alike, have overlooked. Daringly, Professor Turner had compared the New World frontier with the Asian-African-European microcosmos where it had all started: "What the Mediterranean Sea was to the Greeks, breaking the bond of custom, offering new experiences, calling out new institutions and activities, that, and more, the ever retreating frontier has been to the United States directly, and to the nations of Europe more remotely." Taking off in an imaginative leap beyond Turner, Webb proposed the startling theory that *all* of the relatively unoccupied lands across the planet, outside those nations of Europe as they stood in 1500, had constituted a "Great Frontier" into which people moved from what he termed "The Metropolis." The existence of a vast expanse of open land, and the movement across it of a frontier-line, explained not only America's development but much of Europe's as well.

"But never again," Turner had lamented, "will such gifts of free land offer themselves." The same must be true of Webb's larger, worldwide frontier: the "four-hundred-year boom" was over, and unless a "substitute boom-maker" (perhaps science and technology?) came along, Webb concluded his essay on *The Great Frontier* (1952), "we are faced with radical changes indeed."

Historians and philosophers might come to "view the Age of the Frontier as an aberration, a temporary departure from the normal, a strange historical detour in which men developed all sorts of

16

quaint ideas about property for all, freedom for all, and continuous progress." Though society might not—and need not—revert all the way back to the closed-in medieval universe from which it had broken out in quest of its imagined ever-receding West, yet it was "faced with change, much of which we heartily dislike" but must, nevertheless, accept:

> Society as it thickens will become more closely integrated and its members more interdependent. Governments will tend to become stronger, using more compulsion. . . . The loose democracy belonged to a frontier stage of society. The individual will become relatively less important and will tend to lose his identity in a growing corporate life. . . . The passing of free land should be registered by the passing of cheap food.

However, there is no point in moaning and groaning over spilt milk! "If the frontier is gone," Webb concluded, "we should have the courage and honesty to recognize the fact, cease to cry for what we have lost, and devote our energy to finding solutions to the problems that now face a frontierless society."

The Significance of the Frontier in American History is, without a doubt, the single most influential essay ever written by an American historian; influential not merely upon other historians but also upon the public at large—many members of which have grasped, and been moved by, the general idea contained in the essay even if they have never heard the name of Frederick Jackson Turner. Consider the case of Franklin Delano Roosevelt, that crowd-sensitive, ear-to-the-ground master of politics, who in his first presidential campaign in 1932 delivered a major address in which he came as close as he ever did in that election year to forecasting what the proposed "New Deal" might be like—a speech whose conceptual assumptions and rhetoric came straight from Turner's address at the World Columbian Exposition forty years before. "On the Western frontier, land was substantially free," FDR—or his speechwriters—declared. "At the very worst there was always the possibility of climbing into a covered wagon and moving west where the untilled prairies afforded a haven for men to whom the East did not provide a place." Not only did Roosevelt articulate the basic idea of Turner's thesis about the West, he also echoed its downbeat, "never again" conclusion:

> A glance at the situation today only too clearly indicates that equality of opportunity as we have known it no longer exists.

17

> Our industrial plant is built; the problem just now is whether under existing conditions it is not overbuilt. Our last frontier has long since been reached, and there is practically no more free land. . . . There is no safety valve in the form of a Western prairie to which those thrown out of work by the Eastern economic machines can go for a new start. We are not able to invite the immigration from Europe to share our endless plenty. We are now providing a drab living for our own people.
>
> . . . Our task now is not discovery or exploitation of natural resources, or necessarily producing more goods. It is the soberer, less dramatic business of administering resources and plants already in hand.

This somber appraisal, conjoined with Walter Webb's pessimism toward the whole planet's future political economy, reappeared in the 1970s in such concepts as the "zero sum," the "steady state," the "limits of growth." But the spark of American hope for a better world, if not in the mysterious West then *somewhere*, is not easily extinguished. It surfaced for a shining tragic moment in John Kennedy's "New Frontier," and it reappeared in 1980 as common ground between two otherwise sharply polarized politicians, Ronald Reagan and Edward Kennedy, at their parties' respective national nominating conventions. Despite the looming shadows of nuclear darkness, both rejected any "stagnationist" interpretation of the American and the planetary future. Rejecting "an energy policy based on the sharing of scarcity," Reagan called for maintaining "forward momentum"; for "policies that will stimulate our economy, increase productivity and put America back to work." One month later Kennedy picked up almost word for word the same affirmative cry: "I am asking you to renew our commitment to a fair and lasting prosperity that can put America back to work. . . . To all those who doubt the future of our economy, let us provide new hope." When they came down to *how* this hope was to be realized, these two political practitioners came down at diametrically opposite poles; one calling for much more intervention by government into economic and social processes, the other for much less. But both looked beyond the grubby present to a "West" that had become the future. Destiny in America, they agreed, is not something one stoically accepts; it is something one actively makes.

Interlude I

As Niña, Pinta, *and* Santa Maria *ran before the northeast trade winds into the unknown West, each evening just after sunset all hands were called to evening prayers. They said the* Pater Noster, *the* Ave Maria, *and the* Credo, *and then sang the haunting Benedictine chant* Salve Regina mater misericordiae. . . .

In the land toward which they were going there would one day rise—in the Valley of Mexico, on the banks of the Charles—ambitious universities. Their language of instruction and formal disputation, in their earliest years, would be Latin.

Thus, as the voyagers came into the new, empty unknown, they filled it as best they could with what they already knew.

TWO

Caesar's Ghost in America

Although this book is also about science, and religion, and the environment, it is first last and always about republicanism, *as an idea*. It assumes that ideas matter; that they are not simply rationalizations of status or class; that they can be honest efforts to turn experience into meaning, rather than dismissable evidence of "false consciousness" or "mere rhetoric." Thinkers, in this book's view of history, are not bit-players; they are actors. Ideas become ingredients in a national discourse between and among people, and politics becomes an expression of relations between various believing groups. And never was this more the case than in the Revolutionary founding generation, which even from its "new," culturally raw land, reached across the centuries to the forms of classical government and the remembered destiny of Rome.

1. The Roman Heritage

Once there was a city that sat on seven hills. Emerging from tribal obscurity, imagining themselves descended from the defenders of Troy, its people drove out their petty kings and made of their state a republic—then a rare and precious form of government in an otherwise despotic world. Afterward, as they have everywhere, the classes struggled with the masses; but within that republican form of government the patricians and the plebeians over two centuries worked out a constitutional compromise. And then the legions of that small republic marched out, under standards inscribed SPQR, and proceeded to conquer the world.

Senatus Populusque Romanus—the Senate and People of Rome. Of all the legends of Western civilization, theirs is one of the most compelling. At the height of its power all roads led to Rome; even more important, all roads led out from it as well.

To be sure, they did not reach everywhere; Rome's contacts with India and China were fleeting and peripheral, and no Roman roads carried legionaries and merchant-adventurers along the shores of California or across the passes of the Andes. Nevertheless, as generations of Latin teachers in America have valiantly striven to inform their rooms full of bored and uncaring youths, the influence of Rome upon all of us—including, at several removes, those who speak Cantonese or Hindi—has been decisive and profound. The favorite Arab epithet to describe the Western European infidel is still *Roumi*, which is to say, Roman; and it is probably no coincidence that the only East European Communist states to cross the line of planetary polarization and participate in the 1984 Olympic Games were two (Romania and Yugoslavia—*i.e.*, Dacia and Illyria), which at one time had been provinces of the Roman Empire.

Even though America's public schools in the main have given up the struggle for Latin, none of us can really escape from the people who originally spoke and wrote it. We draw salaries (L. *salarium*), and we shell out dollar bills bearing a Great Seal which promises us—in misspelled Latin!—a "new order of the ages," *novus ordo seclorum*. We work out in a *gymnasium*, one of many words and ideas the Romans borrowed from the Greeks. On weekends some of us go to church, and if what we hear is no longer Latin it is likely to be a translation. We come down with diseases, and the doctors diagnose us with Latin names; we sue the doctor, and the lawyers also lead us through a maze of Latinisms. We die, and then our wills, if we have enough heirs, may instruct our executor to distribute our worldly goods *per stirpes sed non per capita*.

The use of such terms is worldwide, or at least West-wide; for into the primeval American Eden or wilderness its European invaders brought, and imposed, their Roman names and institutions. Spanish friars said the Latin Mass before crowds of uncomprehending Indians; French *intendants* (L. *intendere*) displaced the casual Indian approach to land tenure with a system of property ownership and control that was, in its legal origins, Roman; and even the New Amsterdam Dutch bought and sold and traded within a framework of commercial usages many of which Greek or Phoenician or Syrian merchants in the Roman Empire would have found familiar.

Especially the Western world's political life is stamped with its

Latin origins. But America's Latin political heritage differs strikingly from much of Europe's. We nominate (from *nominare*) candidates (L. *candidatus*) for president (L. *praesidens*) who, if elected (L. *electus*) to office (*officium*), promise to preserve, protect, and defend the Constitution (from *constituere*) of a republic (*respublica*) whose very name *America* is a Latinization of that of an Italian geographer. Europe knows many of these names and procedures also, but its own tragic history includes offices as yet unknown here, except in metaphor—notably *dictator* and *caesar* (Kaiser, Tsar).

Forms of government are not guaranteed to be immortal, and history is not a good place to look for happy endings. The Roman Republic did not remain republican forever. Torn apart by social and economic stresses and political abuse which the Roman Constitution could not contain, Rome's government was re-crafted by the subtle Augustus, who combined all the carefully balanced and mutually limiting categories of government into his own person. In the leadership of the regime he founded the wise and clever Emperors were, unhappily, interspersed with voluptuaries, plunderers, and madmen; the flourishing municipal life, which at first they had the wit to leave alone, eventually decayed; the spreading of Roman citizenship and of formal equality under the law coincided with the growth of stifling, sycophantic, and ultimately self-destructive autocracy.

America's revolutionary leaders and state-makers constructed a government for which Rome was the primary blueprint; but one which they hoped might escape Rome's fate. As James Madison argued in *The Federalist Papers*, No. 10, "the greater number of citizens and extent of territory which may be brought within the compass" of a federal republic should insure it against the political excesses both of Athens, under whose town-meeting democracy a democratic majority could lawfully condemn Socrates to death, and of Rome, which in its last republican years got into the absurd predicament of having its city council (i.e., the Senate) attempt to look after the affairs of half the known world. Nevertheless, many of the same eighteenth-century Americans who championed liberty, modernity, and progress had also inherited a Puritan/Calvinist sense of historical inevitability. The founders of the American republic, knowing few contemporary examples of their own political breed save for an occasional quaint survival such as Venice or Iceland, studied the Greek and Roman models with a special intellectual and emotional intensity; haunted by the undeniable historical fact that republics on the whole have been short-lived, and that even the most durable among them—Rome being the supreme example—have proved at last to be mortal. Moreover, political democracy has never been one of the regular and perennial options of humankind. Until the late eighteenth century, at least, its appearance had been rare, both geographically and historically. Rome and Greece, the most renowned examples of the species, existed in a larger Mediterranean cosmos of states ruled by god-kings—except for Ancient Israel, which worshipped a God far too jealous to share divinity with mere kings.

Indeed, the land of Israel got along for generations without kings, and we are told that "in those days . . . every man did that which was right in his own eyes." But in due course Israel's people got themselves a king, "like all the nations." The last and greatest of their judges warned them of what they could then expect: "He will take your fields, and your vineyards, and your oliveyards, even the best of them, and give them to his servants," the prophet Samuel told the folk of Israel. "And he will take your menservants and your maidservants, and your goodliest young men, . . . and put them to his work" (Judges 21:25; I Samuel 8:5, 14, 16). When that day comes, Samuel implied (verse 18), don't say I didn't warn you. Ignoring the warnings Israel got its kings, and the third of them is said to have driven a large fraction of his people into rebellion and separation—under yet another king.

Like the casual rule of Israel's judges, Greek democracy and Roman republicanism also came to an end; and, as we shall see later, the ghost of Caesar was to haunt the American imagination from the Founders' day to our own. At still another point in history the Florentine Republic, whose feisty citizens (as Mary McCarthy has observed) practically invented the modern world, fell into the grasping hands of Lorenzo the Magnificent. And so it went, down to and including the era of the French and American Revolutions.

Those classical historians with whose works the founders were intimately familiar, most notably Polybius and Livy, described the dread declension from democracy to tyranny, from republic to empire as if that transformation is, in the nature of things, foreordained. Lamenting as he did that by the time of Augustus "the old free Roman character no longer existed," the perceptive Tacitus nonetheless conceded that after the Battle of Actium in 31 B.C. "the interests of peace required that all power should be centered in one man." American readers of Tacitus regretfully agreed. Replaying the drama of the republic's defenders versus the empire builders Thomas Jefferson—in a moment of pessimism quite unnatural for him—questioned whether "even Cicero, Cato, Brutus" could have done anything to establish a good government for their country. "They had no idea of government themselves but of their degenerate Senate, nor the people of liberty, but of the factious opposition of their tribunes," Jefferson wrote on December 10, 1819. "No government can continue good but under the control of the people: and their people were so demoralized and depraved as to be incapable of exercising a wholesome control."

John Adams, replying to his old Virginia friend (December 21, 1819), also made short work of the notion "that had Brutus and Cassius been conqueror, they would have restored virtue and liberty, to Rome." The grave civic virtue attributed in the history books to the Roman Republican aristocracy was largely illusory, Adams believed: "Patricians were in general griping usurers and tyrannical creditors in all ages." Nor was the American republic necessarily exempt from some future tragedy similar to Rome's: "I am sometimes Cassandra enough to dream that another Hamilton, another Burr might rend this mighty fabric in twain, or perhaps into a leash." As for exporting the freedoms of the New World back into the Old, John Adams was, to say the least, skeptical: "The French and the Dutch in our day have attempted reforms and revolutions. We know the results, and I fear the English reformers will have no better success."

2. Must All Revolutions Fail?

The failure of the French Revolution, from the viewpoint of an aged American revolutionary, was particularly painful. It was bad enough that Europe's conservative powers had rallied to defeat that Revolution and forcibly re-install the Bourbon kings on their throne; what was even harder to bear was that liberty had been betrayed by forces arising from within the Revolution itself. First the Gracchi, and then Caesar; first the Jacobins, and then Napoleon. Reactionaries could be smug, and cry "What did you expect?"; but for John Adams and Thomas Jefferson, co-drafters of the Declaration of Independence, the march of events that began at the Bastille and ended at Waterloo challenged their own deepest intellectual commitments and political faith.

After democracy, terror; after terror, Caesar; and after Caesar, world conquest. As Caesar had marched through Gaul as far as the Rhine en route to becoming master at Rome, so Napoleon marched through Egypt up the Nile on his way to becoming master at Paris. That was, for many Americans, the lesson of the French Revolution. This dialectic of *ancien régime*–rebellion–new tyranny has its roots in Aristotle's *Politics*; and in the twentieth century it would be elaborated into a formal theory, in Crane Brinton's *The Anatomy of Revolution* (1938). All revolutions, Brinton argued—discreetly sidestepping the American example—tend to fall into a common and repetitive pattern: a moderate, reformist phase; a radical, leveling phase, enforced by a reign of terror; a reaction against the Terror's extremism (Thermidor, so named after the French instance of it); and at the end a man on horseback—Oliver Cromwell, or Napoleon, or Stalin. What devastated eighteenth-century republican sensibilities—and delighted anti-republicans—in the French example was the fresh evidence that revolution, even in the name of freedom, is no guarantee of that freedom.

On a dark November afternoon in 1799, ten and one-third years after the storming of the Bastille, the semblance of French revolutionary democracy that still remained after a decade of terror, military adventure, and corruption came to an inglorious end. With bayonets fixed and drums rolling, Napoleon's grenadiers marched on the national legislature. "A huddled band of red-robed deputies rushed for the doors, leapt out of the windows, and swiftly scattering through the gloom of the trees and bushes were lost to view and to history." In their place (British historian H. A. L. Fisher continues his narrative) came a new government dedicated no longer to *liberté, egalité, fraternité*, but rather to "splendour, comprehension, and efficiency." When at the beginning of the new century this regime was put to a popular vote it carried by a margin of 3,011,077 to 1,562.

Across the Channel George Canning, who was destined for the next quarter century to play a large role in British and even in American foreign affairs, greeted the French coup with an ecstatic "Huzza, huzza, huzza!" The news justified such un-British lack of restraint, he wrote on November 19; "No language but that of violent and tumultuous and triumphant exclamation can sufficiently describe the joy and satisfaction which I feel." The events of the Eighteenth and Nineteenth Brumaire constituted, for Canning, "the lasting ridicule thrown upon all systems of democratic equality,

—it is the galling conviction carried home to the minds of all the brawlers for freedom in this and every other country—that there never was, nor will be, a leader of a mob faction who does not mean to be the lord and not the servant of the people." From thenceforth in any country similar to France in extent, population, and the like, Canning proclaimed, *"republican* and *fool* are synonymous terms."

The founders of the American republic were not, to say the least, fools. But they were persons fully aware that both historical and circumstantial evidence seemed to favor the anti-republicans. When Thomas Paine wrote at the outbreak of the American Revolution that "freedom hath been hunted round the globe," he was not simply indulging in rhetoric; his description of an "old world . . . overrun with oppression" was a factual statement of what political life has actually been like for most people, on most of the planet, most of the time.

When the French Revolution first broke out, many Americans —and especially Thomas Paine!—had welcomed it as a confirmation of the rightness of their own. Even Alexander Hamilton, who was usually mistrustful of any spontaneous mass action by the people, wrote a note of congratulations, of sorts, to the Marquis de Lafayette. "I have seen, with a mixture of pleasure and apprehension, the progress of the events which have lately taken place in your country," Hamilton told his Revolutionary comrade-in-arms on October 6, 1789. "As a friend to mankind and liberty, I rejoice in the efforts which you are making to establish it." However, Hamilton hedged, "I dread the vehement character of your people, whom I fear you may find it more easy to bring on than to keep within proper bounds after you have put them in motion." By 1801, with the Revolution formally proclaimed to be at an end and with Napoleon Bonaparte entrenched as First Consul,—telescoping into one the careers of both Julius Caesar and Octavian—Hamilton was able to write Lafayette and gently inform him, in effect, I told you so. Magnanimous, in the best eighteenth-century sense of that word, toward the Revolutionary activities of his old and dear friend— "No explanation of your political principles was necessary to satisfy me of the perfect consistency and purity of your conduct"— Hamilton nevertheless lectured the Marquis (January 6, 1801) that the American political experiment could not simply be replicated at will, all the way across Europe: "I hold with Montesquieu that a government must be fitted to a nation as much as a coat to an individual; and consequently, what may be good at Philadelphia may be bad at Paris, and ridiculous at Petersburg."

Thomas Jefferson, Hamilton's lifelong political adversary, was inclined to agree with him on at least that one point. Who could have imagined, Jefferson asked in 1802, that the French, of all people, would have proved incapable of self-government? America seemed the only nation capable of living under republican principles. Such a judgment came hard for a man who had spent the pre-Revolutionary years from 1785 to 1789 in Paris imbibing the savory wine of the Rights of Man; but Jefferson would have none of the rationalizations of some of his fellow Republicans, who clung to the idea that because Napoleon built roads, tore down ghettos, and opened careers in his service to people of talent regardless of breed or birth, the Emperor of the French still carried the spirit of the Revolution as some kind of "people's king." Nonsense; Napoleon by his act of usurpation had carried France "from a limited to an unlimited despotism," Jefferson wrote. Better even the hapless Bourbons, suitably checked within a constitutional monarchy, he thought, than this mountebank. A newspaper in the President's home state, *The Petersburg Intelligencer*, emphatically concurred (July 31, 1804): "If there must be a monarchy, perhaps it would be best to have a legitimate one, and restore at once Lewis [sic] the Eighteenth to the throne of his ancestors—the French people could not be worsted." "Resistance to tyrants is obedience to the will of God," said Jefferson; but of what benefit is that to humanity if such resistance is doomed to capture by a leader who means to be the lord and not the servant of the people?

In our own century the legend of the Eighteenth Brumaire would yield to new horror stories, of democratic assemblies fleeing before armed force; of free elections voided by military juntas; of "strong men" holding back the masses in the name of "guided democracy." For one notorious example, on November 18, 1917, the first—and (so far) last—freely chosen government of Russia was sent packing at the end of its first and only session by trigger-happy armed guards. It is well to remind ourselves, for perspective, that a like fate could just as well have befallen the government created by the rebellious British colonies which fought and won the American Revolution. America's Continental Congress, like Russia's elected Constituent Assembly in 1917, found itself beset one day—June 21, 1783—by angry, impatient military men. Powered by a legitimate grievance—their pay was sadly in arrears—fourscore members of

27

the third Pennsylvania regiment marched on Philadelphia, re-cruited four or five hundred more from the local barracks, and sur-rounded the State House. Demanding authority to appoint their own officers, they told Congress it would "immediately issue such authority and deliver it to us, or otherwise we shall instantly let in those injured soldiers upon you, and abide by the consequences. You have only twenty minutes to deliberate upon this important matter."

The members of Congress did not stampede. They sat tight, qui-etly ignored the twenty-minute deadline, and at their customary hour for adjournment rose and filed out of the building through the ranks of jeering, musket-waving soldiers. According to James Madison, who was present, the mutineers were well liquored up; and one angry, drunken trooper firing a shot at that moment could have blown the American Revolution into history. Once safely away from the besiegers, the President of the Congress sent a frantic message off to General Washington, and three days later he called upon Congress prudently to move from the vicinity of those mu-tinous barracks to quieter quarters in Princeton, New Jersey. One has only to imagine an officer more opportunistic and self-seeking than Washington in command of the Continental Army at that mo-ment to realize what a narrow escape the infant American republic had just had.

3. A Revolution Founded on Reason

Republican free government in the eighteenth century had as bad a reputation among conservatives in the West as Marxist-Leninist government has today. Eighteenth-century republicans tried to live down their ill repute in various ways: by appealing to democratic Athens and republican Rome as if one could trace an apostolic succession from the ancient popular assemblies down to the mod-ern revolutionary regimes, somehow bypassing Caesar; by empha-sizing the few modern examples of the type—the German free cit-ies, the Dutch Estates, the Swiss cantons, the Swedish Riksdag; or, at the level of political theory, by positing an original state of na-ture which was, in essence, republican. "In the beginning," John Locke had written, "all the world was America," where everyone had done that which was right in their own eyes. "Being . . . by nature all free, equal, and independent," Locke argued, individuals at history's imagined primordial dawn had founded political societies "by agreeing . . . to join and unite into a community for their comfortable, safe, and peaceable living." To base such a community upon their previous experience of freedom, equality, and independence, far from being "foolish" as anti-republicans like Canning maintained, was the most logical thing they could have done.

Locke himself, embroiled in England's own Constitutional controversies, never quite took that final step into repubicanism, and present-day historians and cultural anthropologists by and large do not believe this is the way civil society and government really began. But colonial Americans—whose historical experience in the empty New World included some actual examples of people joining into communities in such a fashion—found in social contract theory a powerful justificatory idea. "Civil government," John Wise of Massachusetts Bay wrote as early as 1717, "must needs be acknowledged to be the effect of human free compacts and not of divine institution. . . . The first human subject and original of civil power is the people"; and of the three classic "regular" forms of the state (as originally defined by Aristotle)—democratic, aristocratic, and monarchical—democracy "appears in the greatest part of the world to have been the most ancient." Moreover, such apologists contended, the fundamental freedoms enjoyed when all the world was America can not be delegated or bargained away: people "have certain inherent rights," declared the Virginia Bill of Rights in 1776, "of which, when they enter into a state of society, they cannot by any compact deprive or divest their posterity."

They cannot—but they had. Jean-Jacques Rousseau in *The Social Contract* (1762) put it most succinctly: "Man is born free, and everywhere he is in chains." A logical difficulty for all social contract theorists was how to account for the badness of government that they observed in their own day. If human beings had freely entered into the original compact out of rational self-interest, and if democracy was of all forms of government the most ancient, then why were most existing governments tyrannies? The philosophers' answers to this question were, for the most part, awkward. Even Jean-Jacques, when he went on to ask "How did this change take place?", did not propose that the chains be struck off; instead he phrased the problem as "What can make it legitimate?" A few hardboiled realists, most notoriously Thomas Hobbes, contended that oppression is the price one pays for protection; it is insurance against what an actual "state of nature" would be: a "war of all against all." More typically, social contract theorists contended that the original agreement between governor and governed had at some intermediate point in history been broken. Revolution is then justified by a sovereign's bad faith in fulfilling the contract—but not otherwise. So there are good and bad revolutions. But who is to judge, and how?

Thomas Paine, almost alone among the American revolutionary thinkers (but with an assist from that skeptical Scot David Hume) rejected the whole idea of an original compact. Logically consistent in his radicalism, Paine argued that the existing governments, far from having decorously begun in a contract or covenant at the dawn of time, derived ultimately from violence. "It could have been no difficult thing, in the early and solitary ages of the world, for a banditti of ruffians to overrun a country, and lay it under contribution," Paine explained in the *Rights of Man*, Part II (1792). "Their power being thus established, the chief of the band contrived to lose the name of robber in that of monarch." Hereditary government was "an imposition on mankind," camouflaged by pomp and circumstance: "As time obliterated the history of their beginnings, their successors assumed new appearances," Paine continued, "but their principles and objects remained the same. What at first was plunder assumed the softer name of revenue."

There was thus no point in defending modern free government by an appeal to the past; the political past, at least, did not deserve such veneration. Humanity was in a brand-new political era, Paine affirmed, and the makers of a new American government should apply the recent insights of science rather than old conjectures about government origins. Instead of drawing upon an imagined primeval condition of liberty or a real but antiquated Graeco-Roman tradition, modern revolutionaries should transfer the grand simplicities of Newtonian physics over to the craft of state-making: "The revolution in America presented in politics what was only theory in mechanics." Monarchy was not only pretentious and cruel, it was also unscientific: "Nature is orderly in all her works; but this is a mode of government that counteracts nature." Republican government, on the other hand, "is always parallel with the order and immutable laws of nature, and meets the reason of man in every part."

Alexander Hamilton, with his elitism and his commitment to a powerful, coercive government, was at the opposite end of the American political spectrum from Thomas Paine. Yet Hamilton and Paine heartily agreed on the same fundamental point: good government was to be had not by searching out its antecedents in the past but by rational action in the present. It had been reserved to the Americans—Hamilton wrote in *The Federalist*, Number One— "to decide the important question, whether societies of men are really capable or not of establishing good government from reflection and choice, or whether they are forever destined to depend for their political constitutions on accident and force." Human beings—not God, not historical processes, not sociocultural configurations—make government. And they make it not by immersing themselves in tradition, or scripture, or a *Zeitgeist*, or tribal taboos but by thinking and doing.

But that is exactly what is the matter with modern revolutions, the anti-revolutionaries replied. No less a French *philosophe* than Voltaire had cautioned his countrymen against "the insane idea of becoming wholly reasonable," and thinkers who lacked the *philosophes'* faith in reason were quick to deride it as a guide to constitution-making. What holds society together, wrote Edmund Burke—to whose *Reflections on the Revolution in France* Thomas Paine's *Rights of Man* was a reply—is not rational discourse but intangible bonding. When state-makers deliberately sever such bonds—piety, chivalry, filial obligation, "all the pleasing illusions which made power gentle and obedience liberal"—they leave no practicable option for themselves save naked force: "You lay down metaphysical propositions which infer universal consequences," Burke gibed, "and then you attempt to limit logic by despotism." As the art historian Thomas Craven was to write many years later,

> There is something vastly ridiculous in the spectacle of those indomitable French Republicans acting the roles of the old Greeks and Romans, and something vastly courageous in the intensity with which they abandoned themselves, drenched with the blood of slaughter, to the job of creating a new government based upon the dictates of pure reason. . . . A democracy regulated by the intellect, classic in its origin and pagan in its forms! The union of art and politics! What a program, and who, save the French, would have dared it?

4. A Theory for Republicanism

"But theoretic reason," James Madison warned in *The Federalist*, Number 43, "must be qualified by the lessons of practice." The many quotations from classical historians that are sprinkled through the pages of the *Federalist Papers* were intended not so much to link the Americans with the Greeks and Romans in an apostolic feast of pure reason as to point out Graeco-Roman errors which Americans should avoid. American revolutionists might claim the sanction of truths they held to be "self-evident"; but even Jefferson, having said as much, went on to prove the justice of his cause not by formal deductive demonstration but by letting "facts be submitted to a candid world."

If Madison's *Federalist* co-author Alexander Hamilton believed in forming government by "reflection and choice" he also believed in disciplining such reflections. As Hamilton wrote in the sixth *Federalist*, "let experience, the least fallible guide of human opinions, be appealed to for an answer to these inquiries." Even Thomas Paine, who in a rush of rationalistic enthusiasm could thank "the Almighty Lecturer" for "displaying the principles of science in the structure of the universe," found in the course of religious or political debate that he had to justify those principles with evidence. In his rebuttal to Burke's monarchism he relied upon not only theory, but also the horrible examples of hereditary succession one actually saw installed upon contemporary European thrones (and Paine, by the way, was not far off the mark): "one is a tyrant, another an idiot, a third insane, and some all three together." Thomas Paine thus objected to hereditary monarchy not solely as a violation of abstract natural rights but also as a failure by pragmatic test. One got a king not by virtue of his fitness for the job but by an arbitrary shake of the genetic dice: "It requires some talents to be a common mechanic; but to be a king requires only the animal figure of a man."

Thomas Paine's revolutionary manifestoes and the *Federalist Papers* were alike written not simply to proclaim but to persuade: "let facts be submitted." Paine's *Rights of Man*, unlike his earlier *Crisis* and *Common Sense* essays, argued its case in a systematic fashion appropriate for the eighteenth-century mind. *The Federalist* was different; although James Madison's peers in political theory had tended to write formal, thought-out treatises—a *Republic*, a

Social Contract, a *Leviathan,*—the essays which became *The Federalist* were not written in that fashion at all. Commencing to appear in newspapers in New York City on October 27, 1787, the Papers appeared twice each week, until Hamilton realized that in order to cover all the intellectual territory the writers had staked out they would have to double the output to four times weekly. Co-writer John Jay, after contributing half-a-dozen shrewd essays on foreign policy, fell ill and dropped out of the enterprise; thereby throwing all the burden upon the other two authors—who were busy enough on their own account. (Alexander Hamilton, when the winter term of the New York Supreme Court began, took time out to tend to his law practice; James Madison, when not scribbling for *The Federalist,* was ably leading the Virginia delegation to the Continental Congress.) Legend has it that Hamilton composed *Federalist* Number One, with its adjuration to found a government from reflection and choice, in the comparative leisure of a sailing cruise up the Hudson; but for the most part the composition of *The Federalist* was an affair of great haste, sometimes of a printer's devil waiting in the outer room with a galley to be proofed for that day's press deadline while Hamilton and/or Madison dashed off the closing paragraphs of the copy to be set in type for the following day.

Moreover, since Hamilton, Madison, and Jay were writing, in effect, campaign literature to influence a particular body of voters (New York's) to ratify a specific, detailed proposal (the U.S. Constitution), the appeal could not be to an ideal government à la Plato, Thomas More, or Rousseau. Of necessity, *The Federalist* defended the less-than-ideal instrument that had lately come out of Independence Hall in Philadelphia—a document Benjamin Franklin had somewhat lamely defended as the Constitutional Convention drew to a close by saying that he didn't think another fifty-five men, given the cantankerous diversity of human interests and personalities, could have come up with anything better. Nothing could have been further from the abstract political speculations of "sophisters, oeconomists, and calculators" of which Edmund Burke, vis-à-vis France, was to complain.

Yet *The Federalist* did not, and does not, read as if created in slapdash fashion. Steeped in the august, rolling rhetorical tradition of Gibbon and Dr. Johnson—and of Burke, for that matter—the collaborators blended their individualities into a uniform, impersonal style under the soundly Roman Republican pen-name

"Publius." (The original Publius, in Roman folk history, had been the founder of stable republican government at Rome after the expulsion of the Tarquin kings). They submitted their facts—or their adroitly argued opinions—to a candid world, but they also managed to generalize from those particulars to universal propositions about the nature of people, of power, and of the state. *The Federalist* has it both ways: it spoke effectively to the concrete, time-bound situation in which it was written, and it speaks effectively to well-wishers of good government after the passing of two hundred years.

The Federalist, and the Federal Constitution it championed, have often been described as the handiwork of an elite rather than of true-blue revolutionists. Indeed, some influential twentieth-century writers have judged that handiwork as counter-revolutionary. When "Publius" addressed him/themselves to "The People of the State of New York," such critics allege, he/they—and especially Hamilton—did not really mean all the people: "those who are able to take a large view of the subject," to whose judgment "Publius" appealed, added up to only a small minority. Yet Hamilton and his colleagues never made the mistake—so endemic in professional revolutionaries—of believing that only persons who agree with one's own program have opinions one is bound to respect. "We . . . see wise and good men on the wrong as well as on the right side of questions of the first magnitude," Hamilton admitted; moreover, "ambition, avarice, personal animosity, party opposition, and many other motives not more laudable than these, are apt to operate as well upon those who support as those who oppose the right side of a question."

But there *is* a right side; so spoke the eighteenth century. Since fundamental truths—scientific, religious, economic, political—are self-evident to the human mind and heart, the "right" side can be known. Because it can, the "wrong" side need not be proscribed and hounded into silence; it can be routed in full, frank, and civil debate. "In politics, as in religion, it is equally absurd to aim at making proselytes by fire and sword," Hamilton averred. "Heresies in either can rarely be cured by persecution." Revolution, and governments founded on revolution, do not *need* reigns of terror, if they truly have the courage of their convictions.

The fallback position of more thoroughgoing revolutionaries is that Terror is made necessary by the danger of "counter-revolution"; the Americans, not surrounded by an iron ring of hostile

reactionary Great Powers seeking to destroy them and not subverted by diehards seeking to bring back the King, could afford
the luxury of dissent as French and Russian revolutionary governments could not. Napoleon, quite typically, rationalized that France
could not afford a "loyal" opposition on the British model because
a French Opposition would be either Jacobin, wanting its clubs
back, or else royalist, hungering for the *ancien régime.* "There is a
great deal of difference," Bonaparte explained, "between free discussion in a country whose institutions are long established and
the opposition in a country that is still unsettled." This is the standard revolutionary or new-nation argument for despotism; one hears
it today, over and over to the point of weariness, from the Third
World. Still, it is strange to hear frontier America, whose greatest
metropolis (Philadelphia) numbered only forty thousand souls and
whose government was but two decades old, described as a country whose institutions were long established, whereas centuries-old
France, with its sophisticated capital by the Seine resting upon
Renaissance, Gothic, and even Roman foundations, became for
purposes of argument a country that was still unsettled!

In another sense, of course, Napoleon was right. Certain institutions in the former thirteen colonies—the towns, the churches,
commercial relationships—*were* comparatively long established.
"Government of laws and not of men," Hamilton's biographer John
C. Miller points out, had always been high on America's revolutionary agenda, and to the extent that the American revolutionists
had claimed to be fighting not only for Paine's (and Jefferson's)
new and universal Rights of Man but also for legal rights which
historically had been theirs under the Crown, the American revolutionary government did make post-1789 France look relatively
"unsettled." "This attitude toward law," Miller reminds us, "is not
often found among subverters of the established order"; and although "it was held by Americans even in their most revolutionary phase" it was an argument not available at all to the daring
mafioso from Corsica. For revolutionary state-makers such as
Bonaparte, law codes—of which his own *Code Napoléon* is one of
the world's most sweeping examples—have to wait until after the
lawless seizure of power and the equally lawless suppression of
dissent as sedition.

5. The Great Convention

But perhaps all this talk of government by law, established from reflection and choice as qualified by the lessons of practice, is purely ideological camouflage. That is the classic Marxist argument against "bourgeois democracy": representative government is a mask behind which takes place the actual exercise of social—ultimately, of economic—power. It is also the classic "Beardian" argument, as set forth by Charles A. Beard in 1913 in his immensely influential book *An Economic Interpretation of the Constitution.* "At least five-sixths" of the members of the Federal Convention in 1787, both as individuals and as a class, "were immediately, directly, and personally interested in the outcome of their labors at Philadelphia," Beard charged, "and that outcome of their labors was an economic document drawn with superb skill by men whose property interests were immediately at stake." Moreover, in Beard's view, this class-biased Constitution, written in secrecy, was implemented by subterfuge—put over on the unpropertied masses—almost as a *coup d'état*, although admittedly of a less messy kind than Napoleon's. From that standpoint the Philadelphia Convention was in effect the American Revolution's Eighteenth Brumaire, or at least its Thermidor.

It is an attractive argument, especially to the eternal cynic for whom everyone has his or her price and no individuals, groups, or historical generations are morally better than any other. The Constitution *was* debated and written in secret, a fact encouraging an inference that this was but the silence of conspirators sticking together. However, the opponents as well as the supporters of the new Constitution respected the silence; and it would be just as logical to argue, as Charles Warren did in *The Making of the Constitution*, an early rebuttal to Beard (1928), that the success of the framers in preventing leaks out of Independence Hall bears witness not to the self-interest but to the incredible integrity of these men—especially in contrast to political behavior in present-day Washington, D.C., where leaking has become a deliberate instrument of government and where no secrets are safe.

Moving from the secret debates at the Convention to the public argument over ratification, advocates of the economic interpretation commonly have seized upon one celebrated passage in *Fed-*

eralist Ten, written by Madison: "A landed interest, a manufacturing interest, a mercantile interest, a moneyed interest, with many lesser interests, grow up of necessity in civilized nations. . . . The regulation of these various and interfering interests forms the principal task of modern legislation." However, in addition to the division of human society into classes and factions by "the possession of different degrees and kinds of property," Madison/Publius also listed as causes for such division "a zeal for different opinions concerning religion," "attachment to different leaders," and sheer human cussedness: "a propensity . . . to fall into mutual animosities," even into "violent conflicts," over differences that were at bottom "frivolous and fanciful."

However, "if attachments to religious and political values are as basic, as primary, as attachment to economic interest," Jeane Kirkpatrick has argued, "then the quantity and quality of potential factional conflicts are altered and the prospects for a conflict-free society become very dim." This is a surprising conclusion, in a way, for Kirkpatrick, who for a time served a presidential administration whose rhetoric often seemed to envision just such a society, purged of what Reaganites were wont to call "special interests" (i.e., Democrats). But it is not at all surprising in James Madison, with his axiomatic assumption that "the latent causes of faction are sown in the nature of man."

To be sure, Madison recaptured his credentials among economic interpreters of history by conceding that "those who hold and those who are without property have ever formed distinct interests in society," and that of all the sources of factional conflict theirs have been "the most common and durable." But "Publius" did not rest there. In considering how government was to regulate "these various and interfering interests," Madison resisted the easiest temptation, which would have been to leave the matter to the wisdom of future American philosopher-kings: "It is in vain to say that enlightened statesmen will be able to adjust these clashing interests. . . . Enlightened statemen will not always be at the helm." Constitutional government had to be crafted not only to serve effectively under the headship of a Washington, an Adams, a Jefferson, but also to survive the Warren Hardings and the Richard Nixons, who—given Madison's tacit assumptions about "the nature of man"—were inevitably coming down the road. But that problem was political, and in its ultimate assumptions moral and even theological. Beard's theory might be stretched to cover Harding's merry pirate crew, but to interpret the Nixon gang's motives for Watergate in terms of *economic* gain would be grotesque.

Federalist Ten is a rich essay that one turns to again and again. Nevertheless *The Federalist* is not the Constitution, and the question put by Beard can not be resolved solely by proof-texting out of Madison. Going over this polemical territory 45 years after Charles Beard (and 170 years after James Madison), Henry Steele Commager tellingly observed that "the weakest link in the Beard interpretation is precisely the crucial one—the document itself." For all the very real economic powers granted to Congress under that document, Commager argued, "we look in vain in the Constitution itself for any really effective guarantee for property or any effective barriers against what Beard called 'the reach of popular majorities.' " In one crucial institution, the proposed House of Representatives, popular majorities were in fact given greater reach and power than they had ever enjoyed before.

The Articles of Confederation, under which revolutionary America functioned throughout the 1780s, had been even less a "government by the people" than the proposed new regime. The closest modern analogue to the Continental Congress under the Articles would be the General Assembly of the United Nations. Members of the Congress—like members of the UN assembly—were chosen by governments, not by voters. Like UN delegates—and quite unlike U.S. Representatives—they could be, and sometimes were, summoned home for instructions on how to act. As a state delegation they functioned not as individuals but as a unit, and the size of the delegation (ranging from two to seven members) had nothing to do with its clout in Congress, where the rule—as at the United Nations—was one state, one vote.

The Articles of Confederation stipulated that the "delegates shall be annually appointed in such manner as the legislature of each state shall direct." Such language conceivably might have allowed states to direct that their Congresspeople be chosen by popular vote; identical language in the Federal Constitution on the choosing of presidential electors (Article II, Section 1, par. 2) eventually came to be interpreted in just that way. Similarly, the United States government conceivably might someday decide to designate as head of its UN delegation a person chosen by direct popular vote. (If other nations followed suit it would, without altering the Charter, revolutionize the United Nations, which might not be a bad idea.)

However, nobody in 1787 envisioned such an outcome for the Articles government, just as nobody today except perhaps a handful of World Federalists envisions such a transformation of the UN. To believers in popular democracy, therefore, the proposal for a federal House of Representatives chosen directly by the people counted as a definite plus.

Thomas Jefferson, who as the American diplomatic representative in Paris during those years had to watch the constitutional proceedings from afar, confessed to mixed feelings about the new instrument. Elitist enough to worry that a popularly elected house "will be very illy qualified to legislate for the Union, for foreign nations &c.," Jefferson confided to Madison nevertheless (December 20, 1787) that he approved that proposal because it preserved "the fundamental principle that the people are not to be taxed but by representatives chosen immediately by themselves." He was "much pleased too with the substitution of the method of voting by persons, instead of that of voting by states," and he was downright "captivated" by the delicate balance the Federal Convention had achieved between the claims of large states and small. What Jefferson did not like in the new Constitution, he told Madison, was the absence of a bill of rights—"what the people are entitled to against any government on earth . . . and what no just government should refuse, or rest on inference"—and the open-endedness of the election of the President who would probably, once chosen, become "an officer for life." To John Adams he put the same objection even more sharply: "Their President seems a bad edition of a Polish king."

Typically, the Sage of Monticello hesitated and second-guessed his way toward a decision: "There is a great mass of good in it, in a very desirable form," he told another correspondent, "but there is also, to me, a bitter pill or two." Could perhaps a new constitutional convention be called, to repair the mistakes made the first time around? No way, Madison retorted in *Federalist* 49; we had enough trouble getting it more or less right the first time. As the debate over ratification wore on, Jefferson—ever the politician— confessed that the new constitution was gaining ground in his own mind, as in the country, and after George Washington wrote him that their home state of Virginia was likely to fall in line he decided "that its adoption is become absolutely necessary."

Perhaps the key to Jefferson's attitude, and eventual decision, can be found in the third sentence of that letter to Madison from

Paris: "I like much the general idea of framing a government which should go on of itself peaceably." By March of 1789—four months before the fall of the Bastille; one month before the swearing in of George Washington—Jefferson was praising "the example of changing a constitution by assembling the wise men of the State instead of assembling armies"—an example the French, in their very different historical situation, would be tragically unable to follow.

6. Partisanship Through the Back Door

"One of the great dangers in newly organized states," Richard Hofstadter noted in his Jefferson Lectures at Berkeley (*The Idea of a Party System*, 1969), "is that the party in power, which is usually the party that claims credit for the revolutionary liberation of the country and for the successful organization of the new nation, claims for itself the exclusive custodianship of the essence of nationality." Opposition to that party's rule therefore comes to be seen as counter-revolutionary; divisive; unpatriotic; even treasonable. The oppositionists are conspiring to bring back the king, said the French Terror; they are in league with Nazi Germany, said Stalin's chief prosecutor; they are working with the former colonial powers, or with Wall Street, or they are sabotaging our plan for national regeneration and unity, say a host of present-day one-party dictators. The cry of "counter-revolution," in the strict sense, could not be raised in the newly organized state that occupied eastern North America in 1789; nobody was seriously proposing to bring back King George, and the Americans were never to be plagued with nuisances on the order of the Stuart Pretenders (old and young), or Bourbon claimants, or Bonapartist heirs, or unreconciled Romanovs. The other claim, however—that the party in power represented the nation's essence and that opposition to its rule was misguided or wicked—was a ploy that the Federalists who instituted America's new government in 1789 were able to work with considerable skill. So, when it came their turn, were their Jeffersonian opponents.

"Party," in late-eighteenth-century America, was rather a dirty word. It was used interchangeably with *faction*, which Madison defined in *Federalist* Ten as "a number of citizens" motivated by an interest contrary to other citizens' rights, "or to the permanent and aggregate interests of the community." Similarly Hamilton, in *Federalist* One, condemned "that intolerant spirit which has at all times characterized political parties." For most of the anti-Federalists also, during the time prior to ratification, party spirit and tactics were a plague against which a watchful citizenry had constantly to be on guard. It is understandable why late-eighteenth-century Americans should have felt this way about organized partisanship; its immediate model for them was the scurrilous, almost mindless intrigue that had gone on in the British Parliament for the half-century preceding the American Revolution, and they found in the classical historians a venerable and still ominous example of party spirit in the murderous, Republic-destroying maneuvers of the Gracchi and their Roman Senatorial enemies. Both the opponents and the supporters of the new Constitution, therefore, made antipartyism virtually an article of the American political creed.

Yet by adopting the names "Federalist" and "anti-Federalist," as they contested elections for state ratifying conventions to choose the delegates who would vote the new instrument up or down, such political activists became, in spite of themselves, partisans. Furthermore, because the debate over ratification was national in scope, their rivalry was (or became) a national partisanship. Several people who had been "Antifederals" in the debate over ratification were elected to the new Congress under the Constitution: four from South Carolina, two each from Massachusetts and New York, three from Virginia. By a nice historical irony Patrick Henry's anti-Federalist forces, who controlled both houses of the Virginia legislature, defeated James Madison for election to the U.S. Senate; and George Clinton, the powerful and perennial New York governor whose well-oiled political machine (founded early in the Revolution) had done its utmost to prevent ratification of the Constitution by his state, picked up three Electoral College votes—against John Adams and a scattering of other Federalists—in America's first vice-presidential election.

To be sure, few if any political figures after ratification remained *literally* "antifederalist," in the sense of working for a restoration of the former government under the Articles of Confederation. Restorationism has never been a viable American political option, except in jest ("Save your Confederate money; the South will rise again"). Their preferred term was "republican," and they cast themselves as the Constitution's true guardians against their opponents' alleged monarchist machinations. And the growth of this

Republican Opposition was swift and impressive—or, if one were a Federalist, alarming. By the end of George Washington's first term as President the spirit of party and faction had indeed become involved "in the necessary and ordinary operations of the government," as James Madison in *Federalist* Ten had warned it must.

Nobody was more quickly drawn into the partisan whirlpool than Madison himself. Elected (after his Senatorial setback by Henry) to the House of Representatives, he functioned for its first session as an honest broker, trading Virginia votes for federal assumption of the states' war debts in exchange for New York votes to settle the new national capital on the Potomac. But then his *Federalist Papers* co-author Alexander Hamilton, who had become Secretary of the Treasury, proposed chartering a Bank of the United States; his fellow-Virginian Thomas Jefferson, then Secretary of State, opposed it (both basing their positions on carefully reasoned Constitutional grounds); and Madison, unsuccessfully opposing the Bank in Congress with the block of votes he commanded there, emerged in effect as parliamentary Leader of the Opposition.

In March of 1791, after the First Congress finally adjourned, Madison went up to New York City, followed two months later by Jefferson, and the two went on a "botanizing excursion" to upstate New York and New England. The plant they cultivated on that expedition, cross-fertilized between Northeastern and Old Southern genetic strains, sprouted into the Republican, soon renamed Democratic-Republican, Party. On October 16, 1792, there took place what political party historian Roy F. Nichols has termed "the first national nominating conference"; and George Clinton's mere three electoral votes in the previous vice-presidential contest swelled in the 1792 election to an impressive 50 against John Adams's 77.

George Washington, trying to preside over the new government from a vantage point above it all, looked on appalled. As the increasingly militant French Revolution became an issue in American domestic politics, his alarm grew. Overseas, Washington proclaimed strict neutrality as between the French and the British, feeling that a shaky new country in need of "time . . . to settle and mature its yet recent institutions," could ill afford that kind of international partisanship; whether Americans *liked* French revolution or British counter-revolution was beside the point. At home, the first President from a similar motive begged both Alexander Hamilton and Thomas Jefferson, leaders in the emergent rival parties, to stay in his cabinet. The tactic failed; Jefferson left the State Department at the end of 1793, Hamilton departed the Treasury in 1795, and the third U.S. presidential election was frankly partisan, as Federalist John Adams eked out a 71–68 Electoral College victory over Republican Thomas Jefferson.

Most modern commentators upon George Washington's much-misunderstood Farewell Address have treated it primarily as a foreign policy document. But the bulk of its argument is a warning "against the baleful effects of the spirit of party," which—Washington told his fellow citizens—"agitates the community with ill-founded jealousies and false alarms; kindles the animosity of one part against another; foments occasional riot and insurrection"; and "opens the door to foreign influence and corruption." More fundamentally, "it serves always to distract the public councils and enfeeble the public administration." The great temptation for government, at that historical moment, reasoning thus, would have been to suppress all political opposition in the name of national unity; other language in the Farewell Address suggests that Washington himself leaned perilously far in that direction. But surprisingly, in view of what usually happens to post-revolutionary and post-colonial regimes, the only serious attempt at suppression—the Alien and Sedition Acts of 1798—failed; the opposition candidate, Jefferson, was elected and took control of the government.

To be sure, as Ralph Ketcham has argued, Jefferson's inaugural reassurance that "we are all republicans—we are all federalists" may well have signaled a move, subtler than the more forceful effort by the Federalists when they had been in power, to put the opposing party out of business; and under Monroe, who in 1820 gathered in all but one of the electoral votes, the gambit very nearly succeeded. Yet within the next few years the party system, broadened and modernized, would be born again; and since that time —with one traumatic exception—it has never seriously been challenged. Somehow the Americans had devised a mechanism of government capable of both self-criticism and self-correction. Representative democracy had prevailed, in spite of all the weight of historical evidence and of contemporary example to the contrary. The army need not be the final arbiter of political decisions; the cycle of revolution need not always yield a Caesar, a Cromwell, a Napoleon.

Perhaps the exorcism of Caesar's ghost was easier when the

Republic was young, fresh-planted in the empty land, than it would have been in Europe. "We have unwisely considered ourselves as the inhabitants of an old instead of a new country," Charles Pinckney of South Carolina, one of the framers of the U.S. Constitution, told the Federal Convention in Philadelphia on June 25, 1787. "The people of this country are not only very different from the inhabitants of any state we are acquainted with in the modern world; but I assert that their situation is distinct from either the people of Greece or of Rome"—or, one must now add, from their own situation when their state grew older. The dramatic tension in their unfolding story comes from seeing the ghost of Caesar rise again and again and watching Americans cheat destiny, preserving their republicanism in spite of events that seem sure to send them down the road to empire—until the latest bout with destiny, in which we ourselves have been actors.

Interlude II

Before children in the New World could learn about Greek athletes running their hearts out for a perishable laurel wreath or toga-wrapped Roman senators shaking the world with oratory, they first had to master certain fundamentals. "He that ne'er learns his A, B, C, for ever will a Blockhead be"; so the New England Primer *cautioned generation after generation of young scholars. First printed in 1690, the* Primer, *with its wood-block pictures, the Shorter Catechism, and John Cotton's "Spiritual Milk for Babes," saturated young minds for a century, until the first appearance of Webster's "blue-back speller" in 1783. Each letter had a memory-reinforcing scrap of verse, from A—"In Adam's Fall/We sinnèd all"—to Z—"Zaccheus he/Did climb the tree/His Lord to see." And after the illustrated letters came a little anthology of child-oriented poetry, some of which got pretty lugubrious:*

> *I in the burying place may see*
> *Graves shorter there than I;*
> *From Death's arrest no age is free,*
> *Young children too may die . . .*

In 1719—which also saw the first publication in the American colonies of Mother Goose!*—Isaac Watts's* Divine and Moral Songs Attempted in Easy Language for the Use of Children *added its own grim warning:*

> *Tis dang'rous to offend God,*
> *Whose pow'r and vengeance none can tell;*
> *One stroke of his almighty rod*
> *Will send young sinners quick to Hell.*

A person might grow up to reject all such outrageous doctrines; many did. Or the young reader might internalize such teachings, and later in life undergo the wrenching emotional experience of being "born

45

again"; many did that also. In either case, this earliest exposure to cosmic ultimates became embedded in an American's consciousness in a far more primary and coercive way than anything that might afterward be learned about the glory that was Greece and the grandeur that was Rome.

THREE

How Shall We Sing the Lord's Song in a Strange Land?

The fall of Rome, according to Edward Gibbon, occurred in tandem with the rise of Christianity. As Americans launched a republic which they hoped would not go the way of Rome's, their political concerns of necessity became entangled with theology. Is liberty intrinsically irreligious, as frightened conservatives insisted? Does religious faith call for authoritarian politics, as free-spirited radicals proclaimed?

Such questions still plague us today, and still—as in the eighteenth century—prompt hasty, ill-considered answers. But as the song says, "It ain't necessarily so." For many politically active Americans throughout their history, religion has not been an opiate but an energizer. The kind of religion we today would term "fundamentalist" proved compatible with revolution in the eighteenth century and with a powerful anti-slavery impulse in the nineteenth. And even in its most privatized forms, religion has had a way of seeping back into politics.

Organized religion in post-Revolutionary America took on political forms, even while secular political structures were purging themselves of overt, explicit religion. In a complex dialectical interaction, religion and politics both became caught up in America's revolt against destiny.

1. "No Religious Test Shall Ever Be Required"

On April 30, 1789, with "feelings not unlike those of a culprit who is going to the place of his execution," George Washington moved to the chair of government. As he rose to deliver America's first presidential inaugural address his stage fright was painfully evident. "This great man," as a sardonic senator from Pennsylvania

47

observed, "was agitated and embarrassed more than ever he was by the leveled cannon or pointed musket"; he trembled, he had trouble reading his script, and like many other untrained public speakers then or today he couldn't figure out what to do with his hands. But, as had always been George Washington's way, he got through it somehow.

In his second paragraph, the new President set the first of many precedents he would establish for the new government: he invoked the blessing of "that Almighty Being who rules over the Universe, who presides in the councils of nations, and whose providential aids can supply every human defect." To an aristocratic or royalist critic of republican governments, who expected them to pull down religion along with law, property, and respect for one's betters, such conduct in a republican chief executive—a first magistrate who acted also as *pontifex maximus*—must have come as a surprise. Had such a critic scrutinized the new Federal Constitution, it would have disclosed a deeper paradox; for the instrument which Washington had just sworn (on a Bible) to "preserve, protect and defend" also mandated that "no religious test shall ever be required as a qualification to any office or public trust under the United States." No religious test? But such tests had been required of chiefs of state from time immemorial!

A purist might have charged that George Washington, in associating the reverent beliefs of Congress and the people at large with his own in the face of this injunction against religious testing, was already stretching the Constitution more than a little. However, President Washington's gentlemanly "homage to the Great Author of every public and private good" was a long way from the sacramental pomp of a king's coronation oath. Indeed, the same Constitution would have permitted the new President merely to "affirm" its defense, had his own conscience forbidden him to swear a sacramental oath.

So radical a change in the relationship between religion and the state might have been expected to prompt furious debate, if not outright riot. Surprisingly, the ban on religious tests for public office passed through the Federal Convention with scarcely a murmur. It was reported out for a vote late in the Convention's work, when members, anxious to get home, were spending most of their time wrangling over how many states' concurrences—seven, eight, nine or ten—should suffice to ratify. Delegate Roger Sherman thought the test ban unnecessary, "the prevailing liberality being

48

a sufficient security against such tests." Luther Martin—who not coincidentally would end up in the anti-ratification camp—mildly grumbled that "there were some members so unfashionable as to think . . . that in a Christian country it would be at least decent to hold out some distinction between the professors of Christianity and downright infidelity or paganism." But the sense of the times seemed against such distinctions.

Symbolic of that sense is a letter written to the Convention on September 7, 1787—one week after the vote on the religious test —by a Jew in Philadelphia, on behalf of co-religionists who "during the late contest with England, . . . have bravely fought and bled for liberty which they can not enjoy."

Pennsylvania, contrary to the spirit of its own state bill of rights, was requiring of its public office holders a belief in the divine inspiration of the Old and New Testaments. "To swear and believe that the new testament was given by divine inspiration is absolutely against the religious principles of a Jew," Jonas Phillips wrote, "and it is against his conscience to take any such oath." The U.S. Constitution as written would neither hold out a distinction between Christians and others nor leave such matters to the prevailing liberality; it gave non-Christians like Phillips the positive protection of law.

Just to reinforce the point, the new Congress, in its first session, passed and sent around to the states a series of constitutional amendments the first of which declared that "Congress shall make no law respecting an establishment of religion." What arrant folly, an eighteenth-century defender of established—i.e., state—religion might have exclaimed. "Religion is the basis of civil society, the source of all good and of all comfort," Edmund Burke a year later warned sympathizers with French Revolutionary disestablishment. England, he declared, would rather put up with superstition than yield to impiety; its Established Church, although admittedly a "prejudice," was a prejudice involving "profound and extensive wisdom"; and in "taking ground on that religious system, of which we are now in possession, we continue to act on the early received and uniformly continued sense of mankind."

So also had Americans believed when first they settled on their new land. "True religion," proclaimed Nathaniel Ward in 1645, "strictly binds every conscience to contend earnestly for the truth; to preserve unity of spirit, faith, and ordinances; to be all like minded, of one accord, . . . and by no means to permit heresies or erroneous opinions." But should such unity be enforced by the state? Absolutely; "God does nowhere in His word tolerate Christian states to give toleration to such adversaries of his truth, if they have power in their hands to suppress them."

Burke would not have gone so far; nor would some of Ward's own contemporaries. Maryland in 1649, two years after Nathaniel Ward published his justification of intolerance, adopted a Toleration Act—which began, however, by decreeing that any person within the colony who should "deny the holy Trinity . . . or shall use or utter any reproachful speeches, words, or language concerning the said Holy Trinity, or any of the said three persons thereof, shall be punished with death"—a peculiarly cramped and crabbed notion of tolerance, to say the least. But as the seventeenth century wore on into the eighteenth, such harsh usages gave way to gentler practices, and "toleration"—i.e., the mere allowance of some degree of dissent and diversity alongside a state church—gave way in the Revolutionary era to full "separation," whereby the state neither supported the church nor interfered with citizens' religious beliefs and practices.

Massachusetts, with its moralistic-republican dream of a "Christian Sparta," and Connecticut, with its interlocking religious, commercial, political, and social elites (the Federalist/Congregationalist "Standing Order"), clung to their state churches well into the nineteenth century; nor could anything at that time constitutionally have been done about them, because only *Congress* was forbidden to pass laws "respecting an establishment of religion, or prohibiting the free exercise thereof." Not until the Fourteenth Amendment extended the First to the states would it be possible to require separation at the state level. In politically pivotal Virginia, however, after a furious legislative battle during and after the War of Independence, "an act for establishing religious freedom" became law (1786). Written by Thomas Jefferson, and regarded by him as his most important public action after the Declaration of Independence, this statute firmly endorsed the revolutionary view that governments are not handed down from God but crafted by human beings: "our civil rights have no dependence on our religious opinions, any more than our opinions in physics or geometry." In his *Notes on Virginia* Jefferson put it more pungently: "It does me no injury for my neighbor to say there are twenty gods, or no god. It neither picks my pocket nor breaks my leg."

2. The Separationist Creed

How had it happened? Many, then and afterward, saw the implicit logic of Protestantism's "priesthood of all believers" at work, forgetful that the repressive Massachusetts Bay of Nathaniel Ward had also been a Protestant colony. Others, both then and in the heyday of Frederick Jackson Turner, attributed religious (and other) freedoms to the liberating influence of the frontier. "Zeal in Europe is confined; here it evaporates in the great distance it has to travel," wrote Hector St. John de Crèvecoeur in 1782. "There it is a grain of powder enclosed, here it burns away in the open air." Even at its high-and-mightiest, censorious Massachusetts had been subtly checked by the knowledge that the capital of wide-open Rhode Island, founded by Roger Williams with his firm conviction that "a forced worship stinketh in God's nostrils," lay only forty miles away on the Boston Post Road. After the shut-in seaboard settlements erupted into the country back of beyond, and began peopling that country with Moravians, Quakers, Catholics, Scotch-Irish Presbyterians, and other dissenters from the coastal state religions, it became a practical impossibility to establish a continent-wide state church, so the argument runs—even though such churches flourished both in New France and in New Spain.

Sidney Mead, in an influential article on "American Protestantism During the Revolutionary Epoch" and in many subsequent essays and studies, argued that religious freedom in the new American states was the fruit of an unlikely marriage between the scientific skepticism of the Age of Reason and the warm-hearted enthusiasm of the Great Awakening. When the initial wave of revivalism swept over the colonies in the 1730s one of the most acute concerns had been the question of how one tested the *genuineness* of religious emotions; Jonathan Edwards had devoted his narrow but extraordinarily powerful mind to that subject in a deep-probing, 200-page *Treatise Concerning Religious Affections* (1746). Conformity to a prescribed orthodoxy, rewarded by privilege and status in worldly affairs, raised the dismal prospect that such affections might be faked; as Jefferson put it in the Virginia statute, politically enforced religious profession "tends only to corrupt the principles of that religion it meant to encourage." Moreover, "to contend earnestly for the truth," as Nathaniel Ward had urged that believers do, did not necessarily require that they call upon the

51

state to suppress their adversaries. Indeed, many evangelicals came to believe that such state sanctions would only cramp their style. Jefferson got some of his strongest political support from fervent, Bible-quoting Baptists, both in his home state and nationally; and in the crucial Virginia legislative struggle he found an early ally in the staunch Calvinists of the Hanover Presbytery, who memorialized the legislature on October 24, 1776 "that when our blessed Saviour declares his *kingdom is not of this world*, he renounces all dependence upon state power."

Born-again Baptist Isaac Backus, proclaiming in 1779 that "nothing can be true religion but a voluntary obedience unto God's revealed will, of which each rational soul has an equal right to judge for itself," was able to fellow-travel with religiously radical Thomas Paine, who declared in 1794 that "my own mind is my own church." But this marriage of revivalists and rationalists, soon after its fruition in constitutional religious freedom, broke up in an acrimonious divorce. Liberal rationalism, in the turbulent 1790s, came to be equated in conservative American minds with Revolutionary French "infidelity"; and a Second Great Awakening which re-kindled the flames of the First very often took a turn which was religiously orthodox and politically anti-Jefferson.

"The strong sympathy which . . . prevailed here towards those who were leaders in the French Revolution, and towards the Revolution itself, prepared us to become miserable dupes of their principles and declarations," thundered Yale president Timothy Dwight—a grandson of Jonathan Edwards—in 1801. "They were viewed merely as human beings, embarked deeply in the glorious cause of liberty; and not at all as Infidels, as the abettors of falsehood, and the enemies of Righteousness, of Truth, and of God." But by that time it was too late for such fulminations. Dwight might smugly declare that "the liberty of Infidels was not the liberty of New England," and claim that "this part of our country, at least, has escaped the bondage of infidelity, corruption, and moral ruin"; but the rest of the country in the crucial presidential election of 1800, while not necessarily embracing the anticlerical rationalism of Thomas Jefferson, had emphatically endorsed his politics.

Puritan Connecticut and Massachusetts held out against the Jeffersonians for another generation, faithfully voting Federalist in presidential elections until the very last one in which that party offered a candidate (1816). But even they could not hold onto their state churches, and they succumbed at last to full separation in

1819 and 1833, respectively. As the Federalist/Republican political wars faded and transmuted into the Democratic/Whig and Republican/Democratic contests of a later day, and as the Supreme Court came, case by case, gradually to construe Thomas Jefferson's "wall of separation" between church and state as comprehensively shielding the state from church influence and the church (or the religious individual) from state interference, Americans discovered they had created something new in the bitter and sometimes bloody history of church-state relations: a functional separation not based on mutual hostility. It had not been necessary to *attack* the church in order to separate it from the state, nor was it necessary for believers to attack the state in order to safeguard their church. Other modern revolutions left a burdensome political legacy from which the heirs of the American Revolution escaped. Philosophically, Jefferson and Paine were "anticlerical"—mildly so, by European standards—but separation itself did not mandate anticlericalism.

By contrast, in post-Revolutionary times in France down at least through the end of the Third Republic, and in other countries whose revolutions followed the French rather than the American model, a defender of the Republic was almost by definition anticlerical, while a defender of the church was more than likely counterrevolutionary. (In Russia, at least until a subservient church made uneasy peace with an avowedly atheist state, the antithesis was even more severe.) The Americans somehow contrived to have it both ways: mandating no religious test for offices of trust or profit, forbidding establishment of religion, and allowing its free exercise; yet at the same time electing presidents who publicly tendered "homage to the Great Author of every public and private good" and who regularly proclaimed days of national thanksgiving. It would even be possible to argue that although church and state in the United States are constitutionally separated, religion and political culture are not really separated at all.

As church-state separation became accepted as a fact of political and cultural life in America, the more intellectually agile among the conservatives scrambled to adjust to the new situation. Lyman Beecher, whose first reaction to the Connecticut election of 1818 which produced a separationist majority in the legislature was one of thunderstruck horror, soon came to believe that it was "the best thing that ever happened to the State of Connecticut." Nor would he hedge his bet in the manner many religious conservatives, from Ezra Stiles Ely in the 1820s to Jerry Falwell in the 1980s, have proposed: if the state itself can no longer enforce orthodoxy, then at least elect only orthodox persons to run the state. Beecher would have none of this. Christian citizens could "repose confidence in men, for civil purposes, who do not profess religion, or afford evidence of piety," Beecher argued. To suppose otherwise would be to repeat the "mistake of our pious fathers," who had made "the terms of communion and civil trust the same." But since God has created all human beings, Christian or "infidel," as free moral agents, the trait religiously responsible voters must ponder in assessing a candidate's fitness for public office is not orthodoxy but personal integrity.

3. Political Calvinism and Its Religious Critics

Free moral agents? But that, from the standpoint of the Calvinist theology which had intellectually dominated British North America for most of its colonial history, was precisely what human beings on their own initiative were incapable of becoming. "In Adam's fall, we sinnèd all." In the more formal language of the Book of Common Prayer—language that book's users have been trying for three centuries to get rid of—"the fault and corruption of the nature of every person born into this world, . . . deserveth God's wrath and damnation." Orthodox Christians, Protestant or Catholic, were supposed to believe that as a matter of course, and Calvinism added a further twist of the knife: "Adam's" fall meant that our doom, both collectively and as individuals, had been decreed from before the beginning of time. Sin was no mere behavioral lapse; it was, as Paul had grimly put it (Romans 7:19) something ingrained in our character, over which we had no control: "For the good that I would I do not: but the evil which I would not, that I do."

"We sinnèd all"; and "all" meant everybody, regardless of race, national origin, bank account—or even religion. Don't delude yourself into thinking that if you have had a personal religious emotional upheaval you have necessarily been "saved," Jonathan Edwards warned in his relentless, psychologically probing *Treatise Concerning Religious Affections* (1746); "If any one . . . is ready to acquit himself, and say . . . 'I am often greatly moved with the consideration of the great things of religion,' let him not content himself with this." He may only be kidding himself; religious genuineness is not proved by mere vividness or intensity. Such a person might make a profession of faith and be admitted to church membership, and still be eternally ticketed for Hell. The Massachusetts Bay Puritans, in their Cambridge Platform of 1648, had realistically admitted that their godly membership was bound to include "such as . . . may be accounted Saints by calling, though perhaps some or more of them be unsound and hypocrites inwardly." The personal horror of Calvinism was that since God alone decided your ultimate fate you could never, no matter how you felt, reasoned, or acted, really be sure.

Between the Puritan founders and their Revolutionary heirs a full century and a half of theological thinking and teaching had rolled by, and "the views of human existence which resulted from this course of training," wrote Harriet Beecher Stowe—who, growing up in Lyman Beecher's household, had lived through the course—"were gloomy enough to oppress any heart which did not rise above them by triumphant faith or sink below them by brutish insensibility." Strangely, Calvinists during the War for Independence had had no difficulty reconciling this dark view of human motivation and guilt with a belief in revolution and in representative self-government; their leaders—be they Scotch-Irish Presbyterian, Southern Baptist, or New England Puritan—had overwhelmingly supported the patriot side. Calvinists could accept democracy, not as a means for collecting and registering the choice of citizens who were both rational and good—Jefferson's "pursuit of happiness"—but rather as the only means of checking or deflecting the selfishness and power-lust which governors would otherwise assert over the governed.

The germ of this idea can be found in the Puritan political leader John Winthrop's warning to the Massachusetts General Court in 1648 that "when you choose magistrates, you choose them from among yourselves, men of like passions as you are." Winthrop had not gone on to draw democratic conclusions from that premise; but Revolutionary Calvinists did so regularly. Secularized into the dictum that "power corrupts," this insistence that rulers were by nature inherently no better than those they ruled had wide appeal for non-Calvinists as well. Even Thomas Jefferson, with his ordinarily sunny faith in human nature, was capable of taking the darker view held by many of his political opponents and turning it against them: "Sometimes it is said that man cannot be trusted with the government of himself," President Jefferson noted in his first inaugural address. "Can he, then, be trusted with the government of others?" Democracy, a Calvinist could argue, with its capacity to punish its rulers at the polls, was the only form of government with which sinful human beings could entrust each other. As the twentieth-century theologian Reinhold Niebuhr was to express it, "Democracy . . . is not a method which is effective only among virtuous men. It is a method which prevents interested men from following their interests to the detriment of the community."

Calvinism in eighteenth-century America was, however, under fire not so much on political grounds as from within the religious camp itself. Some believers had rejected it from the beginning; the great Quaker apostle George Fox had based his evangelistic appeal not on the premise that "In Adam's fall/We sinnèd all" but rather on the axiom "There is that of God in every man." "Whatever has happened since his creation," wrote a maverick Puritan minister, John Wise, in 1717, man "remains at the upper end of nature, and as such is a creature of a very noble character"; in fact "he is the favorite animal on earth." Some rejected the doctrines of predestination and total depravity on eighteenth-century Enlightenment grounds: a just, reasonable God would not treat rational creatures so arbitrarily. Others found "the awful dread which was constantly underlying life" in a Calvinist community more than could psychologically be borne: these teachings, wrote Mrs. Stowe, "when received as absolute truth, and as a basis of actual life, had, on minds of a certain class, the effect of a slow poison." Many simply found such doctrines morally objectionable: confronted by "the unrelenting vindictiveness with which more than half the Bible is filled," Tom Paine declared, "I sincerely detest it, as I detest everything that is cruel."

However, for every Thomas Paine, who generalized from the harshness of Christian doctrine as typically interpreted to a categorical rejection of Christianity as a whole, there were a thousand Methodists who accepted the Bible and evangelical religion but broke sharply with Calvinistic theology. When they transplanted their religion to the New World, basing their worship service on a form which John Wesley had adapted from the Book of Common Prayer, the American Methodists deleted from the Church of England's Articles of Religion all of the Calvinistic clauses, and substituted instead a declaration that Christians could hope to achieve moral perfection in this world. Catholics also—passing over certain difficult passages in Augustine's *City of God*—rejected predestination; and one distinguished American convert, Father Isaac Hecker, a sometime associate of Emerson and his circle, came to feel that "the withering, soul-destroying horrors of Calvinism" had done much to create "all that is repulsive and hard in the Yankee character." Eventually, although preserving to this day many bastions of theological scholarship and personal piety, Calvinism in America became an object of satire, even of ridicule; readers of Mark Twain's *Tom Sawyer* heard a Calvinist sermon described as "an argument that dealt in limitless fire and thinned the predestined elect down to a company so small as to be hardly worth the saving." The formidable intellectual structure of the "New England theology" founded by Jonathan Edwards became, in O. W. Holmes's whimsical poem "The Deacon's Masterpiece," metaphorically a "wonderful one horse shay," which held together "a hundred years and a day"—dating from the publication in 1755 of Edwards's great philosophical treatise on *Freedom of the Will*— and then, one Sunday morning on the way to church, fell into dust.

This does not mean, however, that Americans had suddenly stopped believing in miracles, Adam and Eve, or the Apostles' Creed. Some of them, by ceasing to indulge in intricate theological discourse on the New England model, may even have become *more* Bible-bound than ever before. "Doctrinal exhibitions," declared Thomas Campbell in 1809, "ought not to be made terms of Christian communication," and "nothing ought to be inculcated upon Christians as articles of faith . . . but what is expressly taught and enjoined upon them in the word of God," *i.e.*, in the Bible. Nor did Americans abandon self-congratulatory political and nationalistic inferences drawn from that word. Since Puritan times they had allegorized themselves as a new Israel, complete with an exodus from Egypt, a time of wandering in the wilderness, the conquest of at least the eastern margin of a Promised Land, and —as Winthrop had preached—a status before the rest of the world as a City Upon a Hill. In their minds, the Revolution and the Constitution only confirmed that status.

In his first inaugural address, George Washington—no Calvinist!—assured the people of the United States that "every step by which they have advanced to the character of an independent nation seems to have been distinguished by some token of providential agency"; and the achievement of their newly settled form of government under the Constitution, by "the tranquil deliberation and voluntary consent of so many distinct communities," could "not be compared with the means by which most governments have been established without some return of pious gratitude." Church and state might be constitutionally separate, but president after president was to restate this essentially theological interpretation of American history, over and over to the point of cliché. Small wonder that G. K. Chesterton, contemplating Britain's former colonies in the twentieth century, would describe them as "a nation with the soul of a church."

4. The Nationalization of Churchmanship

Even in the Republic's earliest years, religion in America exhibited a dazzling diversity. Learned Calvinist divines constructed and delivered intricate, logical sermons; unlettered lay preachers spoke "from the Spirit," without notes. Jewish congregations studied Hebrew; Catholics said and heard Mass in Latin; most Lutherans of that generation worshipped in German. They and the Episcopalians followed set forms, reading or singing words prescribed by the calendar from the traditional liturgical year; others improvised, preaching on whatever topic appealed at the moment and offering extemporaneous prayers. A few, notably the Moravians, sang Bach; many allowed only the Psalms to be sung. Baptists totally immersed their converts under water; Dunkers immersed them three times, once for each person of the Trinity. Many of John Wesley's American followers rejoiced in the name "Shouting Methodists"; some ecstatic believers jumped, barked, or rolled on the ground; Shakers danced; Quakers were silent. And an uncountable number simply stood apart and watched the spectacle.

Americans took the "free exercise clause" of the First Amendment, and its state equivalents, with awesome literalness—barring certain cultural limitations imposed by a society on the verge of becoming Victorian; and even against that barrier some religionists in the early nineteenth-century (the Oneida Community; the Mormons) experimented with sexual practices—plural or complex marriage in particular—which in today's more open climate would still be considered at least picturesque. The "establishment clause," and its state equivalents, meant however that such "establishing"—limiting, organizing, supporting, directing—as these free exercisers wanted would have to be worked out by and for themselves.

Churchgoing Americans, in short, faced the same problems of representative self-government, freedom vs. order, minority vs. majority, local differences vs. national consensus, written rules vs. tacit assumptions, that confronted America's secular political culture as a whole. Perhaps it is not surprising that Americans dealt with religious and political constitutions in a strikingly similar way—but it was by no means inevitable that they do so. A socially and politically open society allows not only for the creation of self-governing churches but also for the rise of charismatic leaders who discipline their faithful flocks with love and terror. The twentieth century has shown us many examples of just such autocratic, personalist regimes, which have ranged from wondrously comic to terrifyingly lethal. Religious authoritarianism, occasionally of an extreme kind, can be found in post-Revolutionary America also; but on the whole that is not the way things happened.

The American Revolution posed immediate problems of reorganization for all faiths, especially those which retained Old World institutional ties. It would no longer do, Dutch Reformed New Yorkers felt, to take orders ultimately from ecclesiastical superiors who sat across the ocean in Amsterdam. But during the war, Holland at least had been benevolently neutral; indeed, its prudent bankers had invested, most helpfully, in the patriot cause. For American Episcopalians, who counted—however loosely—as a province of the Church of England, the issue was obviously more acute. South of Mason's and Dixon's line, planter-controlled vestries and the clergy themselves were enthusiastically patriot; but north of Maryland practically all their parishes were staffed with missionary clergy supported from Britain. Old North Church, from whose steeple hung the lanterns that summoned Paul Revere—"one if by land, two if by sea"—poignantly dramatized the dilemma: below the steeple, down in the church itself, a plaque commemorates the church's Revolutionary-era rector; "driven from his pulpit for King and Country." Many such Anglican churchmen left for Halifax with other British Empire loyalists when George Washington's besieging Continentalers drove the British out of Boston.

With the end of the war, the staunchly Tory Connecticut clergymen of the same faith decided they must send one of their number off to London to be made a bishop, thereby securing a grown-in-America hierarchy. Samuel Seabury accordingly set sail for London, only to find the English bishops unwilling to ordain someone who could not take the Parliament-imposed oath of loyalty to

King George. Undaunted, Seabury proceeded to Scotland, where bishops still functioned in succession to Stuart die-hards who had refused allegiance to William and Mary when the Stuart monarchy was chased from the throne. Meanwhile, American Episcopalians in Pennsylvania, New York, and Virginia had elected additional bishops, two of whom duly proceeded overseas for consecration also—a situation prompting Benjamin Franklin to wonder "that men in America, qualified by their learning and piety to pray for and instruct their neighbors, should not be permitted to do it till they had made a voyage six thousand miles out and home, to ask leave of a cross old gentleman at Canterbury." With enough bishops on hand at home to ordain still more bishops, American Episcopalians would have to ask such leave no longer. Quickly— by the end of the 1780s—their communion became fully nationalized, with a House of Bishops whose members were elected out of their local dioceses, joint lay and clerical concurrence upon all laws and canons of the church, and other "checks and balances" strikingly resembling those in the federal secular governmental model.

The Methodists required the same cutting of an umbilical cord. Founder John Wesley, firmly Tory, had written "A Calm Address to the American Colonies" in a vain effort to convince them of the folly of their ways. Wesley himself, after the bad news from Yorktown, realized that his colonial rule over the American Methodists must come to an end, and so ordained two Americans as "superintendents"—somehow in recrossing the Atlantic they acquired the more exalted name "bishops"—and at a conference in Baltimore in 1784 Methodism also became nationalized. And they too followed the secular political model, with a legislative General Conference (Congress); a multiple executive, the Council of Bishops; and a balance between these national entities and state-level organizations, the annual conferences. In a time of rapid growth in membership and dispersal of the population they also found an innovative method for keeping in touch with their own grass roots: they made their whole church itinerant— nomadic!—from top to bottom. A bishop did not reside by a cathedral church, as in Catholic, European Lutheran, Church of England, or Greek Orthodox usage; he and his colleagues were required to "circulate throughout the Connection," which meant he might be presiding over an annual conference of clergy in New Hampshire and then proceed to his next appointment in South

Carolina. And the lower clergy, similarly, "rode circuit"—covering the ground on horseback, to visit their flocks much as Wesley had in England but on a much vaster scale. To be retired from the ministry, in Methodist parlance, was to be "located"—i.e., grounded.

Methodist bishops retained the ultimate power of appointment, and in that respect Methodism was more centralized and authoritarian than most American religious bodies. The Baptists, as a proscribed and even persecuted sect in their early years, had not to worry about Old World organizational ties (much though all evangelical Americans cherished one best-seller written in jail by the seventeenth-century English Baptist John Bunyan, *Pilgrim's Progress*). By the eighteenth century's end, the Baptist churches had achieved no nationwide organization whatsoever—a state of affairs many Baptists considered one of the glories of their faith.

Most other religious communions felt the need of *some* degree of national incorporation; almost all of them saw that any such broader forms must be generously leavened with local control. Henry Melchior Muhlenburg, the effective founder of American Lutheranism, had seen this coming long before the Revolution. Although insisting that German-speaking Lutheranism in America must be founded upon "the Unaltered Augsburg Confession and other symbolic books," in drawing up a church constitution in 1761 Muhlenburg had specified that the local congregation must have "the right and privilege of electing elders or rulers by majority vote" and of approving any "important transactions, such as buying, dismantling, building, making debts, appointing trustees and elders, or engaging preachers and teachers"—because, already "This is customary in the Protestant churches." It was customary even in Puritan New England at its darkest, one may add; their Cambridge Platform of 1648 had stipulated that "a church being free, cannot become subject to any, but by a free Election . . . and if the Church have Power to chuse their officers and Ministers, then in cases of manifest Unworthiness and Delinquency, they have power also to depose them."

Jews in America found this pattern entirely congenial. Even more constrained to lay leadership than the Protestant sects by the utter absence, at the outset, of *any* clerical hierarchy—in 1773 there were but three rabbis in the New World, none of them in North America—Jews were "congregationalists" from the word go. In some communities Cantors filled in the role which ministers or "charge lay leaders" played in Protestant parishes; after all, it only took ten adult males to hold a canonically legitimate service of worship. Later, as Jewish migration to the U.S. increased, Judaism acquired theological seminaries, rabbinical conferences, all the panoply of organization enjoyed or endured by their WASP (and Black Protestant) counterparts; but by that time the pattern was well set. When the Congregationalists in 1950 got into the civil courts with a lawsuit, litigating whether the national leaders of that communion in seeking merger with another, differently structured church were violating the tenets of the Cambridge Platform, the Jewish presiding trial judge in Kings County Supreme Court, Brooklyn, listened to the litigants and declared he felt right at home.

For Catholicism, the nationalizing process was not nearly so easy. Hierarchy was of its very essence, and the apex of that hierarchy necessarily located itself in Rome—an even longer sea-journey than the one to Canterbury. Nor, realistically, was the option of lay congregations calling and dismissing their pastors available for Catholics as it was for Congregationalists, Baptists, and—within limits—Lutherans. Nevertheless, the passions of nationalism and the spirit of Enlightenment that drove the Revolution to its successful conclusion caught Catholicism up as well.

Like the American Episcopalians, Catholic Americans at the end of the war for independence were stuck with a nominal ecclesiastical superior in London, Vicar-Apostolic James Talbot, who detested their political cause. Replacing this Tory superior with a *French* prelate, as was seriously proposed in 1783, would still have left the American Church in a subordinate, colonial relationship to Europe—not to mention the awkwardness that might have resulted a decade later when the Church in France felt the wrath of the French Revolution! American Catholics desired, Father John Carroll wrote to Rome in 1785, "that no pretext be given to the enemies of our religion to accuse us of depending unnecessarily on a foreign authority." Therefore, he proposed that an American bishop be nominated by the American *priests*—a revolutionary departure from the usual Catholic practice but one which Carroll argued would "remove all ground of objecting to us, as though we held anything hostile to the national independence."

Rome yielded the point; and five years later Carroll himself, chosen by his own fellow clergy—as a Methodist or an Episcopalian might have been in their churches!—was duly consecrated the first Catholic Bishop of Baltimore. The experiment has never been repeated; but at that historic moment it got American

Catholicism past the immediate crisis of national maturation. Moreover, a church which in theory was committed to establishment found itself aligned in practice with the Jeffersonian separationists, beside whom its American members had worked to secure "that glorious revolution," which,—in the words of a Catholic sermon preached to the members of the Continental Congress in Philadelphia on July 4, 1779—"has placed the sons of America among the free and independent nations of the earth."

5. The Religious Schism Over Slavery

Catholics often have argued that Protestantism is by its very nature competitive and divisive; once the mandatory harmony of the *Ura Sancta* was broken, nothing stood in the way to prevent organized Christianity from fissioning into hundreds of sectarian variations. Yet Protestants also enjoyed singing "Blest Be the Tie that Binds." John C. Calhoun in 1850, as the federal Union stood at the precipice of disruption, credited "the unity of the great religious denominations, all of which originally embraced the whole Union," together with "the many and strong ties that have held together the two great parties which have, with some modifications, existed from the beginning of the Government," as the most cohesive and powerful of the bonds that held the republic together—stronger even than the commercial ties which George Washington had hoped would unite Americans for mutual advantage. "All these denominations, with the exception, perhaps, of the Catholics," Calhoun noted, "were organized very much upon the principle of our political institutions, beginning with smaller meetings . . . terminating in one great central assemblage, corresponding very much with the character of Congress." In such meetings, whether called synods, presbyteries, conferences, assemblies, conventions, or councils, "the principal clergymen and lay members of the respective denominations from all parts of the Union met to transact business relating to their common concerns," and all their activities "contributed greatly to strengthen the bonds of the Union."

But even as the words of Calhoun's last great public address were read out before a hushed Senate, those bonds of church and party were breaking. The greatest hazard of republican, self-governing religion lay in the very accuracy of its democratic reflection of its members' convictions—and of their mutual differences. Southern and Northern Methodists might together deride their Baptist rivals, singing

> We've searched the law of heaven,
> Throughout the Sacred code;
> Of Baptism there by dipping
> We've never heard a word,

while Northern and Southern Baptists together answered the Methodists with a hymn of their own,

> Not *at* the River Jordan,
> But *in* the flowing stream
> Stood John the Baptist preacher
> When he baptized Him,

but when the question became whether baptism—of whatever kind—sets people free, and how far, slaveholding Baptists and Methodists found they had more in common with each other than with those of their co-religionists who opposed slavery. "The strong ties which held each denomination together formed a strong cord to hold the whole Union together," Calhoun concluded, "but, as powerful as they were, they have not been able to resist the explosive effect of slavery agitation."

He proceeded to document his argument, case by case: "The first of these cords which snapped, under its explosive force, was that of the powerful Methodist Episcopal Church. The numerous and strong ties which held it together are all broke, and its unity gone." The form which the Methodist schism took aptly illustrates the problem for a representative church when those whom its leaders represent become fundamentally divided. A bishop in that church whose home residence was in Georgia received a slave by inheritance from a will; Georgia law did not permit him to manumit her. His church required him to "circulate throughout the Connection." It also had an antislavery tradition going back to John Wesley's condemnation of slavery as an "execrable villany." Could he, as a slaveowner, preside over one of the militantly abolitionist annual conferences in New England? Northern and Southern Methodists thrashed out the issue at their Church's General Conference of 1844 and decided, after taking a vote to suspend the bishop from his duties which carried on strict North/South lines, that the only practicable course thereafter was "a mutual and friendly division of the Church." It did not remain friendly for long. As Calhoun noted in his speech, the Northern and Southern Methodists "now form separate churches, and, instead of that feeling of attachment and devotion to the interests of the whole church which was formerly felt, they are now arrayed into two hostile bodies, engaged in litigation about what was formerly their common property." (Establishment clause or not, it took a U.S. Supreme Court decision to straighten out that tangle.)

Implicit in Calhoun's description of the "explosive effect of slavery agitation" were both an axiomatic assumption and a political strategy. If it was *agitation* about slavery, and not slavery itself, that strained the bonds of union, then—in many Southern minds—the solution seemed simple: stop the agitation. Congress itself for a time had adopted that strategy, enacting a "gag rule" which prevented slavery from being discussed in its chambers at all. The problem would not go away, however, and after eight years of dogged, single-minded opposition by Congressman and former President John Quincy Adams, the rule had fallen. But that did not stop some churchmen, especially in the South, from proposing the same policy.

In a ploy that has often been used by conservatives to keep the churches harmless, James Henley Thornwell, a professor in the Presbyterian Seminary at Columbia, South Carolina, maintained that the Church "is not . . . a moral institute of universal good, whose business it is to wage war upon every form of human ill, whether social, civil, political or moral." Although its own "healthful operations . . . , in its own appropriate sphere" may indirectly contribute to the betterment of society, "it has no commission to construct society afresh, to adjust its elements in different proportions, to rearrange the distribution of its classes, or to change the forms of its political constitutions." (This thesis could be generalized, to forbid churches to engage in *any* kind of overt social or political action; one heard arguments very like Thornwell's brought to bear against both the religious antiwar protestors of the 1960s and the church-based "sanctuary movement" of the 1980s.) As long as the Scriptures themselves did not explicitly condemn slavery—and they could be proof-texted either way—then the Church, whose "only argument is *Thus it is written*," had no "authority to declare slavery to be sinful," Thornwell concluded. Let the churches tend to their business, and let the planters and slave-traders tend to theirs.

Professor Thornwell's report on "The Church and Slavery" was unanimously adopted in 1851 by the Presbyterian Synod of South Carolina. It would be easy to find Northern religious testimony which simply inverted the Southern. However, Thornwell's injunction to the Church not to meddle in the affairs of the "real world" had also its Northern counterparts. Harriet Beecher Stowe, better known for her scorching attack on Southern slavery in *Uncle Tom's Cabin*, turned her keenly observant eye upon slavery and its defenders closer to home—Newport, Rhode Island—in another of her widely popular novels, *The Minister's Wooing* (1859). Setting her story in the immediate post-revolutionary years, when Newport was still an entry-port for the importation of slaves from Africa—and when Calvinism was a good deal stronger intellectual and social force than it had become by 1859—Mrs. Stowe set up a confrontation between a church deacon who had profited from the slave trade and his pastor, a deadly serious expositor of Calvinist theology after the relentless logical fashion of Jonathan Edwards. Taken aback by this minister's statement "that the enslaving of the African race is a clear violation of the great law which commands us to love our neighbor as ourselves," Deacon Simeon Brown retorts that the saintly Doctor of Theology is "not a practical man." In language that will be heard again in George F. Babbitt's time, and in our own time, the practical Newport businessman further explains that "Ministers are the most unfit men in the world to talk on such subjects; it's departing from their sphere; they talk about what they don't understand." The scene then shifts to the next Sunday morning's service, at which the good Doctor, defying his deacon's warning that "you'll just divide and destroy the church," preaches a rip-roaring sermon—with as many proof-texts (e.g., Habbakuk 12:2, "Woe to him that buildeth a town with blood, and stablisheth a city by iniquity"), as any strict Biblical fundamentalist could have asked for—that indicts "all who have had any hand in this iniquitous business, whether directly or indirectly." That covers a lot of territory. "This trade in the human species has been the first wheel of commerce in Newport . . . and the inhabitants have lived on this, and by it have gotten most of their wealth and riches." For the moment this thunderous tongue-lashing shakes even the affluent Newporters; only after the sermon, prayers, and benediction are over could they begin "to reassure themselves that after all they were the first families, and going on the way the world had always gone, and that the Doctor, of course, was a radical and a fanatic."

6. A. Lincoln: Theologian

Such preachers were still radicals and fanatics from the standpoint of the increasingly militant South of James Henley Thornwell and John C. Calhoun. In the North, however, Harriet Stowe's own brother, the Reverend Henry Ward Beecher, had spent the decade while she was writing her great antislavery novels fighting slavery in other ways; holding mock "slave auctions" from his pulpit in Brooklyn, and shipping guns—"Beecher's Bibles!"— to the antislavery forces in Kansas. "Shall we compromise?" Beecher asked in February, 1850—only a few days before Calhoun's great Senate valedictory—and answered himself with a resounding "No." John Calhoun spoke all too truly for both North and South in declaring that "The cry of 'Union, Union, the glorious Union!' can no more prevent disunion than the cry of 'Health, health, glorious health' on the part of the physician can save a patient lying dangerously ill." A few days afterward, with grim historic appropriateness, Calhoun died.

Some, as the schemes of churchmen and Congressmen to avert the gathering tempest proved unavailing, turned fatalistic. "Sometimes, as the high howling of war threats came shriller," Carl Sandburg sums up the thoughts in 1860 of the man who would soon be presiding over the storm, "Lincoln would speak indirectly as though if a people want to fight there is no stopping them; wars have their own chaotic way of arriving; politicians must acknowledge tidal waves and pent volcanoes." But what then became of the Americans' Revolution-born conviction that they as a people had—perhaps uniquely in human history—taken charge of their own destiny? In religious terms, George Washington had told them at the outset that "no people can be bound to acknowledge and adore the Invisible Hand which conducts the affairs of men more than those of the United States"; but could one see that hand at work in events which now appeared to be spinning rapidly out of control?

Calvinism by Lincoln's time had been discredited in many quarters, both intellectually and morally; but to some, in a time when

Americans were stumbling toward a decision to slaughter one another in great numbers, Calvin's doctrines contained a more adequate explanation of human nature and destiny than the Methodists' exhortation to "all believers to go on to perfection." John Calhoun seems to have thought so; he had been raised in the especially dark version of those doctrines taught by Southern Presbyterianism and, his biographer Margaret Coit conjectures, he had returned to much of that oppressive faith of his boyhood as he faced his own imminent end, and that of the Union (to which he had been true, after his own fashion). On the other side of the deepening gulf in America stood John Brown, "a man of doom, believing in his own right to doom others, and the power of God to doom wrongdoers everlastingly," who after his capture—if Sandburg reports him correctly—could have passed the test of any Calvinist catechism: "Speaking through his bars, he had told one, 'All our actions, even all the follies that led to this disaster, were decreed to happen ages before the world was made.' "

But of all that fratricidal generation which plunged itself into war, perhaps Abraham Lincoln himself best deserves the title of lay Calvinist theologian. Eschewing the "God-on-our-side" rhetoric used by most wartime Presidents, in his Second Inaugural Lincoln called the Civil War a divine judgment against *both* sides that fought it. "Woe unto the world because of offenses! for it must needs be that offenses come; but woe to that man by whom the offense cometh"—as Calvinist a line of Scripture as could have come to hand (Matt. 18:7). "American slavery," Lincoln proposed, "is one of those offenses which, in the providence of God, must needs come, but which, having continued through His appointed time, He now wills to remove, and . . . He gives to both North and South, this terrible war, as the woe due to those by whom the offense came."

Again like a Calvinist, Lincoln did not rebel against this terrible decree but embraced it: "If God wills that . . . this mighty scourge of war . . . continue, until all the wealth piled by the bondman's two hundred and fifty years of unrequited toil shall be sunk, and until every drop of blood drawn with the lash, shall be paid by another drawn with the sword, as was said three thousand years ago, so still it must be said 'the judgments of the Lord, are true and righteous altogether' " (Psalms 19:9) Only then did Lincoln say the words everybody knows—which as carved on the Lincoln Memorial or otherwise read out of context prompt in Americans mainly a sentimental, warm-soggy feeling around the heart. Before *he* earned the right to say "with malice toward none," the President who first said those healing words had to pay his moral dues to the universe. He had begun, in his race for the Senate against Stephen A. Douglas, with a ringing affirmation of human rational initiative in the control of political destiny: "If we could first know where we are, and whither we are tending, we could then better judge what to do, and how to do it." He ended, after four years of dreadful war, by confessing "I claim not to have controlled events but confess plainly that events have controlled me."

Interlude III

The land filled. The forest drew back; the forest's people turned and fled, or stayed and died. In their place came blacksmiths and mill-wrights, schoolteachers and midwives, lawyers and bankers, portrait painters and preachers, barber-surgeons, weavers, prostitutes and pro-curers, bakers, militia officers, stevedores, cobblers, silversmiths.

And slaves. Twenty blacks aboard the good ship Jesus *when it docked in 1619 at Jamestown; then hundreds; then thousands.*

Fields pushed over the land where the forest had been. Stone walls enclosed them in New England; rail fences in Virginia. They filled up with wheat, and barley, and Indian corn; potatoes and "green garden sass"; tobacco and indigo and rice—and, later, cotton. Backs bent, people grubbed at the dirt as they had been doing everywhere for cen-turies. And ever-increasing numbers of those toilers on the South's fertile coastal plains and river bottom land were slaves.

Slave cabins crouched beside George Washington's Mount Vernon, with its great sweep of lawn, and behind Thomas Jefferson's Monti-cello, with its impressive entryway. As young men came to the hand-some Roman buildings that housed Jefferson's University of Virginia, attended by the body servants their fathers owned, the cry of the slave auctioneer echoed from the nation's capital dome.

Along with Bibles and law books, the settlers had brought to the New World the habits and dreams of the Old. In the fresh environ-ment some of those accustomed ways became transfigured; Roman legalism into constitutional democracy, Christian evangelism into re-ligious liberty. But some ancient ways—and one in particular—dis-tended into nightmare. Slaves, and the trade in them, weighed heavily on the hearts of fighters for freedom; "I am drawn along," Patrick Henry miserably confessed, "by the general inconvenience of living without them." And the inconvenience grew, and grew, and the nation nearly broke upon it.

FOUR

It Nearly Didn't Work

Heretofore in this book nothing has been said of labor history, conventional economic or industrial history, strikes, and the like. Republican politics and capitalist economics have thus far been treated as if they were independent variables; perhaps from a present-minded awareness that republicanism, complete with competitive party politics and free elections, can coexist with a wide variety of kinds of economic organization; and conversely that tyranny can choose capitalist, socialist, feudal, or eclectic economic forms. Thus far I have chosen to follow the political rather than the economic vector.

But the slave economy in early-nineteenth-century America cannot be treated in that fashion. Its continuing existence, and growth, called into question two of republican Americans' most crucial definitions: what they meant by "people" and what they meant by "property."

Politicians ducked these intertwined issues as long as they could, deflecting the argument into categories of agriculture versus commerce and industry, foreign adventuring versus isolation, localism versus federal power, even Southern leisure versus Yankee moneymaking. They could not, however, evade forever the political question: just who must be included in the phrase *e pluribus unum?*—or the economic one: does the pursuit of happiness entitle the pursuer to own other people? As a matter of fact it took less than three quarters of a century, since the original drafting of the Constitution with its built-in time bomb regarding slavery, for destiny to catch up with them.

1. One Nation, or Two?

It was a common cliché in the 1960s, among people who played at revolution, that "violence is as American as apple pie." However that may be, Americans have not been notable as a *politically* violent people. At least since the era of Jackson the Duelist, shooting affrays among members of Congress have been uncommon; our presidential assassins, despite strenuous efforts to prove some of them otherwise, have typically been mentally disturbed loners; and even under the most severe of provocations our national party nominating conventions have always managed to transact their business in a peaceable (if sometimes raucous) fashion and get safely home. After one unusually acrimonious presidential nomination— that of William Howard Taft over Theodore Roosevelt in 1912— the genial Kansas newspaper editor William Allen White observed: "An American crowd will have a terrible time behind barricades, or surging up Pennsylvania Avenue to overwhelm the White House. It will probably laugh itself to death on the way." Elsewhere, enraged citizens might storm the palace, tear a prime minister to pieces, or attack one another's party headquarters; Americans got it out of their systems by making speeches, marching in torchlit parades, stuffing ballot boxes, or arguing it out in court.

Except once.

In 1860 the system did not work. The nomination process, and the party system, broke down; a sizeable fraction of the country could not abide the result of an election; the larger fraction could not accept the smaller's bottom-line demands; "and the war came."

The Revolutionary founders had seen such disaster approaching from afar off. George Washington lectured his fellow citizens that they should be aware of "the immense value of your national union to your collective and individual happiness," and should "frown indignantly" upon "every attempt to alienate any portion of our country from the rest." This shouldn't be any problem, he assured them; "With slight shades of differences, you have the same religion, manners, habits, and political principles." Moreover, they had the bonding of a shared Revolutionary heritage: "The independence and liberty you possess are the work of joint councils and joint efforts, and of common dangers, sufferings, and successes." As a backup—for even the most dedicated revolutionaries grow older, and their heirs can no longer fully share the emotions of a generation which had "in a common cause fought and triumphed together"—Washington in the true spirit of the eighteenth century appealed also to their rational self-interest. The economies of the North and of the South were interdependent, he argued, and the West—which in the 1790s seemed a far likelier candidate for secession than the South—could secure its own future growth and comfort only from America's "indissoluble community of interest as *one nation.*"

The famous, and frequently quoted, foreign policy portions of the Farewell Address fitted into this same overview of the Union. "Foreign influence is one of the most baneful foes of republican government," Washington warned, and "the jealousy of a free people ought to be constantly awake against it. But that jealousy, to be useful, must be impartial"—a tacit rebuke both to his own Federalist allies, with their increasingly uncritical approval of Britain, and to the Republican opposition, with its at times doctrinaire commitment to France. Washingtonian isolationism has long since ceased to be a practicable policy, but even in an era of planet-spanning ICBMs Americans can benefit from their first President's caution against "excessive partiality for one foreign nation and excessive dislike of another." In the 1790s such partiality would have been downright ruinous. The statecraft of John Adams, Washington's under-appreciated successor, who was willing to end a quite successful naval war with France that many of his fellow Federalists wanted to continue, may thereby have averted the disaster of U.S. politics becoming subordinated to, and dependent upon, the world-spanning rivalry of the two superpowers of that day. Rural, backwoods America, over against the mighty French and British empires, was in effect a member of a "Third World"; thus Washington's and Adams's nonaligned foreign policy anticipated Jawaharlal Nehru's stubborn refusal, after India won its independence in 1947, to "take sides" in the Cold War.

Thomas Jefferson, when he took office as President in 1801, picked up Washington's noninterventionist stance and erected it into bipartisan dogma: "peace, commerce, and honest friendships with all nations, entangling alliances with none." To push foreign affairs off to the horizon in this peremptory fashion, Jefferson found soon enough, was easier to propose than to do; and the statistics of the presidential elections of 1796 and 1800 disclosed a polarity closer to home that would prove far more difficult to exorcise. Those "slight shades of differences" George Washington had conceded to the American people included a difference over slavery, a difference Washington himself found deeply troubling; and that single exception was fated in the end to undermine all their other similarities in "religion, manners, habits, and political principles."

John Adams won the first of the two Adams-Jefferson presidential contests, Roy F. Nichols has pointed out, "because the northern states had a slightly larger number of electoral votes than the southern." They had that edge, however, as the result of a constitutional compromise: the lame "three fifths rule" by which a slave, for electoral census purposes, counted as three fifths of a free person. Had the entire population been countable, the South would have had an electoral-college majority. In the 1800 rematch, the same narrow balance—eight Northern states having 73 electoral votes, versus eight Southern states with 65—tipped against Adams when Jefferson carried New York. Although the Federalists got eight "border slave state" electoral votes in Delaware and Maryland, and four "upper South" votes in North Carolina, and although local Democratic-Republican leaders commanded vigorous party organizations all over the Northeast, the first two fully partisan national elections were unmistakably regional in character. Nor was this North-South polarity forgotten by the losers, for whom Democratic-Republican ascendancy meant, in practice, a Virginia ascendancy; more bluntly, a slaveowners' ascendancy. Jefferson's wide and deep concern for the rights of man, in bitter Federalist minds, became simply hypocrisy: democracy, Josiah Quincy sarcastically wrote in 1804, was "an indian word, signifying 'a great tobacco planter, who had herds of black slaves.'"

Even the Louisiana Purchase, the great diplomatic triumph of Jefferson's first Presidential term, divided members of Congress on North-South, anti- and pro-slavery lines. The Louisiana windfall was such an obvious bargain that pragmatism prevailed; but not before Federalist Congressman James Hillhouse, in the debate on a motion to bar slavery from the newly acquired territory—a debate destined to repeat itself over and over again, for the next half century—testified that George Washington's nightmare was already coming true: "I did not expect *so soon* to hear on this floor the distinction of *eastern* and *northern*, and *southern* men. Has it indeed come to this—are we to be designated by a geographical line?"

What enthusiastic Southern Republicans failed at the time to perceive was that the expansion of Caesar's authority implicit in the stretching of the treaty-making power by which Jefferson had justified accepting Napoleon's bonanza—for which many conscientious Federalists could find no warrant in the Constitution—would lead one day to consequences far less to the South's liking. "The Pope could as safely trifle with the doctrine of apostolic succession as Jefferson with the limits of Executive power," historian Henry Adams wrote in his classic account of the Louisiana Purchase debate. Eventually the broadening interpretation of other powers of the national government would "lead from step to step, until at last Virginia might cower in blood and flames before the shadowy terror called the war-power." By abandoning the narrow, state's rights construction of the Constitution with which they had started in order to achieve a paramount national purpose, Henry Adams implied, Jefferson and Madison were setting the states up to be crushed in civil war.

In this early clash, however, it was the Northerners who felt themselves to be the beleaguered minority; and a hard core of them seriously considered the same extreme solution that their Southern counterparts would offer half a century later. "*While* I am the representative of a *State* which is *yet* a member of the *Union,* I hope I shall have as much influence as if I was a *southern man,*" Congressman Hillhouse defensively asserted. "A thinly veiled secessionist threat," historian Linda Kerber calls this; and in fact there was, in 1803–4, a serious movement in high New England Federalist circles to secede from the Union, with the hope that the opportunistic Aaron Burr—Jefferson's Vice-President!—would bring New York over to them as well. In one of the many ironies occurring throughout American political history, John C. Calhoun as a senior at Yale, class of '04, first heard secessionist doctrine not from fellow Southerners but in the course in moral philosophy taught by that formidable son of the Puritans, Timothy Dwight. "The people of the Southern States suppose their interests to be different from ours," President Dwight explained. "The Southern States clash with the Northern and Western, and the question is whether a division should be made in the country, that each portion may pursue its own course."

Nothing came of the New England Yankee separatist gambit, and this ominous regional division was obscured for a time as the initial Democratic-Republican victory of 1800 mushroomed into an overwhelming nation-wide majority; even staunch Massachusetts succumbed to a Democratic-Republican governor at the crest of the Jeffersonian tide. But then Jefferson's hand-picked successor, fellow Virginian James Madison, took the nation into a war which re-invigorated a moribund Federalist Party and re-regionalized American politics.

2. The Unifying Gamble of War

What had led the peace-loving Democratic-Republicans, who in Jefferson's first term had opposed the creation of standing armies as engines of despotism and of navies as instruments of imperialist piracy, to launch their ship of state out upon the choppy and uncertain waves of a European war? High statecraft, or low land-grabbing? Many modern historians have opted for the latter interpretation, taking off from Henry Clay's war cry to Congress in 1810 that "the conquest of Canada is in your power." More recently, however, Roger H. Brown has argued that Madison's congressional "war hawks" were moved in large part by fear that the republican principle itself was at stake. "We should all recollect that our Government is in a train of experiment," Vermont Chief Justice Royall Tyler wrote to his Congressman, James Fisk, a month before Congress voted for the War of 1812. "Those of Europe are opposed to it from principle and have no belief in its durability. Every attempt will be made to embarrass, & eventually to destroy it"— and if Congress, having "not resolution sufficient to maintain the national rights," should "sneak out"—*i.e.*, adjourn without a declaration of war—Republicans might well "be led to believe that the Federalists are right, and there is not virtue in the people to support a republican government."

It was, in its way, a powerful argument: don't let the British push us around any longer; use our republican institutions to put them in their place, lest we confirm the traditional authoritarian argument that republics, by their argumentative nature, are incompetent to conduct a forceful, coherent foreign policy. What this Republican war hawk thesis conveniently overlooked was that *both* superpowers in the course of their worldwide struggle had transgressed the neutral shipper's rights of the American newcomer; by a formal *reductio ad absurdum*, therefore, the Americans could logically have declared war upon both. Napoleon, however, semantically quicker on the draw than his British adversaries, had recently led the U.S. government to believe he had removed the

American grievance against France when in fact he had not. From the standpoint of diplomacy the declaration of war showed not only the Democratic-Republicans' "resolution to defend the Constitution," as Tyler put it, but also their gullible willingness to rise all unawares to the continental dictator's bait.

A few maverick Republicans in fact believed that Napoleon, who had subverted republican government in its own name and carried his country further toward a Roman-style Principate than the U.S. ever got, should have been America's arch-enemy; far more so than Britain, whose philosophical basis for opposing Napoleon was not so much formal "counter-revolution" a la Burke as it was opposition to a self-serving upstart who did not play by the traditional international rules. Neither did Britain, when those rules conflicted with national purpose; but the Corsican did not even pretend to play the old game, and may not have really known what it was.

As early as 1806, dissident Jeffersonian John Randolph had told Congress that "with all my abhorrence of the British government, I should not hesitate between Westminster Hall and a Middlesex jury, on the one hand, and the wood of Vincennes and a file of grenadiers on the other." In the temporary insanity of the Alien and Sedition Acts the pro-British Federalists had jailed and fined some of their political opponents, but they had never guillotined or shot them! On the eve of actual war with Britain, Randolph protested that such a choice would make the Americans, in effect, the French Caesar's accomplices. Should Congress declare war, Randolph warned on May 30, 1812, "the last Republic of the earth will have enlisted under the banners of the tyrant and become a party to his cause."

Most Republicans quite evidently didn't see it that way, and some Federalists did: "I dread that above all," declared Connecticut's Benjamin Tallmadge, "which shall link us to the fortunes, & chain us to the car of the French Emperor." This and other motives, commercial and ideological, roused and solidified the Federalist Opposition; "the 12th Congress that voted war included 43 Federalist members," Roger Brown points out, and "of the 40 Federalist congressmen and senators actually voting, all cast votes against war." Brown rejects a sectional interpretation of this vote, noting that nine Federalists who voted against the war resolution came from south of the Mason-Dixon line. But the fact remains that the maritime and commercial states of the Northeast voted for peace, while the votes of Southern and Western states assured a declaration of war.

Royall Tyler had hoped that an actual state of war would break the Federalist phalanx. "A declaration of war will confound the Federalists; . . . derange their present plans; . . . invite many Federalists into the army—and soldiers are always patriotic in time of war; . . . and above all it will place the opposition on slippery ground, and drive them to silence or rebellion." Such a stance raises a serious ethical question, not explored by Brown, concerning the propriety of making war abroad for partisan advantage at home; similar questions have been asked, with great bitterness, about Franklin Roosevelt, Lyndon Johnson, and Ronald Reagan. Henry Adams a century ago raised it about James Madison: "If a strong government was desired, any foreign war, without regard to its object, might be good policy if not good morals; and in that sense President Madison's was the boldest and most successful of all experiments in American statesmanship though it was also among the most reckless." In any event, the immediate effect of the Democratic-Republican President's decision was not to disrupt Federalism but to revive and solidify it—in one of the forms Washington and Jefferson had feared partisanship would take: disagreement over foreign policy, anchored in sectionalism.

In New England, "Mr. Madison's war" was extraordinarily unpopular. Federalists in Providence, Rhode Island, set the church bells to tolling, while in Boston Harbor sailors fought off a Federalist boarding party after their Republican captain refused demands to lower his flag to half-mast. Confounding George Washington's hope that "all the parts combined cannot fail to find in the united mass of means and efforts . . . proportionately greater security from external danger," in the wartime presidential election of 1812 the Federalists in alliance with the antiwar New York Republican leader DeWitt Clinton (nephew of Old George), carried all of New England except inland, non-maritime Vermont, and all the Middle States to the Potomac except Pennsylvania, while Madison won re-election as President by carrying the South and West.

With a more modern technology of communication—a "hot line"—there might not have been a War of 1812 at all; the British government had announced a suspension of its obnoxious Orders in Council two days before Congress declared that a state of war existed. From the standpoint of the United Kingdom, locked in combat with the overlord of Europe, war with its former colonies must have seemed an extraneous nuisance. The sizes of the two wars were absurdly disproportionate; while Canadian general Isaac Brock was attacking Detroit with a force of some two thousand men, Napoleon was moving upon Smolensk with two hundred thousand. Nevertheless, some Englishmen seemed ready by the end of 1813—in the course of the anti-Napoleonic alliance's post-Moscow victories—to couple the two wars together. "The approaching fall of Napoleon threatened to throw America outside the pale of civilization," Henry Adams concluded from the recorded words of some leading Britons, and in their minds "no peace should be made which did not include the removal of both [Madison and Napoleon] from office and power."

For in addition to questions of commerce and power politics, the quarrel between the United States and Britain that had led to the War of 1812 was ideological, and it was deep. During much of this period England's foreign policy was conducted by a man— George Canning—who avowedly detested republican government. The sparring matches of his agents in Washington with their American opposite numbers, veiled of course by the polite language which diplomats affect, remind one of the mutual hostility and incomprehension in the long-winded diplomatic exchanges of Soviet and American envoys in the worst phases of the Cold War, even when softened—as they occasionally were in the earlier case—by the negotiators' personal good will.

This virulent ideological bias on the part of the Tory leadership was obscured from view because that leadership was engaged in a fight to the finish with an even more anti-republican regime in Paris. The imperious Bonaparte, who at one stroke had returned government to the primitive terms of the first person singular, had created so comprehensive a tyranny that when he invaded the Iberian peninsula in 1808, throwing Spain into the arms of England, the resulting alliance between the most reactionary royal family in Western Europe and the high Tories in London could be perceived as a struggle for freedom! The downfall of Napoleon in 1814—preceding his last hurrah at Waterloo—prompted Thomas Jefferson, writing in retirement to John Adams (July 5, 1814), to rejoice at seeing "the Attila of the age dethroned, the ruthless destroyer of 10 millions of the human race . . . the great oppressor of the rights and liberties of the world." Still, Bonaparte's fall left "the tyrant of the ocean [Britain] remaining in vigor, and even participating in the merit of crushing his brother tyrant." Nor did Jefferson relish the spectacle of Tsar Alexander I, Autocrat of All the Russias, dictating terms at Paris: "While the world is thus turned up side down, on which side of it are we?"

Adams and Jefferson in their correspondence over the previous two years had paid surprisingly little attention to the war raging along their own home shores, considering how badly that war had been going. The enthusiastic American invasion of Canada had collapsed in a comedy of errors; Canadians did not welcome the invaders as liberators, and one key battle was lost because New York militiamen, insisting that the terms of their enlistment required them to defend only their home state, refused to cross over into Ontario as reinforcements. Although the Americans halted the British counter-thrusts and recaptured some lost territory, when Napoleon's overthrow freed the Duke of Wellington's regulars for action away from Europe matters rapidly got very serious indeed. Replying to Jefferson on July 16, John Adams observed that "though France is humbled, Britain is not"; the understatement of the year. Thirty-nine days later, British officers were in Washington eating a dinner that had been cooked for James and Dolley Madison.

Militarily, the situation was not quite so bad as the capture of Washington and the burning of its public buildings made it appear. Wellington, invited by his government on the 4th of November to take supreme command in America, made it quite clear he was aware of the strategic limitations upon such a war that his blundering predecessors in the Revolution had ignored. Politically, however, the situation was desperate indeed. For a long, painful moment in the summer of 1814 the government of the United States all but ceased to exist. The treasury was flat; banks suspended payment in coin; enlistments were down because no more enlistment bounties could be paid. Dolley Madison, fleeing the invaders, got turned away by an inkeeper who blamed her husband for helping to bring on the invasion! After the capture of Castine in Eastern Maine (which would not become a state until 1820), Massachusetts put its own state army—the one good, well armed, well equipped militia in all the states—into the field, and Connecticut pulled its militia out of federal service. Other states—New York, Pennsylvania, Maryland, Virginia, South Carolina, Kentucky—were raising their own state armies; Andrew Jackson, having won a war with the Creek Indians, functioned unsupervised by the War Department as, in effect, dictator of the Southwest. As Henry Adams summed them up, the prospects for the very existence of the United States after 1814, had the Peace of Ghent not intervened, seemed doubtful at best: "If the people would not come to the aid of their government at such a moment, Madison felt that nothing could move them. Peace was his last hope."

1814 was also an election year; and from recently besieged Maryland to truncated Maine (whose eastern portion was peaceably paying customs duties into the British treasury), areas which elected more than half the members of Congress, those elections returned 57 Federalists and 51 Republicans. "In every respect as the Federalists looked back at the past twelve years their prophecies had come true," Henry Adams's narrative continues. "The government was ruined in credit and character; bankrupt, broken, and powerless, it continued to exist merely because of habit, and must succumb to the first shock"—so they thought. Grass roots movements in the New England towns and legislatures led to a convention at Hartford to revise a Federal constitution which had apparently proved so unsatisfactory; and that convention's more extremist members were prepared to journey to Boston for another convention "with such powers and instructions as the exigency of a crisis so momentous may require"—including, conceivably, secession.

But peace did come; Andrew Jackson, two weeks afterward, superfluously won the Battle of New Orleans; Britain and its sometime colonies quickly moved toward *détente* (most notably, demilitarizing the Greak Lakes); and Federalism of the sectionalist, states'-rights variety, left high and dry by events, was made to look both unpatriotic and ridiculous. After one more presidential election the party quietly expired. But the political doctrines New Englanders had invoked to defend their regional interests against a Southern national administration could just as readily be adapted to the needs of Southerners defending *their* region—and its "peculiar institution," slavery—against the government in Washington should it one day be captured and effectively managed by politicians from the North.

3. *"Like a Fire-Bell in the Night"*

To men who had been young at the outbreak of the American Revolution, the turn of events in Europe—to which their own military adventures under Adams (vs. France) in 1797 and under Madison (vs. England) in 1812 had been essentially sideshows—offered ground for deep discouragement if not disillusion. How had it happened, Jefferson wondered (January 11, 1816) "that these nations, France and especially England, so great, so dignified, so distinguished by science and the arts, . . . threw off suddenly and openly all the restraints . . . and unblushingly acted on the principle that power was right? . . . the close of the century saw the moral world thrown back again to the age of the Borgias, to the point from which it had departed 300 years before." Replying on February 2, John Adams, as so often in their correspondence, trumped Thomas Jefferson's ace: "Power always sincerely, conscientiously, de tres bon Foi, believes itself Right. Power always thinks it has a great soul, and vast views, beyond the comprehension of the weak, and that it is doing God service, when it is violating all his laws."

Nor could these Revolutionary veterans have taken much comfort from the peace Europe's conservative statecraft was erecting on the ruins of Napoleon's empire—a peace enforced by planting police spies in university student organizations lest they get out of line. The choice for the rising generation in Europe seemed to fall between a dreary statist "conservative" Romanticism whose purpose was to make the world safe for kings and a rabid "radical" folk-nationalist Romanticism whose legacy would be a hostility to cosmopolitan culture. Bonaparte himself, seen from a distance through the eyes of a generation that had not personally known the horrors of war, took on the glamour of a defiant Lucifer fallen from Heaven; and among members of the next older generation both the friends and the foes of the sometime First Consul had to concede that the repressive regimes which had succeeded him in most of Europe were no improvement. France itself, under its restored pre-Revolutionary dynasty, had second thoughts about Napoleon, and about the personal dynasty he had tried to found. Within twenty years after his death in 1821, his remains were brought home from his island of final exile and housed in an impressive tomb adorned with both Christian symbolism and Roman iconography. The image of Napoleon's son "Napoleon II," in a gilt-encrusted toga, is outdone by the Constantinian—or even Egyptian—bas-reliefs of Napoleon himself as Giver and Lawgiver. The trouble with the classical Roman model in art is that it slides so easily from Republic to Principate; and from time to time over the past century and a half that descent from commonwealth to empire has seduced France from its hard-won revolutionary republican ideals. At times it seemed less important to be a Republic than to be Number One—a lesson having warning relevance today for the heirs of the American Revolution as well.

In America, seen from a greater distance than in Europe, Napoleon's attractive power became civilized. "The incarnate Democrat," Ralph Waldo Emerson called the Emperor, confounding the Corsican's energetic amorality with American-style entrepreneurial hustle. "Napoleon is thoroughly modern," the Sage of Concord gushed on (in one of his less inspiring essays), "and, at the highest point of his fortunes, has the very spirit of the newspapers." Under the Napoleonic regime, Emerson assured his modern-minded American readers, "the old, iron-bound, feudal France was changed into a young Ohio or New York." But so had Augustus transformed and modernized *his* inherited, tradition-bound regime; was it not said of the first Roman Princeps that he had "found Rome brick, and left it marble"? There was an implication, unexamined by Emerson, that modernization itself contains an inherent temptation to Caesarism.

Those who study history must always resist a temptation to political and cultural nostalgia. Modernization need not point to Caesarism; it may bring with it different liberties, as old individualisms are replaced by new. In any event Caesarist innovation, from the standpoint of ocean-sheltered nineteenth-century Americans, was a problem for old Europe to worry about. Occasional visions of Caesar's ghost—as when General Andrew Jackson in 1818 over-enthusiastically carried one of his Indian wars across the border into Spanish Florida—became grist for partisan controversy; was Florida, as a military field, an American Caesar's preparatory Gaul? On the whole, however, the politics of modernization in the still young United States turned on such questions as whether governments ought to dig canals and how constitutional was it to charter a bank—questions of great moment, but hardly traumatic. Neither monarchism of the kind then vigorously at work enhancing its power in the Old World nor adventurism on the Napoleonic model seemed likely American scenarios, despite an exaggerated political rhetoric which typically cast one's electoral foes in such roles.

Deep as Thomas Jefferson's pessimism sometimes became, as he contemplated "the Northern triumvirate [*i.e.*, the Holy Alliance] arming their nations to dictate despotism to the rest of the world," he consoled himself that "even should the clouds of barbarism and despotism again obscure the science and liberties of Europe, this country remains to preserve and restore light and liberty to them. In short," he assured John Adams on September 21, 1821, "the flames kindled on the 4th. of July 1776 have spread over too much of the globe to be extinguished by the feeble engines of despotism"—

But what if this country did not remain to preserve and restore those flames?

A year earlier Jefferson had written to Congressman John Holmes, of what was soon to become the State of Maine, concerning the slavery question which had erupted in Congress: "This momentous question, like a fire-bell in the night, awakened and filled me with terror. I considered it at once as the knell of the Union."

Federalism, after holding the diehards in Massachusetts, Connecticut, and Delaware for one last Electoral College presidential vote in 1816, had given up the ghost; and there ensued the partyless period which the textbooks still call the "Era of Good Feelings." That name is itself a subtle concession to the anti-"faction" spirit of the late eighteenth-century; the absence of partisan political contests is by definition presumed to imply the presence of mutual good will. But it hadn't worked out that way at all. Bereft of nationally focused political parties whose members had to bargain together and compromise for a practicable common front against the other party—a point on which John C. Calhoun was to prove so prescient—Northerners and Southerners in the Era of (so-called) Good Feelings had to confront each other directly, far more acutely than they had as Federalists and Republicans.

Calhoun and John Quincy Adams (son of Jefferson's old friend), who were both members of President James Monroe's cabinet, had it out one day while Congress was debating what was to go into the books as the "Missouri Compromise." As Adams recorded their conversation in his diary (February 24, 1820), Calhoun said he didn't expect the present crisis to "produce a dissolution of the Union, but, if it should, the South would be from necessity compelled to form an alliance, offensive and defensive, with Great Britain." (Again, how prescient!—for the hope of a British alliance in the Civil War was to be the cornerstone of Confederate foreign policy). To Adams's observation that "that would be returning to the colonial state," Calhoun replied, "Yes, pretty much, but it would be forced upon them." But might this not force the population of the North, "cut off from its natural outlet upon the ocean," to "move southward by land"? Adams asked. Calhoun's answer was chilling: "Then," he said, "they would find it necessary to make their communities all military." Adams, with a lingering eighteenth-century tact, "pressed the conversation no further."

As it turned out, the Congress a few days later *did* resolve that particular North-South crisis, in terms every American school child used to learn (but apparently does so no longer): Maine, long restive as part of high-and-mighty Massachusetts, admitted as a free state; Missouri, carved from the Louisiana Purchase territory as a slave state; and the remainder of the western territories in effect splitting the difference, so that the division between freedom and slavery past the Mason-Dixon line and the Ohio Valley would (except for the Missouri salient) run to the Pacific Ocean—so soon as American expansionism should carry it there.

Jefferson, in his letter to Maine's John Holmes (April 22, 1820), considered that fire-bell "hushed, indeed, for the moment. But this is a reprieve only, not a final sentence. . . . We have the wolf by the ears, and we can neither hold him, nor safely let him go." And then, for Thomas Jefferson, came an untypical surge of despair: "I regret that I am now to die in the belief, that the useless sacrifice of themselves by the generation of 1776 . . . is to be thrown away by the unwise and unworthy passions of their sons."

His old Revolutionary comrade's son might have retorted that passion is not always unwise or unworthy. After a meeting with James Monroe on March 3, 1820, concerning the Missouri and Maine bills that were on the President's desk for signature and on whose constitutionality Monroe was soliciting the opinion of all members of his administration, John Quincy Adams walked home with Calhoun. From the South Carolinian's condescending description of manual labor (except farming)—"the proper work of slaves," to which "no white person could descend"—so degrading that "if he, who was the most popular man in his district, were to keep a white servant in his house, his character and reputation would be irretrievably ruined"—Adams began to wonder if in his own support of the Missouri Compromise he had done the right thing: "If the Union must be dissolved, slavery is precisely the question upon which it ought to break." What difference did it make, given such militancy in people of the caliber of J. Q. Adams and Calhoun, that Monroe at the end of that same year was re-elected President with all but one of the electoral votes?

4. Liberty versus Union?

In any event the Missouri deed was done, and it became the framework for the politics of the next thirty years. Shortly the Virginia-
Massachusetts dynasty which had administered the nation since
Washington's time broke up. After the unique, fluky five-way presidential contest of 1824—in which the absence of party politics
and organization proved no bar to ill feeling!—the party system
reconstituted itself as National Republicans (soon renamed Whigs)
and Democrats. Many and various were the issues on which they
were to square off over the next three decades: banking and money,
matters still of central concern today; public works spending and
the "pork barrel," of perennial interest in Washington and in the
home districts; the sale of the public lands, an issue for the Continental Congress that would recur again and again throughout our
history down to the spasmodic Interior Department politics of James
Watt and beyond; and the protective tariff, the one issue over which
U.S. parties consistently divided throughout the Republic's history
until the Democrats in the 1980s broke with their own free-trade
tradition. As for slavery, an unspoken agreement among most politicians held it undiscussable, save at arm's length out in the Territories; certainly not in the states where it already existed. Ignore
the issue, John Calhoun had advised Congress in 1817; "bind the
Republic together with a perfect system of roads and canals," and
thereby fulfill George Washington's dream of reciprocating parts
united into a mutually advantageous whole. "The greatest of all
calamities, next to the loss of liberty, and even to that in its consequence," Calhoun cried, was "disunion." But "we are great, and
rapidly growing"; so "let us conquer space," and shut up about
slavery. One is reminded of the dentist's macabre joke: "Ignore
your teeth; they will go away."

Although he was destined to serve the "great and rapidly growing . . . Republic" forcefully and effectively as Vice President,
Secretary of State, and U. S. Senator, Calhoun's unionism was always conditional. In 1830, at a Jefferson Day dinner—then as now
an annual love-feast of the Democratic Party into which Jefferson's
and Madison's political fraternity had evolved—when President and
fellow Democrat Andrew Jackson faced him with a toast to "our
Federal Union—it must be preserved," John Calhoun responded
by lifting his glass to "the Union. Next to our liberties, most dear."

Binding the Republic together with roads and canals was one thing; paying for the nation's expansion with high protective tariffs, at the expense of the agrarian (read: Southern) interests, as Congress had begun to do, was something else again. Reaching into the Jefferson and Madison anti-Federalist heritage—the Virginia and Kentucky Resolutions against the Alien and Sedition Acts of 1798—Calhoun prompted his native South Carolina legislature first to protest, and then to nullify national tariff legislation it considered unconstitutional, with a latent threat of secession should push come to shove.

To the dismay of the whole region, slaveholder and Southerner Andrew Jackson did not behave like a Southern good old boy; he tromped down hard on South Carolina. If their "doctrine had been established at an earlier day," he lectured the people of that state on December 10, 1832, "the Union would have been dissolved in its infancy." If they wanted to raise the flag of revolution that would be another matter; "secession, like any other revolutionary act, may be morally justified by the extremity of oppression; but to call it a constitutional right is confounding the meaning of terms . . . To say that any State may at pleasure secede from the Union is to say that the United States are not a nation." Suiting action to words, Jackson alerted the forts in Charleston Harbor, put the redoubtable Winfield Scott in charge of the army in South Carolina, and dispatched five thousand rifles to Unionist forces in Charleston.

Neither North nor South was really willing to knock the chip off the other's shoulder; at least, not yet. In a flurry of compromises engineered by the wise and devious Henry Clay, Congress simultaneously passed a coercive Force Bill and a repeal of the offensive tariff; South Carolina, having made its immediate point, repealed its ordinance of nullification and then face-savingly nullified the no-longer-needed Force Bill. To contemporary observers it was not clear who had won; the national government had asserted its ultimate coercive authority, but South Carolina had gotten what it wanted—a change in the commercial policy of the whole country, for tariffs stayed low from then until the Lincoln Republicans took command. It was as if two parading hosts had marched up a hill from opposite sides, said "Boo!" at each other at the top, and then marched down again. But they would be back, and next time it would not be an *opera bouffe* affair. "The tariff was only the pretext," Jackson concluded afterward. "The next pretext will be the Negro, or slavery question." Sadly, it was no mere pretext.

87

Andrew Jackson was not the only Southerner who did not share Calhoun's sense of the relative priorities of liberty and union. John Marshall of Virginia, whom John Adams had named to be Chief Justice of the United States in 1801, was still handing down Federalist doctrine from the bench long after the Federalist Party itself was dead—not the regionalist, states'-rights Federalism of the New Englanders who had opposed the War of 1812 but the sweeping economic and legal-political Federalism classically associated with Alexander Hamilton. One year before the Missouri Compromise, Marshall had officially declared (in *McCulloch* v. *Maryland*, 4 Wheaton 316) that the Constitution of the United States was the handiwork of its whole people, not of their separate commonwealths—a notion which state-sovereignty champions found heretical in the extreme. ("What right had they to say, *We, the People*," Marshall's fellow Virginian Patrick Henry suspiciously had asked during the original ratification debates in Virginia, "instead of, *We the States?*") John Marshall was appalled at how far the mind of the South had drifted from its constitutional moorings; misgivings of Henry's kind, aired in 1788 but then presumably settled, were now re-emerging as regional dogma.

Nullification, which Calhoun sincerely thought of as a peaceable constitutional *alternative* to disunion, cut Marshall right down to his Federalist core. "The idea that a state may constitutionally nullify an act of Congress is so extravagant in itself," the Chief Justice wrote to Edward Everett on November 3, 1830, "and so repugnant to the existence of Union between the States that I could with difficulty bring my self to believe it was seriously entertained by any person." Gloomily, he wrote to Associate Justice Joseph Story (September 22, 1832): "I yield slowly and reluctantly to the conviction that our Constitution cannot last."

To John Marshall, this was no arid exercise in constitutional metaphysics. Whatever may have prompted New England Yankees in 1803 and 1814 to dally with nullification or secession, he assured one of them—Timothy Pickering—in 1826, in the South's case the movement toward similar doctrines did not result from deductive reasoning about the Constitution as a revocable compact among sovereign states. Rather it was clearly prompted by the Peculiar Institution, which was also the South's peculiar hangup: "I concur with you in thinking that nothing portends more calamity and mischief to the Southern states than their slave population;

yet they seem to cherish the evil and to view with an immovable prejudice and dislike every thing which may tend to diminish it."

The Chief Justice's son, Thomas, fought in the Virginia legislature to diminish the evil—for the free citizens' own good. "Wherefore, then, object to slavery?" the younger Marshall asked on January 11, 1832, speaking in support of a bill that would have provided for the gradual emancipation of the state's slaves. "Because it is ruinous to the whites," Thomas Marshall argued. "The master has no capital but what is invested in human flesh; the father, instead of being richer for his sons, is at a loss to provide for them. . . . Labor of every species is disreputable, because performed mostly by slaves. Our towns are stationary, our villages, almost everywhere declining; . . . and the entire continent does not present a region for which nature has done so much, and art so little." But that kind of appeal to rational, long-term self-interest, in the wake of the Nat Turner slave insurrection the year before, was foredoomed. Blaming the Turner revolt on the influence upon black Virginians of (in Governor John Floyd's words) "northern incendiaries, tracts, Sunday schools, religion and reading and writing," white Virginians' response was like that of white South Africans to outbursts against *apartheid* in more recent times: further suppression.

5. The Illusion of Greek Democracy

Paradoxically, in the same Southern states that were tightening the iron collar—forbidding manumission, disenfranchising free blacks (who could vote in Tennessee until 1834 and North Carolina as late as 1835), and severely restricting blacks' freedom of movement or assembly—white citizens at the same time were winning full participation in republican government. Of the original thirteen states, elite South Carolina was the *first*—after a brief Revolution-era experiment by Pennsylvania—to establish universal white manhood suffrage. Jefferson Davis's Mississippi abolished property or taxpaying qualifications for voting in 1817, two decades before Lincoln's Illinois. In this movement toward white enfranchisement some led, some lagged; but by 1860 all of the states, Southern as much as Northern, were popularly electing all their state officials, sometimes even their judges, and requiring of them no other test but their approval at the polls.

The rationale, or rationalization, for this society of free and equal citizens in coexistence with chattel slaves was "Greek democracy." As Calhoun explained it in 1837, "there never has yet existed a wealthy and civilized society in which one portion of the community did not, in point of fact, live on the labor of the other." The temples on the Acropolis had rested ultimately on the toilers in the Athenian silver mines; and, by a dizzying inversion of logic, a modern society resting on the toilers in its tobacco and cotton fields could expect similarly to erect its own Parthenons.

Somehow it did not work out that way. If Southern planters replicated Greek buildings on their slave plantations, it was the slaveless Northern towns—home to Emerson, Thoreau, Melville— that came up with what could fairly be compared to Greek ideas. And many of those white-columned temple homes in the South rested upon the Slough of Despond. Traveling in 1842 by rail from Fredericksburg to Richmond, "a district where slavery sits brooding," Charles Dickens noted the "air of ruin and decay abroad, which is inseparable from the system." Dismissed at the time as antislavery prejudice (or simple anti-American snobbery), and perhaps taking insufficient comparative notice of the working-class hovels springing up in the North during the first throes of the Industrial Revolution, Dickens's *American Notes* nevertheless echoed the testimony of countless other travelers and observers—European, Southern, or Northern—in the antebellum South: "the barns and outhouses are mouldering away; the sheds are patched and roofless; the log cabins . . . are squalid in the last degree." Not all of this desolation resulted from slavery; some came from two centuries' soil-exhausting abuse of the environment, an abuse committed elsewhere in North America by nonslave labor as well. And even Dickens took note of less dismal scenes; Richmond, the future Confederate capital, with its "pretty villas and cheerful houses," contrasted brightly with its rundown environs. "But jostling its handsome residences, like slavery itself going hand in hand with many lofty virtues," the English humanitarian continued, "are deplorable tenements, fences unrepaired, walls crumbling into ruinous heaps." As in his native London, the material bleakness aroused Dickens less than did the human degradation. His sharp journalist's eye picked out a toll bridge across the James, which had a notice painted on its gate, "cautioning all persons to drive slowly: under a penalty, if the offender were a white man, of five dollars, if a [N]egro, fifteen stripes." If this was Greek democracy, its model was not Athens but Sparta.

And it may have been that ultimate sanction of the lash which made the conflict finally irrepressible. "It has so happened in all ages of the world, that some have labored, and others have without labor enjoyed a large proportion of the fruits," wrote Congressman Abraham Lincoln in 1847, gathering his thoughts together for a Whig-sponsored Rivers and Harbors Convention in Chicago. "This is wrong and should not continue . . . Inasmuch as most good things are produced by labor, it follows that all such things of right belong to those whose labor has produced them." As a theoretical answer to Calhoun's proposition that all high civilization rests on the labor of an under-class this was not particularly imflamma-tory; but then Lincoln drew the logical conclusion that "to secure to each laborer the whole product of his labor, or as nearly as pos-sible, is a worthy object of any good government." Idleness, and useless labor, were "pensioners"—parasites—upon useful labor, "robbing it of a large portion of its just rights"; and "the only rem-edy for this is to, so far as possible, drive useless labor and idleness out of existence."

The revolutionary thrust of these words of Lincoln's was blunted, for the moment, by their context; as a freshman Congressman he was working up a case for the Whig Party's protective tariff pro-gram, not for slavery restriction. Nor should we assume that a sympathy for productive labor necessarily translated into militant abolitionism. Most Northern whites were not pro-black; quite the contrary. Their emerging political leader, Abraham Lincoln, was a Kentucky poor white, with his region's—and the nation's—prej-udices bred into his bones. It was not black and white inequality at the polling place that would rally a new national party to the cause of antislavery, so much as it was the notion of one portion of the community living upon the labor—the forced labor—of an-other, and using that power to frustrate the labor of the useful free.

Desperately, Stephen A. Douglas—as devoted a Unionist, in his own way, as Lincoln in his—tried to deflect the explosive moral issue into a technical political question: Let the people out in the territories vote slavery up or down, he didn't care which. They had as much right to bring slaves into their new communities as any other kind of property. "This is strictly logical," Lincoln shot back at Douglas in the last of their great debates in 1858, "if there is no difference between it and other property." And if no such difference exists, Lincoln had declared in the first of the debates, then the American Revolution was fought in vain; and "when [Douglas] invites any people willing to have slavery, to establish it, he is blowing out the moral lights around us." If Americans' national premise was the Declaration of Independence, "created equal" was the political bottom line; they could bargain away on banks, tariffs, "sound money," government spending (or non-spending), land sales, commercial regulations—but not on this.

But had not the framers of the Constitution tacitly recognized and legitimatized that kind of property by leaving "each state perfectly free to do as it pleased on the subject of slavery"? Douglas asked in his own opening argument. "They knew when they framed the Constitution that in a country as wide and broad as this, with such a variety of climate, production, and interest, the people necessarily required different laws and institutions in different localities. They knew that the laws and regulations which would suit the granite hills of New Hampshire would be unsuited to the rice plantations of South Carolina." It was a powerful appeal for pluralism, which for moderns enmeshed in a homogenizing corporate culture has its own intrinsic attraction. So also in 1858, and Lincoln answered Douglas as best he could: "The fathers of our government . . . found the institution of slavery existing here," Lincoln acknowledged in his rebuttal after the sixth debate. "They did not make it so, but they left it so because they knew of no way to get rid of it at that time"; and, by providing for abolition of the African slave trade and forbidding slavery in the Old Northwest territory, they had placed slavery in a situation "where they understood, and all sensible men understood, it was in the course of ultimate extinction."

For sensible white men in the South in the 1850s that argument would no longer hold; nor were they much if at all happier with Stephen Douglas's thesis that people in a new territory of the United States could vote slavery down as well as up. In 1850 they had presented their own bottom-line demands, which Henry Clay in his last great feat of political engineering blended into a nationally enactable package: in exchange for giving up California—a free state, even though lying mostly south of the old Missouri Compromise line—they were to get positive federal protection of their Peculiar Institution in the form of an enforceable act for the recovery of fugitive slaves. It was the tearing-up of that carefully crafted

Compromise of 1850 by Douglas himself, in his Kansas-Nebraska bills of 1854, which led thoughtful, moderate Southern leaders like Jefferson Davis to the conclusion that compromise—conventional political bargaining within an agreed-upon constitutional frame— might no longer be possible. Against Douglas, Davis and his Southern Congressional allies demanded not "popular sovereignty" but a positive, protective Federal territorial slave code; and if the slavery-extinctionist Republicans should win the White House, Davis told a cheering Mississippi legislature on November 16, 1858, he would tear his home state's star from the flag, "to be set . . . on the perilous ridge of battle as a sign round which Mississippi's best and bravest should gather to the harvest home of death."

6. Revolution In Spite of Itself

"A geographical line has been drawn across the Union," declared Christopher Memminger—soon to become Secretary of the Treasury in Davis's cabinet—in a manifesto adopted by South Carolina's secession convention (December 24, 1860), "and all the states north of that line have united in the election of a man to the high office of President of the United States whose opinions and purposes are hostile to Slavery." But there was more to it than that. The crucial difference between the slavery upon which the Graeco-Roman leisure class had rested and the slavery which was expected to promote a similar high culture in the American South was, of course, race. In a speech in Atlanta in March 1861, Confederate Vice-President Alexander H. Stephens praised the South's new constitution for having "put to rest, *forever*, all agitating questions relating to our peculiar institution, African slavery as it exists among us,—the proper status of the negro in our form of civilization." Stephens agreed with Lincoln (who, in happier years, had found him a stimulating and agreeable Congressional colleague) that the Founders, including the South's own Thomas Jefferson, had believed that "the enslavement of the African was in violation of the laws of nature" and "wrong in *principle*, socially, morally, and politically"; further, he acknowledged, they had looked forward hopefully to slavery's extinction. But these ideas of the Founders "were fundamentally wrong," Stephens insisted. "They rested upon the assumption of the equality of races." The new Confederate government was founded on the opposite assumption; "its foundations are laid, its corner-stone rests, upon the great truth that the negro is not equal to the white man; that slavery—subordination to the superior race—is his natural and normal condition."

Sweepingly racist statements like that one made Lincoln's constitutional task a good deal easier. Finessing his own racist political hedges in the debates with Douglas ("I have no purpose to introduce political and social equality between the white and the black races," and much more to the same effect), Lincoln was able to go to Congress, when he called it into special session on July 4, 1861, with the argument that "this is a people's contest." His problem was that Jefferson Davis, albeit with a narrower definition of "people," was saying much the same thing.

"The people of the Confederate States," Davis told the Confederate Congress on April 29, 1861, having "determined that the wrongs which they had suffered and the evils with which they were menaced required that they should revoke the delegation of powers to the Federal Government," had done so; and then they had proceeded to form a new government, performing its functions "in accordance with the will of the people." Had not the Northern government interfered "in this legitimate exercise of the right of a people to self government," the Confederate President concluded, "peace, happiness, and prosperity would now smile on our land."

Lincoln himself, from the premises of the Declaration of Independence, had to concede to the South—or anybody else—the ultimate right of revolution. "This country, with its institutions, belongs to the people who inhabit it," he announced in his first inaugural address. "Whenever they shall grow weary of the existing government, they can exercise their *constitutional* right of amending it, or their *revolutionary* right to dismember, or overthrow it." Then he proceeded, with elaborate casuistry, to argue that the "Rebellion"—as Unionists persistently and officially described the conflict—was not a true revolutionary situation.

But it was, as at least one present-day historian has argued. History is written by winners (who ever heard of a course in the History of Carthage?), and the South lost; "thus Sam Adams was a founding father, while Edmund Ruffin was a demented old man. Nevertheless," writes Emory Thomas (in *The Confederacy as a Revolutionary Experience*, 1971), "revolutionaries are revolutionaries no matter how abortive their revolutions." They are revolutionaries even when their goals are "reactionary"; the paradox in

Southern secession, for Thomas, was that a move intended to pre-serve the pre-1860 status quo ended by transforming it out of ex-istence. From their own conservative premises, the South's polit-ical leaders contended that what they were doing was *not* revolution: that South Carolina's ordinance of secession, and those of the states which followed, were drastic but perfectly constitutional acts. Northern rebuttals and Southern defenses of that argument have obscured the more significant fact that the really revolutionary changes in the Confederate States of America occurred *after* seces-sion.

"Within the limits of ability the Davis administration dragged Southerners kicking and screaming into the nineteenth century," Thomas contends. The Richmond government employed more civil servants than its counterpart in Washington; experimented with a rudimentary form of civil service examination; "directly and in-directly managed broad segments of the Southern economy and engaged in income and confiscatory taxation"; and commandeered strategic war materials, including copper tubing from North Car-olina apple brandy stills—a rude interruption of the archetypal Appalachian individualists' most sacredly established ways. Mili-tary expansion prompted urbanization in the formerly overwhelm-ingly rural South; garrisons, hospital patients, camp followers, de-fense workers swelled sleepy Southern towns to double or triple their antebellum size. With the rise of the city came, for the first time in most of the South's history, an industrial, non-slave work-ing class—and with it the strikes for higher wages and better working conditions that happen when such a class begins to sense its latent power. Finally, at the end of the war, a desperately strug-gling Confederate government broke the darkest of antebellum ta-boos: its Congress authorized raising up to 300,000 troops from among the slaves. "In four years," Thomas sums up, "the Southern nation had given up that which called it into being. Independence at the last was no longer means but end. Born in revolution the Confederacy herself became revolutionized."

Convinced states' righters, perceiving the centralist drive of their national government, sabotaged Jefferson Davis's war effort much as New England states'-righters had sabotaged James Madison's. State supreme courts nullified acts of the Confederate Congress, and the Confederacy never got around to creating a national Su-preme Court to which to appeal. State governors refused to allow their militias to fight outside their home states and exempted thousands of their citizens from the draft. Nor was there much, short of outright dictatorship, that Davis could have done to forge them into unity. Paradoxically, as Henry Steele Commager pointed out in an essay "How the Lost Cause Was Lost," the nationalism of the Confederate States of America was "based on a repudiation of nationalism."

This may account in part for the lingering glamour of that "lost cause," even among enlightened moderns who share none of the Confederacy's racist premises. "That the principle of local self-government should have been committed to the cause of slavery, that it was loaded with an incubus certain to alienate the liberalism of the North, may be accounted one of the tragedies of American history," Vernon Parrington wrote at the end of a thoughtful and perceptive essay on Alexander H. Stephens. "It was disastrous to American democracy, for it removed the last brake on the movement of consolidation, submerging the democratic individualism of the South"—and of the North, one may add, thinking of Thoreau—"in an unwieldy mass will." Some of the compassion— the "malice toward none"—which leavened Abraham Lincoln's total-war leadership as he orchestrated and manipulated and deployed that mass will, to the Confederate South's—and slavery's —destruction, may have stemmed from Lincoln's own troubled mind on this very point. In his message to the first emergency session of what was left of Congress, three weeks before the disastrous First Battle of Manassas, or Bull Run, Lincoln with his acute gift for political logic summed up the eternal dilemma for constitutional democrats: "Is there, in all republics, this inherent and fatal weakness? Must a government of necessity be too *strong* for the liberties of its own people, or too *weak* to maintain its own existence?"

Lincoln himself robustly answered that question in the negative. In his best known public statement he dedicated the nation to a high resolve "that government of the people, by the people, for the people, shall not perish from the earth," interpreting the Civil War as a test of whether any nation dedicated to Jefferson's proposition that all men are created equal "can long endure." Southern—and other—critics of Lincoln have dismissed this democratic rhetoric as a hypocritical smoke screen, behind which the new masters of the American economy consolidated a corporate nationalist oligarchy. Moreover, the physical war itself, with its railroad tactics and industrial strategy—in a sense the first truly "modern" war—brutally accelerated the pace of consolidation and invoked the ghost of Caesar in a most terrifying form. "Unappreciated and unmourned," George Dennison has written, "the old republic died giving birth to the republican empire."

Must republics evolve into empires, ceasing in the process to be republics? So to judge America's travail between 1861 and 1865 would be to apply to those terrible years the wisdom of hindsight, which is rarely as wise as it supposes itself. Moreover, historians have a vested interest in cherishing and valuing what was, always at the risk of devaluing what is by comparison. It seems to be one of the most difficult lessons of all to learn: that historical progress is neither inevitable nor illusory—but that its price is pain.

Actually, the way in which the Civil War came, for all the death and destruction it would unleash, constituted a curious, backhanded tribute to America's nonviolent political tradition. Consider: the ablest officer in the United States Army, Robert E. Lee, is offered supreme command of the mighty army Lincoln has called for; he politely declines, rides home across the Potomac, resigns his commission, writes a regretful letter to General Scott, goes to church in Alexandria, notifies the secessionist Virginia governor that he is on his way to Richmond, and duly takes the train—and in the course of all this is not even placed under house arrest! In any other civil war on record, so able an avowed opponent would most likely have been summarily shot. And throughout the war itself, in both the Union and the Confederacy, opposition newspapers viciously attacked their respective presidents, often without reprisal; elections were held; dissidence found many voices, few of which were silenced; and no necessity arose out of America's Civil War, in contrast to Rome's, that (as Tacitus had put it) "all power should be centered in one man." Nor did the postwar years precipitate a rush from republic to empire; not, at least, until the margin of the continent had been reached and the frontier closed. Whatever one thinks of the series of Civil War generals who were elected presidents of the United States for the following quarter-century, not one of those bearded Republican old duffers remotely resembled Caesar.

Interlude IV

Factory whistles screamed at dawn; streets echoed to the grinding of wheels; chimney smoke screened out the sun; top-hatted men and petticoated women thronged into churches, exhibition halls, fairgrounds. Black laborers—slaves before the Civil War; nominal freedmen afterward—chanted at dockside as they rolled cotton bales up gangways onto steamships. Soldiers, lodge members, political partisans marched, shouted, sang. Fiery revivalist preachers, fulsome Fourth of July orators, leather-lunged workgang foremen, drove or charmed or moved or scared their respective kinds of crowds. And yet—beyond the edges of the bustling towns, where the houses separated into isolated farmsteads and the roads dwindled into rutted lanes, the roar of the crowds sank to the whisper of crickets and tree frogs. At night, beyond the circles of flickering light generated by tallow, coal-oil, whaleoil, kerosene, or wood, the land was still dark.

Much of the continent—most of it, west of the great river and north of its glacial lakes—remained wild. Maps still showed a "Great American Desert" barring the way West; not all of it "desert" in the usual sense of dry barrenness, but rather in the archaic meaning: deserted; unsettled; empty. Wagon trains rolled out upon it, horse riders ranged over it; paddlewheelers churned their way up its rivers; it would not stay empty, dark, and silent forever. Yet, while it lay there, stark and trackless, it lured.

"Go West, young man." Go West by yourself, not a few bold souls proposed; "light out for the territory." There lay wealth; danger; escape; perhaps moral regeneration. As the town dwellers in the East began to write and circulate their own poems and stories and plays, in addition to importing such amenities from the Old World they also fashioned the ever-present wilderness beyond their cities and farms into literature.

FIVE

Growing Up, or Running Away?

The moral climate in which Americans first made their public culture—a culture they would continually keep remaking—presented special problems for those citizens whose revolt against destiny took the form of artistic creation. Just where does an artist's responsibility lie? To Art itself, "for art's sake"? To the artist's own urge for "self-expression"? To a public, broad or narrow, knowing or naive? Does the artist seek to amuse that public, or instruct it, or (as Aristotle advised) purge it by inducing emotions of pity and terror?

Historically such questions had been resolved by appeal to standards, aesthetic, religious, political, or technical. It was not yet clear whether in a democratic culture one could speak meaningfully of "standards," in that sense, at all. It *was* clear, however, that such a culture could and did set boundaries. Some of them are still in place.

1. Poetry and Revolution

Financially speaking, a poet's lot is not a happy one. Poets therefore should "choose some gainful trade," wrote Philip Freneau—the poet of the American Revolution—in some heartfelt lines he inscribed on the flyleaf of a book published in 1773 by his fellow revolutionist, Benjamin Rush. Even Shakespeare, "with all the drama in his skull," had as a youth to be "bred to combing wool," rather than to composing soliloquies for Hamlet:

> To steer a boat, or drive a cart,
> To practice some mechanic art,
> Yields something for your pain;

> But poems are in no demand,
> Few read them, fewer understand
> The visions of your brain.

In times past, court patronage had kept a few poets comfortable; in future times, beyond Freneau's ken, foundation grants and university artist-in-residence appointments would similarly subsidize the Muse. But in the plain-spoken, commercially bustling republic born of the American Revolution, Philip Freneau had to confess, "the sheriff only deals in prose." The literary era of Alexander Pope—a time when "statesmen, kings and lords/were poets" (or thought they were), had ended; and

> A poet where there is no king,
> Is but a disregarded thing
> An atom on the wheel.

Exactly so, conservative self-appointed guardians of high culture might have said, as indeed a few of them still do. Paradoxically, the same Jeffersonian right to the pursuit of happiness that freed artistic creators from the constraints of censorship could also extinguish their audience; political equality might generate social leveling of a kind which sought the lowest possible common denominator: in modern educational terms, "dumbing down." From any conventional standpoint, whether aristocratic or democratic, free spirited artists have always seemed possessed by an urge to bite the societal hand that feeds them; that was one reason Plato mistrusted such people. Since Freud, moreover, many have inclined to the belief that alienation is the price for the creation of authentic art.

The tension between artist and audience becomes especially acute in an age of revolution. One can of course peddle hack, monumental "revolutionary art," as in those Stalinist novels where Boy meets Tractor and they fulfill their production quota together; one can also go counter-revolutionary, and lament in elegiac verses the alleged virtues of bygone days. Or, as Philip Freneau advised in "The City Poet," one can give up the struggle to "carry verses up and down" the streets of the uncaring town: "Go home," he concluded the poem, "and mend your shoes." The grandeur in Freneau's oft-thwarted life is that despite his bitter advice to that city poet he never abandoned the struggle to sing his own song, yet he remained true to his own heartfelt revolutionary ideals.

That is, he remained true to them in his own fashion. For a crucial time in his life and in the life of his emerging new nation, Philip Freneau had a serious problem with his own priorities. Coming out of the College of New Jersey (i.e., Princeton) in 1771 as the author of a graduation poem on "The Rising Glory of America," Freneau entered quite naturally into the spirit of revolution in 1775 with an outpouring of anti-British satires, including an imaginary poetic soliloquy by General Gage, the last British commandant of Boston. Freneau's Princeton classmate and close friend James Madison that same year joined a local vigilance committee in his native Virginia and shortly was helping to draft that state's first constitution; Freneau's fellow writer Thomas Paine early in 1776 wrote the opinion-shaking pamphlet *Common Sense*, one of the few literary essays which can honestly be said to have changed people's minds and lives. Paine subsequently joined the Revolutionary army, just in time for George Washington's retreat across New Jersey, and while marching with the Continentalers Paine heartened their morale with the first of his *Crisis* papers: "These are the times that try men's souls. The summer soldier and the sunshine patriot will, in this crisis shrink from the service of his country. . . . Tyranny, like hell, is not easily conquered." But in the very month of *Common Sense*'s publication—January 1776— Philip Freneau quietly shipped out on a packet bound for the Caribbean. For the next year and a half—the bitter months while Washington was being driven out of Philadelphia and taking up winter quarters at Valley Forge—Philip Freneau sojourned on the island of Santa Cruz (St. Croix), in what were then the Danish West Indies. On that neutral ground, Freneau later would argue, a poet could practice his craft:

> What though we own the rude imperious Dane,
> Gold is his sordid care, the Muses mine.

There was no military draft in the American Revolution; nevertheless, a partisan of more recent American wars might be tempted to hang the label "draft dodger" on Freneau. The poet might well have pleaded guilty to the charge; a major literary work he produced out of that time of chosen exile, "The Beauties of Santa Cruz," hovers between self-defense and self-accusation for his summer soldiering. Freneau could not have had recourse to the antiwar rationale of twentieth-century dissidence (as in *Catch-22* or *A Farewell to Arms*), in which a protagonist's resistance or desertion becomes a moral judgment on a war judged to be unjust or absurd; for Freneau was with and for America's democratic revolution heart and soul. His was a deeper existential dilemma, with which American writers and artists have wrestled ever since: how far may, or must, the claims of the public on one's conscience override the demands of one's private Muse? John Winthrop, in his characteristic Puritan way, had set the standard as long ago as 1630: "Particular estates cannot subsist in the ruin of the public." American artists and creative writers have been alternately—sometimes simultaneously—embracing and rejecting that doctrine ever since.

"The Beauties of Santa Cruz," said to have been written on that island in 1776 and first published in the *United States Magazine* for February 1779, is on the face of it a hymn of rebellion against Winthrop's dictum of collective responsibility. Freneau addresses his reader as "shepherd," in the classic pastoral form which modern literature had inherited, like so much else, from Rome, whose poets had appealed—to the point of cliché—from the raucous culture of their metropolis, with its venal law courts and its ugly arena games, to a simpler life among vineyards and olive trees. Thus subtly, the American poet shifts his argumentative ground; rather than directly counsel a retreat from the American Revolution, he appeals to the inhabitant of New York or New England—a region we still denominate the "frost belt"—to flee from that frigid, iron-bound land to a lush, sunlit tropical Eden where the living is easy and, perhaps, less repressive than in the cold Yankee North:

> Sick of thy northern glooms, come, shepherd, seek
> Less rigorous climes, and a more friendly sky:
> Why shouldst thou toil amid thy frozen ground,
> Where half years' snows, a barren prospect, lie . . . ?

"Two weeks with prosperous gales" suffice to bear the shepherd down to this earthly paradise, which Freneau introduces with an adroit mingling of Greek mythological allusion and metaphoric eroticism à la Freud:

> From the vast caverns of old Ocean's bed,
> St. Cruz arising, laves her humid waist,
> The threatening waters roar on every side,
> For every side by ocean is embraced.

This is one moment in the frozen North's long love affair with the tropics (which will recur in Herman Melville's prose), and Freneau makes the most of it. Then, in the midst of cataloguing in careful eighteenth-century fashion all the marine life in the environing ocean and the fruit trees on the island itself, the poet unexpectedly sends his shepherd-reader a more sinister signal. The first of the native trees to meet his scrutiny turns out to bear a fragrant, poisoned little apple, and the poet draws the obvious Judaeo-Christian moral: "Shun the dangerous tree, nor touch, like Eve/this interdicted fruit, in Eden's ground." Then, passing through mangrove and tamarind, oranges and "sweet, spungy plums," cashews and plantains and bananas, Freneau comes at last to "the sweet, uncloying sugar-cane," whence "springs . . . chief the glory of these Indian isles"—mellow, potent West Indian rum. And then his Roman civic inhibitions take over: if you do come to this earthly Eden, Freneau warns, "forbear to taste the virtues of the cane" if you expect ever to get home again: "Whoever sips of the enchanting juice . . . quits his friends, his country, and his all."

The "chief glory" of the West Indies—and, Freneau deftly notes, the source of the planters' wealth—has suddenly transmuted into the mind-numbing *lotos*, from that mythic Homeric shore whence "Ulysses . . . dragged off by force his sailors." The images swiftly darken. The poet lifts up his eyes to a hilltop harvest-field, where a black slave looks longingly off over the ocean and "pants a land of freedom and repose"—which Santa Cruz, for that "Ethiopian swain," is not! In mid-stanza, Freneau changes that subject—"O quit thee then my muse"—and displays before his northern reader some "abject trees" that have been scattered over the plain by the "wasteful madness" of one of those fierce hurricanes which come smashing down upon these islands from time to time "lest Nature should have proved too kind/or man have sought his happiest heaven below."

But the winds pass; the storm subsides; and although his native land is brought to mind, where "murder marks the cruel Briton," the poet almost defiantly embraces his private destiny:

> Contented here I rest, in spite of pain,
> And quaff the enlivening juice in spite of care.

And he invites his far-Northern reader to make the same kind of separate peace:

> Then, shepherd, haste, and leave behind thee far
> The bloody plains and iron glooms above.

> Quit thy cold northern star, and here enjoy
> Beneath the smiling skies this land of love.

In real life, however, this scion of conscientious French Huguenots—a faith as "ought"-ridden by Calvinism as that of the Puritans—could not carry off this plunge into hedonism. Although he ends the poem by encouraging his reader, if not persuaded by these verses to quit his "darksome forests," to remain there and "repel the Tyrant, who thy peace invades," it was Freneau himself who came back to those darksome forests, and to the embattled towns at the forest's edge, to repel the tyrant. Returning to his homeland on July 9, 1778, he enlisted in a militia regiment six days later; afterward served as a privateer captain, capturing a British warship that had been driven inshore by an ice storm; and in turn was captured and confined on the British prison ship *Scorpion*. When the war was over he tinkered with "The Beauties of Santa Cruz" for a new edition in 1786, not always to the poem's benefit; rewriting lines, patching in stanzas from other poems, throwing in pious references to "Judah's tribes" and the "Pilot of the Galilean Sea," adding more Greek literary allusion and, in the midst of his previous discourse on pomegranates and coconuts, interpolating a fresh verse which looked *back* on Santa Cruz with a cry of nostalgia:

> O grant me, gods, if yet condemned to stray,
> At least to spend life's sober evening here.

Was it "the gods" who had condemned Freneau to stray from "yon sheltered bay"? Or his own conscience? In the three-page prose travelogue of the island which preceded the poem's first appearance in 1779, Freneau confessed:

> My agreeable residence at this place for above two years off and on during the wars in America renders the idea of it but too pleasing, and makes me feel much the same anxiety at a distance from it as Adam did after he was banished from the bowers of Eden.

Aside from its frequent hurricanes, what made Santa Cruz not an Eden was its human slavery—worse in the West Indies, Freneau asserted, than anywhere else on the globe;

> and thus the earth, which were it not for the lust of price and dominion, might be an earthly paradise, is by the ambition and

overbearing nature of mankind, rendered an eternal scene of desolation, woe, and horror.

The rest of the Freneau story is better known: how he plunged into the fierce political wars of the 1790s on the anti-Federalist side; how Jefferson, through the State Department, subsidized him as editor of the *National Gazette,* as a counter to the Federalist editor and journal being grubstaked by Hamilton at the Treasury; how the polite literary establishment savaged him, and how President George Washington brushed him aside as "that rascal Freneau"; how he embraced the French as well as the American Revolution, and in a partisan war of letters more vitriolic than we today can imagine gave as good as he got.

What would have happened had Philip Freneau continued making his separate peace, waited out the entire Revolution on Santa Cruz, and embarked afterward upon a nonpolitical poetic career? Bound no longer by the Federalist blinkers of his own literary generation, some twentieth-century critics have come to believe that Philip Freneau had it in him to have launched the Romantic movement in English-language poetry twenty years early. "It is a nice question of literary ethics," wrote Parrington; "but Revolution and not poetry was the serious business of the age, and he chose to have a hand in that business." He wavered, but he chose.

2. A Republican Theater

If the poet in a republic is likely to be "a disregarded thing," the playwright has a further problem. The poet can choose to ignore the public that ignores the poetry, and write primarily for other poets or for his or her own ego; in twentieth-century America— and Europe—many serious, formal poets have done just that. But the writer of plays cannot appease the Muse in any such fashion. There *has* to be a breakout from the writer's charmed circle; no audience, no play.

In a culture whose ethos is heavily anti-theater, the odds become daunting indeed, and American culture in the Revolutionary years was not hospitable to Thespis. The Continental Congress in fact passed a resolution against playgoing. It was hardly enforceable, given the autonomy of the separate states at that time; but it reflected a deep-running current of popular moral opinion. Boston's Puritans had never approved of "the wicked stage"; Philadelphia's Quakers condemned it, along with the novel, as "fictitious," i.e., false to reality; and in other parts of the country—the South, significantly, excepted—the theater seemed a pretentious pastime of a European or Europeanized aristocracy against whose values America was rising in revolution.

In New York the odium was especially acute. The British navy and army captured New York City early in the war and held onto it throughout the conflict, yielding the city only in 1782 after Cornwallis's surrender. Behind siege lines, as it were, theater continued and flourished; indeed, young British officers are said to have acted in some of these wartime stage productions. On the "Broadway" of the 1780s, therefore, to patronize show business seemed not merely decadent, frivolous, or snobbish; it could be viewed as downright unpatriotic, even as collaboration with the enemy.

Into this extraordinarily unpromising theatrical environment in the spring of 1787 came young Royall Tyler, who had never scribbled a line of drama in his life but who promptly—three weeks after seeing his first play, legend has it—wrote America's earliest commercially successful comedy for the stage.

Tyler was of the same generation as Freneau and Madison: born in 1757 into an old Boston merchant family; graduated from Harvard, '72, and practiced law; aide to Revolutionary War hero John Sullivan; engaged for a time to Abigail Adams, daughter of John Adams (an engagement broken, apparently, at the behest of Abigail Senior); and a member of Massachusetts general Benjamin Lincoln's staff during the suppression of Shays's Rebellion. Visiting New York on business in 1787 Tyler saw a performance of Richard Sheridan's *School for Scandal* and made it the model for his own maiden effort at play writing, *The Contrast*.

It would not suffice merely to write an American imitation of the popular British playwright, although structurally *The Contrast* does follow the Sheridan model. A few whole lines of the American play were in fact lifted from *School for Scandal*, and one of Tyler's characters gives a comically garbled account of a production of the Sheridan play he purportedly has just seen. But the American playwright had also to devise a script that would appeal to the sophisticated tastes of an audience which had been going regularly to the theater during half a decade of British military occupation without making the play appear tainted with Toryism.

Tyler solved the problem by exaggerating patriotic sentiment into satire. In the Sheridan tradition of characterizing the players by name (e.g., "Lady Sneerwell" in *School for Scandal*), Tyler gave his New York audience a true-blue, 200 percent American hero named Manly and a jaded Europeanized villain named Dimple, and overdid both of them as comic caricatures. New York theatergoers could thus applaud Colonel Manly's patriotic sentiments, yet distance themselves from them, in much the same way that New Yorkers of a much later era could applaud simplicity, naturalness, and the out-of-doors in a musical comedy like *Oklahoma*, yet covertly put down those same values when they were expressed by a wide-eyed "rube" character in the same show singing "Everything's Up to Date in Kansas City." (Nothing is *ever* up to date in Kansas City, they could assure themselves!) The resemblance between these two very different examples of show business in action is not accidental. Between Royall Tyler and Rodgers and Hammerstein runs a long, durable literary line—it includes writings as humble as *Aaron Slick from Punkin Crick* and as exalted as the novels of Henry James—which ranges unaffected, forthright, often rural, natural American virtue over against sophisticated, devious, artificial European or urban-"Eastern" vice.

Had Broadway showgoers in 1787 not taken all this moralizing with a grain of salt, its implications could have been a bit sinister. Villain Dimple encounters Hero Manly (Act 4, Sc. 1) and tells him in his own worldly wise fashion that "when you shall have seen the brilliant exhibitions of Europe you will learn to despise the amusements of this country as much as I do." To which Colonel Manly retorts: "Therefore I do not wish to see them; for I can never esteem that knowledge valuable which tends to give me a distaste for my native country." Ignorance is Strength!—a forerunner of the self-satisfied anti-intellectualism which has plagued American culture throughout most of its history.

However, had Tyler's audience actually despised European-style amusements, as the actor portraying Manly seemed to urge, they would presumably not have been attending a stage play in the first place. Americans have always enjoyed their political rhetoric just a bit overcooked. In a similar fashion Thomas Jefferson, as civilized a cosmopolite as the Republic produced in the generation next after Ben Franklin's, might list in a letter from Paris in 1785 the disadvantages of sending a youth to Europe for an education ("If he goes to England he learns drinking, horse racing, and boxing"; there and on the Continent "he acquires a fondness for European luxury and dissipation and a contempt for the simplicity of his own country")—but this did not for one moment stop Jefferson from enjoying the cuisine and civilized talk of Paris, nor did it immunize him from the humiliation that is imposed as a matter of principle upon visitors to that city who speak French with an American accent.

Tyler's opus is not simply an antiquarian curiosity; it is also what critics used to call a "well-made play." With judicious pruning of its long-winded speeches and with sound advice to its players on how to say them (e.g., take catch-breaths in the middle in order to punch the ending), this show can even be made to "work," in the theater's sense of that verb. *The Contrast* as one reads it falls into natural scene blockings and built-in laugh lines, clearly intended as such by the author. Moreover, in addition to his somewhat cartoonish Upright Hero and Scheming Villain, Tyler also gave Broadway its first "ethnic" stage character, a New York Dutchman named Van Rough; its first pure and simple rural American comic character of the "Li'l Abner" species, a New Englander named Jonathan; and the hero's sister Charlotte, an urban sophisticate with a primary interest in clothes, money, and men (not necessarily in that order!) leavened by keen wit, whom a present-day actress will still find an interesting and challenging part.

The play was, in its time, highly topical. It contains references to the Battle of Harlem Heights; to Generals Washington and Lafayette; to the Continental Congress's "embarrassments, the natural consequences of a long war," which as Manly explains "disable my country from supporting its credit"; and especially to Shays's Rebellion, which had finally been crushed just weeks before the play opened. Interestingly, Colonel Manly and Jonathan, his "waiter"—not his *servant,* as democratic-minded Jonathan insists ("My father has as good a farm as the colonel")—take opposite sides regarding the Western Massachusetts revolt lately led by Daniel Shays. "I vow, I did think the sturgeons [insurgents] were right," Jonathan confides, drawing from another character the ironic compliment "I thought, Mr. Jonathan, you Massachusetts men always argued with a gun in your hand." But when asked, "Why didn't you join them?", the "waiter" loyally echoes his master's words: "Colonel said that it was a burning shame for the true blue Bunker-hill sons of liberty, who had fought Governor Hutchinson, Lord North, and the Devil, to have a hand in kicking up a cursed dust against a government, which we had every mother's son of us a hand in making."

That was exactly the Federalist view of the matter; and it was into Federalist political pamphleteering and satire—the diametric opposite of Philip Freneau's—that Tyler embarked during the passionately partisan 1790s. (He also found time to write *The Algerine Captive*, which the critics usually count as the first American novel.) Then somehow, in the course of emigrating to the newest of the states—Vermont, admitted to the Union in 1791—Tyler became transformed into a Jeffersonian Republican; eventually (as seen in chapter 4, above) he would become a vigorously anti-Federalist Madisonian. As an Assistant Judge of his adopted state's highest court in 1802 Tyler wrote a landmark opinion (of which many Southern Republicans would have disapproved!) denying the admissibility of a bill of sale for a slave as evidence in court on the ground that under Vermont's constitution "no inhabitant of the state can hold a slave." Later, as Chief Justice of Vermont in 1808, he found himself in the position of enforcing the Embargo Act, the most unpopular measure of any passed by Congress during Jefferson's two presidential terms.

Intent on relieving their economic distress in the time-honored American way, by smuggling, some Vermonters had gotten into a shootout with the crew of a revenue cutter that had pursued them into an inlet of Lake Champlain; they killed the cutter's helmsman and two other government men. Feeling ran high, and Chief Justice Royall Tyler, when he called the state supreme court into special session on August 23, 1808, charged the Grand Jurors to put aside "all those prejudices and partialities which so readily attach to us in private life": both the popular sympathy for the smugglers, on the one side, and "the distress of surviving relatives" of their victims, on the other. Only thus could citizen jurors responsibly play out their part as agents of "a government of our own choice . . . a government which secures its citizens the full exercise and almost uncontrolled expression of private opinion; but a government which has provided wholesome laws to restrain and punish acts of violence and bloodshed"—a government, as Colonel Manly had assured Jonathan, which they had every mother's son of them (both the smugglers and the militiamen!) a hand in making.

3. *Sources of Cultural Blight*

Colonel Dimple's put-down of the amusements of America in contrast to "the brilliant exhibitions of Europe" mirrored attitudes that existed in the real world, away from the make-believe of the stage. The political conflict between European aristocracy and American republicanism was also a clash of cultures, high and low. The Americans, according to one British Establishment paper (*The Courier*, July 27, 1813), "have added nothing to literature, nothing to any of the sciences; they have not produced one good poet, not one celebrated historian!" Throughout the nineteenth century, elite Europeans—especially the English—peppered their American cousins with potshots of this kind. Americans really had no capital-C Culture, Thomas Colley Grattan contended in 1859. They were fit only to "clear the forests, hunt the wild beasts, scatter the savage tribes . . . till the soil, dig in the mines, and work out the rude ways of physical existence." "America," complained the great Matthew Arnold in 1888, "is not *interesting*."

Smarting under such insults, Americans could quite properly have countered them from their own republican ideology: one citizen is as good as the next, and it is as honorable to dig in a mine or to till the soil as to engage in polite letters. New World republicans often, however, wanted to have it both ways; to be a people who cleared the forests, hunted the wild beasts, *and* wrote the Great American Novel. Indeed, creating a national literature and art was a high priority for a people still in the process of finding its own identity.

"We have listened too long to the courtly muses of Europe," cried Ralph Waldo Emerson in 1837. Henceforth, "please God . . . we will walk on our own feet; we will work with out own hands; we will speak our own minds"—bold and oft-quoted words, from that day to this. The problem was that none of the "young men of fairest promise, who begin life upon our shores," for and to whom Emerson spoke, had any desire to be—like Philip Freneau's City Poet— "a disregarded thing/An atom on the wheel." The author of a Great American Novel ought properly to receive some great American royalties. The catch was that the only place where one could earn them, in the republic's early years, was England.

This meant that a writer had to run the gauntlet of the English literary critics; which is to say, the recognized interpreters of the courtly muses of Europe. Washington Irving, America's first great literary success, is a case in point. His early work in America, including that roistering parody of the historical grand style, *Diedrich Knickerbocker's History of New York*, caught the attention of the London literary Establishment as well as of Irving's own countrymen. When he began to turn his notebooks from a visit to England (after the War of 1812) into essays, Sir Walter Scott, no less, saw to it that Irving's *Sketch Book of Geoffrey Crayon, Gent.* got the full media treatment in London. But the *Sketch Book* is, in content, an overwhelmingly *English* piece of work.

Washington Irving had it in him to have written keen, biting satire; after reading "Diedrich Knickerbocker's" mock-Homeric description of the climactic battle between the Swedes and the Dutch for control of Nieuw Amsterdam (complete with interventions by the appropriate Greek gods and goddesses!), readers may find it hard to go back to Homer and again take the earnest, heroic, knuckleheaded brawlers in *The Iliad* quite so seriously as they take themselves. Alas, none of the mordant political and social humor of Irving's Old New York Dutch persona found its way into the almost suffocatingly gentle essays in the *Sketch Book*. Moreover, of the thirty-four essays or stories in the work, only five are recognizably "American" in locale or theme.

Two of this handful dealt with the Indians, who had become acceptable in Europe as examples of the New World's quaint freshness. Another was a politely worded complaint against "the literary animosity daily growing up between England and America," in which British writers' "illiberal spirit of ridicule" Irving carefully balanced against the "querulous and peevish temper" to which Americans felt driven in reply. Only two of the sketches—"Rip Van Winkle" and "The Legend of Sleepy Hollow"—called on Diedrich Knickerbocker's comic American muse. Even these great made-in-the-U.S.A. folk tales, if one compares them with "The Spectre Bridegroom" in the same volume, have unmistakable European resonances; and almost everything else in this international best seller of Irving's was Tourist British: "Rural Life in England," "The Country Church," "A Sunday in London," "Westminster Abbey," "Stratford-on-Avon," and five long-winded essays on the British way of celebrating Christmas. Charles Dickens was shortly to do all that sort of thing much better.

The British chorus of critical praise for Washington Irving, literary historian William Kelly points out, carried with it a note of condescension: "here at last, Irving's reviewers implied, was an American who wrote like an Englishman." Some of Irving's fellow Americans accused him of, in effect, going after brownie points in the U.K. "See Irving gone to Britain's court/To people of *another sort*," gibed the aged Philip Freneau in some sarcastic stanzas he addressed "To A New-England Poet" in 1823. The sometime bard of the American Revolution saw Irving "with the glittering nobles mix/Forgetting times of seventy-six"; and ironically—with, perhaps, a touch of sour grapes—Freneau suggested that the person he addressed in the poem go and do likewise:

> Why pause?—like Irving, haste away,
> And England will reward you well,
> When you some pompous story tell
> Of British feats, and British arms . . .

and you will have the further satisfaction, Freneau savagely added, that

> In England what you write and print,
> Republished here in shop, or stall,
> Will perfectly enchant us all.

Emerson's advice to young Americans to work with their own hands and speak their own minds found the other arts in no better case than literature. Lorenzo Da Ponte, the librettist for *Don Giovanni* and *The Marriage of Figaro*, emigrated to the United States in 1805, where he became professor of Italian literature at Columbia and sponsored opera performances; but he found in New York no American Mozart. Serious music performers born in America had, throughout the nineteenth century and well into the twentieth, to make European concert reputations before becoming fully acceptable in their own country. Similarly with painting. John Singleton Copley, who painted Paul Revere; Gilbert Stuart, who painted George Washington more or less as he appears on the dollar bill; and John Trumbull, who painted the Battle of Bunker Hill, all sharpened their skills at the London studio of the American expatriate Benjamin West—the official historical painter to King George the Third!

They labored, moreover, under paralyzing inhibitions. American painters in the nineteenth century, art historian Oliver Larkin points out, notoriously did not paint nudes; Raphaelle Peale's *After the Bath* (1847), in which bare feminine arms and feet coyly appear from behind a realistically rendered opaque sheet or curtain, was about as saucy as U.S. pictorial art permitted itself to get. As with painting, so with sculpture, poetry, the theater, and the novel. Horatio Greenough's heroic seated statue of George Washington, half-draped in the Grecian fashion, had to be banished to the Smithsonian's basement because of objections to the father of his country's bared manly torso; and characters in novels or short stories given to mild profanity had to be contented with "d---d," "d---l," and "h--l." Prudery ws as much a distinguishing mark of American popular culture then as sexual sleaze is now.

However much Americans may have emancipated themselves politically from Britain, Queen Victoria—with her much-quoted put-down of an off-color joke told in her presence, "We are not amused"—reigned even more effectively over the former colonies in sociocultural matters than she did over England. But American free spirits had local wet blankets to contend with also. Most especially, writes Ann Douglas, they suffered under an unholy alliance that linked lower-bourgeois writing women, then rising in influence and popularity, with liberal clergymen who were losing their more traditional kind of authority. Together, according to Douglas, these relentless sentimentalists in the antebellum years engaged in a "feminization of American culture," systematically vitiating and corrupting the national taste. One may skeptically object to the term "feminization"; surely Douglas's thesis does not imply that an ideally vital national culture ought to be male-macho, nor should we infer that in Victorian America only females and clergymen were prudes! Still, *something* evidently worked to censor the American artistic psyche; it is not at all difficult to imagine an American equivalent of Charles Dickens, but it is very hard to imagine an American equivalent of George Sand.

Even more crippling than outright censorship—which an American could legitimately have challenged as an interference with Jefferson's "free market of ideas"—was a pervasive insistence that art had to be "good for" something other than itself. It had to edify, inform, enlighten, inspire; teach moral lessons; redirect Americans' attention to the Finer Things of Life. It must appeal democratically to the people, and so must not be complicated, symbolic, or obscure; but it must portray them as they ought to be rather than as they necessarily were—not unlike the similarly motivated "socialist realism" which in the Stalin era would make a wasteland of Soviet painting, music, and literature.

113

"Concern for refining the national character . . . to a great extent determined the forms and subject matter of American art in the nineteenth century," Lillian Miller sums up; and "Americans, believing they ought to be optimistic and cheerful, accepted the art that portrayed them in this way." Even today we have not quite gotten away from the dreary notion that certain kinds of books, music, and art works must be taken in for our improvement, like bad-tasting medicine, rather than simply enjoyed. In the words given to an imagined high-society clubwoman by the comedienne Anna Russell, "We are going to get culture even if it *kills* us."

4. Society and Solitude

"The figure of Rip Van Winkle presides over the birth of the American imagination," wrote Leslie Fiedler in his provocative study *Love and Death in The American Novel;* "and it is fitting that our first successful home-grown legend should memorialize, however playfully, the flight of the dreamer from the shrew—into the mountains and out of time, away from the drab duties of home and town toward the good companions and the magic keg of beer." By a nice irony Washington Irving, the very writer whom Philip Freneau accused of having sold out to the British, thus managed in a small but significant fraction of his own work to inaugurate a truly revolutionary American departure from the canons of Europe's courtly muses.

When a fictional European youth sets out into the world to seek his fortune, "the world" commonly turns out to be Paris or London; while he is winning or losing fame, fortune, or his light-of-love he is likely to be surrounded by a cast of thousands. Tolstoy launched *War and Peace* with a gala Moscow party, which introduces so many people by name all at once that many a well-intentioned reader of the Russian classic gets discouraged and reads no further; the reader who persists to the end will find in the concluding chapter the same hostess giving another party, and despite all the deaths in battle and otherwise that have taken place during Napoleon's invasion of Russia most of the people who were present in chapter 1 are still there for the close. In like manner Charles Dickens populated his pages with scores of colorful characters drawn from all walks of life; and Honoré de Balzac planned 120 novels, of which he finished 90, that encompassed the entire spectrum of contemporary French society. By contrast, the heroes created in classic American literature from Cooper's time to Hemingway's, rather than faring forth into the crowded crossways and halls of civilization, typically have gone off into the wilderness. Alone, or in the company of a bosom buddy of the same gender but a different race, they have fought Indians or descended into maelstroms or harpooned whales. Their closest European literary kin is not the street-smart Figaro but the self-sufficient Crusoe.

Critic Fiedler judges such writing as a sign not of self-sufficiency but of immaturity; "The great works of American fiction are notoriously at home in the children's section of the library, their level of sentimentality precisely that of a pre-adolescent." The flight to the frontier is not so much heroic adventure or spiritual pilgrimage as it is a recoil from sexual commitment, the family, and one's responsibility to society; the wanderer in the wasteland is "more motherless child than free man." But perhaps that judgment is unfair. Such fictional characters may simply have been rejecting an over-prescriptive society's "don'ts." Don't go fishing when all the other kids are on their way to school, Huck Finn; don't neglect to wash behind your ears, Tom Sawyer—a reflection and translation of the galling constrictions upon their creators' own cultural-political freedoms: Don't deviate from what European critics define as "good" art; don't offend your Paul Prys and Mrs. Grundys at home; above all, don't write, or sculpt, or paint, or compose unless your handiwork improves people's minds, morals, or manners. To which a cacophonous chorus of American artistic individualists have always shouted, "No!"

The more thoughtful among them are likely to add that the culture-prescribers' "dos" and "don'ts" are intrinsically self-defeating. "Trust thyself," Emerson warned; you cannot create the great American novel by following a committee's novelistic guidelines, or even by emulating the great writers of a (presumed) committeeless past: "Meek young men grow up in libraries, believing it their duty to accept the views which Cicero, which Locke, which Bacon have given; forgetful that Cicero, Locke, and Bacon were only young men in libraries when they wrote these books." To cut oneself off from one's past, or from one's peers, *is* immature; but it may be the immaturity of the kid in Hans Christian Andersen's folk tale, gleefully pointing out that the Emperor has no clothes. "Let him not quit his belief that a popgun is a popgun, though the ancient and honorable of the earth affirm it to be the crack of doom," said Emerson; like the baseball umpire, we cannot take another's word for what we see. In order to court one's national or personal Muse with integrity it may even become necessary, spiritually if not physically, to take Huckleberry Finn's advice and "light out for the territory."

"Strict science," Emerson insisted, "finds underneath our domestic and neighborly life" a "tragic necessity" for solitude, "irresistibly driving each adult soul as with whips into the desert, and making our warm covenants sentimental and momentary." Yet in the next breath the Sage of Concord admitted that "this banishment to the rocks and echoes no metaphysics can make right or tolerable." Humans *are* social creatures (like other primates), Emerson knew; we "must be clothed with society, or we shall feel a certain bareness and poverty." With the pragmatic Yankee prudence that always subtly checked his highest Romantic transports, Ralph Waldo Emerson resolved the dilemma in a manner enabling him to have it both ways: "Solitude is impracticable, and society fatal. We must keep our head in the one, and our hands in the other."

American writers have balanced the equation between society and solitude in various ways. Some, like Royall Tyler when writing *The Contrast*, took most of their cues from Society but manipulated its biases to their own advantage; others, like Henry David Thoreau, opted for Solitude but drew strength therefrom for confronting Society. The solitary Edgar Allan Poe lit out for a territory which existed mainly within the confines of his own head; yet even Poe, when not writing horror stories, deeply engaged himself with at least the *literary* society of his own day, and in the pages of its media battled vigorously against the educators and improvers. (Poetry, which Poe defined as "the rhythmical creation of Beauty," had "no dependence, unless incidentally, upon either Duty or *Truth*"; the trouble with poets like Longfellow was that far too often they developed a valid poetic image or idea only to spoil it at the end with a moral.)

Yet another balance between Society and Solitude was struck by Nathaniel Hawthorne, who fled, not down the Mississippi or out into the desert, but back through two centuries of New England antiquity, to translate the theological tenets of seventeenth-century Puritanism into a quite startlingly modern psychological equivalent (what the malign Roger Chillingsworth does to poor Arthur Dimmesdale in *The Scarlet Letter*—a "black psychoanalysis" whose purpose is not to heal but to destroy—can be taken as a left-handed anticipation of Freud). Yet Hawthorne prefaced his fictional pilgrimage to the past with a wistful, fifty-page look at the raucous, vital, commercial culture which surrounded him in 1850—and conceded that "a better book than I shall ever write was there," in society rather than in solitude.

Some European Romantic writers opted at times for Solitude: "I wandered lonely as a cloud," sang William Wordsworth. But the English lake country which inspired Wordsworth and his friends did not open out into endless wilderness; while tramping across it you were never very far from a hot meal, a clean bed, and a bath. To be sure, Americans had already begun to discipline or destroy their wilderness in the Roman manner, with roads and aqueducts and canals. One fine summer day in 1844, as Nathaniel Hawthorne recorded in his notebook, the "startling shriek" of a train whistle rudely broke the Sabbath quiet of a rustic pathway near Concord, bringing "the noisy world into the midst of our slumbrous peace." As Leo Marx has observed, the same kind of sudden invasion of a garden by a raging machine recurs again and again in classic American literature.

Nevertheless, and despite such ominous interruptions, it was still relatively easy in Hawthorne's time to get away from the noisy world. "In one-half hour I can walk off to some portion of the Earth where a man does not stand from one year's end to another," declared Henry Thoreau as late as 1862; "I can easily walk fifteen, twenty, any number of miles, commencing at my own door, without going by any house, without crossing a road except where the fox and the mink do." Thus he could get away from the train's whistle, "harsh above all other harshness," which had so upset Hawthorne.

What such walking thinkers could *not* get away from was the civilization-trained consciousness they brought with them on their walks. Fenimore Cooper in his "Leatherstocking Tales," as Henry Nash Smith has shown, oscillated constantly between a devotion to the wild freedom of unspoiled Nature beyond the frontier and a stolid commitment to the forces of social order. Ralph Waldo Emerson seemed rather less hung up on Order than Cooper—"whoso would be a man, must be a nonconformist," and much more to the same effect—yet Emerson's high flights into the Over-Soul somehow always landed him back within the walls of his own library. Indeed, he tacitly conceded the point when he affirmed that "the

117

ancient precept, 'Know thyself,' and the modern precept, 'Study nature,' become at last one maxim."

Henry Thoreau, on the other hand, was willing to hike and bushwhack his way to a terrific spiritual confrontation with something which was patently *not* himself. Neatly inverting Governor Winthrop's Puritan rejection of the "natural" liberty "common to man with beasts and other creatures" in favor of "civil or federal" liberty, defined by Winthrop as the freedom to do "only that which is good, just, and honest," Thoreau at the outset of his great essay "Walking" (1862) spoke "a word for Nature, for absolute freedom and wildness, as contrasted with a freedom and culture merely civil." He wished "to regard man as an inhabitant, or a part and parcel of Nature, rather than a member of society." It did not by any means follow, however, as it did for Emerson, that Nature is a part and parcel of man.

Traveling in 1846 to the highest mountain in Maine, which involved arduous poling and portaging along wild rivers and frigid ponds before the climb could even begin, Thoreau felt that "some part of the beholder, even some vital part, seems to escape through the loose grating of his ribs as he ascends." The Nature one found at the summit of Mount Katahdin was not Emerson's or the English lake poets' kind, with which one could easily commune; "there was clearly felt the presence of a force not bound to be kind to man." (As the old hands still warn the novices in hiking and climbing clubs, the mountains *don't care*.) Thoreau devoutly believed it was necessary to our own souls that we see "pure Nature" thus, "vast and drear and inhuman." As Philip Freneau's personal vision-quest had taken him to tropical Santa Cruz, and Melville's to the far Pacific isle of Nukuheva, Thoreau's had carried him into the north woods; but "the prevailing tendency of my countrymen," he acknowledged, was toward the western frontier: "That way the nation is moving." Thoreau's West was not that of the plundering pioneer or his obscene descendant the "developer." "The West of which I speak is but another name for the Wild; and . . . in Wildness is the preservation of the World."

It might be the preservation of the world, but as the land inexorably filled up, Wildness was going to have less and less to do with Americans' daily life. A literature that continued to confine itself to the wild frontier was going to miss a greal deal of what was going on. Of the "classic" American writers it was paradoxically that ultimate isolate Edgar Allan Poe who told us so, in one dark flash of insight. The narrator of his short story "The Man of the Crowd"—a tale unusually subdued in tone for Poe—follows through the streets of London a mysterious, anonymous figure who leads him from the bustling boulevards of the well-to-do to the shadowed haunts of poverty and crime, seeking always to mingle with people regardless of their class or condition as if fearing ever to be alone. After twenty-four hours of this fitful chase the fugitive ends up right next to the streetside coffee house where it all started, and it dawns upon his pursuer that this goalless journey will go on and on, day after day, night after night, world without end. Recalling a legendary German book that was said to be so terrible it did not permit itself to be read, the narrator dubs his quarry "the man of the crowd," of whom it can truly be said that *"es lässt sich nicht lesen."* One cannot imagine this person on a forest trail or in an open boat at sea. Today we know him, or her, not as a darkly Romantic figure out of Poe's ghost stories, and not—alas —as an ordinary human individual, but as that social abstraction we call "the homeless." We *could* read the book, if we would; most better-off Americans frankly don't care to.

5. *"Let Them Be Sea-Captains, If You Will"*

"Whoso would be a man, must be a nonconformist," said Emerson. What happens when we change that wording to "whoso would be a woman"? If a man should light out for the territory, he could return a hero and write a book; such was the genesis of Melville's instantly successful *Typee*. Should a woman light out for the territory, according to the pitiless double standard of Victorian American culture, she was instantly "lost." In the frantic scramble of homemaking, she very likely could not even gain the temporary relief of going out for a walk, Thoreau-style. "How womankind, who are confined to the house still more than men, stand it I do not know," bachelor Thoreau sympathetically observed, "but I have ground to suspect that most of them do not *stand* it at all."

Most of the fictional roles held up for readers of the classic American novels—deerslayer, harpooneer, river rafter—were heavily male-gendered; where a novel's protagonist was a woman she could expect not to Do but only, stereotypically, to Endure. Just before the climax of *The Scarlet Letter* Hester counsels her doomed lover—unsuccessfully—to follow the forest track outward from the grim settlement which has been their common social prison, "deeper into the wilderness . . . until, some few miles hence, the yellow leaves will show no vestige of the white man's tread"; and after poor Arthur's death Hester herself quits Boston long enough, we infer, to get their illegitimate daughter safely married into the European aristocracy. But in the end she returns, moves back into her cottage at the edge of town, and sets up practice as a counselor to whom the people bring "all their sorrows and perplexities . . . women more especially." Particular estates cannot subsist in the ruin of the public, Governor Winthrop had said, but the converse does not necessarily follow. By a paradox of Christian self-sacrifice the ruin of a particular estate may redound to the public's benefit, and such is the tragically redemptive way Hester finally balances her own equation between Society and Solitude.

This was not the kind of solution, however, which American society at that time—or any time!—typically expected of men, who, endowed (as Jefferson had told them) with inalienable rights, have been free guiltlessly to pursue happiness. Some day, Hester assures the women who come to her cottage with their problems, "when the world should have grown ripe for it, . . . a new truth would be revealed, in order to establish the whole relation between man and woman on a surer ground of mutual happiness"; and "the angel and apostle of the coming revelation must be a woman." Contemporary with Hester's creator lived at least one candidate for such apostleship; an apostle, moreover, by whom men like Nathaniel Hawthorne and Ralph Waldo Emerson apparently felt threatened in the way a man—even an "emancipated" male intellectual—still commonly feels when directly confronting a keen, brainy, vital, independent-minded woman. *The Blithedale Romance*, a fable which Hawthorne derived from his brief stay at Brook Farm (the Boston and Concord intellectuals' genteel experiment in socialism), presented as one story character the brilliant, enchanting, subtly menacing, ultimately doomed Zenobia; in real life her name was Margaret Fuller.

Born in 1810, educated on the then-heretical assumption that girls could be the intellectual equals of boys, Fuller entered and lived in the world of New England letters with staggering self-assurance; "I now know all the people worth knowing in America," she once told Emerson, "and I find no intellect comparable to my own." (At that exact moment in American intellectual history she may well have been right!) Although she successfully edited the prestigious *Dial*, contributing to it among other things some of the best Goethe criticism ever penned in America, Margaret Fuller—like Benjamin Franklin before her—found the narrow culture of Boston too cramping. She emigrated to New York, where she wrote for Horace Greeley's rightly renowned *Daily Tribune*. During her New York stay, she expanded an essay she had written in her Boston years on the *Dial* and published it in 1845 as *Woman in the Nineteenth Century*.

Moderns sometimes have trouble with this book of Fuller's. She wrote in the same ornate, roundabout way men did at that time, especially men schooled in New England; and her large excerpts from Italian, British, Greek, and German literature may now put off a reader nurtured in a culture which is far less conversant with those literatures than hers was. Nevertheless, there are passages still so relevant to the human condition that they practically leap off the page. What woman really wanted, Margaret Fuller argued—against a gambit that has been used on them since creakiest antiquity!—was "not life-long sway" over men; "it needs but to become a coquette, a shrew, or a good cook to be sure of that." "Some little girls like to saw wood, others to use carpenters' tools," even if their elders think "such things are not proper for girls," she observed. "I think women need . . . a much greater range of occupation than they have, to rouse their latent powers." If anyone asked her what offices women might properly fill, Fuller's reply was "Any. . . . let them be sea-captains, if you will"—a sea captain having then the kind of macho glamour a spaceship pilot now commands.

For a woman in the nineteenth century, locked into a system of economic dependency, educational disability, and lack of autonomy, Emerson's trumpet-call to "self-reliance" was on the whole a summons to futility. "Though women were taught the same things in school" as men, one recent student of Fuller concludes, "they were not really being taught anything, because they were never called upon to put it to use." And put it to use Margaret Fuller dramatically did. Not even reporting for Horace Greeley's liberation-minded *New York Tribune* sufficed; she decided she must act in history. Journeying to Europe in 1846 she threw herself into the cause of Italian independence, took an Italian lover, converted him away from conservative politics, bore his child, and in the great revolutionary upheavals of 1848 tended the sick and wounded soldiers who were defending Rome. (Symbolically she had chosen the most radical of all the 1848 revolutions in Europe, since a complete victory for that short-lived Roman Republic would have required the overthrow of the Papacy itself.) Like Philip Freneau, Margaret Fuller left her safe literary harbor for the tempestuous seas of democratic action; unlike Freneau, she paid for that choice with her life. Within sight of Fire Island, the ship upon which she, her child, and her husband were returning to America in 1850 after the Roman Revolution's defeat broke up in a storm.

Also lost in the wreckage of that ship was a manuscript; a history of the Italian revolution—*not*, be it noted, a Great American Novel. Fuller had rejected fiction writing, which she judged "too feminine" a form of expression, and a present-day reader of the Victorian lady novelists (British or American) can readily understand that judgment. Nevertheless, the Muse has a way of finding a voice and telling a story, no matter how paralyzing the societal circumstances. Nonconformism and moral improvement need not always be opposites, and "women's fiction" of the kind practiced by Harriet Beecher Stowe or Louisa May Alcott may contain values a male-dominated literary establishment has hitherto missed. Moreover, best sellers, of which women writers have contributed more than a few, cannot be neglected in seeking to understand the American past. "*Vox populi*, if something less than *vox dei*, is at least a voice to which we must hearken," wrote Frank Luther Mott in his pioneering history of American best sellers *Golden Multitudes* (1947). "A profound respect for people in mass, or for the wide streams of life, is by no means inconsistent with an appreciation of lone genius, or of the highest development of ideas. Indeed the two must go along together." Of *Uncle Tom's Cabin*, so easily dismissable as "mere propaganda," Mott said, "If you wish to know why millions once read it, go and hunt it out of the shelves, and, putting aside all modern sophistication, read it for yourself."

Ever the iconoclast, critic Leslie Fiedler did just that, astutely noting, for example, that instead of the forest and the prairie and their metaphoric equivalent the ocean—the romping grounds of Cooper and Melville—*Uncle Tom's Cabin* celebrates "the most compendious gallery of *homes* in all American literature, ranging from the humble Kentucky habitation which gives the novel its name . . . to the elegant New Orleans villa of the St. Clares . . . , and from the prim New England farmhouse of Miss Ophelia's family . . . to the squalid and decayed mansion of Simon Legree." Absent from both "classic" and popular fictional chronicles of the lone, heroic, inarticulate male American, the subtle interplay of families and generations—no problem for a male European writer!—became in nineteenth-century America a task delegated or relegated to writing women. To a great extent it still is.

Civilization, wilderness; society, solitude; intensely complicated interpersonal relationships, lone pilgrimages; sisterhood, male bonding; perception, action—the American literary dialectic in each such case requires both of the antitheses. Set *Moby Dick* alongside that other novel of Mrs. Stowe's, *The Minister's Wooing;* and enjoy both Melville, minutely describing the production of whale oil, and Stowe, with equally loving care describing the production of a wedding dress. The respective climaxes of *Moby Dick*, in which the mad captain leads his boat crews in a three-day chase to their destruction in the ocean, and of *The Minister's Wooing*, in which the supposedly drowned young James comes *back* from the sea hale and sound just in time to save his Mary from the dutiful but loveless marriage her mother has schemed for her, are alike authentic distillations of American experience. If the Great American Novel were ever to be written it would have to encompass both, or all, such distillations; and as the Republic year by year grew larger and more varied, the challenge became correspondingly greater. As always, the essence of America lay elusively beyond the horizon.

6. Toward a World Audience

Out of the two-hundred-year span during which Americans have been writing stories and poems and plays, two decades in particular carry special glamour: 1845–1855 (approximately; those dates mark the respective publications of Poe's *Tales of the Grotesque and Arabesque* and of the first edition of Whitman's *Leaves of Grass*) and 1919–1929. They were in many respects as different as two literary epochs could well be: the one typified by writings that were ornate, long-winded, euphemistic, given to lecturing and preaching; the other by language that was direct, concise, frank, and inclined to make its point by "showing" rather than "telling." Yet each of these ten-year intervals is commonly considered a great creative peak in American letters. For all its Victorian repression, bourgeois stuffiness, and (except for Poe) relentless moralizing, the earlier period—out of which came *Typee* and *Benito Cereno*, *The Scarlet Letter* and *The House of the Seven Gables*, *Walden, The Ore-*

gon Trail—must have been doing something right; its output is still what one means when referring to the "classics" of American literature. And the later span that we call "the Twenties" speaks for itself, in *Winesburg, Ohio*, which opened the decade and in *A Farewell to Arms*, which closed it; and, in the years between, *This Side of Paradise, Main Street, Giants in the Earth.*

Not all American literary productions usually considered masterworks date from those two narrow eras. The so-called "Gilded Age" that followed the first period claims as its own the ex-riverboat pilot Mark Twain and that passionate recluse Emily Dickinson. The second period also, as Henry F. May has convincingly shown, was preceded by an "innocent rebellion" whose literary and cultural innovations—those of Amy Lowell and Carl Sandburg and Willa Cather—were in place well before the First World War. Nevertheless, to move from the world of Longfellow and Whittier to that of e.e. cummings and Ezra Pound required nothing less than a literary revolution.

Edmund Wilson, the acknowledged dean of literary criticism in America, contended in 1960 that even the greatest writers in the classic tradition—Hawthorne, Melville, Poe—"embroidered, or, perhaps better, coagulated, their fancies in a peculiar clogged and viscous prose characteristic of the early nineteenth century." Such a vitiating prose style infected the essay, the sermon, the political address, the novel, even the short story; and it tends to make antebellum literature slow going for the modern reader who is conditioned to a different stylistic standard. Nor could the canons of "fine writing" laid down by that magniloquent school have led to a Lewis, a Hemingway, even a Faulkner, had not something rather drastic intervened to change them.

Wilson suggested in his compendious, provocative book *Patriotic Gore*, which is something of a literary history of the Civil War, that the war itself had something to do with the shaking-up of literary gentility. "The relative lack of movement" in the works of the antebellum writers, he argues, "is quite in keeping with the tempo of secluded lives, of men in a position to live by themselves, usually in the country, to write about country manners which they try to think traditional and stable," despite the upsetting subversiveness of some of their fantasies and dreams. After the War Between the States, Wilson implies, that kind of ivory tower way of doing literature simply ceased to be possible. This critical judgment is hardly fair to some of the writers we have been considering; Freneau, Tyler, Thoreau, Fuller, Stowe, even Poe in his own fashion, were acting, judging participants in the public life of their day.

More persuasive is Wilson's judgment that the Civil War revolutionized the *language* used by American writers. If "the medium is the message," the medium of the 1860s was the telegraph; and its use, he implies, changed perception as much as the use of television changed perceptions a hundred years later. The war was told telegraphically to a newspaper-reading public, and the telegrapher's and the newsdesk writer's virtues—clarity, compression, concreteness—were inconsistent with the leisurely belle-lettristic style of the antebellum years. But it was not simply the "media" of that day that wrought this transformation, Wilson was quick to acknowledge. Out of the secession crisis and the war's cauldron came not only the vernacular fiction of Mark Twain, who did serve a newspaper apprenticeship (as would Ernest Hemingway after a later war), but also the *Memoirs* of Ulysses Grant, who, utterly unlettered in the formal sense, managed to produce a set of military commentaries as economical and to the point as Caesar's; and, above all, the public prose of Abraham Lincoln, who distilled from the Bible and Shakespeare and the folk vernacular of rural Illinois those renowned state papers, whose simple yet elegant diction puts them on a different plane from those of any other president. With a critic's glee Wilson contrasted the lengthy oration of Edward Everett, who "opened" the dedication of the Gettysburg battlefield cemetery in November 1863, with the 269 carefully chosen words with which the President closed the proceedings. Everett's oratory is quite deservedly forgotten; but nothing Abraham Lincoln ever said was *less* true than his disclaimer "the world will little note nor long remember what we say here."

It would be the height of American exceptionalism, however, to conclude that the impact of the Civil War completely and uniquely transformed American prose—and its subject-matter—from its classical to its modern form. America, never quite as provincially isolated as its detractors supposed or as some of its own partisans would have preferred, shared a cultural database with at least the entire Western world. Darwinian evolution; physiological psychology; functionalist architecture; impressionism in music and painting; non-Euclidean geometry; the motion picture; the acceleration of the movement of goods and ideas—these were historical experiences shared by all of the Euro-American peoples, and by many in the awakening world elsewhere. Yet when Americans took up these widely shared models and motifs—literary naturalism, for example—they would retain much of the "classic" outlook against which some of them thought of themselves as being in revolt. Their novels, short stories, and plays, and later on their films, would continue to describe the journey into the wilderness, the humorous deflation of self-important pomp, the regenerative/destructive power of physical Nature. And even in the midst of nihilism and disillusion, they would still find ways to moralize.

One of the most marked differences between antebellum "classical" writing and the literature of the 1920s would be its relationship to the culture of the rest of the world. No longer on the defensive, no longer anxiously seeking the blessing of the courtly muses of Europe, American works were themselves becoming a standard. German pedants wrote doctoral dissertations on Melville, as ponderous as the ones they had previously produced on Kant. French *vers libre* bards emulated e.e. cummings. If the literary artifices of Proust and Joyce became models for a new insurgent generation, so did those of Faulkner and Hemingway; and after World War II book-oriented young Frenchmen would talk and try to act like Hemingway characters. When a novelist/philosopher as undeniably *avant-garde* as Jean-Paul Sartre in his novel *The Reprieve* (1947) used literary devices—e.g., the quasi-cinematic "shock cut" from one story line to another, sometimes in midsentence—that had been pioneered by John Dos Passos in *Manhattan Transfer* (1925), the Americans may be said to have gone Emerson one better. *They* had become muses for others, although "courtly" would hardly have been the right word to describe them.

When one moves from the polite letters that have been the subject of this chapter to the livelier arts, the American impact on the rest of the planet becomes overwhelming. Neither the British music-hall singer nor the French *chanteuse*, although both have their devotees, ever became naturalized outside their homelands to a degree remotely like the universal pervasiveness of American musical comedy and jazz. On ideological grounds the socialist countries resisted for a time this invasion of capitalist *Kulturbarbaren* (as East German state radio once termed it!), but eventually they too gave up the ghost. In due course, Soviet-bloc ice dancers would be competitively skating—and winning—to the lively sound of American show tunes; even, at times, to rock 'n' roll.

Interlude V

Scattered over the river bluffs like discarded packing boxes, five dozen ugly, unpainted buildings stood in ragged ranks along streets that were thick with dust, which during rainstorms turned into a slimy yellow paste. Conjured up from the harsh alkaline earth at the command of the railroad builders as they pushed their way west, the town of Green River Station, Wyoming Territory, sprawled beside the river from which it took its name, a classic American example of boom and bust. The population, two thousand strong in September of 1868—the year of the settlement's founding—had dwindled by the following spring to a scant hundred dispirited drifters and hangers-on.

May 10, 1869, hundreds of miles on down the iron road at Promontory Point, Utah Territory, saw more activity. Surrounded by an excited crowd, two big-smokestacked locomotives faced each other while the bridge-building and track-laying crews that had been hammering their way toward each other from east and west at an incredible eight miles per day joined their prodigious handiwork into North America's first transcontinental railroad. The next day, May 11, back up the line, two Union Pacific trains rolled into Green River Station with freight and passenger cargoes that were destined to bring that raw, virtually abandoned village dramatically back into history.

The first train's flatcars bore boxes of scientific instruments and four sturdy, double-ribbed and double-ended boats; the second train's passengers included a one-armed Civil War veteran named John Wesley Powell. Half a mile downstream from the town, half a dozen men awaited their arrival. On May 24 the men in the boats shoved off down the Green River to the Grand (as the Colorado used to be called), and thence to the previously unexplored Grand Canyon.

The arid Southwest, when Powell and his crew ventured into it in their boats, was the last major blank spot on the North American landscape. The latest government maps showed a great, white four-

hundred-mile gap crossed only by dotted lines conjecturing where the Colorado and its upper tributaries might join. The first complete crossing of that unknown space fired Americans' imaginations, reminding them that a world spoiled by numbing work routine and sleazy political corruption and heartless racial oppression nevertheless held wonders yet untold.

SIX

The Age of the Dinosaurs

As the American nation prepared to close out the first century of its independent existence, it still perceived itself as a new kind of community in a New World not yet quite filled up—and it still combined the spirit of a Hebrew prophet with the mind of a Roman lawyer.

But now, upon the American stage, a new actor moved into the spotlight. Politics and Religion had to make room for Science, which—some feared, and others hoped—might upstage both the older players. That science and religion staked conflicting claims upon some of the same territory was, by the time of the American first centennial, an old story; that science might lay similar claims upon the domain of politics was a novel and deeply unsettling idea.

1. An Untamed Immensity

People like John Wesley Powell—soldier and explorer, social activist and science bureaucrat—were to the nineteenth century in America what people like Neil Armstrong have been to the twentieth: figures of high romance in the tradition of Columbus or Polo, or of those explorers not yet born but imagined on *Star Trek* who "boldly go where no one has gone before," yet at the same time organizers of romance into reality. Powell, though soldier and scientist, could write of the remote canyonlands he loved to explore in Victorian poetic language strikingly different from the flat, laconic diction of the soldier-scientists, Soviet and American, who were to rocket into space a century later. "It is the land of music," he exclaimed. "The river thunders in perpetual roar. . . . With the melody of the great tide rising and falling, swelling and vanishing forever, other melodies are heard in the gorges of the lateral can-

129

yons, while the waters plunge in the rapids among the rocks or leap in great cataracts. Thus the Grand Canyon is a land of song." However, Powell was first and foremost a scientist; and although he could write warmly of the canyon's wild music and gloomy solitudes he also saw that country with a scientist's keen and probing eye.

So it had been at the siege of Vicksburg, where, when not working his artillery pieces up toward the Confederate lines, Major Powell was collecting fossil sea shells uncovered in the army trenches, wrapping the precious mollusks in cotton for safekeeping, and sending them home for study; and so it was when his three boats (one of the four with which they started had smashed itself on the rocks at a place they named Disaster Falls) pulled into shore at the junction of the Grand River with the Green on July 17, 1869. While most of the crew were turning over and recaulking the boats, drying out their soaked clothes, running their dampened and lumpy flour through a mosquito-net sieve, or just simply resting, Powell and a companion scrambled over boulders and up a fissure, climbing "as men would out of a well," to emerge into a world of unspeakable grandeur—and saw, facing them on the opposite canyon wall, "rock forms that we do not understand." The expedition's business in that remote place was precisely to understand them. "Unraveled the mystery of the rocks," the Major wrote of another puzzling formation a few miles and several hard portages further downstream. He climbed (despite the lack of the arm he had lost at Shiloh!) and geologized the upper Colorado, not only as a romantic thrill-seeker but also as a hard-headed investigator; his findings, and those of other explorers in the American West, would illuminate our knowledge of a billion years of Earth's past, much as the Apollo astronauts and the Voyager probes have opened up new vistas into the even more ancient past of our solar system.

The Grand Canyon is a cross-section of the history of the earth. In our time that has become a truism; it was not at all obvious in 1869. Rather than having been cut by a river through ages-old layers of rock as they rose, the Canyon might have been a great crack that suddenly broke open when the earth cooled, or an underground river whose roof fell in. Legend has it that one old cowboy, coming unexpectedly for the first time upon the Canyon's edge, exclaimed: "Something has happened here!"—a happening which must have been cataclysmic and, by geological standards, swift. Common sense "in a creature who instinctively measures things on a scale related to his own experience," writes Joseph Wood Krutch, strongly pointed toward such an explanation; "it just didn't seem possible that anything had endured so much longer than man or the history he knew." (The other way some visitors to the Canyon cope emotionally with this people-dwarfing phenomenon is to insist that anything so impressive in scale could not be natural; it must have been built by human hands.)

Geologists themselves, at least until the publication of Sir Charles Lyell's *Principles of Geology* (1833), were fiercely divided in their answers to questions such as the Grand Canyon posed. "Uniformitarianism" and "Catastrophism"—the very names of their conflicting schools of geological interpretation suggest squabbling religious sects. From the latter school of thought we have inherited a few terms that still appear occasionally in science textbooks, such as the description of the process by which a mountain range is built as a *revolution*, a word Webster also defines as "a sudden, radical, or complete change." (The more ambiguous word *orogeny* is coming to be the more common scientifically accepted term.) On the whole, however, except among special creationists, the Uniformitarians have long since carried the day, with their argument that the slow, normal, daily, and yearly operations of weather and climate—"little drops of water, little grains of sand," as a *Mc Guffey's Reader* verse puts it—suffice to make and mold even the mightiest of natural formations, if given a long enough time span. "There is no *a priori* or philosophic reason for ruling out a series of natural catastrophes as dominating earth history," geoscientist George Gaylord Simpson observed in 1963. "However, this assumption is simply in such flat disagreement with everything we now know of geological history as to be completely incredible." (Today, however, Simpson's defense of Lyell and gradualism is crumbling, at least as far as extinction theory is concerned; of such is the ebb and flow of scientific thought.)

A century before Simpson not so much of geological history was known; at the time of Powell's first expedition down the Colorado probably a majority of working geologists in America were Catastrophists, despite Lyell. The field work done in between shooting rapids and drying out clothes was thus a direct and major contribution to the debate. The canyon of the Colorado is, by human scale, staggering in its size; "pluck up Mt. Washington by the roots to the level of the sea," as Powell vividly put it, "and drop it into the Grand Canyon, and the dam will not force its waters over the

131

walls." So vast a gulf seemed to demand a clear-cut explanation in terms of one geologic hypothesis or the other; either as the climax of gradual natural processes, with the river having started to cut the canyon between ten and twenty million years before our own time, or else as an upheaval mighty enough to have created the Canyon but brief enough to fit within a calendar that began a comparative eye-blink ago. John Wesley Powell, in a short report published soon after the expedition's return and at greater length in his *Geology of the Eastern Portion of the Uinta Mountains* (1876), wholeheartedly embraced the Uniformitarian cause with a confident sureness as to what he had found. The faulting, flexing, and dissection by erosion had rendered "the whole region . . . an open book to the geologist," he reported, and in studying that book "we have been able to arrive at conclusions, both quantitative and qualitative, with some degree of certainty."

Much more than geology was at stake. "Whenever modern philosophers talk about mountains," the Rev. Clement Moore had warned as early as 1804, "something impious is likely to be at hand." For those with a religious commitment to a shorter time span— scant centuries, rather than millions of years—geologic uniformitarianism was a clear and present danger; something as impious as Darwinism, if more subtle. If it had simply contradicted the Bible, apologists might have dealt with the problem (as some of them still do) by a generous interpretation of what the Book of Genesis meant by the word "day." This new vision of earth's history, however, had the philosophical effect of shrinking human beings and all their works into an overwhelming immensity of landscape and time. To this day special creationists, intent on preserving the high status of their species—"a little lower than the angels"—insist not only on a nonevolutionary explanation for the appearance of life on earth but on the Bible's one-week timetable as well.

George McCready Price, a geologist and Fundamentalist upon whose writings creation-science advocates still drew in the 1980s in their battles for equal time in school curriculums, dismissed as "cunning inventions" John Wesley Powell's accounts of how the Green River had cut through the Uinta Range and how the canyon of the Colorado had come to be. The quarrel epitomized by Price and Powell had lurked unknown on North America's agenda since the first Europeans came ashore into its wilderness and set down their cultural luggage. "What has Athens to do with Jerusalem?" the second-century Latin church father Tertullian had asked; what had Greek scientific rationalism to do with Hebraic prophetic insight? Nineteenth-century science now rephrased the question: what had either Athens or Jerusalem—either the human-scaled Greco-Roman cosmos or the ethical Judaeo-Christian universe—to do with the vast, silent, and impersonal timescape of the Colorado Plateau?

2. The Coming of the Bone Hunters

On the whole, science and religion in America had theretofore been on civil speaking terms. Puritan Boston, although founded at about the same time as Galileo's troubles with the Inquisition, had learned to live comfortably with the new astronomy Galileo described. The formidable Cotton Mather, preaching one Sunday in 1714 on the text "Trust in the Lord" (Psalms 37:3), "spake of the sun being in the center of our system," parishioner Samuel Sewall noted in his diary, though the practical-minded Sewall grumpily added: "I think it inconvenient to assert such problems." Throughout the eighteenth century proper Bostonians, their relatives in Connecticut, and their rivals in Philadelphia—many of them clergymen—discovered comets, built optical instruments, sketched sunspots, and otherwise joyfully pushed back the dizzying depths of space which some of Galileo's contemporaries—the mathematician-philosopher Blaise Pascal, for example—had found "frightening." However, such inquirers had yet to conjoin those ever-receding gulfs of astronomic space with equally terrifying abysses of time. Less orthodox Americans, like Thomas Jefferson, seem still to have had no inkling how old were the land and its relics to which they devoted so much loving attention; it still loomed in their minds as a *New* World. Even so free a spirit as Herman Melville, heretic enough to have prompted one modern critic to write a study titled *Melville's Quarrel with God*, did not question the short Mosaic chronology of world history. At the end of *Moby-Dick*, after "a sullen white surf" had closed over the doomed *Pequod*, its sole survivor tells us, "the great shroud of the sea rolled on as it rolled five thousand years ago" when time presumably began, rather than hundreds of millions of years farther back in the past.

Melville's contemporary, Ralph Waldo Emerson, however, in one of those flashes of insight which often illuminate his rambling writings, sensed the deeper meaning in the new geology: "The book of Nature is the book of Fate," he wrote in an essay probably completed in 1852:

> She turns gigantic pages—leaf after leaf—never re-turning one. One leaf she lays down, a floor of granite; then a thousand ages, and a bed of slate; a thousand ages, and a measure of coal; a thousand ages, and a layer of marl and mud: vegetable forms appear; her first misshapen animals, zoöphyte, trilobium, fish; then saurians. . . . The face of the planet cools and dries, the races meliorate, and man is born. But when a race has lived its term, it comes no more again.

Even high-and-mighty *Homo sapiens*, Emerson hinted, might expect in due time to become but one of the fossil notes Nature scribbled on the page, for "the population of the world is a conditional population; not the best, but the best that could live now."

Such were the pages opened for study by the erosive action of the Colorado. "Down by the river the walls are composed of black gneiss," Powell wrote. Broken, vertically seamed with dull rose quartz and sparkling with mica, these are some of the oldest rocks exposed anywhere on Earth; two billion years of age, and more. "Over the black gneiss," the explorer continued, "are found 800 feet of quartzites, usually in very thin beds of many colors, but exceedingly hard," dipping uncomfortably from the rocks above and below; "set up," Powell metaphorically described them, like "a row of books aslant." Both of these ancient formations are now judged to be exposed roots or stumps of great mountain ranges, once Alpine or Himalayan in majesty, then beveled flat by erosion; "risen and vanished," notes Krutch, "before life had got further than the protozoa and the jellyfish," although in the younger of the two strata life has left its mark in algal colonies' fossil remains.

Higher, at the lip of the Canyon's Inner Gorge, a mere half-billion years ago, coarse sands, then mud, and finally limy skeletons were deposited in a deepening tropical sea; its floor abounded in living things, notably Emerson's "zoöphyte" and "trilobium"—but as yet no fish. Still higher, in Permian times—only a quarter-billion years ago—alternating shales and sandstones marked advancing and retreating seas; a former mud flat at shore's edge still displays ripple marks, rain drops, fern fronds, worm trails. Higher yet, windblown sand became compacted into the fine yellow-white Coconino Sandstone, whose cross-bedding reveals former desert dunes—and the footprints of small animals, plodding always *up* the dunes because on the downward side their prints would have been quickly obliterated by sliding sand. Finally at the top of the Canyon two more limestone layers, the Toroweap and Kaibab formations, mark two more invasions by seas—and by clams, corals, sponges, the ubiquitous trilobite (a crustacean-like creature which ruled the world for 200 million years before vanishing utterly), and—as evidenced by their teeth—sharks. On land, by that time, scorpions crawled, amphibians splashed, dragonflies flew; the earth was green with club mosses and horsetails and giant ferns. But there were no flowers; no birds; nothing we would now recognize as the "higher" plants and animals—Nature had not yet turned those pages.

Lift one's eyes to the Vermilion Cliffs which border the Colorado River upstream from its plunge into the Grand Canyon, however, and one is in Mesozoic times—the years of the dinosaurs. Evidence for those "terrible lizards" (which is what "dinosaur" literally means, in Greek) had been piling up for decades. Captain William Clark may unwittingly have described a dinosaur bone which he found cemented into the rock face at Pompey's Pillar on July 25, 1806, while the Lewis and Clark expedition was wending its long way home—the "rib of a fish" he called it, three inches in circumference and three feet long. The site, on the south bank of the Yellowstone River in eastern Montana, would later yield numerous dinosaur bones. In England in 1824 cleric and Oxford don William Buckland described *Megalosaurus*, a forty-foot reptile with fearsome, bladelike teeth; one year later another Briton, the physician Gideon Mantell, wrote of *Iguanodon*, whose first relic his wife had picked up from a rockpile by the side of the road one spring day, waiting outdoors while her husband visited one of his patients. From 1835 onward the pious Edward Hitchcock, Professor of Natural Theology and Geology and president of Amherst College, collected dinosaur footprints from the Triassic sandstones of the Connecticut Valley, although he thought to the end of his life that they had been made by birds; Valley folklore indeed described them as the prints of "Noah's raven." Other dinosaurs turned up in a lovely dale in southern Germany; in the Red Beds of South Africa; at the bottom of a coal mine in Belgium. But the findings that really fired the Victorian imagination came from the semi-arid North American Rocky Mountains and Great Plains.

A personal feud helped stimulate the great bone hunts of the 1870s. Othniel C. Marsh, securely based at Yale, and Edward Drinker Cope, who for most of his life worked independently, stormed and rampaged against each other in learned societies and at fossil excavation sites for three decades. Independently wealthy—Cope the son of a Philadelphia Quaker shipowner; Marsh the nephew of a self-made millionaire—they could indulge both their scientific curiosity and their personal animosity in the style of builders of other kinds of Gilded Age empires: "scientific robber barons," Howard S. Miller has called them, "fitting contemporaries of Daniel Drew and Commodore Vanderbilt." And, just as the cutthroat competition characteristic of America's Gilded Age economy seemed only to yield bigger economic aggregations, so the rivalry of Cope and Marsh seemed only to yield greater troves of dinosaur bones.

"I wish you were here to see the bones roll out and they are beauties too," wrote excavator Bill Reed in 1878 to Marsh's assistant Samuel Wendell Williston from Como Bluff, a long east-west ridge parallel to the Union Pacific's main line in southern Wyoming. In subsequent years, both Marsh's men and Cope's came to Como Bluff, feverishly shoveled away the surface deposits to get at the fossil treasures, learned to preserve the fragile skeletal remains by first wrapping them in strong paper or cloths steeped in paste, and loaded the bandaged and boxed bones into wagons to be hauled to the nearest railroad siding. Back East the remains were assembled and mounted; fierce-jawed *Allosaurus* with its clawed hind feet and tiny forearms; tiny-headed *Stegosaurus*, with triangular vertical plates along its back and a subsidiary brain in its hindquarters to power the lethal, spike-equipped tail; mighty *Brontosaurus*, in life seven times the weight of an elephant, with long neck and tail and a snakelike head; and many more.

In addition to feeding and fighting on land, the Mesozoic reptiles also invaded air and sea, including the great salt-water body which in Cretaceous times covered Kansas. Edward Cope, gleaning the findings of F. V. Hayden's Interior Department-sponsored geological survey in 1871 (the year also of Powell's second trip down the Colorado), described *Elasmosaurus*, a carnivorous sea reptile, and the airborne *Ornithochirus*, in language of a kind one does not expect to find in the dusty pages of a government report:

The extent of sea to the westward was vast, and geology has not yet laid down its boundary. . . . Far out on its expanse might have been seen in those ancient days, a huge, snake-like form which rose above the surface and stood erect, with tapering throat and arrow-shaped head. . . . Then it would dive into the depths, and naught would be visible but the foam caused by the disappearing mass of life. Should several have appeared together, we can easily imagine tall, twining forms rising to the height of the masts of a fishing fleet, or like snakes twisting and knotting themselves together. This extraordinary neck—for such it was —rose from a body of elephantine proportions; and a tail of the serpent-pattern balanced it behind. . . .

The flying saurians . . . flapped their leathery wings over the waves, and often plunging, seized many an unsuspecting fish; or, soaring at a safe distance, viewed the sports and combats of the more powerful saurians of the sea. At night-fall, we may imagine them trooping to the shore, and suspending themselves to the cliffs by the claw-bearing fingers of their wing-limbs.

It reads like science fiction, and that is exactly the point; the discovery of the dinosaur was a startling inversion of usual assumptions about the progress of knowledge from colorful fantasy-invention to prosy proven reality. "In addition to their obvious biological interest dinosaurs have an enviable mythical importance and an epistemological resonance of primary significance," writes the Spanish philosophy professor Fernando Savater. "It was the astounding hypothesis that was revealed as the most convincing one. The dinosaurs proclaimed the supremacy of imagination as opposed to the mutilating self-censorship of rationalist common sense, for which 'mediocre' means 'probable'." Some took offense at the doctrine that such splendid beasts lived and died millions of years before any man or woman was born; "There is no possible line of scientific reasoning to convince us that any single type of fossil is older than the human race," creation-scientist George McCready Price sturdily proclaimed in 1913. Others, however, greeted this news with a kind of fierce Romantic joy.

3. Progress and Extinction

To another formal evaluator of the data from the Hayden geological surveys, John S. Newberry—professor of geology in Columbia University's School of Mines—North America's Tertiary era when "a warm and genial climate prevailed from the Gulf to the Arctic Sea" seemed an Elysian interlude between the savage dinosaur epoch which had preceded it and the grim ice age which would follow. In Tertiary times "man, the great destroyer, had not yet come" to this pristine land; "no human eye was there to mark its beauty, no human intellect to control and use its exuberant fertility. . . . Fruits ripened in the sun, but there was no *hand* there to pluck." The imagery, of a kind common in New World descriptive writing (see chapter 1), is unmistakably that of Eden before the Fall. Newberry, however, was writing in 1871, the year of publication of Darwin's *Descent of Man*. Geologic investigators could find nowhere in the long history of North America any peacable kingdom where the wolf had dwelt with the lamb and the calf with the young lion (Isaiah 11:6). "Not all was peace and harmony in this Arcadia," the writer regretfully had to conclude. "The forces of nature are always at war, and redundant life compels abundant death."

Many sensitive Victorians found this natural state of affairs shocking and tragic. Nature as described by Darwin and his kind is "red in tooth and claw," Lord Tennyson exclaimed:

> So careful of the type she seems,
> So careless of the single life.

Others, however, found Charles Darwin's doctrines bracing, even inspiring. "The generation that acclaimed Grant as its hero," wrote Richard Hofstadter, "took Spencer as its thinker"—referring to Herbert Spencer, the best-selling British sociologist/philosopher who championed and popularized Darwinism. It was Spencer, not Darwin, who coined the phrase "the survival of the fittest," and he applied it not only to the world of wild Nature but to human society as well. Natural selection and the struggle for existence are givens, whether one be a beast hunting for food, a worker looking for a job, or a capitalist in quest of customers. Little or nothing can or should be done either by government or private agencies to mitigate the situation; remedial legislation or massive charities will only make matters worse, penalizing the "fit" and rewarding the "unfit." Jefferson, asserted Spencer's leading American disciple, William Graham Sumner, had been wrong; a person's "right to the pursuit of happiness is nothing but a license to maintain the struggle for existence if he can find within himself the power with which to do it." This doctrine of "Social Darwinism," as it has since been called, became for many (and has remained for not a few) an intellectual justification for social indifference and personal greed.

Social Darwinism in Europe fueled emerging racial and national chauvinist mass movements destined to erupt into twentieth-century totalitarianism. A host of pseudo-scientists in Germany, England, and France (with some disturbing American echoes) asserted that oppression and aggression should be regarded as benign agencies of natural selection. In England to some degree, in entrepreneurial America to a far greater extent, Social Darwinism also breathed new life into the economic doctrine of "free enterprise." Founded in the eighteenth century on axioms its founders presumed analogous to the mathematical assumptions of Newtonian physics—a "law of supply and demand," an "iron law of wages," and the like—the laissez-faire school found its deductive dogmatic logic inadequate to describe the booming, rapidly changing late-nineteenth-century corporate economy. Biological evolution, however, seemed to give it a dynamic and more modern rationale.

The "law of competition," Andrew Carnegie affirmed in 1889, "may be sometimes hard for the individual," but "it is best for the race because it insures the survival of the fittest in every department." Professor Sumner at Yale put it more cosmically: "The law of the survival of the fittest was not made by man and cannot be abrogated by man." And in his old age John D. Rockefeller, in an address to a Sunday School class, touchingly likened the Standard Oil Company he had created to the American Beauty rose, which achieves its "splendor and fragrance . . . only by sacrificing the early buds which grow up around it." The growth of any big business firm, Standard's founder generalized, "is merely a survival of the fittest."

Edward Kirkland, in *Dream and Thought in the Business Community* (1956), cautioned modern readers against overrating Social Darwinism as a motivation for the actual behavior of Gilded Age tycoons. Except for Andrew Carnegie, who was not only a self-made millionaire but also a self-made intellectual steeped in canny Scots logic, businessmen (then as now!) had little time to read books, Darwin's or anybody else's, and as yet they possessed insufficient routinized organization to hire others to do such reading for them. Typically they had not gone to college, and their personal ideologies (Kirkland concluded, after extensive reading in their diaries, letters, and after-dinner speeches), came down to homely maxims of the Ben Franklin sort, which they had copied into school notebooks in their boyhoods before the Civil War—and before Darwin.

Nevertheless, the sons of such men often as not *did* go to college, and members of succeeding generations of America's corporate elite—college-bred or not—did use the language of Social Darwinism. By the 1920s one could hear it at salesmen's pep talks, political rallies, and Rotary Club dinners all across the land. The essays of William Graham Sumner, pungently written—and given provocative titles such as "What Social Classes Owe to Each Other" (answer: nothing) and "The Absurd Effort to Make the World Over," found a receptive public far wider than Sumner's initial Yale undergraduate classrooms. When Mario Cuomo, keynoting the Democratic national convention in 1984, accused the then-incumbent deregulation and laissez-faire-minded Republican administration of practicing "Social Darwinism," clearly a large fraction of his mass national TV audience grasped what he meant—and, judging by the subsequent election returns, just as clearly rejected his argument.

Significantly Charles Darwin himself did not make the leap from biological to Social Darwinism. In a letter to Sir Charles Lyell he scoffed at a newspaper editorial which insisted he had "proved 'might is right,' and therefore Napoleon is right, and every cheating tradesman is also right." So also his colleague and advocate Thomas Huxley maintained in his Romanes lectures of 1893 (published as *Evolution and Ethics*) that the ideal metaphor for human society is not a strife-filled jungle but a well-tended garden; "social progress means a checking of the cosmic process at every step." Americans also were not lacking to combat the dark Spencer/Sumner world view. From a really rigorous laissez-faire standpoint, sociologist Lester F. Ward sarcastically argued, one ought not to build a dam across a creek lest one interfere with water's "natural" tendency to run downhill, nor confine steam within a boiler and frustrate its natural tendency to expand. John Wesley Powell, hard-headed scientist and social scientist though he was, likewise denied Social Darwinism; "'The Survival of the Fittest,'" he charged, "is inscribed on the banner of every man who opposes any endeavor to ameliorate the condition of mankind." Should Herbert Spencer's passive sociopolitical inferences from evolution prevail, "modern civilization would lapse into a condition no whit superior to that of the millions of India," Powell told a meeting of the Anthropological Society of Washington in 1881. "When man loses faith in himself and worships nature, and subjects himself to the government of the laws of physical nature, he lapses into stagnation."

Powell, Ward, and the pioneering anthropologist Lewis Henry Morgan attacked Social Darwinism by challenging its premises; the maverick economist and culture-critic Thorstein Veblen deflated it by provisionally accepting those premises and showing that they led into *reductio ad absurdum*. Suppose for the sake of argument that the present ruling elite has risen into power by natural selection, Veblen proposed in *The Theory of the Leisure Class* (1899). Protected by wealth and prestige it then proceeded to shelter itself from the very process of evolution which had gotten it there; and the institutions it created, "adapted to past circumstances," could be "therefore never in full accord with the requirements of the present." Such a successful social class, once exempted from the struggle for existence, thereafter "will adapt itself more tardily to the altered general situation," and, since evolution presumably does not stop, by virtue of its inherent conservatism this sheltered elite will render itself increasingly and disastrously out-of-date. "The characteristic attitude of the class may be summed up in the maxim 'Whatever is, is right,'; whereas the law of natural selection, as applied to human institutions, gives the axiom: 'Whatever is, is wrong.'"

If one must use animal behavior as a model for human, Veblen implied, perhaps the Social Darwinists had been using the wrong animal. Rather than the wolf-pack, romantically idealized by writers of Darwinist fiction (Jack London's *White Fang* is a choice example), the cautionary model might well be the dinosaur, beautifully adapted by natural selection to its environment and by the end of the Cretaceous times lord of all it surveyed until its material circumstances changed; the swamp dried up, or whatever—the returns are not yet all in on just what happened—and it died. Darwinism seemed to have reassuringly hitched the relatively short span of human historical progress onto a great sweep of biological development up from the primeval mud; yet just beneath its affirmations lay a quiet terror. The mighty dinosaur, majestic, cruel, brainless (perhaps a metaphor also for the giant Gilded Age corporation?) was after all *extinct*.

If evolution described life's triumphant march, as many of the Victorians believed, it also newly defined life's transiency. As he brooded over "The Ancient Lakes of Western America" for the Hayden survey in 1871, geologist John Newberry, a staunch uniformitarian (judging from some of his other, more technical publications) noted that the present Great Lakes at no geologically distant time "will have shared the fate of those that once existed at the far West." The thought led the writer on to some melancholy reflections on the presumable future of Chicago, Sandusky, Cleveland, and Buffalo, startlingly at variance with normal Gilded Age American boosterism:

> The cities that now stand upon their banks will, ere that time, have grown colossal in size, then gray with age, then have fallen into decadence and their sites be long forgotten, but in the sediments that are now accumulating in these lake basins will lie many a wreck and skeleton. . . . These relics the geologist of the future will doubtless gather and study and moralize over, as we do the records of the tertiary ages. Doubtless he will be taught the same lesson we are, that human life is infinitely short, and human achievement utterly insignificant. Let us hope that this future man, purer in morals and clearer in intellect than we, may find as much to admire in the records of this first epoch of the reign of man as we do in those of the reign of mammals.

4. Toward a Culture of Science

To one of those Gilded Age American boomtowns not yet gray with age, John Wesley Powell came back from his wanderings in the West—rather than to the quiet Illinois campuses where he had taught since the Civil War: Washington, D.C., the political cockpit of the nation. In 1873 the shabby, overgrown village beside the Potomac was still a place where farm animals shared the streets with the new horse-drawn streetcars. The not-yet-finished Washington Monument, topped by a derrick, brooded over a discordant blend of ostentation and squalor; this was a town where, in Allan Nevins's words, "shining carriages laden with sealskins and diamonds stuck in the mudholes of unpaved streets." But all of that was rapidly changing. The notorious corruption of Ulysses Grant's presidential regime carried with it an incidental benefit of civic beautification; brick or wooden sidewalks suddenly appeared along residential streets and gangs of laborers swarmed all over the city, digging, fixing up, repairing. Alexander Robey ("Boss") Shepherd, the flamboyant grafter who ran the District of Columbia's Bureau of Public Works under Grant, undertook at last the tree-planting Major Pierre Charles L'Enfant had envisioned along the boulevards when submitting his plans for the building of Washington in 1791—a "natural arcade, green for a large part of the year" as urban planner-critic Lewis Mumford has described the result, which "mercifully hides some of Washington's worst architectural misdemeanors without seriously obscuring the more comely buildings."

Politics has always been Washington's life blood, and its practice a high art. Critics, however, from time to time have faulted the city for its lack of other kinds of culture. Science in particular, after a great start under Jefferson, had languished in the capital's antebellum years. President John Quincy Adams in 1825 had laid out an ambitious scientific program in his first annual message to Congress, lecturing his countrymen that "liberty is power"—power to accomplish great things. But power, for that scion of Puritan and Roman Republican values, carried with it also responsibility: "In assuming her station among the civilized nations of the earth it would seem that our country had contracted . . . to contribute her share of mind, of labor, and of expense to the improvement of those parts of knowledge which lie beyond the reach of individual acquisition, and particularly to geographical and astronomical science." Should not Americans emulate the Russians, the British, and the French in devoting national "genius . . . intelligence . . . treasures . . . to the common improvement of the species?" Well, no, they shouldn't, influential editors, Congressmen, and members of Adams's own cabinet replied. From the republic's beginning, Hunter Dupree points out, Americans have been ambivalent about science; "its freedom and the withering of superstition under its examination" appeal to their anti-authoritarian tradition, but "the inaccessibility of its lore to the untutored masses" puts them off.

In the anti-elitist "common man" atmosphere of Andrew Jackson's America, Adams's metaphoric reference to astronomical observatories as "light-houses of the skies"—misread, he ruefully acknowledged later, as "light-houses *in* the skies"—drew choruses of raucous laughter, and the President's proposal for government-sponsored science, along with most of Adams's other programs, soon lay in ruins. The same animus against government science continued after British chemist James Smithson left to the United States in his will half a million dollars—then no small sum—to create "an Establishment for the increase and diffusion of knowledge among men." The bequest, received by the United States in 1838 and invested in state bonds (which after the Panic of 1837 weren't doing very well), depreciated for several years while Congress debated whether it was useful or proper to accept a gift for any such purpose. Some of Calhoun's friends wanted to send the money back to England, and we owe it to the dogged persistence of some of Adams's friends that a Smithsonian Institution exists at all.

By Powell's time, however, the intellectual mood of the capital had changed almost as much as its physical setting. Although the tobacco-spitting Congressmen of the Grant era were (to say the least) no improvement on their equivalent in Adams's and Jackson's time, the status of science in Washington had become greatly enhanced, at least as judged by that ultimate political measure, Congressional appropriations. Still on the job at the Smithsonian, its first secretary Joseph Henry—after whom the *henry*, the unit of electrical inductance, is named—had enjoyed considerable success in promoting research, nationwide data and artifact gathering, and science popularization; a consciously undertaken program by Henry, Curtis Hinsley writes, "to diffuse among Americans not only scientific knowledge but the pious experience of doing science." It was a piety which could become as deep as that which drove other Americans to "do" religion or art or money-making.

It had even become possible, in the changed climate of the 1870s, for a serious practicing scientist deliberately to choose a government job over a position in the private sector, both in order to facilitate work on particular problems and to advance a professional career. Despite friendly advice from Grant's Secretary of the Navy, G. M. Robeson—"Don't remain in the government service a day longer than you have to. A scientific man here has no future before him, and the quicker he can get away the better"—the distinguished mathematical astronomer Simon Newcomb astonished Harvard's formidable President Charles W. Eliot in 1875 by turning down the headship of the Harvard Observatory, preferring to stay with the Naval Observatory and the *Nautical Almanac* both for personal/professional reasons and, Newcomb stated in his *Reminiscences of an Astronomer* (1903), because he "did not believe that, with the growth of intelligence in our country, an absence of touch between the scientific and literary classes on the one side and 'politics' on the other, could continue."

144

Today we are accustomed to think of "the scientific and literary classes" as being constantly at loggerheads; Sir Charles Snow in his memorable BBC lectures on *The Two Cultures* (1956) described the sciences and the humanities as if separated by an unbridgeable gulf of mutual incomprehension and hostility. Such was emphatically not the case in Gilded-Age Washington. The nation's capital, like all American towns great and small, abounded in cliques and clubs, ranging in purpose from philanthropy to drinking; one such, the Literary Society of Washington, for its sessions on alternate Saturday evenings, not only drew upon novelists and other literati, resident and visiting (the elder O. W. Holmes, Mark Twain, Bayard Taylor, George W. Cable, and on one occasion Oscar Wilde) but also—quite unlike literary societies elsewhere in the republic of the kind classically described in the novel . . . *And Ladies of the Club*, with their endless recyclings of Browning—tapped the bounteous reservoir of scientific talent then descending upon Washington: Joseph Henry on the philosophy of science, John Wesley Powell on native American costume, Edward M. Gallaudet on his pioneering work in the eduction of the deaf. Moreover, "The Literary," as it was familiarly known, had firm ties to the political community; former Confederate Vice-President Alexander Stephens, Mrs. Rutherford B. Hayes, Secretary of State John Foster, and House Speaker James A. Garfield were all members. Similarly, the scientists' own formidable scholarly and social organizations—the Philosophical Society of Washington, founded in 1871 with the ubiquitous Henry as president, and the Cosmos Club, dating from 1878 and presided over by the equally omnipresent Powell—included as a matter of course people who did not practice the so-called "hard" sciences: General Sherman and Chief Justice Chase belonged to the former, while a banker, a patent attorney, several career military officers, the sociologist Lester Frank Ward, and (interestingly) freelance thinker Henry Adams were members of Cosmos.

From a careful study of such clubs by J. Kirkpatrick Flack (1975) one realizes that intellectuals have congregated in Washington not only under liberal Democratic presidents but also during regimes administered by bearded Republican heroes of the Civil War. Like Franklin Roosevelt's brain trusts or John Kennedy's New Frontiersmen, Gilded Age savants relished their association with the capital's transient political elite and consciously sought to influence national policy. There were limits, however, to how much could be accomplished in that direction by clubbing; *nouveau riche* Gilded Age America was not upper-class Victorian England. In addition to the scholars' own drive toward professionalization and specialization (part of the broad societal sweep Robert Wiebe has characterized in late-nineteenth-century America as *The Search for Order*), and aside from the proliferation of their disciplines in the rapidly rising German-style research universities, scientists sought also to institutionalize their work in the structure of government itself, more intimately than in the detached, quasi-private status of the Smithsonian and more comprehensively than with the special case of the Naval Observatory.

The Department of Agriculture, in existence institutionally in Lincoln's time although not receiving Cabinet status until Cleveland's, launched studies in chemistry, horticulture, entomology, animal disease control, and botany. Another result of this kind of organizational effort was the consolidation of the existing four surveys of the Western lands by different (and often conflicting) agencies into a single United States Geological Survey. Clarence King, who had launched the whole series of postwar scientific explorations with his great Fortieth Parallel survey begun in 1867, became the new agency's first director, succeeded in 1881 by Powell, who headed (and shaped) the USGS for its next thirteen formative years. Thus what had begun as a madcap adventure down the Colorado became a plunge into the toils of Washington bureaucracy.

5. Politics and Scientific Reality

Had John Wesley Powell contented himself with being the kind of bureaucrat usually dubbed "faceless," he might have faded securely away into institutional history. But that was never Powell's way. Ever since his return from the first Colorado expedition he had used his enhanced visibility before the public as a platform for voicing opinions that clashed with many cherished American beliefs. Even had he not been so outspoken he would have been controversial as a symbol. At about the time Emma and John Wesley Powell were settling into their home in Washington, the venerable Princeton Seminary theologian Charles Hodge asked "What is Darwinism?" and answered himself: "It is Atheism." Bat-

tle was joined, and geologists—particularly the fossil hunters—
were inescapably part of Darwinism's shock troops.

If God had created all species of living things fixed and immutable, there could be no "missing links"; but missing links were
turning up all over North America. O. C. Marsh—"Big Bone Chief,"
as he was known among Indians in the West—turned up ancient
fossil birds which possessed teeth and other reptilian features, and
put together a sequence of fossil skeletons which convincingly
showed the evolution of the native North American horse from its
five-toed progenitor *Eohippus* in Eocene times (to anti-evolutionists the North American Tertiary fossil mammals were in a sense
even more dangerous than the dinosaurs, which could always be
dismissed as having been among the clean or unclean beasts Noah
had not seen fit to load on board his Ark). Powell hired Marsh to
head the Geological Survey's division of vertebrate paleontology,
thereby becoming guilty of bone-hunting by association.

If Powell's ideas about the history of the land appeared to some
Victorian Americans to threaten their souls, his ideas about its
present condition and future prospects threatened their pocket-
books and their ideals. Since the Land Ordinance of 1785, debate
over the "public domain"—the vast stretches of land owned by the
national government itself (or, as Calhoun and his friends had insisted, by the states collectively) had turned on the question of how
rapidly it could be gotten rid of and on what terms. From the spruce
forests of northern Maine to the buffalo-grass country across the
Mississippi, government land for more than ninety years had been
neatly sliced into square townships and sections, with long pie-
shaped pieces (called "gores," analogous to the pleats in a skirt)
inserted between the rows of townships in order to make a two-
dimensional grid survey fit onto the curvature of the Earth, and
then put up for sale. In a curt, 30-minute bombshell of a speech to
the National Academy of Sciences in April of 1877 Powell warned
that this simple system, once so productive of national growth, had
had its day: "All the good public lands fit for settlement are sold.
There is not left unsold in the whole United States, of land which
a poor man could turn into a farm, enough to make one average
county in Wisconsin." So much for the brave promise of the Home-
stead Act, one of the planks on which Powell's Republican Party
had ridden into power in 1860, that had seemed to promise free
land and a new start in the West for everyone.

In his famous *Report on the Lands of the Arid Region,* printed the following year, Powell warned Congress that the carefree expansionism Americans had enjoyed ever since they arrived on the Eastern seaboard must soon come to an end. Most of the remaining public land could not be "redeemed for agriculture, except by irrigation"; some of it ought to be retired from use altogether; and all of it should be reclassified from an earth-sciences rather than a real-estate point of view. Empowered by an 1888 Act of Congress authorizing an irrigation survey, Powell proceeded to do just that—and the Attorney-General of the United States ruled that until the land had been so reclassified, entries of claims would not be permitted upon it. Yet in earlier years the government had derived the great bulk of its revenues from land sales; Webster retains to this day the metaphorical term *land-office business,* meaning "rush of sales or transactions." Now, suddenly, at the end of a century's land boom, the General Land Office itself was in effect put one of business until Major Powell gave the word. It was too abrupt a halt to the American sky's-the-limit booster tradition; Westerners' anger roared through the halls of Congress and the Irrigation Survey was quickly gutted. Nobody loves a prophet who destroys their dreams, even if he be a scientist trying to speak the truth.

The key to the arid lands, Powell insisted, was water. Intelligible boundaries for a political community in the water-hungry West must be mountain watersheds and hydrographic basins rather than arbitrarily drawn straight lines that met at right angles. Nor could water become a commodity to be traded on mercantile exchanges, with results like the Gilded Age's notorious "corners" in wheat, oil, and gold. Like the land it barely sufficed to nurture, it would thenceforth have to be managed as a public trust, not for the "bottom line" but for the long term. "Fix it in your constitution," he told the convention delegates who were drafting a state constitution for North Dakota in 1889, "that no corporation—no body of men—no capital can get possession of the right of your waters. Hold the waters in the hands of the people."

Powell's biographer William Culp Darrah argues—rightly, I think—that the Geological Survey, with its "sense of possession, protection, and stewardship," constituted a pilot project for a quite new political concept in America: "the first significant venture of the government as a 'welfare state.'" But Powell's assumptions could also lead to more radical conclusions. If scientific necessity foreclosed certain kinds of financially rewarding activity; if (as Powell testified in 1886) "the laws of political economy do not belong to the economics of science and intellectual progress" because whereas "possession of property is exclusive, possession of knowledge is not exclusive"; then the question arose whether science, applied to human political and economic affairs, logically and unavoidably required socialism. Gilded-Age entrepreneurialists, seeing science and especially Darwinism as a rationale for laissez-faire, of course disagreed; and Powell himself never made clear what kinds of "corporations" for administering water and other natural resources ought to prevail—private or public, nationally sponsored or locally controlled. He had, however, raised some deeply unsettling questions. At the very least, he intimated, the wild freedom celebrated in the mythical West—and in America at large!—would have to yield to a new necessity to cooperate; to anticipate; to plan—a lesson many in the nation a century later still seemed unable to learn.

The Geological Survey's director had also, both by virtue of his combative temperament and ex-officio as a bureaucratic empire builder, made enemies. To befriend and support O. C. Marsh, for example, meant inevitably to incur the enmity of E. D. Cope, who in 1890 spread over a page and a half of the *New York Herald* an accusation that Powell and Marsh were conspiring to control all government scientific work through a Tammany-like political machine. Powell was, moreover, an active, partisan Republican; a war crony of Grant (who saw to it that the first Colorado River expedition got free Army rations) and a Radical, moved ultimately by his abolitionist Methodist family's prewar commitment against slavery. When the pendulum in Washington swung away from Radical Republicanism, and especially when the disheveled Democratic Party of the postwar years finally got its act together and began winning elections, a Republican-appointed bureaucrat became fair game.

The GOP of a century ago, strange as this may sound to modern ears, was the more congenial of the two parties toward what we would term "big government" policies; government subsidies for railroads, government land grants for colleges, government spending on science—policies which the Democracy in its antebellum days of power had opposed either on Southern states'-rights grounds or on the Jacksonian principle of minimal governmental interference with the economy. Indeed, backlash against spending by the

Republican-controlled "Billion Dollar Congress" elected with Benjamin Harrison in 1888—so named because it was the first Congress ever to appropriate a sum of money so horrendous—had a great deal to do with creating the lopsided Democratic majorities in the House of Representatives over the next two sessions. In that political atmosphere Geological Survey Director Powell became even easier to caricature than John Quincy Adams had been. As one Democratic Representative, John L. Wilson of Washington, put it in 1892:

> We make appropriations everywhere to give the Geological Bureau an opportunity to ascertain the variety and number of butterflies and to stow away in dusty volumes the result of their examinations into prehistoric times and report whether the birds that existed in that era lived with or without teeth, but the home builder, the settler, who is developing new country, building towns and villages . . . is almost totally neglected.

Some of this polemic doubtlessly reflected a serious ideological worry about government paternalistic control. "The Congress of the United States is about to seize the last power that was reserved to the states and the people," cried Congressman W. W. Dickerson, an old foe of the Geological Survey. "We are centralizing until we are now looking after the health of the people by taking charge of their food" [by implication, through the just-aborted Irrigation Survey]. But much of it rose from a homespun conviction that Powell's kind of activity was simply frivolous, a waste of taxpayers' money. "There is no end to paleontology, there is no end to geology," lamented Alabama Representative Hilary Herbert; "and when the morning of resurrection shall come, some paleontologist will be searching for some previously undiscovered species of extinct beings. . . . No other government in the world appropriates as much money as we do for science." Motivated also by the great economic depression that had descended upon the country in 1893, such Congressmen vowed to appropriate less—much less; and the damage-control measure Powell felt he had to take, in order to save his Bureau, was to resign.

In the following century the status of science in political society was destined for drastic change. Along with Big Business, Big Government, and Big (more politely, "mass") Society, willy-nilly, came Big Science. Especially after the Manhattan Project and Sputnik, scientists' involvement with government became extensive and expensive. That involvement remains controversial; Gilded Age Congressional objections to butterfly-counting and bone-hunting have echoes in latter-day Senatorial snipings at the space program. On the whole, however, it became a ground for pride, not indignation, that "no other government in the world appropriates as much money as we do for science"—and that very acceptance carried with it a profound historical irony. Gilded-Age science, with its lingering faith in Baconian "hard facts," had a moral and intellectual commitment to truth-telling; and even in our own relativized and phenomenalized scientific era the knowing falsification of data remains for a scientist the sin of sins. In retrospect, the real danger in government science after Powell's time, rather than that society would come under the control of the scientists, as the Congressmen feared, turned out to be that science's truth-telling function would become compromised by political priorities and goals.

Less acutely than in Hitler's Germany, where Einstein's theory of relatively was discounted as "Jewish physics," or in Stalin's Russia, which rejected the same doctrine as inconsistent with dialectical materialism, science in America nevertheless has sometimes found the hard-won factuality of its data subordinated to, even set aside by, economic and political agendas. (For example, how factually feasible are the optical and engineering physics that would be necessary to implement "Star Wars"?) Against the heavy hype of theater politics as practiced in contemporary America, the high hope of elucidating social problems by "the dry light of science," as Lester Ward in 1893 proposed, "as though it were the inhabitants of Jupiter's moons, instead of those of this planet, that were under the field of the intellectual telescope," seems hardly to stand a chance. Social scientists, however, should not be smug about this historical development among their "hard"-science colleagues. Their own forebears in economics, history, and sociology, in their struggle for professionalization during the forty years following the Civil War, largely abandoned the broad-gauged concerns of Gilded-Age science and social science, Mary Furner writes, and in the main ceased to "bring expert skill and knowledge to bear on cosmic questions pertaining to society as a whole." Perhaps, in the appallingly vast and impersonal universe described by Gilded Age science, the contemplation of cosmic questions in relation to human society had become far too painful even for experts to bear.

Interlude VI

Hunching down from the north, the great glacier enfolded Canada and the Great Lakes and New England in its icy grip. Cold water rolled out from under its forward edge, to drop dirty debris in rows and piles that were located by the dictates of gravity and the lie of the land. Near its eastern end, where bergs calved off and fell thundering into the salt sea, a strip of mucky tundra underlain by permafrost nourished mosses and lichens, herbs and dwarfed trees; farther west, stands of hardy spruce and fir marched up near the glacier's very edge. And across this wintry land roamed beasts, the like of which America has not known for the past ten thousand years.

Woolly mammoths and giant beaver crashed through the subarctic forests near the glacier's front; farther from the ice sheet tapirs browsed, and camels, and native American horses. From some of these peaceable browsers the saber-toothed cat made his living, and among them slowly moved the ponderous, uncouth ground sloth. Of all the continents only Africa has known so grand a variety of wild creatures as did Pleistocene North America. "What an interesting continent ours would have been," the Canadian geologist A. P. Coleman wistfully wrote, "if somewhere in the wilds we could have seen the ground sloths uprooting the trees or the mammoth or mastodon clothed in long hair and with gleaming recurved tusks." But it was not to be. As the ice melted and the earth warmed, that great menagerie melted away also, in a bare heartbeat of geologic time. In only ten centuries, according to one calculation—a span of years shorter than that of the Roman Empire—much of the animate host that had roamed America unchallenged for a million years was gone.

What happened to that host? Perhaps, as the ice drew back and the climate suddenly became warmer and drier, America's grassland steppes turned into desert where overspecialized grass-croppers could no longer live; or, in more humid regions, the forest canopy may have grown up and closed over the animals, screening away the lifegiving sun from the forest-floor cover which had been their habitual food. But in the course of that million years the ice had advanced and retreated three previous times with no such wholesale and irreversible dying-off of wildlife as happened in this last climate change. Furthermore, many of the extinct late-Pleistocene fauna in North America would be perfectly natural as inhabitants of that same continent today. One can readily imagine mastodons faring well in Missouri; ground sloths on the Kaibab Plateau in Arizona; camels in West Texas; giant beaver in Northern Maine; the great cats in western Montana —provided, of course, that people left them alone.

Four times the great glaciers marched out over the land, and four times they fell back. The one new factor in the North American life-equation, the fourth time, was man.

SEVEN

World Wreckers or Planetary Custodians?

Early in this book, gentle reader, you were warned that one of its themes was going to be finiteness—that ultimate deterrent to any revolt against destiny, whether an individual's or a nation's. For their first two centuries the new people, the Americans, were able to decline that challenge by telling themselves, "There'll always be more"—of water, food, fuel, land, whatever—"where that came from."

By the end of the nineteenth century they were beginning to know better. However, to know is not necessarily to act. "A sense of security springs more often from habit than from conviction," George Eliot wrote. For Americans, their abundant land had given that habitual sense a long time to settle in. Science could give them the tools and the rational method—but not, of itself, the sense of urgency—to wrestle with this new incarnation of destiny.

1. Extermination as a Way of Life

Whether or not science follows an inner logic of its own—a matter concerning which there is considerable debate—it takes shape and color from the culture out of which it comes. The astronomical and mathematical revolution of the seventeenth century happened in a setting of global exploration and the organization of conquest; nineteenth-century Darwinism arose in a context of international competition, class conflict, and social misery. After the twentieth century's harvest of holocausts and pogroms, it was thus quite natural for a historically remote problem in Ice Age paleozoology to be tackled by analogy with more recent human beings' systematic inhumanity toward their own kind. The "statistics of deadly quarrels" between 1820 and 1945, Paul Martin told a glacial geology

154

class in 1978, reveal that human creatures during that time span killed off about 60 million of their own species; should one expect them to have behaved any more tenderly, back near the dawn of human time, toward a species other than their own?

During the last glaciation of the northern hemisphere, such savants have reasoned, the ice cap locked up so much of the ocean's water that the Bering Strait was high and dry; in places it was much as 900 miles wide. And most of Alaska was never glaciated. Thus, while most of North America was under ice, human immigrants from the Old World could have wandered down the Alaskan and British Columbian coasts. They could not, however, have gone on into the central steppes and prairies until a corridor opened between the Cordilleran (i.e., Rocky Mountain) and the Laurentian (i.e., Continental) ice sheets. As the ice melted, such a corridor did open, and—some archaeologists have theorized—North America's "gregarious and fearless megafauna were for the first time . . . confronted by spear- and fire-equipped man."

Human hunters, schooled by a million years of chasing after big game all the way across Asia, Paul Martin hypothesized, would have "found it duck soup to kill ground sloths in North America." Moving on from frontier to frontier as the hunted creatures vanished before them, he has calculated, a wave of human predators starting out on foot from the vicinity of Edmonton, Alberta some 11,500 years ago could have reached the Isthmus of Panama halfway through their first millennium, and by the end of the first thousand years have marched all the way down to Cape Horn. The projected dates of their successive invasions of new regions across both continents ominously coincide with the *known* dates at which fossil remains of the hapless megafauna in those same regions abruptly cease to exist.

The statistics are not merely cold; they are chilling. Judging by the 130 million head of livestock in present-day North America, such "overkill" theorists contend, the carrying capacity of that continent in prehistoric times was indeed great—"but a very large biomass, even the 2.3×10^8 metric tons of domestic animals now ranging the continent, could be overkilled within 1000 years by a human population never exceeding 10^6," Martin bleakly sums up (*Science*, March 9, 1973). "We need only assume that a relatively innocent prey was suddenly exposed to a new and thoroughly superior predator, a hunter who preferred killing and persisted in killing animals as long as they were available."

It is a depressing portrait—man, at best a heedless plunderer and at worst a willful destroyer, hounding the rest of the Earth's creatures to their doom even in primordial, one would like to think Edenic, time. Understandably, therefore, this overkill thesis has met with spirited rebuttal: "Almost totally conjectural," the skeptics reply. Human beings, they contend, were in the New World much earlier than Martin's "Clovis hunters" (so named after artifacts of theirs found in Clovis, New Mexico). If this is the way human newcomers overran the New World, the objectors ask, why do we not find their kill sites? If they wiped out all the big game, why did the bison escape? Why did those ancient marauders not leave records to commemorate their prowess, comparable to the Paleolithic cave paintings in France and Spain or the ivory animal carvings found in the mammoth-hunters' camps along the Don?

Because, Paul Martin argues in reply, "the big game was wiped out before there was an opportunity to portray the extinct species." We do not find their kill sites because the inexperienced prey found by the new human predators were not granted enough time to learn defensive behavior, so that the hunters in order to take them would not have had to build traps or organize cliff drives of the kind the later Indians unleashed against the buffalo. And the impact of people prior to the Clovis hunter-culture, Martin argues, was ephemeral. The debate continues to rage; in 1983 Martin and Richard G. Klein edited an 800-page blockbuster of a book, *Quaternary Extinctions*, in which supporters and rebutters of the rival theories on the cause of the Pleistocene extinction—climate versus human overkill—had at one another with evidence gathered not only from the Americas but from the planet as a whole. Whatever the paleo-Indians had to do with the sudden disappearance of the woolly mammoth from North America, they can hardly be faulted for the demise of the giant moa bird in prehistoric New Zealand!

The pros and cons of the overkill hypothesis are phrased in terms of logical inference from empirical evidence; but that argument crackles with ideological electricity, left over from the ecology/energy/growth controversry of the 1970s. The "native American," who eventually descended from the paleo-Indians of the late glacial age and who has had to endure successive stereotyping as the Savage (noble or ignoble), the Drunken Indian, or the Vanishing American, has lately taken on yet another: the Ecological Indian, who is said to have lived in harmony with the world of nature. According to this view, the Indian on the hunting trail was no predator; he revered, or at least prudently respected, the animal he slew as "a conscious member of the same eco-system" with himself. The serpent in Eden was not the rampaging postglacial horde who may have been the Indian hunters' remote ancestors, but rather those more recent immigrants who corrupted him with the cash-values of early modern Europe. Merchant-adventurers unknown to him, far away in London or St. Petersburg, spun webs of credit that drew him into the fur trade; and his participation in that trade, writes Calvin Martin (no relation to Paul) in *Keepers of the Game* (1978), "drove the Indian . . . into a position of uncompromising callousness toward Nature, as he progressively shifted his allegiance from the spirits of his handicrafts to the secular commodities of Western Europe. The function of the Indian within his ecosystem had now changed from conservator to despoiler"; and despoil he did, armed by the new technology—the steel traps, steel knives, rifles—for which, along with kettles and trinkets and whiskey, he traded his hard-won beaver skins and, ultimately, his birthright.

Tu quoque; "you're another." Such controversies, however scientific and dispassionate their intention, easily and speedily slide into a routine of the pot calling the kettle black. However much the scholars debate who was responsible for overkilling North America's game—whether the Clovis hunters behaved as Paul Martin believes they did, or whether the later Indians "despiritualized" their relationship with their prey as Carl Martin contends—the *fact* of such overkill can hardly be gainsaid. And not alone in North America; the old Europe-Asia-Africa triad had its own prodigalities. Think of the animal cages that trundled up the Appian Way toward Imperial Rome, stripping North Africa and Asia Minor of their noblest wild beasts for slaughter in the gladiatorial arena; food not to nourish the Roman masses' bodies but to entertain their bloody souls. Think of how European high fashion, rather than American carelessness, dictated the near-doom of the North American beaver, victim of the curious conceit that wealth and social prominence can be measured by the height of one's hat; and of how a change in fashion's irrational decree—the invention (appropriately, in Paris) of the tall silk hat—spared the same intelligent and enterprising quadruped into the present century.

Endangered species have perished or capriciously survived as readily in the Old World as in the New. The decline of the American bison, from the vast herds one eyewitness described during the Civil War as "a monstrous moving brown blanket" covering

157

the ground "as far as the eye could reach" to the few hundreds of fenced-off, carefully protected bison that survive today, can be paralleled in the equally sad story of their European equivalent the *wisent*, whose last specimens in what remained of the Hercynian Forest described in *Caesar's Commentaries* (where they had once flourished) fell to hungry peasants and soldiers—some armed with machine guns—in the chaos that engulfed the Eastern Front after the First World War. That European bison, however, had been in slow retreat for centuries before he met his *coup de grace*, whereas the sheer speed and magnitude of what happened to his American cousin staggers the imagination. Siegfried in the *Nibelungenlied* is said on one occasion to have slain one *wisent*, along with a moose, four aurochs bulls, and a wild stallion; but that exploit pales to triviality compared to the methodical mowing-down of American bison by Buffalo Bill. The dream of the West—that virgin paradise America that lay beyond the historic ken of Europe, Africa, and Asia—became a walking (or railroad-riding) nightmare, as the prairies came to be dotted with heaps of stinking, abandoned flesh.

Yet so pristine, so unspoiled were those prairies that one might cross them without any awareness that the bare act of crossing was a portent of coming doom. As the "two thousand Americans, some of them illiterate and ignorant, all of them strong, taking with them law, order, society, the church, the school" trudged from the prairie up to the High Plains in Emerson Hough's fictionalized acount *The Covered Wagon*, they saw "a wild, free world" which, to the wondering eyes of Hough's young heroine, seemed eternal:

> The ceaseless wind of the prairie swept old and new grass into a continuous undulating surface, silver crested, a wave always passing, never past. The sky was unspeakably fresh and blue, with its light clouds, darker edged toward the far horizon of the unbounded, unbroken expanse of alternating levels and low hills. Across the broken ridges passed the teeming bird life of the land. The Eskimo plover in vast bands circled and sought their nesting place. Came also the sweep of cinnamon wings as the giant sickle-billed curlews wheeled in vast aerial phalanx, with their eager cries, "Curlee! Curlee! Curlee!"—the wildest cry of the old prairies. Again, from some unknown, undiscoverable place, came the liquid, baffling mysterious note of the nesting upland plover, sweet and clean as pure white honey.
>
> Now and again a band of antelope swept ghostlike across a ridge. A great gray wolf stood contemptuously near on a hillock,

gazing speculatively at the strange new creature, the white woman, new come to his lands. It was the wilderness, rude, bold, yet sweet.

2. *"Not to kill twenty and eat one"*

The New World set an insidious trap for the hunter—or the miner, or the sodbuster—by seducing his hopeful and greedy mind into confusing *new* with *inexhaustible*. If a bison herd truly covered the ground in a miles-wide moving brown blanket, what harm could there be in trimming off a little of the blanket's edge for buffalo robes? If the passenger pigeons darkened the sun in flocks trustworthy observers estimated in the thousands of *billions*, who could grudge the hungry settlers along the flight path a few atoms out of all that mass to make into pigeon pie?

When the passenger pigeons flew over one village in upstate New York in the spring of 1794, as later reported in James Fenimore Cooper's *The Pioneers* (1823), the inhabitants mobilized as for war, with "every species of fire-arms, from the French ducking-gun with a barrel near six feet in length, to the common horseman's pistol," as well as bows and arrows and a small piece of field artillery. Fenimore Cooper's ludicrous inaccuracies about Indians have been known since the time of Mark Twain, but the white men's and boy's antics he depicted in *The Pioneers*, one fears, were all too real:

> The reports of the fire-arms became rapid, whole volleys rising from the plain, as flocks of more than ordinary numbers darted over the opening, shadowing the field like a cloud; and then the light smoke of a single piece would issue from among the leafless bushes on the mountain, as death was hurled on the retreat of the affrighted birds, who were rising from a volley, in a vain effort to escape. Arrows, and missiles of every kind were in the midst of the flocks; and so numerous were the birds, and so low did they take their flight, that even long poles, in the hands of those on the sides of the mountain, were used to strike them to the earth. . . .
>
> "Fire!" cried the Sheriff, clapping a coal to the priming of the cannon. . . . The roar of the gun echoed along the mountains, and died away to the north, like distant thunder, while the whole flock of alarmed birds seemed, for a moment, thrown into one disorderly and agitated mass. The air was filled with their irregular flight, layer rising above layer, far above the tops of the highest pines, none daring to advance beyond the dangerous pass;

when, suddenly, some of the leaders of the feathered tribe shot across the valley, taking their flight directly over the village, and hundreds of thousands in their rear followed the example, deserting the eastern side of the plain to their persecutors and the slain.

In the midst of all this ruckus, Cooper's archetypal character Leatherstocking stalks onto the field, declares "It's wicked to be shooting into flocks in this wasty manner," and quietly takes one bird for his supper. "If a body has a craving for pigeon's flesh, why, it's made the same as all other creatur's, for man's eating; but not to kill twenty and eat one." Ominously, Leatherstocking warns the trigger-happy sportsmen of the danger in blazing away at the heavens in that fashion: "Well! the Lord won't see the waste of his creatures for nothing, and right will be done to the pigeons, as well as others, by and by."

Not to kill twenty and eat one; like many other self-denying resolutions, such advice is easy to give and seemingly very hard to take. "Man has too long forgotten that the earth was given to him for usufruct alone, not for consumption, still less for profligate waste," cautioned George Perkins Marsh, four decades after Cooper, in *Man and Nature* (1864). "Nature . . . has left it within the power of man irreparably to derange the combinations of inorganic matter and organic life," Marsh wrote. Man, whether prehistoric big game hunter or civilized pigeon-shooter, "is everywhere a disturbing agent," and "he wields energies to resist which, nature . . . is wholly impotent." He wields those energies not only against pigeons and buffaloes, but also against the land that nourishes man, pigeon, and buffalo alike—and he seems unable to stop himself from doing so.

Two thousand years ago, Pliny the Elder noted in his *Naturalis Historiae* that "destructive torrents are generally formed when hills are stripped of the trees which formerly confined and absorbed the rains." Such torrents were formed when hills were stripped in Pliny's time, and in Marsh's time, and in our own time; and when the floodwaters recede we promptly run up tacky housing on the flood plain and sell it, hoping that the next inundation will mercifully not arrive until we have taken our money and run. All, of course, in the name of progress, whose "elementalistic champions," William Vogt sarcastically observed (in *Road to Survival*, 1948), "cry, over and over again, 'Free enterprise has made our country what it is!'

"To this an ecologist might sardonically assent, 'Exactly'."

Pliny's torrential rains wash away much besides the real estate developers' absurdly ill-located buildings. Vogt noted that "American civilization, founded on nine inches of topsoil," had already lost one-third of that soil to water and wind since the European voyages of discovery. Such destruction is less spectacular than that of woolly mammoths or bison herds; the earth, when it is raped, does not cry out. Yet that kind of ravage may be ultimately the more momentous. "There are parts of Asia Minor, of Northern Africa, of Greece, and even of Alpine Europe," George Perkins Marsh warned in 1864, "where the operation of causes set into action by man has brought the face of the earth to a desolation almost as complete as that of the moon; and though, within that brief space of time which we call 'the historical period,' they are known to have been covered with luxuriant woods, verdant pastures, and fertile meadows, they are now too far deteriorated to be reclaimable by man." During twenty centuries while undiscovered, thinly settled North America suffered but little physiographic change, "man had changed millions of square miles, in the fairest and most fertile regions of the Old World, into the barrenest deserts." If Americans would avoid the fatal mistakes of Rome, which let its North African grain fields be swallowed up in the Saharan sands, they must get promptly to work. Yet America—fresh, verdant America, the heavenly garden West that seers and poets had dreamed of for many centuries in Alpine Europe and Greece and Northern Africa and Asia Minor—was moving along the same fateful track that the Old World had trod.

From earliest colonial times, land along the Eastern Seaboard was abandoned almost as rapidly as it could be cleared—largely because of its very abundance; "We can buy an acre of new land," Thomas Jefferson worriedly wrote, "cheaper than we can manure an old one." By Jefferson's time, only twenty years after the American Revolution, travelers were describing mile after mile of once-fertile lands in Virginia and Maryland as "flat and sandy, wearing a most dreary aspect . . . worn out by the culture of tobacco, overgrown with yellow sedge and interspersed with groves of pine and cedar trees"—in the midst of which stood "several good homes which shows that the country was once very different from what it is now." A tablet in Jamestown's old church celebrates Pocahontas's husband John Rolfe, whose discovery of the commercial possibilities of tobacco, says a National Park Service sign, revolutionized Virginia's economy for one hundred and fifty years. "This," William Vogt bitingly comments, "is a major piece of understatement. Virginia has not yet recovered from the effects of John Rolfe's brainstorm, nor is it likely to for many years to come."

As the plunderers moved on westward, the damage got worse. "The West doesn't heal the way Vermont, let us say, heals," Western writer Wallace Stegner has warned us: "You can tear the hell out of Vermont woods and pretty soon, five years, you can't tell the loggers have been there. It's all come back to woods. And you can do almost anything to Vermont grass and it comes up grass again. But you can't do that in the West." Sadly, for most this lesson seems insurmountably hard to master. In the farthest West, the searing aridity of the desert wilderness ought to have made people "learn how to take care of the range," but "they didn't learn in time." Instead of becoming "irrigators rather than just plowers of the land," Stegner observes,

> they turned most of the ranges into sagebrush and shad scale and rabbitbrush. There's hardly a range in the West that isn't fifty percent deteriorated from what it was in the beginning. Even down in southern Utah, where some of that country won't carry any animals at all now, there used to be stirrup-high grass. It was sparse, but it was stirrup-high. Most of the grass reproduced from seed; when it was overgrazed it was gone. In some areas such as the Escalante Basin you've got not even shad scale and sagebrush but bare rock. Grass and soil just blew away.
> Such things have to be learned.

3. Deserts in the Sky: A Cautionary Tale

Some Eastern Americans, ignoring warnings like Stegner's (or Powell's; see chapter 6), continued to trek westward in search of greener pastures. Others, fleeing crowded urban centers in search of open space, in turn formed new crowds as they stood in line or peered over one another's heads at Old Faithful or the Grand Canyon's South Rim; to accommodate such pilgrims the graceful shade trees along the navigable parts of the Colorado were cut down to provide fuel for steamboats, and trains offered them transportation in comfort along new railroad cuts that eroded terrain and befouled fishing streams. Still others came—or sent their money —in quest of wealth; many sought health; and more than a few, scientific knowledge. One proper Bostonian with impeccable family credentials—Amy Lowell, the avant-garde poet, was his sister; A. Lawrence Lowell, for many years President of Harvard, was his brother; James Russell Lowell, crusading activist against slavery and against the Mexican War, was a cousin—emigrated in search of air clean enough to let him study the planet Mars. Astronomer Percival Lowell, like many other Eastern Establishment types who came out West for inspiration, recreation, or profit, afterward proceeded, subtly but powerfully, to influence the way the rest of the nation thought and felt about the West—and, eventually, about itself.

From any astronomer's point of view the advance of civilization across our planet has had its disadvantages. "Not only is civilized man actively engaged in defacing such part of the Earth's surface as he comes in contact with," Lowell lamented in 1906, "he is equally busy blotting out his sky." London, Cologne, Milan, and America's own urban centers vied with one another in obliterating the view beyond this Earth, "so that today few city-bred children have any conception of the glories of the heavens which made of the Chaldean shepherds astronomers in spite of themselves." In Europe, places which earlier in Lowell's own lifetime had housed important astronomical observatories had become unusable; and in his own country "not till we pass beyond the Missouri do the stars shine out as they shone before the white man came."

In 1894 Lowell's young assistant A. E. Douglass, armed with a six-inch telescope, boarded a train to look for an astronomical site in the trans-Missouri West. Douglass tested the atmosphere in Wyatt Earp's Tombstone; in Tucson, where astronomers make the same complaint about sky pollution today; in Tempe, Phoenix, Ash Fork, and finally Flagstaff, Arizona Territory, then a ranching and lumber town of some 800 souls. Their enterprising Board of Trade saw to it that a brass band met him at the train station; they wined and dined him at the best local hotel, and offered him land for Lowell's proposed observatory, together with a pledge to build and maintain between the site and the depot "a good wagon road." There, on a spot which soon became locally known as "Mars Hill," they built the Lowell Observatory. The boosters' strategy paid off. Within a few years Flagstaff had become "known wherever Man reads his daily paper," Percival Lowell later boasted—known largely from the furor over the discoveries about Mars, real and imaginary, that he had made there.

Impressed, like many other newcomers to the region, by the Southwest's dryness and what seemed to them its emptiness, Professor Lowell incorporated and transferred this sense of desolation into the epic tale he told, in his many books and academic papers and public lectures, about the planet Mars. "Deserts already exist on earth, and the nameless horror that attaches to the word in the thoughts of all who have had experience of them . . . is in truth greater than we commonly suppose," Lowell declared in 1908. "For the cosmic circumstance about them which is most terrible is not what deserts are, but what deserts have begun to be." Desert Mars is, in short, a prophetic warning of a future desert Earth. "Beautiful as the opaline tints of the planet look, down the far vista of the telescope-tube, they represent a really terrible reality. . . . That rose-ochre enchantment is but a mind mirage," Lowell wrote. "All deserts, seen from a safe distance, have something of this charm of tint. . . . But this very color, unchanging in hue, means the extinction of life." The planet-girdling Martian Saharas inevitably remind us of our own, and "to this condition that earth itself must come, if it last so long."

The grimness of Lowell's vision deepened into tragedy; for across the arid Martian landscape that shimmered through the Flagstaff telescope's refracting lenses the astronomer believed he had found convincing evidence of doomed intelligence. The tracks his Mars-watching predecessor Giovanni Schiaparelli thought he had discerned on the Red Planet and named *canali*—in Italian, literally "channels"—the American described with a similar sounding but much more exciting word. Lowell, more than anyone else, popularized the idea of Martian "canals"—planet-spanning irrigation ditches carrying meltwater from the polar caps in order to postpone a high civilization's inevitable end.

Historical circumstances nourished the acceptance of Lowell's ideas, for the turn of the twentieth century was a highly canal-conscious era. People considered the Suez one of the wonders of the modern world, and the public argument over the reality of Lowell's canal-building Martians almost exactly coincided with the controversy over the forcible taking of the land across which the United States was to build the Panama Canal. Land reclamation, also, was a subject very much "in the air"; In 1902 Congress at Theodore Roosevelt's urging passed the Newlands Act for that purpose, and in the same year Britain was spending millions of pounds for irrigation in India and for new dams and other works along the ancient Nile. America's own Nile, George Wharton James wrote in 1917, was going to be the Colorado; "the Mohave, Colorado, Arizona, and Sonora Deserts that it crosses are enough like Egypt to suggest it in everything save its pyramids, sphynx, ancient ruins, and modern fellaheen." Thanks to government-financed irrigation, agricultural extension work, and dam-building (which in the long run was going to create at least as many problems as it solved), the new Nile was already beginning to resemble the old: "Date palms wave over fields of cotton, alfalfa, wheat . . . while the same pure sky and insistent sun overarch the scene during the day and the rich velvety pall of bluish black, studded with brilliantly scintillant stars, covers it during the night."

That early, long before Paul Ehrlich and others made us conscious of the ticking "population bomb," worries were already being voiced about the ratio of people to arable land, even in that arid corner of the U.S. "As population increases and the need of land for cultivation becomes greater, the question arises, 'How can a country so dry be made to yield food?'" Yale geographer Ellsworth Huntington wrote in 1911. Not yet was Earth's civilization in need of measures for yielding food so heroic and desperate as on the Mars of Percival Lowell. "Perchance some day," Huntington continued, "when the denizens of Mother Earth become like Lowell's Martians, we shall distill the water of the sea with solar engines and pump it hundreds of miles to irrigate lands that now are dry. Meanwhile we must try other methods." Near Tucson, he noted, the Carnegie Institute in 1903 had established a Desert Laboratory (still in business today, administered by University of Arizona scientists) to study "how the plants perform their functions under the extraordinary conditions existing in deserts" and even to conduct experiments in actual plant evolution. If enough water could not be brought to the desert to make it bloom like the rose, perhaps without adding any more water it could be made to bloom like the cactus.

But that kind of adaptation to the land and its limits has not been typical. Only in our time, as more people have become aware of the exciting possibilities of usable desert plants like the *jojoba*, has the philosophy of the Desert Laboratory begun—as yet just barely—to show practical economic and social consequences. However, the more usual procedure for the allegedly most intelligent species on this planet has not been to adapt to the environment, as Huntington suggested, but to change it. "Already man has begun to leave his mark on this globe in deforestation, in canalization, in communication," Professor Lowell wrote. "So far his towns and his tillage are more partial than complete. But the time is coming when the earth will bear his imprint, and his alone"; and then, when he has "partitioned so regularly the surface of the earth as to impart to it an artificiality of appearance," this planet will be truly viewable from space as an abode of sentient life.

The Viking Lander which touched down on the surface of Mars shortly after America's bicentennial in 1976 found no Martians, and the Mariner probe which swung around the Red Planet in 1971–72, taking 7200 superb pictures, uncovered no canals. Percival Lowell was wrong; on the planet at which he stared from his mountain in Arizona there appears to be no high, dying civilization—although some observers interpret certain strikingly regular formations on its surface as tantalizing hints of such a presence in Mars's past. Yet in another sense Lowell, the dreamer, was more right than the practical people who developed the American Nile, attracted even more settlers to live there, and paved the way for a far more severe water crisis in the now not very distant future. Planetary resources *are* finite, and neither money nor boosterism can make them otherwise. "Intelligent interference with nature," such as Lowell believed he discerned on the face of Mars, is limited by what nature itself permits—and "one of the things that makes Mars of such transcendent interest . . . is the foresight it affords of the course earthly evolution is to pursue." Through Lowell's dark Darwinist vision of the future, however, glimmered a ray of utopian optimism; for a species capable of organizing a planet's water supply from pole to pole, Lowell believed, must long ago have outgrown war and other forms of selfish gain.

4. "On a Certain Blindness in Human Beings"

Humanity's own agricultural works—the "methodical rectangles" of wheatfields in Kansas or the Dakotas, for example—probably "would be the first signs of intelligence to one considering the earth from far," Percival Lowell argued in 1906. "Fields for miles turning in hue with the rhythm of the drilled should impress an eye, if armed with our appliances, many millions of miles away." But ought human beings to look forward with such enthusiasm to a time when the Earth would bear their imprint, and theirs alone?

For that matter, need anyone's psychological reaction to a desert necessarily be one of horror? Another Eastern intellectual who migrated to the arid Southwest, John Van Dyke—an erstwhile librarian and professor of art history from New Jersey—had a reaction to "the land of little rain" that was the diametric opposite to that of the Proper Bostonian astronomer Lowell. "The waste places of the earth, the barren deserts, the tracts forsaken of men, and given over to loneliness, have a peculiar attraction of their own," Van Dyke wrote in the opening chapter of his nature-classic *The Desert* (1901). "The weird solitude, the great silence, the grim desolation are the very things with which every desert wanderer eventually falls in love."

It is Emerson's old dialectic of Society and Solitude, worked out in terms of a new setting. The "conservation" movement that emerged in the era and largely under the tutelage of Theodore Roosevelt, historian Donald Fleming has pointed out, was—and is— in reality *two* movements; Fleming named them respectively *preservationism* and *conservationism*. The conservationist wants to manage natural resources in the interest of future generations, by prudently cropping national forest trees, for example, in the same spirit with which a careful farmer conserves the soil. "Wise forest protection does not mean the withdrawal of forest resources, whether of wood, water, or grass, from contributing their full share to the welfare of the people," Roosevelt proclaimed in his first annual message to Congress in 1901. "The fundamental idea of forestry is the perpetuation of forests by *use*." In sharp contrast, the preservationist believes that future generations are better served by locking up the wilderness and leaving its irreplaceable values uncorrupted; an echo of Henry David Thoreau's dictum which is still the slogan of the Wilderness Society, that "In Wildness is the preservation of the World."

Both movements have legitimate historical roots in that moment, celebrated by Frederick Jackson Turner and rationally expounded by John Wesley Powell, when the American frontier finally closed. However, although they have numerous agendas in common (TR in that same message to Congress spoke, for example, of the need for "preserves for the wild forest creatures," if only to save a few of them for future recreational shooting!), they have also—especially in recent years—collided at times as heated political opponents. The preservationist is often accused of anti-democratic elitism, of seeking to deny most of the people access to their heritage; while the conservationist is frequently charged with being a public-relations front for corporate developers who merely postpone or slow the pace of environmental destruction. Conservers and preservers clash in this fashion in large part because Americans have never coherently answered the political question Powell long ago said they must: Who shall decide who uses, or does not use, water, minerals, forests, desert life or land, and for what purpose?

"Any fool can destroy trees. They cannot run away," said John Muir, a pioneering wilderness advocate, in the course of a long political and economic struggle to save the mighty ancient redwoods of California from the dynamiters and the timber thieves. "I hope for the preservation of the groves of giant trees simply because it would be a shame to our civilization to let them disappear." But should such groves be preserved at the expense of the homes which their lumber would otherwise have provided for that civilization's ever-increasing millions? "I do not believe there is either a moral or any other claim upon me," Senator Henry Teller of Colorado told Congress in 1909, "to postpone the use of what nature has given me, so that the next generation or generations yet unborn may have an opportunity to get what I myself ought to get." Senator Teller's negative credo, if proclaimed today, would sound like no more than a justification for greed—get mine, and to hell with my posterity, if any. Take what we need for the present generation and—distorting Scripture somewhat—"take no thought for the morrow." Teller, however, definitely was not one of the apostles of plunder and progress so ubiquitous in his times or in ours. For the Senator also championed the most plundered of all the inhabitants of America, its Indian natives; and to his country's fateful venture into overseas imperialism in 1898 he successfully interposed a Congressional resolution—the "Teller Amendment"—which foreswore any intention of annexing Cuba to the United States. Teller's refusal "to postpone the use of what nature has given me," therefore, could be interpreted not in imperial exploitive terms but as a Jeffersonian liberal claim on behalf of the living, as against either the dead or the unborn.

Even for those who advance the claims of the unborn, if not of the dead—Burke in opposition to Paine, if you will—just *what* one decides to conserve is heavily conditioned by conflicting values. William James testified to that conflict in one of his acutest essays,

"On a Certain Blindness in Human Beings." Traveling through the mountains of North Carolina near the turn of the nineteenth century, that professorial New Englander passed by several recently cleared farmsteads, where the smaller trees had been cut, leaving only their charred stumps, and the greater trees girdled and killed. Among the chips at irregular intervals grew Indian corn, and in the remaining woods pigs and chickens grubbed and foraged. "The impression on my mind," the cultivated Harvardian confessed, "was one of the unmitigated squalor. . . . The forest had been destroyed; and what had 'improved' it out of existence was hideous. . . . talk about going back to native!—I said to myself, oppressed by dreariness, as I drove by." But then the mountaineer who was driving him gently rebuked the professor's tacit snobbery: "Why, we ain't happy here, unless we are getting one of these coves under cultivation."

"I instantly felt that I had been losing the whole inward significance of the situation," James admitted:

> Because to me the clearings spoke of naught but denudation, I thought that to those whose sturdy arms and obedient axes had made them they could tell no other story. But, when *they* looked on the hideous stumps, what they thought of was personal victory. The chips, the girdled trees, and the vile split rails spoke of honest sweat, persistent toil, and final reward. . . . In short, the clearing, which to me was a mere ugly picture on the retina, was to them a symbol redolent with moral memories and sang a very paean of duty, struggle, and success.
>
> I had been blind to the peculiar ideality of their conditions as they certainly would also have been to the ideality of mine.

Even the sacrifice of the passenger pigeon and the buffalo might be ascribed to the "peculiar ideality" of the sacrificers' conditions. In 1952 Amiya Chakravarty, a distinguished scholar from India who was serving as an exchange professor at the University of Kansas, told of a transcendent moment when for the first time he had stood on the hilltop in Lawrence, Kansas that overlooks the High Plains and seen, as far as the flat, distant horizon, nothing but endless fields of wheat. "Can you possibly imagine," he asked one group of affluent Americans, "what *that* sight would mean to an Asian?" Confronted with the South Asian subcontinent's wretched malnourished reality, even the purest of wilderness advocates might balk at contending that all those wheatlands ought to have been left in buffalo grass to shelter the antelope and the grey wolf, the upland plover, and the giant curlew. Although thought of (and sung about) as if complementary, America's amber waves of grain and its purple mountain majesties are to a great extent *opposing* values; and the claims of its (alas, never built) alabaster cities in turn clash with both. This is not a matter simply of being "for" or "against" "the environment," or "for" or "against" "growth" as polemicists on both sides typically insist. Overkill of wild game *is* abomination, but so also is human starvation in Calcutta or the Sahel.

"Hunger," the second Roosevelt's Civil Works Administrator Harry Hopkins declared in 1934, "is not debatable." Coming off the experience of the Great Depression, the New Deal's energies were applied more in the direction of "conservation" than of "preservation". Civilian Conservation Corpsmen built picnic tables and opened forest trails, whereas more purist wilderness advocates today favor closing down the campgrounds to relieve users' pressure on fragile ecologies. Many of the conservation issues of the 1930s —soil erosion, dramatically climaxing in the "dust bowls"; rampaging floods along the nation's rivers; dwindling energy reserves, already foreseen by Interior Secretary Harold Ickes decades before the "oil crunch" of the 1970s—were understood primarily as engineering problems: build dams, dig ditches, generate electric power. *The River*, an impressive conservationist motion picture by Pare Lorenz, which was produced by the Farm Security Administration in 1937, begins with an elegy to the looted, long-gone North American forests, narrated in Whitmanesque poetry; but the film's final triumphant image is of high-voltage transmission lines.

The New Deal also left unresolved a question of the relationship between environmentalism—of either the "preservationist" or the "conservationist" sort—and democratic values. Economic historian Broadus Mitchell, in an otherwise rather critical study of the New Deal, wrote most warmly of the great social experiment FDR's administration had launched in the Tennessee Valley. "A group of farmers in a county council, consumers of electricity meeting to manage their cooperative, construction workers making a wage bargain with the TVA—these are all more democratic than anything that has happened in a Tennessee, Alabama, or Mississippi courthouse in a round century. . . . The democracy of the physical frontier, long since dwindled, has been revived in the democracy of the social frontier, and the second is stronger and richer than the first." But the year before Mitchell offered that testimony a hard-bitten Republican, while conceding the integrity, rationality, and comprehensiveness of the Tennessee Valley Authority in comparison with the rationed scarcity practiced by certain other New Deal agencies, found in TVA nonetheless an ideological flaw —of a kind which a democratic socialist could have faulted as readily as any free-enterpriser. Each of the dams and power stations along that regenerated waterway bears an inscription: BUILT FOR THE PEOPLE OF THE UNITED STATES; how much better, that independent citizen observed, had those plaques said BUILT *by* THE PEOPLE OF THE UNITED STATES.

V. Life Shapes Its World: The Lesson of Vernadskii

Long before the advent of television, Americans tended to have remarkably short attention spans. The psychological advantage of having migrated to and settled in a "New World" was that it relieved them of centuries-hallowed prejudices; the disadvantage was that it ruptured their connection with the past. Both their hopeful/fearful comparisons of themselves with the ancient Romans and their invocation of a still-potent Biblical tradition can be interpreted as not entirely successful attempts to reconnect themselves. More recently, their Revolutionary Bicentennial observances in 1976 constituted another such attempt, also not quite successful; for rather than trying to make conceptual sense out of the process by which America had gotten from "then" to "now," ad hoc Bicentennial committees instead rummaged in national and local attics for symbolic antiques to place on display. (Apparently what Americans collectively decided to do in 1976 was to take a day off to celebrate their *entire* past since the Revolution, lumping it all together regardless of logic or chronology, garage-sale style—thereby clearly implying that none of that hallowed history had anything to do with the practical present. "History" became equatable with "dead and gone," as in the hard-boiled video epithet "You're history, buddy.") Only within the time covered by one's own conscious memory, this kind of reasoning assumes, has anybody ever been concerned with racial justice, militarism, budgetary deficits —or the environment.

For both "preservationists" and "conservationists" in recent years, this absence of historical memory has been crippling. "Like women's liberation, the environmental movement *began* in the sixties," didactically stated an American history textbook that was produced in 1988 in all seriousness by a major publisher of such works. That would have been news indeed to John Wesley Powell, Theodore Roosevelt, or John Muir; not to mention Alice Paul, Elizabeth Cady Stanton, or Charlotte Perkins Gilman. The writer of that textbook, whose lines presumably would be memorized by college students and repeated on their exams, went on to report that around 1970 "a new word, 'ecology,' came into common usage to mean the interrelatedness of all things in nature"; however, to Joseph Wood Krutch (*Henry David Thoreau*, 1948), Aldo Leopold (*A Sand County Almanac*, 1949), Rachel Carson (*The Sea Around Us*, 1951), and their thousands of devoted readers, "ecology" was *not* a new word.

Nor was it a new notion that public policy ought to be based not only on economic benefits but also on ecological concerns. As early as the 1920s, scientists under League of Nations auspices, responding to disastrous news from Danish and other North Sea fisheries, were studying—and issuing worried reports about—the impact of industrial dumping upon the oceanic food chain. But that from the viewpoint of the most powerful non-member of the League of Nations was something going on somewhere else, far away; and if the vision of far too many Americans was constricted in time, it was similarly shriveled in geographic space. Even Americans' best friends have had at times pointedly to remind them that when one takes the entire planetary environment into consideration, "American" problems—of waste disposal, radioactive contamination, energy shortages—can no longer be understood solely as American. Canada recently, even under a government highly congenial in economic outlook and general ideology to the conservative Republican regime then occupying the White House, nonetheless found itself at odds with its southern neighbor over the ravages of U.S.-produced acid rain; "It's ruining our lakes, it's killing our rivers, it's ruining our forests," Prime Minister Brian Mulroney complained (*Time*, April 11, 1988). "Friendship has inescapable costs. One of them is bearing whatever burdens are required to avoid polluting your neighbor's property." Good fences may make good neighbors, as poet Robert Frost observed, but not if one of the neighbors is upwind of the other while burning trash.

Some American environmentalists, conditioned by the radicalisms of the 1960s and 1970s, wistfully imagined that in those parts of the planet beyond the clutch of American capitalism all would be different; abolishing the profit motive would clear the way for a rational yet caring policy toward the environment. Sadly, it does not seem to have worked out that way. "The destruction of the environment by the socialist industrial states does not fall behind the environmental destruction of the capitalist industrial countries," wrote Jürgen Moltmann, a politically concerned West German theologian, in 1985. In evidence he cited a Central Committee report in 1971 to a party conference of his Communist German neighbors to the East, replete with calls for "rapid development of socialist production, increased efficiency, further scientific and technological progress," without any consideration of the ecological cost. "Towards the different political systems, the ecological crisis is apparently neutral," Moltmann warned. "Whether nature is destroyed by capitalist expansion or by socialist increased productivity makes no difference to nature."

Fortunately for the future prospects of the species, such concerns were and are shared in the Soviet Union—by people, Douglas Weiner has argued, who have managed in the face of considerable difficulty to make their voices heard and felt as a factor in national policy. "When the Bolsheviks took power in late 1917 a modest conservation movement was already established in Russia," Weiner writes. It was divided into three factions, each of which had its ideological counterpart in the West: pastoralist, corresponding to "preservationism" in the U.S., whose ideal in its purest form would have been "a world without civilization"; utilitarian, corresponding to "conservationism" of the Theodore Roosevelt variety, known in Russia also as "wise use"; and ecological, whose defenders—mostly natural scientists—viewed nature as a web of interdependence, emphasized its fragility, and warned [in 1917 already!] "of the possibilities of an ecological collapse."

Under Lenin the working ecologists enjoyed modest success; but in the grim Stalin era, with its narrow vocationalism that made theoretical science subordinate to social ideology and practice (most notoriously in the elevation to power of that genetic charlatan Trofim Lysenko), its concept of humans "as beings in whom culture so outweighed biology as to almost efface it," and its "commitment to breakneck industrialization," they went into partial eclipse. (In effect, the managers of the successive Five-Year Plans were telling them: you can't have that tract of land for a wildlife reserve;

we're going to run cattle on it.) What the future holds for environmentalism in the USSR's era of *perestroika* remains to be seen. Even under Stalinism, however, one great champion of the ultimate theoretical rationale for environmentalism, Vladimir Ivanovich Vernadskii—despite having had a son who defected to the West to teach Russian history at Yale!—did his scientific work apparently unchallenged and died in 1945 loaded with honors, academic and otherwise. He has since become something of a cult figure in the' Soviet Union. He had been trained long before the Revolution, matriculating at St. Petersburg University in the same year John Wesley Powell took charge of the U.S. Geological Survey. (What a pity those two intellectually wide-ranging, socially concerned savants never met!) In the course of a long scientific career Vernadskii published in a dozen or more disciplines and founded two or three others, making major original contributions in crystallography, mineralogy, radiogeology, hydrology, soil sciences, the study of permafrost, the history of science, biogeochemistry, and much else. In 1926 he wrote a work titled *The Biosphere—another* word that was not coined the day before yesterday!—which is only beginning to be known, as it should be, in the West.

If Vernadskii had one scientific specialty, it was the geology—more specifically the geochemistry—of living organisms in the earth's crust; the processes by which bacteria fix iron ores, calcareous marine microorganisms deposit limestone, green algae by liberating oxygen make possible the predominance of silicates in the Earth's surface rocks, and organic decay forms oil and coal. In effect Vernadskii turned the assumptions of nineteenth-century Darwinism upside down. Life does not passively take its shape from the pressures of its material environment; it actively enters into that environment and changes it. The appearance of birds in the Mesozoic era was a more momentous event than the rise and fall of their spectacular contempories, the dinosaurs, because birds did far more to accelerate the tempo of biogenic migration than the lumbering saurians. More generally, the appearance and disappearance of plant and animal speicies does not have the all-importance it had for advocates of "struggle for existence" and "survival of the fittest": "One can equally . . . observe and study in living forms not their *variability* but their extraordinary *stability*," Vernadskii wrote. The total mass of living matter on Earth has not changed appreciably since the pre-Cambrian era; the greater part of it is composed of green plants, and photochemically the most important fraction of that is in the ocean. "The biosphere in its fundamental features has not changed in the course of geologic epochs since the Archeozoic Era," for at least two "milliards" (i.e., billions, in U.S. terms) of years. As a recent Soviet biographer of Vernadskii summed him up, "The geochemist visualizes the Earth's crust not as an inert stone mass, but as a sophisticated mechanism entraining inorganic matter into the 'whirlwind of life.'"

Vernadskii's Soviet admirers have done their utmost to tie him safely into the canons of conventional Marxist dialectical materialism. But there isn't an ounce of that kind of jargon in *The Biosphere*. Instead, there is more than a little poetic biogeological and cosmological Romanticism. Despite his stress on "the importance of quantitative study," Vernadskii gives away his underlying attitude by writing, for example: "The ancient religious institutions of humanity which considered the terrestrial creatures, men in particular, as *children of the sun* were closer to the truth than they think who see in terrestrial beings only ephemeral creation, the blind and accidental play of matter and terrestrial forces." To which Vernadskii's devoted Russian biographer R.K. Balandin chimed in, after paraphrasing the passage: "The fancies of the ancient people were a far cry from science. But they were not far from truth."

And now that stable regimen of Earth, unchanging for millions of years, has been revolutionized. The biosphere yields to the "noösphere," or sphere of thought—a word Vernadskii got, interestingly, from the devout French Catholic evolutionary scientist-priest Pierre Teilhard de Chardin!—and "the thought of *homo sapiens faber* is a new fact which overthrows the structure of the biosphere after myriads of centuries. . . . This process has been effected very rapidly in a space of insignificant time. The face of the earth has been transformed in an unrecognizable fashion," Vernadskii concluded, "and yet it is evident that the era of this transformation is only beginning."

The advent of human civilization "has been prepared by all paleontological history"—a surprisingly teleological statement from a hard-headed scientific materialist—and, once established in the noösphere, "human thought changes in an abrupt and radical fashion the course of natural processes, and modifies what we call the laws of nature." (Who here was in revolt against a predetermined destiny—the Americans, or this extraordinary Russian?) It is in this soaring and imaginative spirit, not in any crass Stalinist (or American techno-capitalist!) assertion of "mastery over nature," that people must approach their new task as the biosphere's care-takers and conservators. Humankind has begun to have an impact upon its home planet comparable to that of the profoundest natural geological processes; therefore, Vernadskii concluded, we ought to conduct ourselves responsibly as if we *were* collectively the equivalent of a mountain-building revolution or an Ice Age.

Interlude VII

Seven miles upstream along the Düssel, a minor tributary of the Rhine, lies the gorgelike Neander Valley. It takes its name from Joachim Neander, a seventeenth-century composer of hymn lyrics and tunes, most notably Lobe den Herren, den Mächtigen König der Ehren— *"Praise to the Lord, the Almighty, the King of Creation"—which congregations far away from the Rhine still sing. In the Felshofer Cave above that valley, quarry workers in 1856 while cleaning off a thick layer of loam found bones, including the vault of a human skull, but one that was not, it seemed,* exactly *human. It was large, but low, with a retreating forehead, a flat back, massive brow ridges, huge teeth, and a receding chin.*

The man, or creature, had possessed disproportionately short arms and legs; short, stubby hands and feet; a ribcage that anchored massive muscles; and thigh bones that were thick, curved shafts. And it was tens of thousands of years old. To the churchly composer-poet after whom the site was named, for whom history had begun a scant six millennia ago with the creation of Adam, such a disclosure would have been profoundly shocking; it is ironic that the place named in that religious writer's honor, the Neander Valley—Neander Tal, or Thal—*should have given its name to* Homo neanderthalensis, *as the scientists came to call him; Neanderthal Man.*

After vanishing utterly from Europe more than thirty thousand years ago, Homo neanderthalensis *fearsomely reappeared in the civilized modern imagination as the archetypical "cave man." Because the first investigators did not put his bones together quite properly, this pre-Adamite character seemed even more different from modern humanity than he really was; stooped, shambling, with his head hanging forward on a bull neck—"an aberrant side line in evolution," the* Britannica *called him as late as 1959. Nowadays we view him less condescendingly, as a variety of* Homo sapiens, *not a separate species;*

we in fact may contain some of his genes. However, as the first-found example of truly ancient man, he remains a challenge to all who still date humanity's arrival on this planet around 4004 B.C. A century ago, he became the first real test of Darwin's theory of evolution as applied to human beings.

Professor Rudolf Virchow, Germany's most renowned medical research scientist, who had examined the first Neanderthal find and pronounced it not an ancient fossil at all but a deformed specimen of relatively modern man, remained unsatisfied. "There exists a definite barrier separating man from the animal," he told an international congress on prehistoric anthropology in Moscow in 1892; the Darwinist's "missing link" between ape and man "remains a phantom." Fundamentalist Christians who would have been appalled at Virchow's hard-headed medical materialism—life, he asserted, was "merely the sum of physical and chemical actions"—took spiritual comfort from this authoritative negative pronouncement on Darwin, and quoted and requoted him in their own religious polemics for years afterward.

In the New World as in the Old the conviction was growing that our human ancestors had first appeared at a time far too remote to be derived by stringing together the genealogies one finds in Genesis 5 and 11. But also, in the New World as in the Old, conspicuous holdouts rejected this growing human-evolutionist consensus—holdouts who, if they lacked Professor Virchow's impressive academic credentials, rivaled him in political clout. Rudolf Virchow, a dogged opponent of Bismarck's rearmament policies, chaired for many years the powerful finance committee of Germany's Reichstag; William Jennings Bryan, an equally determined foe of Woodrow Wilson's rearmament policies, received three times his party's nomination for President of the United States.

EIGHT

The Majority Has Always Been Moral

The American nation, historically considered, abounds in tensions and contradictions: religion *and* rationality; revolution *and* order; science *and* free will. But the American people as a whole have not found it necessary to make a choice between any of these. In fact, although perhaps unconsciously, they have found it necessary *not* to make a choice, but to keep each of these polarities going as proof against the declension of either part of each dualism—science into paralyzing determinism, revolution into anarchy, religion into superstition. The indivisibility of the "one nation" to which they pledge allegiance is that of a three-legged stool; take away any one of the legs, and the stool cannot stand.

1. Politics in the Language of Religion

"We meet in the midst of a nation brought to the verge of moral, political, and material ruin." The words could have been spoken in America during the late 1970s or early 1980s by any of a dozen nationally televised evangelists on the religious Right. But in 1892 they were the rallying cry of an insurgent movement on the political Left. Its manifesto continued in language those religious rightists a century later would have considered heretical in the extreme: "The fruits of the toil of millions are boldly stolen to build up colossal fortunes for a few. . . . From the same prolific womb of governmental injustice we breed the two classes—tramps and millionaires."

The delegates to the first and, as it turned out, last presidential nominating convention of the People's (Populist) Party, meeting in Omaha on the Fourth of July, 1892, greeted the reading of this fiery preamble and of the successive planks of their party's platform—

government ownership and operation of the railroads under civil service, a graduated income income tax, free coinage of silver at a ratio to gold of 16 to 1— with an enthusiasm Populism's first formal historian, John D. Hicks, aptly likened to "a regular Baptist camp meeting chorus." There should be "little wonder," Professor Hicks affirmed, "that a platform so christened should come to have among Populists a sort of religious sanction. These demands were not like ordinary political demands—they were a sacred creed."

Rather than debate a political proposal on its merits as policy, Americans have always shown a tendency to translate it into other terms; for example, into a constitutional case that can be tried in court. In addition to that jurisprudential bent they have also manifested an urge to translate political questions into *moral* ones. Thus, to oppose a desired course of political action comes to be judged by its adherents not merely as unwise or impractical but as downright sinful. Nor have politically concerned Americans stayed within a carefully circumscribed "civic" morality, their Constitution's First Amendment to the contrary notwithstanding. As the Populist example makes evident, political discourse in America can quite naturally fall into the vocabulary and rhythms of a specific religious tradition.

Toward the end of the solid, 450-page debater's brief he produced for the 1892 campaign, the People's Party's first and only presidential candidate, James B. Weaver—a sometime Civil War general, like most Republican and one or two Democratic presidential nominees of that generation—described the movement he headed as "the religion of the Master in motion among men." For the coexistence of abject poverty and ostentatious wealth in the modern world Weaver found in the New Testament a metaphor in the figure of the poor beggar Lazarus in heaven and the rich man Dives in hell (Luke 16: 19–26): "two representative characters" who, the candidate argued, appear and reappear throughout history, "side by side in disturbing contrast just before the tragic stage of revolution is reached." In the Old Testament, Weaver found imagery for Americans' political and economic plight as of the 1890s in the Book of Exodus: "In their flight from their task masters the people have about reached the Red Sea. . . . Either the floods will be parted for us and close, as of old, upon our pursuers, or a life and death struggle will ensue between oppressors and oppressed."

General Weaver, like many other politically tough-talking Americans then and afterward, stopped short of actually proposing revolution. That extreme expedient, he hopefully prophesied, should not be necessary, because "thanks to the all-conquering strength of Christian enlightenment we are at the dawn of the golden age of popular power." Not revolution but fusion was Populism's ultimate destiny. Four years after Weaver's campaign the party, although indulging itself in a separate vice-presidential nomination, threw its presidential hopes in with the Democrats and William Jennings Bryan—who had already electrified the Democratic National Convention of 1896 with a speech that propelled him from merely regional notability to national fame; a speech capped by the frequently quoted punch line which transformed it from a political argument into a sermon: "You shall not press down upon the brow of labor this crown of thorns, you shall not crucify mankind upon a cross of gold."

Bryan's political style easily shifted from a specific religious confession to a more generalized ethical judgment. "The day is past," he defiantly proclaimed after the disastrous election of 1920, "when the liquor machines and Wall Street interests . . . can successfully dictate to the great moral majority of the nation." To my best knowledge this is historically the first use by an American politician of the specific phrase "moral majority"—a startlingly different definition of the term, however, from that given it by those who have so labeled themselves since Jerry Falwell founded Moral Majority, Inc., in 1979. Falwell and many of his partisans would have agreed with what Bryan said about the "liquor machines"—but, Wall Street? In the Reagan era, when the stock market—throughout almost all of the eighties— rode high and wide, if not exactly handsome? Hardly; they would have seen an attack on that capitalist shrine as radical and unAmerican.

Radicalism—or, more precisely, what conservatives perceived as radicalism—and evangelical religion had been allies long before Bryan; think of the preachers who were mobbed and sometimes murdered for standing against slavery before that stance became expedient or fashionable in the North. But conservatives in Bryan's time or earlier had their own religious rationales. William McKinley, Methodist and Republican, Bryan's victorious opponent in 1896 and 1900, was as pious as the Great Commoner, albeit more stodgy. If Populists, Democrats, and Progressive Republicans could castigate the "malefactors of great wealth"—Theodore Roosevelt's term—in language borrowed from the prophets of ancient Israel who preached doom upon those who "beat my people to pieces, and grind the faces of the poor" (Isaiah 3:15), conservative Republicans such as George F. Baer in 1902 could defend those same alleged malefactors as "Christian men to whom God in his infinite wisdom has given the control of the property interests of this country."

It may well be that American politicians, Left, Right, or in-between, have had to employ religious imagery perforce, for want of any other kind. Rejecting the aristocratic symbolisms available to cultures long existent in the Old World (e.g., the glorious pomp of a British coronation), Americans had tried for a while to make do with republican symbols derived from classical antiquity, housing their governments in Greek temples or Roman forums and debating each other under pseudonyms like Caesar and Cato, Publius and Brutus. Unfortunately for that purpose—and despite their anxiety lest Roman republican history repeat itself in America (above, chapter 2)—a two-thousand-year gulf lay between the Americans and the hands-on politics of republican Greece and Rome. Nor was the nineteenth century as attuned to classical values as the eighteenth had been. Some few United States Senators might have looked grand decked out in togas—Calhoun, perhaps, or more recently Arthur Vandenberg; most would simply have appeared ridiculous. And aside from their own Constitution, which after a century's use was beginning to take on a patina of age, what other historical resource did late-Victorian Americans have to draw on in common, except the Bible?

Very occasionally in nineteenth-century America an important political figure might have been classically christened Hannibal or Ulysses or Lucius Quintus Cincinnatus, but they were far outnumbered by people named Gabriel or Levi or Benjamin or David or Samuel or Nathan or Noah or Stephen or Joseph (Supreme Court justices, all!); or Timothy, Daniel, Abel, Jeremiah, Lot, Isaac, Amos, Gideon, Aaron, Zachariah (all given names of cabinet members), if not an occasional Matthew, Mark, Luke, or John. It was a culture, moreover, which *knew* the original Biblical provenance of such names, in a far more intimate way than it knew the Apology of Socrates to the Athenians or the Struggle of the Orders in ancient Rome. A politician threfore could employ a metaphor from the Bible, as Bryan did with the Crucifixion, and come across to a mass audience not as a rummager in antiquities but as an articulator of its own deepest folk values.

To be sure, in the heat of oratorical battle this kind of appeal could get out of hand. A poignant example occurred in the campaign of 1932 when incumbent President Herbert Hoover was standing for re-election. Buffeted by the storms of Depression, Hoover struck his partisans as fitting to a T the much-overworked image of the captain at the helm of the Ship of State. Roscoe Conkling Simmons of Illinois, in seconding Hoover's nomination for another term, so characterized him: "I watch him on the bridge. I note him most when the storm is wild." Then, daringly—and, some might have thought, with questionable taste—Simmons compared Hoover to "the Captain of the vessel of eternal hope" who, "once begged by his followers to speak to the loosened elements that shook the sea . . . smiled the sea into ripples and the winds into zephyrs"—prompting from those voyagers on the Sea of Galilee (according to Mark 4:41) the cry "What manner of man is this, that even the wind and the sea obey him?" Even so, the Republican orator in Chicago in 1932 declaimed, "Around our captain now rolls the sea of circumstance. . . . The winds of a disturbed world beat upon his face. But mark him. Unwearied and unmoved he stands . . . What manner of man is he?" Surely a man as devout, and as basically modest, as Herbert Hoover might have blushed.

In that same city of Chicago two weeks later Franklin Roosevelt broke with historic tradition by flying out to accept in person the Democrats' nomination to oppose Hoover. Taking office the following March, Roosevelt delivered a short, rousing inaugural address, or sermon, that abounded in Biblical references or paraphrases: "plague of locusts" (Exodus 10:14–15); "when there is no vision the people perish" (Proverbs (29:18); "The money changers have fled from their high seats in the temple of our civilization" (Matthew (21:12); "not to be ministered unto but to minister" (Mark 10:45). That this kind of homily continued to hit home to an American political congregation—and no politician as intuitively sensitive to that congregation's hopes and fears as FDR would have played upon that particular set of emotional chords had they *not* been effective—furnishes evidence yet again for G. K. Chesterton's characterization of America as "a nation with the soul of a church."

2. Democratic Choice Along the Sawdust Trail

Franklin Roosevelt's personal religion—insofar as he would or could put it into words—was of a decorous sort, taught to him in boyhood by his Groton headmaster and embodied in the stately language of the Book of Common Prayer. That had emphatically not been the kind of religion practiced by most WASP and Black Protestant Americans during the century within which FDR had been born. For countless thousands of them, being "born again"—or, more starkly, "saved"—had been a wrenching conversion experience, sometimes undergone in agonized solitude, more often in the company of excited crowds. Televangelism today at its most vehement can hardly match the nineteenth-century tent revivals' or camp meetings' fervent hymn singing, shouts and cries, leaps and swoons, lengthy extempore prayers, and bombastic preaching. (Abraham Lincoln once remarked—whether deferring to popular taste of his own day or truly expressing his own preference is hard to say—that he liked to see a minister deliver his sermon as if he were fighting bees!) According to that revivalist tradition, religious conversion comes as a crisis, not unlike that of a fever; sudden, dramatic, and manifest in a complete transformation of character, or at least of one's emotional state.

William James, in the two chapters on "Conversion" in his classic *The Varieties of Religious Experience* (1902), described and documented many examples of such transformations. He pointed out also that in those churches which were founded or focused upon a revivalist understanding of religion, "unless there has been a crisis of this sort, salvation is only offered, not effectively received"; some of them premised admission to membership upon a person's having undergone such a crisis. James, with his usual pluralistic caution, took note of other kinds of religious believers in America who "have set no such store by instanteous conversion". Instead, they regularly participated in an accustomed liturgy, or acquired religious convictions gradually by precept and example from family and congregation, or put themselves by calm introspection "in tune with the Infinite"—or simply spent their Sabbaths with a large newspaper or a long fishing pole. Nevertheless William McLaughlin, an acute historian of the revival movement (and biographer of Billy Sunday and Billy Graham), does not too much exaggerate when he claims that "revivalism has so permeated American culture from its beginning that to write a history of revivalism would be to write a history of America."

More specifically, revivalism has permeated America's *political* culture. Americans have tended to characterize political choices not merely as moral judgments but as "decisions," in the way the

Billy Graham Crusaders use that word; that is, as either/or absolutes. Not typically, and not normatively, perhaps; Henry Clay's classic defense of pragmatic political accommodation—"all legislation, all government, all society, is formed upon the principle of mutual concession, politeness, comity, courtesy. . . . I bow to you to-day because you bow to me"—may more accurately describe the way Americans have handled their political differences, most of the time, than do General Weaver's cataclysmic alternatives or W. J. Bryan's moral absolutes. "Let no one who is not above the frailties of our common nature disdain compromises," Clay cried. However, a previous speaker in that same great Senate debate in 1850, William H. Seward—like Henry Clay a serious presidential contender—had declared: "I think all legislative compromises radically wrong and essentially vicious"; and presumably viciousness has no rights that righteousness is bound to respect.

Choose the right, reject the wrong; shun temptation and be "born again." "Once to every man and nation/Comes the moment to decide," James Russell Lowell wrote in the course of the furious debate over slavery in the 1840s; "In the strife of truth with falsehood/For the good or evil side . . . And the choice goes by forever/Twixt that darkness and that light." Although no revivalist in his personal, rather dusty Boston Brahmin religious creed, Lowell in his poem "The Present Crisis" boldly compounded religious with political revivalism. Political enough to be quoted in full forty years later by lifelong radical activist Wendell Phillips in a speech advocating—among other things—woman suffrage, the overthrow of the Tsar, and the independence of Ireland, these stanzas were also evangelical enough to have found their way in the twentieth century into many a "mainline" Protestant hymnal, often set to a stirring Welsh march-tune:

> Truth forever on the scaffold,
> Wrong forever on the throne;
> Yet the scaffold sways the future:
> And behind the dim unknown
> Standeth God, within the shadow,
> Keeping watch above His own.

"For we wrestle not against flesh and blood," St. Paul proclaimed, "but against principalities, against powers, against the rulers of the darkness of this world, against spiritual wickedness in high places" (Ephesians 6:12). How tempting it often has been, when American political controversy becomes close and hot, to characterize one's opponents not as "flesh and blood"—sharing desires and aspirations concededly similar to one's own, differing only in the tactical details proposed for achieving them—but as malign counter-forces: "monarchists" or "mobocrats" in one era, agents of "the Communist conspiracy" or of the "the power structure" in another. (Indeed, against such principalities and powers as Nazism or South African apartheid compromise can certainly come to seem, in William Seward's words, "radically wrong and essentially vicious.") Against such opponents, at a peak of political confrontation such as the 1840s or the 1960s, the warrior for the faith puts forward not bargaining points but ultimatums; in 1960s political terminology "non-negotiable demands." What counts in such a situation is not rational construction of a convincing case but emotional commitment to a cause.

As long as revivalism tinged the secular political culture, its style of behavior and rhetoric would continue to invigorate (or infect!) American politics. Its folkways would persist even in milieus from which its specific religious vocabulary had vanished. In the 1960s, often, a political congregation responded to a radical speaker's demand for freedom now (*right* now, this instant) with cries of "Right on!"—cries which came at pauses in the oratory where, earlier in the nation's history, audiences would have shouted "Praise the Lord!" or "Amen!" At the apex of the radical insurgency came George McGovern, who, upon being nominated for president in 1972, proceeded to deliver an acceptance speech which was structured like a revival sermon, complete with altar call. "Come home, America," that Methodist-preacher's-son-turned-presidential-candidate invited, and under those words could be heard echoes from an old gospel hymn used in the Dwight L. Moody evangelistic campaigns a century before, with its haunting refrain, "Come home, come home. . . . Ye who are weary, come home." (Indeed, the clustering of many and various radical causes in 1972 around that very conventional minister's son from strait-laced South Dakota is one of the more surprising ironies in American political history.)

Revivalism constituted a militant form of the evangelical Protestantism which for generations had considered itself the national norm; normative not only for religious doctrine but also for personal behavior, public morality, and cultural values. Even in Bryan's time that claim could no longer so confidently be made. Not only had it increasingly to share the stage with other religious

186

persuasions—Catholic, Jewish, Christian Scientist, and the faiths of the Far East—but also with a world view that challenged *all* religions. For many of the intellectual generation rising to maturity in and after the 1890s, in the words of their chronicler Vernon Louis Parrington, God had vanished from their ken and "a benevolent, egocentric universe was become unthinkable." The cosmos newly being unfolded by chemistry and physics—"vaster and colder" even than that disclosed a generation earlier by historical geology and evolutionary biology—seemed "a vibrating mechanism shot through with energy. . . . impersonal, amoral"; and within that mechanism a human being "is but a single form of imprisoned energy, localized for a brief instant and rising to momentary consciousness in the eternal flux." Gone were the optimisms, whether materialist or idealist in outlook, that had sustained such thinkers' Victorian forebears. "At a stroke the benevolent cosmos of the fathers, wherein for generations men had been providing themselves with sure refuges, was swept away," Parrington wrote;

> and with its passing passed the old faiths—faith in freedom of the will, in a purposive providence, in a universe that had been long in travail to bring forth man, its last and dearest offspring for whom all things work together for good. And with the decay of the traditional faiths the younger generation was left to wander as best it might upon the bleak tablelands of impersonal energy.

The old-time religion in America, from then onward, could expect to be buffeted by much chillier winds of doctrine. "We have grown used . . . to a Godless universe," Joseph Wood Krutch would write three years after the Scopes "monkey trial," "but we are not yet accustomed to one which is loveless as well, and only when we have so become shall we realize what atheism really means."

3. Tablelands of Unbelief

Every young generation tends to overdramatize its own predicament, as if nothing so daunting had ever happened to anyone else. But those tablelands had been visited before. "When I consider . . . the little space which I fill, and even can see, engulfed in the infinite immensity of spaces of which I am ignorant, and which know me not, I am frightened, and am astonished at being here rather than there," Blaise Pascal wrote more than three hundred years ago. "Man is but a reed, the most feeble thing in nature. . . . A vapour, a drop of water suffices to kill him." Nevertheless, Pascal bravely added, a human being is nobler than the universe which crushes him because he is a *thinking* reed; he knows the advantage the universe has over him, and this the universe does not know.

"All our dignity consists, then, in thought," the eloquent French scientist-theologian concluded. "By it we must elevate ourselves, and not by space and time which we cannot fill. Let us endeavor, then, to think well." But the icy winds sweeping over those high, dark plateaus of speculation late in the nineteenth century might carry with them the power to extinguish even Pascal's small gesture of dignified defiance. For if, as Parrington put it, "men are physical beings who can do no other than obey the laws of the physical universe"; if "in the vast indifferentism of nature they are inconsequential pawns in a game that to human reason has no meaning or rules"—then that bending reed in the wind might possess only the *illusion* that it was thinking.

"From the magnet which chooses between steel and zinc, to the philosopher who chooses between good and evil, the difference is one of degree, not of kind," wrote a contributor to a list of "Notes on the Progress of Science for the Year 1869"—the same year in which John Wesley Powell made his epic journey down the Colorado. The philosopher's field of mental activity was implicitly no more exalted a realm than the magnet's field of force. In both cases *choice*, in the sense of an action consciously taken of one's own accord, did not really exist—and Billy Graham-ish "decisions," whether at political rallies or at revival meetings, became simply meaningless. To attach ethical value to the insensible movement of a compass needle toward magnetic north would be absurd; given a magnetic field of sufficient strength, could one then count up a "moral majority" of compass needles?

On June 29, 1870, in an address to Harvard's Phi Beta Kappa Society titled "Mechanism in Thought and Morals," Oliver Wendell Holmes, Senior—"the autocrat of the breakfast table"— paid tribute, in his own bookish, long-winded fashion, to the disconcerting notion that all mental work can thus be reduced to, even identified with, mechanical impulse. "The flow of thought," he argued, although "incidentally capable of being modified to a greater or less extent by conscious effort," was "like breathing, essentially mechanical and necessary." Mental qualities, he suspected, were "as susceptible of measurement as the aurora borealis or the changes of the weather." "The effect of age, of disease, of a blow, of intoxication" showed "how intimate is the alliance of memory with the material condition of the brain." Sudden changes of emotional states were "automatic, involuntary . . . entirely self-evolved by a hidden organic process." Half buried in Holmes's diffuse, endlessly digressive discourse lay some questions that sounded startlingly modern; in fact, neurologists are still asking them, albeit in more sophisticated ways:

> The brain being a double organ, like the eye, we naturally ask whether we can think with one side of it, as we can see with one eye; whether the two sides commonly work together; whether one side may not be stronger than the other; whether one side may not be healthy, and the other diseased; and what consequences may follow from these various conditions. . . . We have a field of vision; have we a field of thought?

In the experimental laboratory founded at Leipzig five years later, from which would emerge a relentlessly mechanistic physiological psychology, Wilhelm Wundt and his disciples would have considered Holmes's modest heresies old hat. In Victorian Boston, however, one still had to apologize, even to an audience of scholars, for studying the brain at all. But Holmes—who in addition to writing poems, novels, and essays, also occupied the Parkman Chair of Anatomy and Physiology at Harvard Medical School—insisted upon the necessity for such study: "A slight congestion or softening of the brain shows the least materialistic of philosophers that he must recognize the strict dependence of mind upon its organ in the only condition of life with which we are experimentally acquainted."

Little did genial, gentle Oliver Wendell Holmes suspect how far such researches were destined to go. Holmes referred to the brain as the mind's organ; Patricia Smith Churchland in *Neurophilosophy* (1986) declared flatly that "the mind *is* the brain"—and not even the "highest" part of the brain at that. Nor did mind possess even the autonomy of emergence out of something less, as other philosophers of mind insisted. According to Churchland modern experimental neurology was blowing away much more than the immaterial "soul"; such "deeply felt folk psychological concepts" as memory, learning, and consciousness "are either fragmenting or will be replaced by more adequate categories." From a proposed algebraic solution of the problem of sensorimotor coordination, for example, this reductionist writer believes, can be derived—eventually—all the activities of the human intellect; and thus the ultimate achievement of Pascal's "thinking reed" would be to demonstrate its own nonexistence.

"What is man, that thou art mindful of him?" It remained possible in Holmes's (or Parrington's, or even in Churchland's) time to answer that question in the old-fashioned way—but it had become a great deal harder. Holmes tried to fight the logical consequences of his own inquiry, maintaining that while thought by 1870 had come to seem more mechanical in nature, morality now seemed far less so—a parting shot at the Calvinist theology which by Holmes's time was in full retreat in his native New England. What had started out as an investigation at the cutting edge of the new experimental neuropsychology had transformed itself into a *confessio fidei:* "I claim the right to eliminate all mechanical ideas which have crowded into the sphere of intelligent choice between right and wrong."

But the idea which has been unceremoniously booted out the front door has a way of sneaking in through a back window. Harriet Beecher Stowe, despite having worked her way (as all of Lyman Beecher's children had to) out of her morally paralyzing ancestral Calvinism, yet had to confess that the new scientific outlook might carry implications equally paralyzing: "Nature in her teaching," Stowe observed in 1869, "is a more tremendous and inexorable Calvinist than the Cambridge Platform." The theological predestination which had undermined human freedom in Jonathan Edwards's time was returning in the guise of scientific determinism; and the deterministic conclusions to which the neurologists were coming seemed reinforced, as Parrington pointed out, by what was going on in physics and chemistry. Even Emerson, as vigorous a champion of untrammeled human free will as ever lived in America, conceded a great deal to this rising tide of necessity, secularizing the former Calvinistic predestination into impersonal "Fate," in an essay bearing that title: "If we thought men were free in the sense that in a single exception one fantastical will could prevail over the law of things, it were all one as if a child's hand could pull down the sun."

4. Science: Calvinism's New Guise

"A common opinion prevails that the juice has ages ago been pressed out of the free-will controversy." Not so, countered William James in 1884. Quite the contrary: "I know of no subject less worn out." The tortuous theological defenses of determinism by Calvinist divines, long since rejected by a wide variety of nineteenth-century Americans (above, chapter 3) had given place to a tough-minded philosophical and scientific argument "that those parts of the universe already laid down absolutely appoint and decree what the other parts shall be." To the dismay of many, this newer kind of determinism, unlike the kind Calvinist sermons had made familiar to Americans of earlier generations, advertised itself as frankly— even belligerently—nonreligious. *Qué sera sera*—dictated not by divine decree but by pressures of the physical environment, by the inescapable patterns of one's genes, by electrochemical firings within one's skull, or by the compulsion of one's glands.

"The dilemma of determinism," to use James's own title for his discourse on the subject, was that a world of human experience from which science seemed to have banished all vestiges of the supernatural appeared devoid of morality as well. To make his point, James recounted with macabre humor the confession of a recent wife-murderer in Brockton, Massachusetts, whose victim—after having been shot four times—asked him: "You didn't do it on purpose, did you, dear?" To which the killer, "as he raised a rock and smashed her skull, replied . . . 'No, I didn't do it on purpose.'" From what James described as "the mild . . . self-satisfaction" of that statement it is but a short step to the excuse, offered by young criminal gang members to Officer Krupke in *West Side Story*, that they do what they do not out of any intrinsic malice in their hearts but because "we're sociologically distoibed." Many—today as much as in William James's time—would agree with the philosopher's reaction to this kind of predestination, "that, although a perfect mechanical fit to the rest of the universe, it is a bad moral fit"— as bad, in its own way, as Jonathan Edwards's grim insistence that if God before you were born had doomed you to Hell, there was absolutely nothing you could do about it.

Life being what it is, "we constantly have to make judgments of regret"; yet if the determinists are right such judgments are inherently irrational. Humanly we want to call the murder "bad," which "means, if it mean anything at all, that the thing ought not to be"; determinism, however, "in denying that anything else can be in its stead, virtually defines the universe as a place in which what ought to be is impossible." To stand by our moral conviction and insist that "though it *couldn't* be, yet it *would* be a better universe with something different from this Brockton murder in it," is in effect to espouse a deep metaphysical pessimism á la Schopenhauer—"It is absurd to regret the murder alone . . . What we should regret is [the] whole frame of things"—or else be forced into the fatuous optimism of Dr. Pangloss in *Candide:* whatever is, is right; all is as well as possible in the bests of all possible worlds. How can there be a moral majority, or even a moral minority, James was asking, if there can be no such thing as responsible choice?

Earlier in his own personal odyssey, contemplating this bad yet seemingly inescapable condition of life, William James had fallen into deep depression, which climaxed one hideous night in "a horrible fear of my own existence," so wounding an experience that "for months I was unable to go out into the dark alone." James recorded his turn back toward the light in a passage in his diary (April 30, 1870), in which he cried out—against all reason as he then understood it—that "my first act of free will shall be to believe in free will." *Here I stand; God help me, I can do no other*, as Martin Luther had said before him.

"But you didn't need to jump prematurely to such a depressing conclusion about the cosmos," a few of James's own scientific contemporaries might have assured him; nor have seized so desperately anti-rational a way out. The assumed physical foundations of the "block-universe" determinism James so detested were about to transform themselves into something very different. The thoughts and experiments of people like Albert Michelson, the Polish immigrant's son from Murphy's Camp, Nevada, whose disproof of the existence of any light-bearing "ether" would irretrievably shatter one pillar of that mechanical block-universe, or the shy, profound physical chemist Willard Gibbs, who argued in 1876 that the inexorable erosion of the world by entropy was not quite so fearsome a destiny as at first it had seemed, were beginning to modify prevailing notions about the universe (as Gibbs's biographer puts it) "in a direction away from the almost Calvinistic determinism so prevalent in the scientific thinking of the nineteenth century." The science of the twentieth century would deal not in steel-hard substance moving in mathematically predetermined patterns but in ghostly, elusive quanta into whose movements had to be factored a formal mathematical principle of uncertainty.

Practitioners of "softer" disciplines such as sociology or experimental psychology, however, would prove more reluctant than physicists to abandon determinism. Indeed, a deterministic mindset continues to express itself even today in many freshman "psych" or "sosh" or even "poli sci" textbooks. The spirited but ultimately sterile debate that raged for half a century or more over "nature" versus "nurture"—asking which is more decisive in shaping character and behavior, heredity or environment—was, strictly speaking, not a debate at all; for both sides in that debate assumed that something external to the person, be it genes, instincts, Oedipal fixations, conditioning, or membership in a given socioeconomic class, bound and molded what that person really was.

James, however, was not about to abandon his hard-won existential freedom. Conceding, as the professor of psychology he was, that "the acts we perform are always the result of outward discharges from the nervous centres, and that these outward discharges are themselves the result of impressions from the external world," William James insisted nevertheless that down at the bottom of the stimulus-response loop there had to be an autonomous "x" capable by its own volition of turning the response in one direction or another. "Any mind, constructed on the triadic-reflex pattern," he wrote in 1881, "must first get its impression from the object which it confronts; then define what the object is, and decide what active measures its presence demands; and finally react." To dismiss this element of willed choice as mere subjectivism, as the more consistent mechanists insisted we must, was to miss the point. "So far as we can see, the given world is there only for the sake of the operation," James insisted:

> To bid the man's subjective interests be passive till truth express itself from out the environment, is to bid the sculptor's chisel be passive till the statue express itself from out the stone. Operate we must! and the only choice left us is that between operating to poor or to rich results.

At that time psychology and philosophy had not yet fully separated themselves as disciplines. Thus it was both logical and easy for someone like James to move from one kind of study of "the mind," as embodied in 1890 in his trail-blazing *Principles of Psy-*

chology (still important, though neglected by most present-day psychologists), to the other kind, as expressed in the public lectures he gave in 1906 and 1907 that were subsequently published as *Pragmatism*. In philosophy as in psychology it is the results, rich or poor, of our operations that really count, James would argue. "Truths" consist in the consequences of actions: "Truth *happens* to an idea." One finds truth not by intuiting or deducing it but by doing something, and learning from the experience. James's own way of finding out just how truth happened was fundamentally individualistic; in many respects his master spirit was still old self-reliant Emerson. But his younger contemporary John Dewey socialized the process: the meaning of truth would be disclosed in the consequences of our *collective* action, disciplined by one another's shared experiences and—Dewey hoped—by the agreed-upon data of science. Even without the sure refuges of the old benevolent cosmos, regretfully dismissed by Parrington, human beings through their pooled social intelligence could deal with the cold universe on at least equal terms. Although in coming decades many American social scientists would strive for a "value-free" social science—such that by the 1930s, as William Graebner sums up their conclusion, "it no longer seemed possible or reasonable to justify democracy as a function of values or moral assumptions"—John Dewey dissented, continuing to insist throughout his long and embattled life that a freely communicating democratic social intelligence could achieve results properly describable as "moral" or "good". Nor did such an ethical stance necessarily require one to embrace traditional religion as its sanction. William James might daringly bridge world-views which seemed forever put asunder by titling one of his key essays "Reflex Action and Theism," but few in his own philosophical camp followed James toward that redeveloped Promised Land. As one distinguished professor of American history and responsible political activist who admired John Dewey told some of his students early in the 1950s, "I am a pragmatist because it lets me make moral judgments without invoking spooks."

5. The Great Educator and the Great Commoner

The political implications of philosophical pragmatism, at least of Dewey's sort, were momentous. Indeed, against the many erosions of practicing republicanism in our own time John Dewey's resolution and synthesis of science and politics may still be the only program that might work. In his vision for the future, democratic decision-making meant something after all; no matter what various fatalists said, you could discuss the options, make your choice, count the votes, and abide by the result. You were not forbidden to make political judgments by your lack of expertise, as elitist social scientists were beginning to insist, nor were you foreclosed from entire areas of legislative experimentation by deterministic tenets of "natural law," as the hardboiled Social Darwinists claimed. As one bright high schooler in an honors American History class in 1987 summed up that classic controversy, "If you believe in evolution, you just let it happen; if you believe in pragmatism, you do it yourself."

However, pragmatic social democracy such as John Dewey professed had set itself an all-but-impossible intellectual goal: to revalidate, in acceptable modern scientific terms, a kind of politics that had been founded upon truths held to be self-evident, while denying on scientific grounds that *anything* can be self-evidently true. "Our thoughts and beliefs 'pass' so long as nothing challenges them," William James had observed in the sixth of his lectures on *Pragmatism;* but sometime, somewhere, if they were to claim the status of truths they had to be verified. And how, pray tell, a critic of pragmatism could properly have asked, does one go about verifying the proposition that people, created equal, are endowed with unalienable rights to life, liberty, and the pursuit of happiness? "Truth forever on the scaffold/Wrong forever on the throne," James Russell Lowell had declaimed. Could one continue to cry out against enthroned injustice and martyred innocence if words like "truth" and "wrong" no longer carried the meaning they had had for Jefferson and Lincoln and Paine?

The social determinists—except for those who professed Marxism, of whom there were not yet very many in America—were of not much help in resolving this difficulty. Their dean, William Graham Sumner, published *Folkways,* his magnum opus, in 1906 (one year before James's *Pragmatism*). The logic of that book has been enormously influential in the ongoing push toward ethical relativism, even among people who have not read it or who reject Sumner's laissez-faire economics. Sumner titled one of his chapters "The Mores Can Make Anything Right and Prevent Condemnation of Anything"—cannibalism, incest, the killing of the old, human sacrifice, gladiatorial games; or in other settings, civil liberties or equality before the law. Mores, the author wrote in his preface, "arise no one knows whence or how"; "they very largely control human undertakings"; and they can be purposefully modified "only to a limited extent." John Dewey's faith that society could be changed at the grass roots through progressive education must fail, Sumner argued, for the mores ultimately would determine what should be considered "progressive." The only kind of education that counted, in Sumner's view, was in the scientific method or, more broadly, "the critical faculty," which *might*, he hinted, gradually permeate society and become habitual. Meanwhile all one could do was stoically wait for the mores to change.

As previously noted, moral and political judgments had always been difficult for Americans to disentangle. Now their judgments in those areas had to pass scientific muster as well. In other historical periods in America, democratic moralism and rational liberalism had been able to overcome their inherent mutual tensions and go hand-in-hand. Southern Baptists had worked faithfully to carry out Jefferson's political agenda (including its insistence on church-state separation!); later on, fervent evangelicals in the North and West had allied themselves with intellectuals, not only in the antislavery crusade but also—as Timothy Smith has convincingly shown in *Revivalism and Social Reform* (1957)—in a host of other humanitarian and reform causes. But in John Dewey's time this historic alliance seemed to have broken down. When push came to shove, many who were both morally motivated and politically activist seemed inclined to take the morality and let the science go. What one found in America, the educator summed up in a 1922 essay titled "The American Intellectual Frontier," was "social and political liberalism combined with intellectual illiberality."

Dewey paid a handsome tribute to the Midwest, "the prairie country . . . the center of active social philanthropies and political progressivism," the chief home of "the church-going classes, those who have come under the influence of evangelical Christianity"; people who, according to Dewey, embodied "the spirit of kindly goodwill toward classes which are at an economic disadvantage." This class had "followed Lincoln in the abolition of slavery, and it followed [Theodore] Roosevelt in his denunciation of 'bad' corporations and aggregations of wealth." However, it had "never had an interest in ideas as ideas, nor in science and art for what they may do in liberating and elevating the human spirit. Science and art as far as they refine and polish life, afford 'culture,' mark stations on an upward social road, yes: but as emancipations, as radical guides to life, no." Such folk in the 1920s, unlike the discontented literary intellectuals who scorned them, felt no need to be emancipated from or radically guided toward anything; and the contemporary political figure who most aptly symbolized their aspirations and limitations, Dewey asserted, was William Jennings Bryan.

Make no mistake about it, Dewey cautioned: "Mr. Bryan is a typical democratic figure. Economically and politically he has stood for and with the masses, not radically but 'progressively' " in revolt against privilege, and justice demanded that his usefulness in that role be recognized. He had, moreover, not turned reactionary in sour old age, as most interpreters of Bryan's role in the Scopes "monkey trial" have tended to assume. He wanted the Democratic Party platform of 1920, for example, to endorse government ownership of the railroads—an old Populist demand—to which he added the telegraph, telephone, and merchant marine as well; in a speech in Louisiana that same year he came out for government ownership and development of the nation's water power, anticipating by a dozen years the creation of TVA. In a more reflective mood in 1922 Bryan declared, attributing the idea to Jefferson, that there existed "naturally two parties in every country, one which drew to itself those who trusted the people, the other which as naturally drew to itself those who distrusted the people." It was, and in some quarters still is, orthodox Democratic Party doctrine—and the passage occurs in a book by Bryan titled *In His Image*, the main purpose of which was to rebut and overthrow the theory of evolution! "Civilization is measured," he declared in the same book, "by the moral revolt against the cruel doctrine developed by Darwin."

These ideas of the Great Commoner, John Dewey warned, and those of his constituent folk, could not be neatly separated into religious versus political categories; "There is a genuine and effective connection between the political and the doctrinal directions of his activity, and between the popular responses they call out." Dewey might have added that the anti-evolution crusade, so easily dismissable by "modernists" as a regressive survival of an outmoded attitude, had its popular social-democratic side.

Bryan had raised the Darwin issue as early as 1904, in his widely delivered lecture "The Prince of Peace," and he raised it in a characteristic and significant way. The Great Commoner objected to

Darwinism not only because he believed it would cause people to lose "the consciousness of God's presence" in their daily life but also because it represented them as having reached their present state of existence "by the operation of the law of hate—the merciless law by which the strong crowd out and kill off the weak." A year later, having just read Darwin's *The Descent of Man*, Bryan confessed his misgivings to the sociologist E. A. Ross: "Such a conception of man's origin would weaken the cause of democracy and strengthen class pride and the power of wealth." At that time Bryan was still considered presidential timber; his opponent in the election of 1908 would be the temperamentally conservative William Howard Taft—who was theologically heretical enough to have been turned down for the presidency of Yale, and who *did* believe in evolution. Given the track record of both men, a beleaguered politically liberal intellectual of a later generation might well look back and judge—however wincing at the thought!—that the fundamentalist Bryan would have made a better president than the Unitarian Taft.

World War I, which prompted Bryan's resignation as Secretary of State in protest at Woodrow Wilson's war-trending policies, gave him an opportunity to say, in effect, "I told you so": "There are only two attitudes that man can assume in relation to his fellow; . . . he is either restrained by the consciousness of the ties of kinship, . . . or he hunts for prey with the savage loathing of a beast," Bryan wrote in 1916, the year of the unspeakable battle of the Somme. "I believe that the fundamental question that the people of the world have got to ask and answer is whether man is to be a brother or a brute." After the war he heard, to his dismay, that in quiet classrooms across the land students were being told that man after all *is* a brute; and thus—on political as much as on religious grounds—Bryan plunged into his last crusade. A belief in evolution enabled human beings to accommodate to the world as it existed, Bryan declared in "The Menace of Darwinism," (1921); a religious belief in the redemptive power of love made them reformers. Lawrence W. Levine, a close and careful student of the Great Commoner's activities during his last decade of life, concludes: "Bryan joined the anti-evolutionists not in order to retreat from politics, but in order to combat a force which he held responsible for sapping American politics of its idealism and progressive spirit." (But suppose, the nagging voice of science continued insistently to whisper, just suppose that evolution is *true?*)

Passion and idealism of Bryan's kind can be found in American politics today—but such a witness in Left politics for most of the eighties was drowned out by the TV-hogging Right. Much had changed between William Jennings Bryan's homilies to believing Democrats and George McGovern's to their political descendants. Evangelicals in George McGovern's time could not so confidently have affirmed the futurist positivism which such believers in the Bryan era had found not at all inconsistent with their religious heritage; the sense, as General Weaver put it, of being "at the dawn of the golden age of popular power." Even McGovern, with his "come home" appeal, implied a coming *back* to a previous national standard from which the nation had fallen away—a subtle concession to the rising tide of conservatism. During the course of the twentieth century, evangelicals have wavered between stridently asserting that their creed continued to be the core of American civilization, and defensively digging in as a beleaguered minority against a secular society they perceived as hostile—and against a scientific Establishment which seemed to reinforce that hostility.

The mentality of a state of siege does not combine easily with that of social innovation; a difficulty all but foreclosing the combination of Biblicist evangelicalism with *radical* politics, George McGovern's example to the contrary notwithstanding. "Evangelicals in this century," charges Jim Wallis—an evangelical activist who personally has kept faith with radicalism—"have a history of going along with the culture on the big issues and taking their stands on the smaller issues"; on the really big questions—war, poverty, social equality, economic justice—they "have accepted the culture on its own terms." The religio-political activism of the generation next after McGovern's, with certain distinctive exceptions—most notably the Rev. Jesse Jackson—was going to have a strikingly different agenda from that of McGovern or Bryan; one of rolling back New Deal experimentation, curtailing unconventional lifestyles, and venerating a presumed "original intent" of the framers of the Constitution.

Echoing John Dewey's observations about Bryan's constituency, Justice Antonin Scalia in his dissent from a 1987 Supreme Court decision that outlawed the teaching of "creation science"—the much more sophisticated anti-evolutionist doctrine which had replaced the kind of statute tested in the 1925 Scopes "monkey trial"—noted that "Political activism by the religiously motivated is part of our heritage." Such people ought not to be cut off from participation

199

in the political process, Scalia argued; "today's activism may give us the Balanced Treatment Act [the creation-science statute which the Court's majority was striking down], but yesterday's resulted in the abolition of slavery, and tomorrow's may bring relief for famine victims." Surely the point was well taken—but it was made in the context of a deep-running cultural, political, and constitutional conservatism quite alien to the spirit either of the secular-minded Dewey or of the religiously motivated Bryan.

6. "God Does Not Take Sides in American Politics"

If William Jennings Bryan could comfortably and naturally use the words "moral majority" to describe his political constituency, it was Jerry Falwell who gave the term formal, legal status as "Moral Majority, Inc." The distance between Bryan and Falwell is a measure of what had happened to political religion in the half century following Bryan's death.

A caution is in order here: to classify religious believers primarily by their politics would be to distort one's understanding of them. Many twentieth-century Fundamentalists, despite Justice Scalia's caveat, contended that religionists as such should take *no* stand on political questions; their business was to save souls, period. Sociopolitical criticism and action—what Protestants called the Social Gospel—was something religious "modernists" did; people who rejected the Fundamentalist belief that "the entire Bible from Genesis to Revelation," as Jerry Falwell once put it, "is the inerrant Word of God, and totally accurate in all respects." Falwell himself in his early ministry shared in the conviction (an old one in America; see chapter 3) that the church should not get mixed up in politics, even in order to combat what it took to be moral evils. "We are not told to wage war against bootleggers, liquor stores, gamblers, murderers, prostitutes, or any other existing evil as such," Falwell declared in a 1965 sermon on "Ministers and Marchers." "I would find it impossible to stop preaching the pure saving gospel of Jesus Christ, and begin doing anything else—including fighting Communism."

Fifteen years later, however, at a press conference on the eve of the 1980 presidential election, Jerry Falwell repudiated what he had said in that sermon as "false prophecy." In the meantime he had taken on a vast array of political causes: for voluntary prayer in schools, free enterprise, balanced budgets, military strength, aid to Israel; against the Equal Rights Amendment, pornography, abortion, homosexuality, pari-mutuel betting, and rock and roll. "If you would like to know where I am politically," he exclaimed in 1979, "I am to the right of wherever you are. I thought Goldwater was too liberal!" (And on certain crucial issues Barry was in fact more liberal than Falwell, a point the Arizonan made pungently clear.)

In part this dramatic shift in strategy, which Falwell shared with other prominent religious conservatives, was a response to the circumstance that those "modernists" had, at one level, succeeded all too well. Politically conscious "social gospel" liberals, as well as non-liberals like Reinhold Niebuhr who shared the social gospel agenda for action, had captured much of the public relations machinery of the "mainline" Protestant denominations. They had produced documents such as the Social Creed of the Churches (1912; revised 1932 in a New-Dealish direction), more or less normative in those churches that subscribed to it, whose program—the right of labor to organize; a living wage, "the highest wage that each industry can afford"; "the right of the workers to some protection against the hardships often resulting from the swift crises of industrial change"—believers in an unregulated "market economy" felt bound to reject. If religious liberals and their allies engaged in political and social action, religious conservatives would have to do the same thing. Although some of those conservatives' "inerrant Bibles earlier told them inerrantly not to try to legislate morality," Martin Marty wryly notes, "now just as inerrantly they were told *to* legislate it."

They found their weapon for counterattack in religious radio, which had experimented for a time with unpaid, "sustaining"—non-sponsored—public service broadcasting, carefully noncontroversial in content—a CBS "Church of the Air," for example. It was tepid fare indeed by contrast with the lively and markedly sectarian radio programs the Fundamentalists and their listening audiences were willing to pay for, such as Charles E. Fuller's Old-Fashioned Revival Hour—a program successful in prime time and, by his own testimony, an important boyhood influence on Falwell. After the television revolution, one could *see* the troubled faces in the audience and the people filing down through the aisles at the altar-call while the choir sang, just as in the old-time tent revivals. The crudeness early fifties televangelism shared with all early-fif-

ties TV yielded to slick, smooth professionalism, often employing
established show-business personalities to carry the gospel message. Then in the seventies the Federal Communications Commission decided that paid-for religious programs would satisfy the
"public service" requirement all broadcasters had in theory to meet.
That revolutionized religious broadcasting; in many places cost-
conscious local stations in effect drove the moderate "mainline"
preachers off the air by selling their Sunday morning time to the
Fundamentalists. Into that formerly placid Sabbath hour came ex-
horters who made Falwell seem the voice of sweet reasonableness
by comparison. The message was very often millennialist ("This is
the terminal generation before Jesus comes," Falwell himself has
said); stridently sectarian and, in at least one notorious case, specifically anti-Catholic and anti-Semitic; and, on secular issues,
consistently and virulently right-wing.

Although Jerry Falwell shared in the general objectives of the
emergent political conservatism of the 1970s—and indeed had received chastisement from Billy Graham, by that time the gentlemanly dean of evangelistic broadcasters, for preaching on "secular, nonmoral issues like the Panama Canal"—it was not the
liberals' stands on taxes, economic regulation, or labor-manage-
ment relations that really triggered Falwell's ire. In addition to
"godless Communism" one of the archfoes of Falwell and other
evangelical conservatives was "secular humanism"—which they
defined as a belief that human beings through social, educational,
economic, and (heresy of heresies!) government action can solve
all their own problems without the help of God. (Such humanists
quite properly could have replied that they, believing as they did,
had to act accordingly; it would be hypocritical to them to posit
God as their sanction merely on the ground that it would be a good
thing *if* He existed.) The evangelicals' anti-"humanist" polemic went
beyond combatting the scientific heresies about traditional religion, however; it was also a blunt rejoinder to the "value-free" relativistic social science which had indeed by that time made major
intellectual conquests in America, leading to a widely shared conclusion that, as *Time* expressed it in a typical essay, "it is O.K. to
be divorced, O.K. to be a single parent, O.K. to be different"—
conclusions which countless other, non-Fundamentalist Americans
found not threatening but liberating.

As vehemently committed folk are prone to do, many of the religious Rightists saw all this relativism or "situationalism" not as

the consequence of a rational inquiry, the seemingly inevitable conclusions of which troubled some of the investigators themselves (further below, chapter 10), but rather as a deliberate conspiracy pervading the stage, the screen, the universities, the news media, the schools, and indeed the non-Fundamentalist churches. Jerry Falwell said he founded Moral Majority as "a coalition of God-fearing moral Americans" in order to "reverse the politicization of immorality in our society." To accomplish that goal, political leaders in America must be religiously and morally committed; and Falwell came close at times to saying they must be committed to *his* kind of religion. Those whose faith was less rigid than his own he consigned to outer darkness: "The liberal churches are not only the enemy of God but the enemy of the nation." Holding up a Bible at one political rally in 1979, the founder of Moral Majority reportedly said: "If a man stands by this book, vote for him. If he doesn't, don't"—a startling rejection of old Lyman Beecher's hard-won dictum (chapter 3 above) that Christians in the Republic could safely "repose confidence in men, for civil purposes, who do not profess religion, or afford evidence of piety."

It is difficult to assess the extent of Jerry Falwell's contribution, or that of Pat Robertson and others of the same school, to the wave of political conservatism that crested in 1980 in the election of Ronald Reagan together with the first Republican-controlled Senate in 26 years, a Senate many of whose new members ousted liberal Senators who had been specifically targeted in mudslinging Moral Majority TV commercials. Surely it is substantial. Certainly Falwell and ministers like him, using his slogan "Get them saved, baptized, and registered," got many people out to register and vote who had never previously participated in America's political life at all. "Instead of being typified by a business man on the golf links," Frances Fitzgerald wrote in 1981, "the Republican party leadership was now looking more and more like William Jennings Bryan."

But Bryan, who as noted above also used in his day the term "moral majority," had energized his followers for *liberal* causes—anti-imperialism, trust-busting, aid to farmers, the League of Nations. Many who shared Jerry Falwell's brand of warm-hearted evangelicalism resented having it equated with right-wing partisanship; Jimmy Carter, whose presidential administration Falwell savagely attacked in his book *Listen, America!* (1980) was as legitimately a born-again Baptist as Falwell was. In religious as in sec-

203

ular matters conservatives (like some liberals!) have an exasperating tendency to make pre-emptive claims of virtue. During the long, hot Iran-Contra hearings of 1987 one Senator who happened to disagree with Oliver North's—and the Reagan Administration's—stand on Contra aid, George Mitchell of Maine, exclaimed, "God does not take sides in American politics. . . . I still love country and God just as much as you do, Colonel North."

This pre-emption was manifestly unfair to the rich political variety among Fundamentalists themselves—or evangelicals, as they nowadays prefer to be called. As Robert Booth Fowler has shown in a careful study of evangelical political thought during the late 1960s and early 1970s, there were pro- and anti-Vietnam evangelicals; pro- and anti-ERA evangelicals; even pro- and anti-capitalist evangelicals. Even in the Falwell-Robertson era the religious Right was not quite the monolith it professed itself to be; in the showdown of the 1988 presidential primaries, Jesse Jackson's brand of revivalist politics rolled up many more votes for national party convention delegates than Pat Robertson's. Moreover, the tradition of American folk evangelism could still be drawn on for nourishment by people who totally rejected its theology, as James Russell Lowell had similarly done during the slavery controversy. At one protest rally for the largely church- and synagogue-supported "sanctuary movement" in 1985, folksinger Joan Baez, a champion of feminism and civil disobedience—movements the religious right detested—led the congregation at the close in singing "Amazing Grace," and playfully added: "Eat your heart out, Jerry Falwell."

Interlude VIII

What the mountains and high plains were to inland dwellers, the ocean was to young people who grew up among fishing nets and lobster pots: a frontier. From the barren sand-and-scrub strands of Nantucket and Cape Cod, from the tree-shaded inlets of the Chesapeake, from the splendid harbor of New York; from Wilmington and Charleston and New Orleans; from the Golden Gate and from Puget Sound, they ventured out onto the trackless sea. In squat, ugly steamers or in clipper ships of incomparable beauty, Americans found their way to the ends of the Earth.

Back from their journeys came sealskins and whale oil, mahogany and gold dust, spices and tea. Into airless Victorian "front sitting-rooms," offsetting to some degree their hideous and unsittable horsehair sofas, came Ming vases, sandalwood, peacock feathers, delicately carved ivory. And in village cemeteries, alongside the markers for Civil War soldiers, mothers who perished in childbirth, babies carried off by fever, stood not a few stones that marked no actual graves, but were inscribed instead with the legend "lost at sea."

Seven-eighths of the planet is covered with water. A ship alone in that aqueous emptiness faced an isolation greater than human beings could know anywhere else until they began venturing into space; and no voyager across that expanse, before the discovery of electromagnetic waves, had the comfort or annoyance of constant contact with a Mission Control. Yet the crossing and recrossing of the oceans shrank the world nonetheless. Sea lore abounded in strange coincidences; on a dank frigid day in 1820, for example, Nathaniel Palmer, a young captain out of Stonington, Connecticut, lying-to under a heavy fog near the Antarctic Peninsula as close as one could then get, literally, to "the ends of the earth"—hundreds of miles from inhabited land, thousands of miles from civilization—heard the startling sound of another ship's bell. The fog, as it will, whisked away, and the little

205

American vessel found itself in company with two imposing men-o'war of the imperial Russian navy.

Palmer and the Tsar's Admiral Bellingshausen parted amicably; having learned to their surprise, however, that no matter where you go on this Earth, you can't get away from other people. And some of the voyagers, flying rival national flags, inevitably wanted some of the same things—perhaps enough to fight for them. An American admiral in 1890, Alfred Thayer Mahan, wrote The Influence of Sea Power on History. *The name of the game, it seemed, was empire.*

NINE

Imperial Rome and Progressive America: The Ghost of Caesar Walks Again

The ongoing struggle of republicanism against Caesarism in various forms, from Napoleon to Mussolini, links this book with the new understanding historians lately have achieved concerning the intellectual and moral climate in which Americans first created their political culture. The same historians have had difficulty, however, in getting that republican debate past the early nineteenth century; indeed, sometimes we seem implicitly to have consigned America's historic republican creed to an irrecoverable past. It is the contention of this book, on the contrary, that the nineteenth century—not only its science and industry but its essential democratic values as well—can be connected to the twentieth again, and that Americans in their political choices and actions during the century now ending successfully made that connection.

1. Welcome to the Club

"A breakaway federation of sparsely populated farming and trading colonies entered the nineteenth century," the Marxist critic H. Bruce Franklin has written. "What came out at the other end of the century was modern America, a global power." Quietly, during the years of isolation, American statecraft had moved toward a global reach: in 1867, purchase of Alaska and annexation of Midway; in 1884, acquisition of the naval base at Pearl Harbor from a native Hawaiian government which in 1893, with the help of United States Marines, American settlers in those islands undertook to overthrow; and in 1889, after a three-way Great Power collision of naval forces at Pago Pago was averted only because a hurricane wrecked the contending warships, an agreement to place the islands and people of Samoa under American, British, and German joint control. Then, dramatically, the United States burst out openly upon the world stage by intervening in Cuba—undoing a previous, highly skilled Secretary of State's success in *staying out* of an earlier Cuban-Spanish conflict (1868–1878)—and enthusiastically went to war with Spain, a war from which the U.S. emerged almost painlessly with an overseas empire.

Rudyard Kipling, that archpriest of British imperialism, welcomed the Americans to the club, as a junior member. "Take up the white man's burden/Send them the best ye breed," the poet admonished. "Go bind your sons to exile/To serve your captives' need." You're a grown-up country now, and must take on adult responsibilities; these include looking after "your new-caught, sullen peoples/Half-devil and half-child"—for their own good, of course. Put behind you the carefree years when your sheltering oceans protected you from the real world; come out and earn respect as a mature power among powers—"cold, edged with dear-bought wisdom/The judgment of your peers!" Not a few influential Americans stood ready to take the advice offered them by the author of *The Jungle Books*. "From a nation of shopkeepers we became a nation of warriors," proclaimed white-mustached, bushy-eyebrowed "Marse Henry" Watterson, editor/publisher of the *Louisville Courier-Journal* and a major regional and national political force. "From a provincial huddle of petty sovereignties we rise to the dignity of an imperial republic incomparably greater than Rome."

Most Americans still like to think of themselves as non-imperial; indeed, by virtue of their successful revolution of 1776, as a nation and people which is anti-imperialist on principle. Mexican and Native American appraisals of that claimed principle have understandably been sarcastic. In extenuation, paleface Americans contended that they had previously expanded only into land that was empty—well, *almost* empty; and only the kind of expansion that jumped off the home continent, they argued, could properly be put down as imperialism. Grover Cleveland took that traditional view of overseas expansion when he abruptly withdrew from the Senate's consideration a treaty negotiated by the previous U.S. administration (Harrison's) with the new, revolutionary settlers' government in Hawaii—a regime which, Cleveland explained in his usual no-nonsense fashion, "owes its existence to an armed invasion by the United States." The native Hawaiian monarchy of Queen Liliuokalani—"the lawful Government of Hawaii"—had been "overthrown without the drawing of a sword or the firing of a shot," the President declared, "by a process . . . directly traceable" to his Presidential predecessor's envoy to that government, who had also instigated "the landing of the United States forces upon false pretexts respecting the danger to life and property."

To drive home his point, Cleveland pulled the battle fleet out of Pearl Harbor, thereby testing whether the provisional "Republic of Hawaii" under Sanford B. Dole (founder of the pineapple dynasty) could survive without direct American military support. As matters turned out, it could and did; a counter-revolution by the Queen's adherents failed. President Cleveland was roundly criticized in his homeland for having removed the Navy from the islands, leaving them likely prey for some other power—probably Japan. In 1898, under the McKinley administration, almost as a sideshow in the furore over the Spanish-American War, a Congressional joint resolution made Hawaii an American possession. Imperialism had become the order of the day.

Could the old republican order survive such a transformation? In acquiring by conquest possessions outside of North America "Uncle Sam changed his sex and became a mother country" (as one contemporary wit put it); which is to say, the American government became ruler over people who were *subjects* of the United States without necessarily being *citizens*. Thomas Jefferson had foreseen this ominous possibility of creating two legally distinct political classes, and forestalled it—he believed—by the statecraft of the Northwest Ordinance of 1787, which provided that territories owned by the U.S. should evolve by a regular and orderly process into states. To certain of the territories added after the Civil War the Northwest Ordinance principle would in due course be applied; Alaska and Hawaii became states in the 1950s on an equal basis with the rest. (The same prospect—unless the examples of Fidel Castro and Daniel Ortega offer a more attractive alternative—may also be the political destiny of Puerto Rico.) Other possessions, however, inhabited by those "new-caught, sullen peoples" of whom Kipling condescendingly spoke, might be expected *never* to go through the Northwest Ordinance process; and unless and until they did, the benefits and protections of the Constitution did not apply.

In the Philippine Islands in particular some of those new peoples were not yet quite "caught." They had had a revolution of their own going against Spain when the Americans showed up, and their leader, Emilio Aguinaldo, had supported the United States in the joint military effort that captured Manila under the assumption that the islands' fate would be independence, not annexation. When he learned otherwise, he and his followers rose in rebellion, and the "splendid little war," as Secretary of State John Hay called the Spanish-American conflict, was followed by a dirty little war that involved some fifty thousand American troops and dragged on for three years: America's first military invasion of Southeast Asian villages, but tragically not its last. What will the Americans do with the Filipinos? the fictional "Mr. Hennessy" asked "Mr. Dooley," the philosophical bartender in Chicago who was the literary persona for the shrewd, widely read political satirist Finley Peter Dunne. "They'll give them a measure of freedom," Mr. Dooley replied.

"But when?" Hennessy persisted.

"When they'll stand still long enough to be measured," said Mr. Dooley.

That "measure," when it came, was narrowly conceived. Congress, in enacting a law for the government of the Philippine Islands in 1902, after the insurrection ended, exempted that portion of the new overseas empire from the provision in the Revised Statutes of the United States which gave force and effect to the Constitution and laws of the U.S. in its territories as much as elsewhere. The Constitution, said the Supreme Court on a 1904 appeal from the Philippines (*Dorr* v. *United States*, 195 U.S. 138), did not require that even such basic rights as trial by jury be automatically carried to the new imperial domains.

Eventually this terrible constitutional ambiguity would have to be resolved by setting the Philippines free, with consequences hazardous in the extreme; but few in 1902 considered that a serious option. The United States for the foreseeable future was going to have an overseas empire of dependent peoples, and in that assumption the old fears of a Roman parallel revived. The ghost of Caesar, it seemed, was again walking abroad in the land.

Can a republic govern a distant empire without corrupting itself? Some thought it could; the British, after all, seemed to be moving toward popular democracy—the reform of the House of Lords in 1911, for example—without letting go of their imperial domain. (The Irish, of course, saw the matter quite differently.) Others were not so sure. After America's easy military triumph over the Spanish Empire in 1898 William Graham Sumner, the hard-headed, conservative sociology professor at Yale, wrote an appraisal of that conflict ironically entitled "The Conquest of the United States by Spain." Sumner argued that by snatching an imperial domain from the faltering hands of the Spaniards the United States had in effect surrendered to Spanish principles. Other renowned Americans, highly diverse in outlook—House Speaker Thomas B. Reed, former President Grover Cleveland, Samuel Gompers of the A.F. of L., the steel magnate Andrew Carnegie, the philosopher William James—opposed the new imperialism as a subversion of the old republican ideals.

Early in 1900 Carl Schurz, a political refugee from the unsuccessful democratic revolution of 1848 in his native Austria-Hungary and afterward a distinguished American adopted citizen (U.S. Senator, Civil War general, Secretary of the Interior), voiced his fear of Roman imperial consequences from America's Philippine adventure in a letter to his fellow anti-imperialist Charles Francis Adams, Jr. In reply the Boston patrician warned that signs of a Rome-ward political trend could be found much closer to home than Luzon: "The real seat of disease is right at your own door. We could slough off the Philippines;—can you slough off New York city?" Nations did not die of their external excesses, Adams insisted; they decayed from within. "The trouble with Rome wasn't in the colonies and the empire; it was in the Senate and the forum," this scion of the Boston Adamses continued, applying the precedents of ancient history to modern politics much in the spirit of old John, his Revolutionary ancestor: "We cant about imperialism, and look for the 'man-on-horseback,' and all that nonsense. Our Emperor is here now, in embryo; even we don't recognize him, and we scornfully call him a 'boss.'"

Americans less elitist than a Boston Adams might not have perceived the city boss as a Caesar prototype; in fact, the boss system had some resources within it for the revitalization of democratic values, as Al Smith and Anton Cermak were soon to show. "That system takes the politically untrained foreign-born and grafts them upon the Republic," asserted Richard Croker, for fifteen years head of Tammany—the oldest, gamiest political machine of them all. "Who else would do it if we did not?"

The Caesars, however, had built on something else besides mere civic corruption. In addition to machine politics, the enthusiastic militarism of America's new political generation roused fears that martial glory might enable an American Caesar to bulldoze his way

211

to power. Misunderstanding Theodore Roosevelt, as many historians still do, Emperor Wilhelm II of Germany, who already possessed the title of Caesar (Kaiser), publicly welcomed the man he took for his American equivalent into the imperial fraternity. In 1910, on horseback, they reviewed the German troops together. A photographer snapped them, mounted and shaking hands, and across the back of a print he gave to TR the Kaiser wrote: "When we shake hands we shake the world."

2. Urbes *Ancient and Modern*

We shook the world, with our bombs, our battle wagons, our thundering big guns; but also with our jackhammers, our blowtorches, our clanging steam shovels. The silent and empty New World found by the first wandering Europeans was long gone; the dark green forest that once greeted the Dutch on Manhattan Island had given way to mansions and tenements, churches and warehouses, El tracks and the Brooklyn Bridge. And the El Dorado in the West which for centuries had haunted the Old World's dreams was giving place to a reality which increasingly resembled the Old World and echoed its history—not the Old World of castles and tournaments, monks and troubadours, but an earlier Old World, of stadiums and forums and aqueducts. "We understand Augustus and his times much more readily than we do the times of Charlemagne," the distinguished Italian historian of ancient Rome Guglielmo Ferrero told an American audience toward the end of the Lowell Lectures he gave in Boston in 1908. "Look about you: what do you see? A world that looks more like the Roman empire than it does the Middle Ages . . . We are returning to a vaster world, to the condition of the Roman Empire at its beginning."

One great common link, for Ferrero, between modern Euro-America and the early Roman Empire was urbanization. The Latin language had created the very word that denoted "this marvelous and monstrous phenomenon of history, the enormous city, the deceitful source of life and death—*urbs*—the city." Americans in the old republican-agrarian tradition, who deeply distrusted the city and all its works, would not have been reassured to be told that "the countless *urbes* which the grand economic progress of the nineteenth century has caused to rise in every part of Europe and

America look to Rome as their eldest sister and their dean." Imagine Jefferson's reaction—or Bryan's!—to Professor Ferrero's peroration:

> In the Rome of the days of Caesar, huge, agitated, seething with freedmen, slaves, artisans come from everywhere, crowded with enormous tenement-houses, run through from morning till night by a mad throng, eager for amusements and distractions; in that Rome where there jostled together an unnumbered population, uprooted from the land, from family, from native country, and where from the press of so many men there fermented all the propelling energies of history . . . ; in that changeable Rome, here splendid, there squalid; now magnanimous, and now brutal; full of grandeurs, replete with horrors; in that great city all the huge modern metropolises are easily refound, Paris and New York, Buenos Ayres and London, Melbourne and Berlin.

And what of America? Was it also finding in its own new, smoky, fast-sprawling cities their eldest sister's horror and grandeur? "In many matters the United States is nearer than Europe to ancient Rome," Ferrero declared, in the preface to an American edition of his multi-volume work *The Greatness and Decline of Rome* (1909). ". . . An American understands easily the working of the old Roman state because he is a citizen of a state based on the same principle."

Notice, however, one all-important difference between Ferrero's appraisal and that of concerned Americans such as Schurz and the younger C. F. Adams: it was the Roman *Republic*, not the *Principate*, of which the Italian historian judged America to be the political heir. Moreover, he hinted, that political inheritance might have ceased to be any longer an option for Europeans. With no inkling as yet of the social and political revolutions about to sweep across the planet, Ferrero looked back to the downfall of democratic institutions in the wake of Napoleon and concluded "that the Republic, the human state considered as the common property of all—the great political creation of ancient Rome—is reborn here in America, after having died out in Europe." As he brought his course of lectures to a close, Ferrero paid his American hosts a handsome compliment: "I do not believe that you are superior to Europe in as many things as you think, but a superiority I do recognize, great and, for me at least, indisputable, in the political institutions with which you govern yourselves. The Republic . . . is the true political form worthy of a civilized people, because the

213

only one that is rational and plastic"—a sentiment with which James Madison, or John Dewey, could have heartily agreed.

But would America's political institutions remain instruments of self-government? Or would they become hollow forms, legalistic trappings behind which—as in Rome—government would simplify itself into the unlimited exercise of power? Another European visitor to America in that first decade of the new century, H. G. Wells, saw "a strong parallelism between the present condition of the United States and the Roman Republic at the time of the early Caesars" from which "one might venture to forecast the steady development of an exploiting and devastating plutocracy, leading perhaps to Caesarism." In America in 1905, however, Wells discerned "forces of recuperation and construction" unknown to the Roman world: "There is infinitely more original and originating thought in the state, there are the organized forces of science," and—above all else, for H. G. Wells—"a habit of progress, clearer and wider knowledge among the general mass of the people"— with very little hint in America of that debilitating tendency in the classic Roman writers, strikingly pointed out by Ferrero in his first lecture, to equate *corruption* with what moderns meant by *progress*.

There had been a germ of truth in that pessimistic equation, the Italian visitor conceded, "just as there is a principle of error in the too serene optimism with which we consider corruption as progress"—but in the ancients that pessimistic perspective had clearly gotten out of control, as when the Latin poet Horace "covers with invective, as an evil-doer and the corrupter of the human race, that impious being who invented the ship, which causes man, created for the land, to walk across waters," and excoriates the legendary Daedalus, who made artificial wings and ascended where humans were not meant to go. "'Caelum ipsum petimus stultitia,' [we petition heaven itself in our stupidity] exclaims Horace—that is to say, in anticipation he considered the Wright brothers crazy." That kind of reactionary Luddite snobbery, H. G. Wells believed, the inventive, mechanically minded Americans would never commit. In his own inimitable Cockney-philistine manner Wells argued that while moderns could perhaps learn from late republican Rome's politics—at least as a warning of what not to do!—they could gain little or nothing from its formal culture:

> New York is not simply more interesting than Rome, but more significant, more stimulating, and far more beautiful, and the

214

idea that to be concerned about the latter in preference to the former is a mark of a finer mental quality is one of the most mischievous and foolish ideas that ever invaded the mind of man.

What impressed H. G. Wells again and again about America, in contrast not only to ancient Rome but also to the social *vis inertiae* he diagnosed in his fictional portrayals of his native England, was its vitality. Thus it was appropriate that Wells's first American visit should be topped off with a call upon that most bumptious of Americans, Theodore Roosevelt. In the White House garden Wells poured out his hopes and fears for America and the world to his hearty host, and recorded the President's reply: "He hadn't, he said, an effectual disproof of any pessimistic interpretation of the future . . . only he chose to live as if this were not so." Mentioning "a little book of mine, an early book full of the deliberate pessimism of youth"—the best selling *Time Machine*, that dark Romantic fable of the inevitable doom of humankind—TR got "gesticulatory"; his voice rose. "With one of those sudden movements of his, he leaned forward on a garden chair . . . and addressed me over the back. 'Suppose after all that should prove to be right, and it all ends in your butterflies and morlocks. *That doesn't matter now.* The effort's real. It's worth going on with. It's worth it—even then.'"

Alas, the strenuosity of Theodore Roosevelt, who not long before Wells's visit had added the Panama Canal Zone to the American empire, was perceived in some quarters not as part of the solution but as part of the problem. If he was never quite the candidate for Caesar some bitter partisans supposed—if, as Richard Hofstadter put it, "the man on the white horse turned out to be just a graduate of the Harvard boxing squad, equipped with an immense bag of platitudes, and quite willing to play the democratic game"— yet it would have given one pause to hear his followers at the Progressive party convention in 1912, which nominated him for President for the third and last time, chanting:

> Thou wilt not cower in the dust,
> Roosevelt, O Roosevelt!
> Thy gleaming sword shall never rust,
> Roosevelt, O Roosevelt!

—although, to the man's credit, we are told, when this sort of thing happened "his face took on a look of bewilderment."

Woodrow Wilson, the candidate who beat both Roosevelt and incumbent Taft that year, would have been embarrassed at such emotional excess. But the preacher-teacher Wilson may have had his own Caesar-potential. "The valuable element in monarchy," Wilson wistfully wrote early in his career, was "its *cohesion*, its readiness and power to act." The American people, "this vast and miscellaneous democracy, must be led; its giant faculties must be schooled and directed." And who better to school them, he wrote on the eve of his own entry into politics, than a president who knows what ought to be done, more concretely and effectively than the people themselves? "His office is anything he has the sagacity and force to make it. . . . If he rightly interprets the national thought and boldly insists upon it, he is irresistible, and the country never feels the zest for action so much as when its President is of such insight and calibre"—a zest for action which in a few short years would propel millions of young men into the shell-swept trenches of northern France.

3. World War and Political Fatalism

For most of the present century, the world has become hardened to bouts of international mass slaughter. People spent the interwar years 1919–1939 in effect waiting for the other shoe to drop. Then, only five years after the end of World War II, another international armed collision began in Korea, and since that time war has followed bloody war with dismal regularity. In contrast, World War I had been preceded by 99 years during which there had been no general conflict involving all the major powers. Peace seemed the normal state of humankind, war an interruption; only a few incredibly old people could personally recall Napoleon's *Grand Armée!* Wars had been localized (as in the Crimea), or they had been short (for example, the Franco-Prussian), or they had taken place out at the edges of empire (Kitchener's march to the Sudan). The two bloodiest—the American Civil War and China's Taiping Rebellion (1851–1864)—were domestic affrays. As the nineteenth century turned into the twentieth, if one ignored the vastly accelerating arms race and the commitments implicit in the pattern of military alliances, it was possible to look selectively at the growing interdependence of modern society and the seeming onward march of literacy, public health, and representative institutions—even in countries like the Kaiser's Germany—and conclude that a nonviolent Golden Age had dawned. "We confused rapidity of change with advance," John Dewey confessed after the guns of August 1914 blew that golden age away, "and we took certain gains in our own comfort and ease as signs that cosmic forces were working inevitably to improve the whole state of human affairs." Cosmic forces, Dewey knew, just don't work that way.

Thirty million men marched toward the future chanting a hymn of progress and suddenly they marched straight over the edge of a cliff. "The cubist war," Stephen Kern has called World War I, arguing that the modernist consciousness which had quietly incubated in Europe since the 1880s burst in 1914 into giddying, disruptive reality. The horrors of that war—three hundred thousand lost *on each side* at Verdun, six hundred thousand on each side at the Somme—seemed all out of proportion to any conceivable objective for going to war. "They brought weapons of a strange and terrible effectiveness to the settlement of what were in comparison small and antiquated disputes," H. G. Wells later wrote; armies organized not very differently from the Roman legions cut each other to pieces with machine guns, war gases, and wickedly accurate artillery. Yet the leaders played their age-old political and diplomatic game against each other "with a sort of terrified inevitability," and millions of their followers, with surprisingly little resistance, "marched indeed right out of civilization . . . with a sort of fatalistic pride." For people who resisted that fatalism— who believed with Woodrow Wilson that this holocaust would "make the world safe for democracy" or even "end war"—their continuing faith in progress truly was the substance of things hoped for, the evidence of things not seen. Those who had fought in the war came out of it in the mood of an alcoholic coming off a three-day drunk; sick and hung over and vowing never to do *that* again—but bleakly aware that one is going to.

In the gloomy and cruel aftermath of the First World War and the Peace of Versailles—or as he also termed them, "the Great War and the Petty Peace"—H. G. Wells, badly shaken by what he termed "the international catastrophe of 1914," read in the furious discontent of the European masses in the wake of such a war and such a peace "a state of mind comparable to that which had rendered possible the debacle of the Roman Empire." Yet his *Outline of History* (1920)—the most widely read historical book of its day and surely one of the most influential—nevertheless argued that the governments, republican and otherwise, which had launched and (thus far) survived that catastrophe were a long advance over Re-

217

publican Rome, where "there were no newspapers," and where education was "the freak of the individual parent, and the privilege of wealth and leisure." To be sure, a modern reader of Roman history found "in the Senate and the popular assembly a conflict of groups and personalities, an argumentative process of control," which seemed familiar and assimilable. But if such a reader tried to interpret Rome's history "in terms of debates and measures, policies and campaigns, capital and labour," he or she must from time to time come upon shocking reminders of that earlier culture's real raw primitiveness: "We talk of a legislative gathering, and the mind flies to Westminster; but how should we feel if we went to see the beginning of a session of the House of Lords, and discovered the Lord Chancellor, with bloody fingers, portentously fiddling about among the entrails of a newly killed sheep? . . . If republican Rome was the first of the modern self-governing national communities," Wells concluded, "she was certainly the 'Neanderthal' form of them."

Human beings had learned *something* since those hapless times, H. G. Wells believed: "Clumsily or smoothly the world, it seems, progresses and will progress." The revolutionary upheavals and military disasters since 1914 were but the birth-pains of a rational, peaceable, prosperous, and free world community. But others then alive read the signs of the times quite differently. The First World War was not the opening round of the struggle for a true World State, as Wells believed; it was the signal for the oncoming downfall of Western civilization. So argued Oswald Spengler in *The Decline of the West* (1918), a book whose general thesis had an impact far wider than upon the comparatively few readers masochistic enough to plow through its many pages of turgid prose. ("In Germany," warns H. Stuart Hughes—a sympathetic student of Spengler—"a book that is not hard to read is scarcely considered worth reading.")

Civilizations, according to Spengler, have life cycles resembling those of living organisms: youth, maturity, senescence. In youth, tribalism and epic poetry; in maturity, cultural cosmopolitanism and great systems of philosophy; in old age, world empires and gigantic buildings. Spring, Summer, Fall; and then in the Winter phase Caesar comes. "We are civilized, not Gothic or Rococo, people; we have to reckon with the hard cold facts of a *late* life, to which the parallel is to be found not in Pericles's Athens but in Caesar's Rome." Forget Leagues of Nations, and abandon all hope of writing plays like Shakespeare's, Spengler advised; the proper vocation of a young person moving with the tides of history in the late Fall or early Winter of Western Civilization lay in soldiering or engineering, to prepare oneself to go to work for Caesar. Devote yourself "to technics instead of lyrics, the sea instead of the paintbrush, and politics instead of epistemology," Spengler exhorted:

> He who does not understand that this outcome is obligatory and insusceptible of modification, that our choice is between willing *this* and willing nothing at all, between cleaving to *this* destiny or despairing of the future and of life itself; he who cannot feel that there is grandeur also in the realizations of powerful intelligences, in the energy and discipline of metal-hard natures, in battles fought with the coldest and most abstract means . . . must forego all desire to comprehend history, to live through history, or to make history.

Where would the new Caesar come from? Spengler throughout *The Decline of the West* left broad hints that he really ought to be a German. On the other hand Max Weber, the great German sociologist, found in the 1918 armistice proof that Germany had already resigned the *imperium* into other hands: "America's world domination," Weber declared, "was as unavoidable as that of Rome after the Punic War. It is to be hoped that it will not be shared with Russia." And there were Americans prepared to respond to this call to arms. Their own Brooks Adams, in *The Law of Civilization and Decay* (1895), had in fact anticipated Spengler's grim prophecy. Civilizations do not even possess the intrinsic coherence of living organisms as Spengler thought; their history, Adams argued, is essentially a process of accumulation and dispersal, presided over—sometimes peacefully; more usually violently—by administrative intelligence. When the administrative genius of a particular society's governing class reaches its limit, and becomes unable to manage "the bulk and momentum of the mass to be administered . . . disintegration sets in, the social momentum is gradually relaxed, and society sinks back to a level at which it can cohere."

Sharply disagreeing with his brothers—Charles Francis, who as we have seen resisted America's drift toward imperialism, and Henry, who renounced the whole modern game to pursue a personal vision of the Virgin of Chartres—Brooks Adams insisted that Americans, or their ruling elite, had only the starkest of choices between two destinies. "The United States," he wrote in 1902, "has become the heart of the economic system of the age and she must maintain her supremacy by wit and by force, or share the fate of the discarded." How melancholy, and ultimately false, a choice that would have seemed to those two tough old republicans, Grandfather John Quincy Adams and Great-Grandfather John.

4. New Rome in the Old World?

The actual advent of a claimant to Caesar's mantle came in 1922 as an almost comic anticlimax when Mussolini's blackshirted legions marched on Rome, where it had all started. In Italian Fascism, taking its very name from the bundle of rods with protruding axe-head which the Roman *lictores* had carried as a symbol of the state's authority (we used that same Roman symbol also, on the reverse side of the old liberty dime), one distinguished American historian of ancient Rome, Frank F. Abbott, saw a "remarkable revival . . . of the old Roman spirit and of certain Roman political institutions." Like Ferrero before him, Professor Abbott drew parallels between Rome and America: "If an immigrant from ancient Rome of the first century before our era should disembark in New York tomorrow, he would need less training in understanding our political machinery than many of our contemporary immigrants do, because the Anglo-Saxon and the Roman show the same characteristics in their political life." To assert that parallel in the context of the March on Rome, however, rather than of the parliamentary and relatively peaceful time when Ferrero proposed it, was to open the alarming possibility that Caesar's bully-boys, America's ward heelers, and Mussolini's Fascisti were all political cousins.

"Both peoples"—the ancient Romans and the modern Americans—"are opportunists," Abbott went on; and it is logically possible to move from opportunism to Machiavellianism to sheer naked *Realpolitik*. The Italian dictator professed himself a disciple of the American philosopher William James, whose gentlemanly Harvard variety of pragmatism Mussolini caricatured into Fascist-style "direct action." At least one American political scientist took the proffered bait: "Mussolini, Prophet of the Pragmatic Era in Politics," W. Y. Elliot called *Il Duce* in the June 1926 number of the *Political Science Quarterly*. What he glossed over, in praising the

Italian dictator for employing "the psychological pragmatism of Machiavelli," was the brute, gangster-style power which enforced the psychology.

Other writers quickly picked up the New Roman theme. "Mussolini, Garibaldi or Caesar?" asked the *Literary Digest* on November 18, 1922. "New Romulus and New Rome," wrote B. H. Liddell Hart in the *Atlantic* for July 1928. And in 1935, when Mussolini took his first step toward rebuilding the Roman Empire by attacking Ethiopia, another writer for the same respected magazine, F. H. S. Simonds, took Mussolini and his regime very seriously indeed: "From the very start he had dismissed peace as the last and particular blessing of the fed and sated nations and had accepted war as the inescapable necessity of countries like his own, which were at once hungry and strong. . . . So does history repeat itself in the region which Ancient Rome proudly described as *mare nostrum* and Fascist Italy now claims as its own."

Il Duce himself worked such parallels for all they were worth, building a replica of the Roman Forum several subway stops away from the crumbling original and sponsoring in 1937 a bimillennial anniversary of the birth of Augustus—to the disdain of people like John Buchan (Lord Tweedsmuir), author of an excellent biography of Augustus published that same year, who admired the first Roman Emperor but not his grubby reputed heir. It was an American journalist, however, who most effectively blew the whistle on the new Roman *imperator*. In 1935, while others were still depicting Mussolini as a colossus who bestrode Africa and Europe, George Seldes wrote a debunking biography that summed him up as "totally unscrupulous . . . a genius at assimilating the ideas of other persons and making them his own . . . a tremendous will but an inferior mind." Seldes aptly titled this critique *Sawdust Caesar*.

In Germany meanwhile, something far more sinister than the grandiloquent Italian Fascist regime had swept into power. "Once again," John Buchan concluded, in the modern era as in Augustus's time, "the crust of civilization has worn thin, and beneath can be heard the muttering of primeval fires." To personalize those fires, as if the Fascist dictators represented nothing beyond opportunistic, amoral individual power-grabbing—to perceive Hitler and Mussolini merely as unusually successful Al Capones—would have been to miss the immensity of the tragedy that was in the making. Nor, despite Hitler's fascination with the apocalyptic "twilight of the gods" in Richard Wagner's lushly orchestrated op-

221

eras, could Fascism have simply equated itself with the last act of a dying Western civilization. It was a *new* Rome that Mussolini proclaimed, breaking with the old Christian calendar in order to do so and dating future years from the advent of Fascism. It was a *New* Order that Nazism envisioned for Europe and the world; theirs would be a "thousand-year Reich." Their Caesar, they proclaimed, came not at the end of a civilization but at its beginning. Significantly, Oswald Spengler in 1924 and again in 1932 belittled Adolf Hitler with a quip that the *Führer* of a national movement ought to be a "hero," not a "heroic tenor," and when the Nazis came to power they returned the compliment by banning Spengler's latest book.

They also did their utmost to smash German Communism, which to anti-republicans on both the Left and the Right seemed Germany's only other available option. But Communism, like Fascism, believed itself to be a society's birth-pangs, not its death-throes. Marxists as a matter of course rejected any theory of cyclical recurrence, by which the whirling wheels of history's slot machine must inevitably in time again bring up Caesar's number. History for them was unmistakably a movement onward and upward; interrupted by dialectical zigs and zags, to be sure, but always ultimately for the better. So marked a defeat for humane political culture as Mussolini's Fascism, therefore, and the far more menacing version of that creed which had just captured Germany, the Marxists had to understand as mere temporary setbacks; as "the last stage of capitalism" just preceding the redemptive world revolution.

To have called this last stage "Caesarism" in the full sense would have been a denial of their own progressive hopes; for in the comparable historical situation the dictatorship of Julius Caesar and the Principate of Augustus had not been followed by anything remotely resembling an expropriation of the expropriators or a dictatorship of the proletariat. Attempts such as that of Karl Liebknicht and Rosa Luxemburg to make the gladiators' revolt under Spartacus in 73 B.C. some kind of precursor of more modern revolutions ignored the grim object lesson of that revolt's end: six thousand captured rebels crucified along the Appian Way, leaving not a spark of revolutionary tradition behind them for the coming imperial centuries. To describe the economic policies of subsequent Roman emperors as "socialist" because they fixed prices or created state monopolies, as many twentieth-century commentators have done (e.g., the chapter in Will and Ariel Durant's widely read popular history *Caesar and Christ* entitled "The Socialism of Diocletian") is to ignore the crucial fact that under the Empire—the Republic is of course a different story—the processes creating that kind of "socialism" in no way involved mass action by the people. There surely was a "proletariat" in imperial Rome, but it had—with the arguable exception of the early Christian Church—no ideological vanguard; a proletarian's one long-shot chance at achieving enough status to have any leverage on public policy was to "work within the system" by joining the army.

Marxism did, however, have an important impact on the way modern writers discussed ancient Rome. Previous analyses of just what happened to the Roman republic had tended to be political and military rather than economic: the breakdown of an orderly constitutional check-and-balance system; the raising by late-republican political leaders of their own private armies. Yet the struggles at the end of the republic between *optimates* and *populares*—between "the best men" (i.e., the old patrician class) and the champions, sincere or not, of relief for the masses—had always had an economic agenda, as the classical historians themselves had perceived. If one were to make meaningful comparisons—hopeful or anxious—between late republican Rome and modern Euro-America, therefore, it would be necessary to ask what might have been the Roman equivalents of the corporate manager, the troubled farmer, and the industrial worker.

Although personally anti-Marxist, expressing his judgment on the Russian Revolution by "voting with his feet" and leaving the country, the Russian emigré historian Michael Rostovtzeff in his monumental *Social and Economic History of the Roman Empire* (1926) asked just such relevant and necessary questions. In his account of the fall of the republic and the rise of the Caesars Rostovtzeff alluded, for example, to the role of a "city bourgeoisie" in the urban centers of the Roman world. He wrote on the consequences of the development between Rome and its provinces of an unfavorable balance of trade. His description of absentee-owned, cash-crop producing *latifundia* and their disastrous effect upon the "family-sized farm" (as we would term it), which could not compete with slave labor or with the multiple tenancy system which later replaced it, has striking resonances with the social impact upon rural America of what today we would term "agribusiness." Furthermore, Rostovtzeff throughout his study regularly used the term *capitalism*. He carefully distinguished between the capitalism of antiquity and its more sophisticated modern forms; "the fact that many shops of the same kind belonged to one man did not transform them into a factory in the modern sense of the word." But he also asserted that the Hellenistic and Roman entrepreneurs who "introduced for the first time a mass production of goods for an indefinite market" brought their states—Rome included—"very near to the stage of industrial capitalism that characterizes the economic history of Europe in the nineteenth and twentieth centuries."

The kinds of comparison Michael Rostovtzeff made between ancient and modern economic life require caution. In the late Republic "money was freely used by unscrupulous aspirants for office," Frank Abbott conceded in his monograph on *Roman Politics* (1923), but there was a vast difference between that statement and the assertion "that capital played the important part in directing the policy of the state which certain modern writers ascribe to it." Indeed, under the patrician regime it really couldn't, since the recognized aristocracy was forbidden—by both custom and law—to indulge in something so vulgar as trade or manufacturing. *Wealth* they defined as land or plunder; the notion of creating it rather than simply accumulating and displaying it, while not totally absent from the Roman world, would have struck the kind of Roman who could denounce the inventor of shipbuilding for corrupting society as no activity for a gentleman. The Roman patriciate would have considered American entrepreneurs of the generation which had seemed to Ferrero so Roman in temper—the Rockefellers and Vanderbilts and Goulds—as "plebeian" in both the political and cultural senses of the word; as, indeed, many of them were. It was "reasonably certain," Abbott concluded, "that 'big business' did not have the political power in Rome which it has with us today."

The most powerful impact of Rostovtzeff's kind of inquiry upon modern Euro-American thinking about Rome, however, came from his account of the *alimenta* (read: food stamps!) and other measures designed for the relief of an underclass which post-republican Roman government resigned itself to deal with as permanently unemployed. Chronic before 1929, acute after the Crash, the kind of poverty sociologists today call "structural" remains with us as a rebuke to modern high-tech civilization—and the innovative totalitarian states of the 1930s claimed to be able to abolish it. While the rest of the world starved, it was said, full employment existed under Stalin's Five-Year Plans; or as John Kenneth Galbraith once quipped, Hitler solved Germany's unemployment problem, and then proceeded, by going to war, to solve America's.

Many in the democratic West shared Anne Morrow Lindbergh's sense "that somehow the leaders in Germany, Italy, and Russia have discoverd how to use new social and economic forces." Anne Lindbergh's *The Wave of the Future* (1940), written after the grey Nazi machine had rolled over Holland, Belgium, and France, was not a pro-Fascist apologia; civilized Americans, she believed, had to feel more affinity for Big Ben and the Paris sidewalk cafes than for the bullying goosesteppers Rome and Berlin had unleashed on the democracies. "The tragedy is . . . that there is so much that is good in the 'Forces of the Past,' and so much that is evil in 'The Forces of the Future.' " But there was no stopping those new forces, any more than the Roman Republic's defenders could have stopped the march of the Caesars, who brutalized and terrorized the wretched common folk of Rome—but fed them. "There is no fighting the wave of the future, any more than as a child you could fight against the gigantic roller that loomed up ahead of you suddenly," Lindbergh despairingly cried. "All you could do was to dive into it or leap with it. Otherwise, it would surely overwhelm you and pound you into the sand."

5. The Republic Gets Another Chance

If Fascism was, from a radical perspective, the last stage of capitalism, then democracy was no more than a forlorn evasion of reality. Nontotalitarian politicans in the democratic states struck good Communists (and Fascists) as suspicious, naive, or simply contemptible characters: either as wishy-washy compromisers with the Powers of Darkness or as would-be Caesars themselves. That line of reasoning tainted political discourse in the democracies as well. In the U.S. during recent decades we have become hardened to the use of the epithet "Communist" to describe political opponents on one's left; but in the 1930s and 1940s the word "Fascist" to describe the opposition to one's right was almost as promiscuous a term. The New Deal, in particular, was denounced by some of its enemies as both Communist *and* Fascist; the Latin word *dictator*, as applied to FDR by Roosevelt-haters, connoted both Hitlerism and Stalinism—and it was as grotesque a caricature as the word *monarch* had been when applied to George Washington and Andrew Jackson by the more excitable of their political foes.

The political "bosses" of the Roman republic's last centuries, and the Triumvirs and Caesars who followed them, commanded large armies; and "veterans who had served under these commanders," Frank Abbott concluded, "naturally accepted the political leadership of their former officers." Abbott then proceeded to draw the ominous modern parallel: "We are familiar in this country with the great influence exerted at the end of several of our wars by compact organizations of ex-service men." The Cincinnati, the G.A.R. (Grand Army of the Republic), and the American Legion had all functioned in a politically conscious way, and had secured tangible benefits for war veterans: after the Revolution, land grants; after the Civil War, liberal pensions; after World War I, G.I. insurance, mustering-out pay, care of the disabled. "All of these plans were tried by the Romans," Professor Abbott pointed out; "the bonus system was adopted, in a formal way, by Augustus in 7 B.C." The parallel worked for much of the world that had been at war between 1914 and 1918—as witness the Fascisti, the *Stahlhelm*, the *Freikorps*—but for the United States it manifestly broke down. Presidents as much at odds politically as Herbert Hoover and Franklin Roosevelt vetoed veterans' bonus bills, and Congress overrode them both. Moreover, World War I was unique among American wars up until that time in *not* producing from among its military leaders a serious, viable presidential candidacy. The only conceivably electable nominee, General Pershing, made it emphatically clear he was not interested; and General Leonard Wood was snookered out of the Republican nomination in 1920 by that ultra-civilian Warren Harding. Even combat veteran Theodore Roosevelt, Jr.—whose name alone carried potency—failed to repeat his father's feat of having won the governorship of New York by charging up San Juan Hill; he was defeated by Al Smith in 1924.

As for the military muscle of ex-servicemen, which indeed flexed frighteningly in American Legion repressive and vigilante activities after World War I ended, it in no way entered into the political coalition out of which arose the New Deal; if anything, the Legion's politics belonged with the Republican Opposition. In any case, *coups d'état* were foreign to American political experience; even the states that became the Southern Confederacy had made their "revolution" by statutory legislative action. In sharp, painful contrast is a speech delivered by Mussolini in 1921—the year before the March on Rome—in which the Fascist leader argued, like other twentieth-century tyrants, that his rule over his fellow citizens would be not only in their own best interest but also on their own acknowledged behalf, whether they wanted it that way or not: "I declare that my desire is to govern if possible with the consent of the majority, but, in order to obtain, to foster, and to strengthen that consent, I will use all the force at my disposal."

So the Caesars had operated, professing to be forceful champions of the Roman *populus* against the reactionary old patrician class. One can therefore understand the disquiet of conservative Americans—and, perhaps, of others not so conservative!—at a newly inaugurated President's declaration in 1933 that if the existing constitutional structures did not suffice to bring relief to a "stricken nation in the midst of a stricken world," he would ask Congress for "broad Executive power . . . as great as the power that would be given to me if we were in fact invaded by a foreign foe"; a disquiet reinforced by the great applause he drew from the Inauguration crowd for saying so. What subsequent critics of Franklin Roosevelt have overlooked is that *he never came back to Congress and asked for that power,* even though a desperate country might very well have granted it to him; much as democratically chosen French executives, in the same period, were frequently given the power to govern by decree.

Aha, said vigilant Roosevelt-watchers; then he is not Julius, violating law and custom to cross the Rubicon and march on Rome, but Augustus, adroitly blending the forms of republican constitutionalism with the substance of autocratic control. "Shrewd ol' Gus," wrote one late convert to the New Deal after a lifetime as a reactionary, the science fictionist H. P. Lovecraft, in 1936; "he had himself 'elected' consul of the 'republic' year after year, whilst the conscript fathers doddered emptily on in the old Hooverite (or Catonian or what-have-you) way without any further power to cause poverty and mischief and revolt!" In the long run, some observers felt, constitutional democracy was threatened less by the prospect of militants marching up Pennsylvania Avenue than by the growth of administrative regulation at the expense of judge-interpreted law. That was, in large part, what the Supreme Court "packing" fight of 1937 was about. In that controversy "Caesar" is usually said to have lost the battle but won the war; yet he won it in a way which eventually shifted such decisions back into activist judges' hands.

But that was not the end of the argument. From time to time critics and observers of the American scene continued to compare the innovative domestic institutions of the New Deal with those of the Roman Principate. Thus H. J. Haskell of the *Kansas City Star* produced a book entitled *The New Deal in Old Rome: How Government in the Ancient World tried to Deal With Modern Problems* (second edition, 1947). Forgetting that a metaphor is by definition a comparison between two things that are *un*like except at the point being compared, Haskell credited a Resettlement Administration to the Gracchi and then to Julius Caesar, a PWA to Augustus, a Home Owners' Loan Corporation to Tiberius, an Agricultural Adjustment Act to Domitian, a Farm Credit Administration to the Antonines, and at the last, to Diocletian, something very like an Office of Price Administration. Far-fetched as many of these comparisons doubtlessly were, they point to a concern—not limited to partisan Republicans—lest the enormous expansion of the scope of government under the New Deal make "Caesarism," or something like it, far more possible structurally than it had ever been before. "If our civilization is to continue on the present complex basis," that philosophical New Dealer Henry A. Wallace wrote in 1934, government would of necessity be managing far more of the economy than Americans were accustomed to have it do. Perhaps, then, FDR was neither Julius Caesar nor Octavian, but Claudius, the fourth emperor, creating and deploying an effective bureaucracy that would persist through rain or shine, plagues, civil wars, or barbarian invasions, for centuries.

In 1940, when "that man in the White House" sought and won an unprecedented third presidential term, the gambit somehow seemed different from previous third-term attempts such as Grant's in 1880 or Theodore Roosevelt's in 1912. Not only the conspiracy-minded alarmists but also a politician as broad-minded and good-natured as Wendell Willkie, contesting the third-term election on the Republican ticket, described the contest in ways that drew scare headlines even in the verbally inhibited *New York Times* (September 17, 1940): WILLKIE PREDICTS DICTATORSHIP HERE IF ROOSEVELT WINS. Conceding as a good sportsman that Roosevelt wasn't doing this on purpose, that he doubtless thought of himself as a small-d democrat, the challenger nonetheless charged that his opponent "has strained our democratic institutions to the breaking point. I warn you— . . . if, because of some fine speeches about humanity, you return this administration to office, you will be serving under an American totalitarian government before the long third term is finished."

The long third term was followed by a fourth; yet the institutions of democracy survived. The American republic's traditional constitutional forms and procedures turned out to have considerably more strength and resilience—and, as it turned out, capacity for creative adaptation—than many people had supposed. More than that. None of the other democracies—not even Britain—felt able to stage a serious partisan election in the midst of a perilous all-out war. Willkie's indictment of Roosevelt in the summer of 1940 has to be set in the context of an action that same summer by the democratically elected French government, which on July 10, 1940, without even being nudged to do so by the occupying Germans, meekly voted itself out of existence, together with the republican constitution which had given France its longest-lived regime since the great Revolution itself.

Willkie's presidential candidacy gave no comfort, however, to Americans who *approved* of New Deal policies but saw them jeopardized by Roosevelt's foreign policy; for on the all-important question of support for the Western Allies the two candidates saw eye-to-eye. Much of historian Charles A. Beard's bitterness toward President Roosevelt, which after the war would lead Beard to launch the revisionist or "FDR personally dropped the first bomb on Pearl Harbor" school of historical writing, sprang from a conviction that the New Deal, having creatively fused "the severe economic analysis of the Hamilton-Webster tradition with the humanistic democracy of the parallel tradition" (of Jefferson) in a grand synthesis which could have brought America into a true blending of political with industrial democracy, had blown it all away by going to war. John Dewey had similar misgivings about going to war in 1939: "It is quite conceivable," he wrote in an essay titled "No Matter What Happens—Stay Out," "that after the next war we should have in this country a semi-military, semi-financial autocracy, which would fasten class divisions on this country for untold years. In any case we should have the suppression of all the democratic values for the sake of which we professedly went to war."

The Blitz changed Dewey's mind; he did not have to wait for Pearl Harbor to decide that the march of the dictators must be halted and turned back. But it put him, and other good-willing Americans, into an intolerable dilemma, deflected from consciousness for a time by the all-absorbing whirlwind of actual war. In due course the deferred awareness of that dilemma would exacerbate the "generation gap" that would open between Americans shaped by the experiences of the 1940s and those who shared in the insurgencies of the 1960s. To the slogan "Make love, not war," one possible rejoinder was "Okay, kids, so what are we supposed to have done about Hitler?" In order to *stop* Caesar, it seemed, one had to *become* Caesar. The ghosts of Spengler and Brooks Adams must have grinned.

Interlude IX

From a moon-orbiting spacecraft as it looks across an ash-grey landscape to the lunar horizon, the Earth as it ascends into a black sky seems little. From a sail-powered hull as it rises and falls on the sea-swell, the same world appears immense. Great also, for most of human history, has been the time required to span that immensity. Herodotus, the Father of History, states that Phoenicians sailing under Pharoah's flag took three years to sail all the way around Africa—pausing long enough, in two successive seasons, to plant and harvest enough food crops to keep them going. Two millennia later, Magellan's surviving crew members managed to circumnavigate the planet—"the first earth orbit," it has aptly been called—in just under two years. Eventually, as a byproduct of the industrialization of commerce and the competition for empire, speed records would fall and fall and fall again.

Jules Verne's mythical Phileas Fogg in 1873 made it Around the World in Eighty Days. In 1889–90 in real life, the intrepid young American journalist Nellie Bly cut that to seventy-two. In 1942 former and future presidential candidate Wendell Willkie on a goodwill mission around the globe logged 30,000 miles in forty-nine days—thirty of which he spent on the ground, visiting, exhorting, observing.

The voyage of the converted warplane Gulliver had to be highly circuitous, for in 1942 most of the planet was at war. Skirting the vast stretches of Africa, Eruope, and Asia which then flew the flags of the Rising Sun or the Nazi crooked cross, the aircraft touched ground in Cairo, which Willkie said President Roosevelt had warned him might be in the hands of Rommel's Afrika Korps by the time the Gulliver got there; in Kuibyshev on the Volga, among pine trees and "wheat land rolling down the river to Stalingrad, where Russian soldiers were holding a mass of rubble" against the Wehrmacht's assault; in Chungking, Kuomintang China's rugged wartime capital far up the

Yangtze, then regularly being bombed in Japanese air raids after each of which the people emerged from the intricate caves they had dug into the city's red loam hills and, with incredible patience and energy, commenced to rebuild.

The war must end one day, Willkie knew; and the peace that followed would have to be planned for an emerging world that would, this American pilgrim passionately hoped, be "free alike of the economic injustices of the West and the political malpractices of the East. . . . I mean," Willkie summed up after his return, "quite literally that it must embrace the earth." Thus he turned the insights of Vladimir Vernadskii and other whole-earth-minded scientists into their political equivalent: "Continents and oceans are plainly only parts of the whole scene, as I have seen them, from the air," and the shrinkage of the planet must continue. That much of human destiny not even enterprising, willful Americans would be able to defy or set aside; for distances which in the Gulliver's time were measurable in days would become measurable in minutes in the era of the long-distance rocket bomb.

TEN

World Revolution—World Empire— World Community

The Wilderness had become the City; the empty land had become an industrial dump; the formerly dispersed settlements of human-kind were flowing together into, if not a "global village," then perhaps a global shopping mall. Americans, whether they liked the idea or not—and many of them didn't—must henceforth rub shoulders with the other villagers or shoppers.

Had their Constitution and other political forms prepared them for that kind of planetary consciousness? More urgently, with that village/mall seeming constantly on the verge of feud or riot, could that Constitution and those forms stand the strains of a continual state of war or semi-war, with at last the prospect of an instantaneously launched, world-shattering war-cyclone, after which the crowded land could become empty wilderness again?

1. One World: Easier Said Than Done

Flitting from airport to airport on a VIP tour is no way to get to know a country—including one's own, as a flock of U.S. presidential candidates have learned in recent years—especially when most of one's time is spent hobnobbing with other VIPs. On his plane hops along the United Nations/Axis frontier in 1942 Wendell Willkie spent a large part of his time talking with the likes of General Montgomery, Charles de Gaulle, the Chiangs of China (and, by way of balance, Communist China's Chou En-Lai), the Premier of Iraq, the Shah of Iran, and the President of the Council of People's Commissars of the autonomous republic of Yakutsk. Like many other Americans, then and now, Willkie put more faith in personal contact and *bonhomie* to unravel complex political and social questions than historically weary Asians or Europeans ever would; reporting with relish, for example, Josef Stalin's reaction after their first long private conversation: "Mr. Willkie, you know I grew up a Georgian peasant," said the Master of the Gulags. "I am unschooled in pretty talk. All I can say is I like you very much."

However, the American capitalist did not spend all of his ground time in state dinners and motorcades. President Roosevelt had known exactly what he was doing when he gave his blessing to this global tour by the man who two years earlier had accused him of heading the nation toward dictatorship. Although as CEO of an electric utilities firm Wendell Willkie had fought and won a battle for his stockholders against the New Deal's great experiment in public power, the TVA, he was far more open-minded and free from entrepreneurial cliches than most U.S. business executives of that era, some of whom in clinging to their private-enterprise platitudes had gotten the country into the fix which made the New Deal necessary. Willkie brought that same freshness of outlook with him overseas.

Part of Wendell Willkie's political charm lay in his wide-openness. But alongside the man's "gee-whiz," lumbering big bear manner he carried a keenly observant mind and eye. He noticed the "underfed and scrawny children playing in the dirty streets of the old city of Jerusalem"; the "Egyptian boys not ten years old pumping water into irrigation ditches with pumps as primitive as the first wheel"; the couples in the audience at a "gypsy opera" performed in Yakutsk, parading between the acts arm in arm as was the custom of the country. Willkie did not simply watch such people; more important, he listened to them. In addition to VIPs, the American visitor talked with a grade-school teacher in China, a veiled woman in Baghdad, a carpet weaver in Teheran, a fur-capped pelt hunter at the edge of the Siberian forest—and, wherever possible, with young people. The disconcerting message he brought back from them, beyond the expected ritual assurances that "our side" was going to beat "the other side" in the war, was that they wanted *all* the foreign occupiers and administrators off their soil; not just the Germans and the Japanese, but the British and the French as well.

Willkie may have been the first major American political figure to sense what was happening in what we now name the Third World. He saw, and said, of the Second World War what Woodrow Wilson had never been quite willing to accept about the First: that the planet was engaged not just in war but in revolution. "I am only reporting that a great process has started which no man—certainly not Hitler—can stop," Willkie summed up in the book he published six months after his return, appropriately titled *One World:*

> After centuries of ignorant and dull compliance, hundreds of millions of people in eastern Europe and Asia have opened the books. Old fears no longer frighten them. They are no longer willing to be Eastern slaves for Western profits. . . . The big house on the hill surrounded by mud huts has lost its awesome charm.
>
> Our Western world and our presumed supremacy are now on trial. Our boasting and our big talk leave Asia cold. Men and women in Russia and China and in the Middle East are conscious now of their own potential strength. They are coming to know that many of the decisions about the future of the world lie in their hands.

America, Willkie believed, had a vast "reservoir of good will" in the rest of the world (and where, one is forced to ask, has *that* disappeared to in the last forty-going-on-fifty years?). It did not follow, however, that the "profound and violent" changes that could be expected after the war would automatically "be in our favor. The magic of our Western political ideas has been sharply challenged. . . . [Others] have watched us now at close range, for almost a generation, while we have been fighting each other and ourselves and questioning the central structure of our beliefs. Everywhere I found polite but skeptical people, who met my questions about their problems and difficulties with . . . ironic questions about our own."

One World is a political tract, not a philosophical treatise. Much of its analysis is superficial, much of its argument outdated. Nevertheless it touched hearts and consciences in its day, and if it had not the transforming effect of *Common Sense* or *Uncle Tom's Cabin*, still it stands today as a reminder to Americans of the road sadly not taken after 1945. "America must choose one of three courses after this war," Willkie counseled, "narrow nationalism, which inevitably means the ultimate loss of our own liberty; international imperialism, which means the sacrifice of some other nation's liberty; or the creation of a world in which there shall be an equality of opportunity for every race and every nation."

Nationalism in the "narrow" sense, which in Willkie's time (and in his own political party) meant isolationism, perished in the rising roar of the first German V–2 rocket test-fired at Peenemünde and in the first nuclear fireball over New Mexico. Americans in the postwar years sometimes wistfully looked back at that kind of nationalism, when they had been all alone in "God's country," but recognized in more realistic moments that galloping technology had made it obsolete. Nationalism in our own time has become interventionist, intrusive, willing to take risks unimaginable in the age of Washington and Jefferson. International imperialism in the old, formal, possessive sense Americans also forswore. Except for the formerly Japanese-held islands scattered across the "Trust Territory of the Pacific" the U.S. after World War II annexed no overseas territories; even before the Union Jack and the Tricolor came down over great stretches of Africa the Stars and Stripes were coming down in the Philippines. But imperialism, like nationalism, has changed its face; expressing itself not as outright ownership and governance, but as economic penetration, as the acquisition of airfields and launch sites, as the deployment ten thousand miles from home of missile-equipped fleets, as the forcible support of "friendly" governments and the overthrow of "unfriendly" ones; in short, as *power*.

As for Willkie's third option, to create a world of equality, that was supposed to be a job for the just-born United Nations—whose potential for success rested on the assumption of a postwar greatpower cooperation which simply did not come to pass. Stalin had said he liked Wendell Willkie very much, and Harry Truman reciprocated—and got himself into hot water politically—by saying "I like old Joe"; but that did not stop either superpower leader from doing his bit to launch the Cold War. Let us not play historical games here, either of the Right's "the Communists started it all" sort or of the Left's "It's all the American capitalists' fault" variety; both superpowers abused the veto in the United Nations and/or circumvented the UN's nominal authority. When the United Nations themselves sought to repair the damage by shifting that authority from the deadlocked, superpower-dominated Security Council to the more open forum of the General Assembly, they found that they had subtly sabotaged Willkie's equality of races and nations into an equality of *governments*, many—nay, most—of which failed to qualify as "democratic" by even the most generous semantic stretching of that term.

America, born in revolution, found itself at mid-century in a revolutionary world—and, tragically, could not accept the fact. Such had not been the case in the nineteenth century, when many

Americans—and at times their government's leaders—had praised the revolutionary activities of Garibaldi and Kossuth, of South Americans and Irishmen, of Greeks and Russians and Poles. Even Woodrow Wilson had pushed for "self-determination," of a correct and proper, nonrevolutionary sort; and the Franklin Roosevelt administration had pressed the British very hard on their future role in places like India, prompting Mr. Churchill's famous retort, "I did not become His Majesty's first minister in order to preside over the liquidation of the British Empire." In that exchange the Americans had the last word, but the British had the last ironic laugh. Churchill's immediate successors in the U.K. did, in effect, liquidate the British Empire—and they left the United States with many of the traditional British imperial commitments and goals, one of which, long before the advent of Communism, had been to Stop Russia. Wrackingly, in Southeast Asia America would become the French legatee as well.

The Second World War was dual in nature. It was, as Willkie said, a war of liberation. But it was also, in William Appleman Williams's suggestive phrase, a "war for the American frontier," a frontier of ever-continuing, planet-wide economic expansion. When Frederick Jackson Turner's continental frontier ended, we had had a chance to do otherwise, Williams has argued; we could have turned away from that tempting horizon, faced ourselves, solved within America's own borders the problem of maldistribution of wealth. Instead, we had turned outward and spread the problem all the way around the globe.

One well-intentioned publicist of that time defined the Chinese as *400 Million Customers*. Other people overseas were similarly perceived in America as *markets* rather than as autonomous agents with economic goals they set for themselves. "Having defined overseas economic activity as essential to the welfare of the United States," Williams continues, "American policymakers were exceedingly prone to view social revolution in those countries as a threat to the vital national interests of their own nation." Against that threat in the postwar years Americans would intervene in ways that at times proved downright reactionary. So had Rome performed, when moving into Greece militarily and politically in the second century B.C.; in the perennial, never-settled quarrels within the various Greek city-states between democratic and oligarchic factions Rome, with one eye on a possible military menace further to the East, regularly as a matter of policy sided with the local aristocracy. Local "city bourgeoisies," as Rostovtzeff would call them, approved. It was better for business that way.

2. The End of Ideology?

For Americans categorically to have condemned *all* revolutions would have been to reject their own revolutionary heritage. Ranged against a superpower which also claimed revolutionary sanction, soon to be joined by a China which had not gone at all the way Wendell Willkie and countless others had expected (although Chou En-Lai during Willkie's China visit had dropped a few broad hints as to what might be coming), Americans in the postwar years faced the same knotty problem with which Locke and Burke and Paine had wrestled: how to distinguish "good" revolutions from "bad." Adlai Stevenson, in the Godkin Lectures he gave at Harvard in 1954 after visiting even more countries than Willkie had—and, like Willkie, avoiding those in hands most Americans perceived as hostile—contended that the choice facing the emergent Third World would not be between revolution and counter-revolution but between the revolution symbolized in Thomas Jefferson and the revolution which pledged allegiance to Karl Marx.

Like efforts of Adlai's in certain other directions, this was a good try. One problem with such an approach, however, was that the intellectual context for Jeffersonian democracy was long gone. Not without reason has Daniel Boorstin written of the *lost* world of Thomas Jefferson; a great loss indeed, for even Jefferson's archaic agrarian biases could have spoken to the condition of a Third World that was—and still is—overwhelmingly rural. It is worthy of note that Sukarno, the liberator of Indonesia from the Dutch, made it a point during his first visit to the U.S. to make a personal pilgrimage out to Monticello. Another Asian revolutionary leader who, like Sukarno, used Jefferson's "all men are created equal" phrase, in his own declaration of independence from imperial control, was Ho Chi Minh.

At home, however, categorical imperatives of Jefferson's kind—abstract, axiomatic "rights" to life, liberty, and the pursuit of happiness—had been sapped and undermined by the findings and analyses of American social scientists for at least two generations (above, chapter 8). World War II, and the march of Fascism which had led to it, had been a great shock to the "value-free" social psychology, political science, and other relativist disciplines which resulted from that disintegrative process. Suddenly people wanted to be able to assert that certain things going on in the world— racism, police terror, the suppression of political opposition, aggressive war, genocide—were wrong; not just historically inappropriate, or unscientific, or contrary to an informed consensus, or inconsistent with the mores, or culturally dysfunctional, or against one's personal preference, or neurotic, or ignorant, but actually, ontologically *evil*. The emergency abroad was also a formidable intellectual challenge at home, Edward Purcell writes in *The Crisis of Democratic Theory* (1973): "Rational justification was urgently needed at the very time when it seemed impossible to accomplish. . . . While their scientific predispositions had led many intellectuals in one direction, their moral beliefs and political attitudes pulled them strongly in another."

Apparently it was a crisis not only for intellectuals; writers highbrow, middlebrow, and low also rang journalistic changes throughout America's participation in World War II on the theme that Americans "don't know what they are fighting for." (As one widely circulated jest expressed it, British soldiers fought for the lifeline of Empire, Germans and Italians for the Fascist New Order, Russians for the workers of the world, Japanese for their Emperor—and Americans for souvenirs.) The simplest—and most dangerous—response to that felt gap would have been simply to absolutize the American nation-state without reference to any formal principles upon which it might rest; "my country, right or wrong." From that standpoint America was neither a set of self-evident truths nor a principle of constitutional government; what "the boys" were fighting for could be summed up as the flag, the land, and Mom's apple pie.

Somehow, even at the elementary level of the Hollywood propaganda film, that didn't seem quite enough. The nation's essence also had to be expressed as a special, historically unprecedented way in which diverse peoples got along together. The war movies of the 1940s, as Jeanine Basinger has shown, very quickly developed a formula in which the "typical" U.S. military outfit in combat always included a Dodger fan from Brooklyn, an Ozark or Appalachian hillbilly, a Polish immigrant steelworker, a wizened veteran of World War I (usually Irish), a bookish young man who writes poetry (usually killed), and one, two, or three ethnic representatives, also customarily killed off early in the script. It seemed

239

that Americans had an ideology in spite of themselves; their answer to the Nazi "master race" theory was, within certain limits, *e pluribus unum.*

Powerful though that egalitarian ideology undeniably was, it was not strong enough to prevent Americans while fighting a racist enemy abroad from committing racist acts at home, most notoriously against Americans of Japanese ancestry. And as a foundation for the theory and operation of a democratic government, *e pluribus unum* gave them precious little of a practical nature to draw on. The Emperor Caracalla in 212 A.D. granted blanket Rome citizenship upon all the free native inhabitants of the empire, an act making the Roman peoples truly *e pluribus unum* and conferring upon them pro forma equality before the law—but "in fact," Michael Rostovtzeff cautions, "Caracalla's grant did not help anyone and had no real social or political importance." Momentous though the principle of *de jure* equality would eventually prove, both in the formulation in the eighteenth century of republican political theory and in the achievement of civil liberties and civil rights thereafter, it had no direct or immediate impact upon the plight of the free but poverty-stricken citizen, or upon the eternal political question of who gets what, when, where, and how.

A more sophisticated solution to the perceived vacuum in American political values consisted of taking the anti-ideological relativism the social scientists had been forging for two generations and transforming it in turn into an ideology. Philosophical absolutism implies *political* absolutism; for decades John Dewey, to the dismay of various Thomist and Platonist academic colleagues, had been saying just that. "When freedom is conceived to be transcendental, the coercive restraint of immediate necessity will lay its harsh hand upon the mass of men," the educator had argued as early as 1908. "The diversion of intelligence from discrimination of plural and concrete goods . . . and from devising methods for holding men responsible for their concrete use of powers and conditions, has done more than brute love of power to establish inequality and injustice among men." (Incidentally, this consistent, and at the time typical, use of the generic term "men" for "people" can perhaps be more readily excused in John Dewey than in most of his contemporaries; for when it came down to the application of his educational philosophy to gender—how boys and girls should be educated and in what—John Dewey was decades if not generations ahead of his time.)

240

After the advent of Hitler in 1933 and after the Stalin terror culminating in the purges of 1937, Dewey was able to say, in effect, I told you so; totalitarianisms are absolutisms, embracing closed systems of ideas which they then force people to accept. Conversely, a democracy is by definition a country which doesn't have an ideology. By the late 1930s, largely in response to the challenge of Fascism (and, with more argument about it, of Stalinism), American intellectuals had begun "to develop the clear outlines of a broadly naturalistic and relativistic theory of democracy. Abandoning the idea of logically demonstrating the validity of democratic government," Edward Purcell sums up this school of thought, "they moved toward a pragmatic interpretation of the social consequences of absolutist versus relativist political theories." This transvaluation of values would not satisfy the frustrated longing for certitude which would eventuate in the Moral Majority, but for the time being it seemed to satisfy a lot of intellectuals; not only "secular humanists" (as John Dewey, for one, would have proudly acknowledged himself to be), but even a few theologues. Reinhold Niebuhr, for one, whose name was one to conjure with in the immediate postwar years, contended in *The Irony of American History* (1952) that "our actual achievements in social justice have been won by a pragmatic approach to the problems of power."

Niebuhr—or Dewey—would have added that you can't just do "realistic" social criticism or attempt case by case to redress specific grievances; you have to have a program and be willing to bet on it politically, otherwise you simply capitulate to Things As They Are. But right there, according to Purcell, lies the fatal flaw in this anti-ideological ideology. History is always playing cruel tricks on people; what the relativizing of American democratic ideology had unexpectedly accomplished was to transform 1940s-style liberal intellectuals into conservatives! Their consensus about America was both *pre*scriptive and *de*scriptive; it prescribed relativism as the democratic norm and then defined *existing* American society as the embodiment of that norm.

But what a powerful means that could become for the paralysis of all criticism! In the Cold War polarization between "America" and "anti-America," domestically whatever is, is right, and whatever "they" do "we" must not do; socialism, in particular, even of the non-Marxist British or Swedish kind, virtually ceased to be a thinkable American option. And abroad, seriously flawed regimes which professed—often cynically—allegiance to the "free world"

241

became all but insusceptible to criticism. McCarthyism as a means to conformity was hardly necessary, Purcell implies; the brokers of ideas had already done that to themselves. Small wonder, with such a mind-set, that there was a reaction against it in America in the sixties,—a reaction into Marxism, which insisted that you *do* need a coherent ideology, not just a rule-of-thumb program; and into civil rights militancy, on the part of long-suppressed Americans who could not calmly relativize their condition: as their advocate Martin Luther King, Jr. tried to explain, *"We can't wait."*

3. *The Strong Man Armed*

The right to trade freely with those purported four hundred million Chinese customers, regardless of imperial interference from any other quarter (and, perhaps, regardless of any desire on China's part to develop an internal market and economy of its own), the American State Department had formulated in 1900 as the "Open Door Policy." In due course that policy clashed with the aims of another country that had an expanding frontier, which that other nation defined as the "Greater East Asia Co-Prosperity Sphere." The price Japan exacted from the United States for continuing to insist on the Open Door after Japan's massive invasion of China in 1937 was Pearl Harbor.

The subsequent short-lived Japanese breakout across the Pacific Ocean, checked though it was after six months at the Battle of Midway and then turned back in bitter, to-the-last-man struggles on island after island, showed Americans—or *ought* to have shown them—that the indefinite mercantile expansion across the world, which they had expected would go on cheaply and peacefully forever was in reality not going to happen without cost. Rudyard Kipling, the poet of the world-empire then in process of leaving the stage, had implicitly warned them what to expect: "If blood be the price of Admiralty,/Lord God, we ha' paid it in full." To undertake such a burden as the British were about to lay down required a kind of ongoing military commitment America had never engaged in before.

Americans theretofore had fought their wars on an ad hoc basis, improvising immense armies virtually *ex nihilo;* as William Jennings Bryan had asserted as an argument against any need to impose a draft in World War I, "I have but to stamp my foot and a million men will spring to arms." Typically Americans had mobilized, rapidly, confusedly, but effectively; gone off and fought their war; and then demobilized as speedily as possible. The Union army which after the Civil War could in all probability have taken on any power in Europe soon shrank to a force barely sufficient to cope with the Indians along the frontier, as George Armstrong Custer, for one, learned. The nearly four million troops raised for World War I, half of whom got overseas in the relatively short time between the war declaration and the Armistice—a formidable levy by any standard—dwindled during the interwar years into a Regular Army the size of Denmark's. FDR, always sensitive to what people might be politically willing to take, evidently expected a similar outcome from World War II. Mindful that his opponent in the 1944 election (Thomas Dewey, a pale replacement for Willkie) had charged that the government, fearing the political consequences of renewed unemployment, was plotting to "keep men in the army" after the war, Roosevelt told Stalin at Yalta that he did not think he could hold American ground forces in Europe for more than two years.

The Cold War changed all that. "During modern times, and especially in the United States, men had come to look upon history as a peaceful continuum interrupted by war," C. Wright Mills observed in *The Power Elite* (1956). Now however, "men in authority are talking about an 'emergency' without a foreseeable end." After the German and Japanese surrenders the American armed forces did indeed come home quickly, as they always had before. However, as crisis followed renewed crisis—so acutely that Harry Truman, privately after a briefing during the Berlin blockade and airlift of 1948 wrote, "I have a terrible feeling . . . that we are very close to war"—American military power ceased to be a temporary improvisation for occasional use and became instead a permanent, structured part of American life.

In 1948, for the first time in the nation's history, Congress—against surprisingly little resistance—enacted a peacetime draft. The cozy, incestuous relationship that had developed during World War II between business, government, and the military, as exemplified in the corporation executive who either put on a uniform and entered the Quartermaster or Supply Corps to negotiate contracts for war materiel with his "former" employer or else accepted a job as a government economic regulator and then bent the procurement and bidding rules in favor of the large corporations' supposed greater efficiency of scale, became simply a fact of life; eventually leading Dwight Eisenhower, who may have felt himself caught in a Dr. Frankenstein's role for having helped create this monster, to denounce it as the "military-industry complex."

From the standpoint of the Revolutionary and Constitutional fathers, such a development would have amounted to counter-revolution. "Standing armies"—permanent military establishments—they regarded as instruments of the traditional authoritarian state, designed not only for the prosecution of its own, not popularly chosen, foreign policy goals, but also for the intimidation and coercion of its own people. The whole point of the Second Amendment—so tenaciously misunderstood by today's gun fanatics—had been to avert such centralization of force by diffusing military power through "a well regulated militia," locally controlled.

The Founders were also aware of the political mischief to which a state of emergency could lead. The ever-perceptive James Madison warned Jefferson in 1798, when partisans of an incumbent administration were using a war crisis to discredit and silence their opposition, "that the loss of liberty at home is to be charged to provisions against danger, real or pretended, from abroad." Abraham Lincoln also, although as war leader he would himself play fast and loose with liberty in the Union states to provide against the danger he perceived from the Rebellion, pointed out earlier in his career that the claimed prerogatives of a Commander-in-Chief could put the Republic in mortal danger. "Allow the President to invade a neighboring nation whenever he deems it necessary," Lincoln wrote to his friend and law partner William Herndon during the Mexican War,

> and you allow him to make war at pleasure. . . . If today he should choose to say he thinks it necessary to invade Canada to prevent the British from invading us, how could you stop him? You may say to him, 'I see no probability of the British invading us'; but he will say to you, 'Be silent: I see it, if you don't.'

—precisely the rationalization President Lyndon Johnson would employ against his opponents, again and again.

But those had been emergencies of brief duration; the naval war of 1797–98 with France was in process of settlement almost while Madison wrote, while the war with Mexico was concluded in less than two years from its declaration. But "an 'emergency' without a foreseeable end," as Mills described the Cold War, enormously multiplies the danger Madison and Lincoln foresaw; many a person who can resist an occasional or infrequent temptation to stray, if that temptation becomes insistent and unending, will succumb. Danger, real *and* pretended, from abroad has since 1945 become a way of life; and the stratagems devised by American leaders to deal with successive foreign crises have suggested to alarmed small-r republicans the possible gradual rise of an American Caesar far more subtle than the simple man-on-horseback who was saluted by Kaiser Wilhelm II. Perhaps indeed he will not be a "he," but a faceless, corporate "they."

Only once during the past forty years has Caesar's ghost seemed to materialize in his classic form, and that was a very special case. When Douglas MacArthur strode down into the well of the House of Representatives to give account of his proconsulship over Japan, he turned and raised his arm to the applauding members of Congress in a gesture as old as the legions. It did give television watchers who had read some Roman history a scare. But that was the end of it. U.S. foreign policy has always been peculiarly a prerogative of the civilian executive, tempered at times by the Senate; and even so bitter a Senatorial foe of Harry Truman as Robert A. Taft had to concede that in a constitutional showdown the President, not the General, was in charge. What bothered thoughtful critics like Taft was the enormous increase in the power, if not the authority, of the President himself, with or without consultation with Congress, to commit the country to a course of action anywhere in the world. Yet at the same time, as the Caesars had also known, a nation once expanded cannot, without risk of chaos, simply pack up its legions and go home.

Moreover, not all such commitments to action necessarily pointed toward Caesarism. Arnold Toynbee, whose *Study of History* had a vogue in the post-World War II years even greater than that of Spengler's *Decline of the West* after World War I, saw the foreign policy initiatives of the 1940s and 1950s—the Coal and Steel Community, the United Nations, the Common Market, and the like—as creative and democratic responses to an unprecedented international challenge. A "movement for the unification of Europe . . . has now received powerful encouragement from America in the terms of the Marshall Plan," Toynbee proclaimed early in 1948, and "the eagerness and earnestness of the response which the Marshall Plan has evoked on the European side are indications that Europe does realize her danger." Spengler was wrong; history

245

need not repeat itself. "We cannot cast a horoscope of our own future," said Toynbee in his Reith Lectures of 1952, "by observing what happened in Graeco-Roman history in the period of decline, and then mechanically translating this Graeco-Roman record into modern Western terms."

Nevertheless the Roman experience carries a sharp warning to any nation whose field of action suddenly inflates beyond all previous limits ("we shall pay any price, bear any burden, meet any hardship, support any friend, oppose any foe"—JFK): once launched upon an initiative, warlike or otherwise, whose scope embraces the entire known world, it becomes very difficult to know when or where to stop. Not every land lying in the disputed area between the superpowers could be Americanized, no matter how many soldiers or how much foreign aid be shipped in. Similarly, in antiquity, not every land could be Romanized; Germany was not Gaul, as three of Augustus's legions found out in 9 A.D. when they were led into ambush and annihilated in or near the Teutoburg Forest. The parallel goes one long step further. The *Teutoburger Wald* disaster had the effect upon Rome that the Tet offensive in Vietnam had upon America; it sharply changed the direction of a nation's foreign policy. Six years later, after an inconclusive strike with eight legions across the Rhine at Mainz was checked by a resolute and skillful German foe, the Romans never again tried to establish their kind of social order in that long-contested corner of the world. One can well imagine a following generation of Roman second-guessers, like their post-Vietnam equivalent in America, grumbling that if their invincible legions had only been permitted to hang on longer in that tangled, guerrilla-infested wilderness they could have won. The most striking political difference between the two events is that afterward Augustus, unlike LBJ, did not feel he had to step down.

4. From Criticism to Insurgency

Douglas MacArthur's return from the Far East occurred at the beginning of the 1950s, a decade many persist in thinking of as a time of calm and security in contrast to the turbulent and anxiety-ridden years which were to follow—forgetful that *any* time period, even one that experienced a world-convulsing war or a great depression, gets misremembered in the same hazy nostalgic way once it has receded twenty or thirty years beyond present reality.

The fifties in fact produced far more sharp and pertinent criticism of society's shortcomings that the period usually gets credit for. That was after all the decade of *The Power Elite* and *White Collar*, of *The True Believer* and *The Organization Man*, of *Brown v. Board of Education* and Dr. King's *Stride Toward Freedom*, of *The Affluent Society* and *Rebel Without a Cause* and the first American publication of Beauvoir's *The Second Sex*. In such an age of social dissection, much of it acute, some of it profound, it should not occasion surprise that the America/Rome comparison would come up again—or that this time around the comparison would be more with the Principate than with the Republic. "Certainly there were disturbing parallels between the history of the Graeco-Roman world and the state of Western civilization," Arthur Ekirch wrote in a typical Jeremiad, *The Decline of American Liberalism* (1955). "Even if dire predictions of new Caesars and more wars proved false, there were other illiberal pressures derived from modern technology, mass psychology, and collectivist economics. . . . modern civilization might already be in the midst of the decline that had overtaken all previous civilizations and cultures."

In support of this argument Ekirch quoted a leading American historian of ancient Rome, Chester Starr. "The perfect democracy of the Roman Empire," as Starr ironically called it, came down to no more than the Romans' attempt "to camouflage to their own hearts the full nature of their autocracy"; and "the saddening fact is that people were almost universally ready to accept this state of affairs"—as (implicitly) Americans might be getting ready to accept a social system far more authoritarian than the open, popularly controlled regime it still professed itself to be. Starr was but one of several formally trained historians of antiquity who occasionally took time out from mulling over their coins and inscriptions to join in this American-Roman comparison game. Writing on "Roman Economic Problems and Current Issues" in the *Classical Journal*, Kenneth D. White declared that he found "the story of Rome's decline and fall . . . a far more profitable subject of study for the present generation than it was in Gibbon's day." White saw "an important parallel between the finished record of Rome and the incomplete story of our Western civilization" in the modern world's "problems of reduced incentives to work, of restrictions upon free enterprise, of an expanding bureaucracy which puts a premium on 'safe' thinking and discourages initiative and the development of new ideas." It sounds almost like Republican entrepreneurial rhetoric, foreshadowing Reagan's—save that corporate enterprise also, loaded down with unimaginative MBAs, seemed as devoted to stifling routine as its governmental equivalent, if not more so.

That was in 1958. A decade later another American historian of ancient Rome, Frank Bourne, although disclaiming any prescriptive authority—"I do not think that classicists are about to be drafted as presidential advisers"—suggested that "study and reflection about" the maladies of Rome in decline "might at least broaden our grasp of and concern for possibilities inherent in our own situation." Like Ferrero before him, Professor Bourne—a Down-Easter who ran his Maine farm on the principles laid down in the elder Cato's *De Re Rustica*—focused on what was happening to the city, arguing that in this respect twentieth-century America's dilemma "closely resembles" that of Rome:

> Not only the middle class and well-to-do leave for the suburbs, but so has much industry—as the quantities of industrial parks along our highways testify—and to these the urban poor do not have access. The flight of the powerful, and sometimes whole villages, to the self-sufficient economy of the Late Roman villa was very materially instrumental in the decline of the city in the Late Empire. One does not have to belabor the similarities of the resultant problems in taxation, welfare, education, and structural decay in a place such as New York without wondering how many of the counter-measures taken by the conscientious Roman bureaucrats will be taken—unconsciously of course—by our own.

A new note was struck in the fifties, of cultural exhaustion; the diametric opposite of the previously more typical kind of America criticism (that the U.S. is gawky, adolescent, immature, youthfully vigorous but sloppy and careless, et cetera ad infinitum). The Rome part of this comparison was not with the early Principate under Augustus, nor with that later century under the Antonine emperors which Edward Gibbon hailed as the peak of ancient civilization, but with the waning years under the Dominate when the well of classical learning ran dry. Surprisingly, and unprecedently, radicals joined with conservatives in this threnody. Ray Ginger, for one, concluded an excellent book on the lively Chicago culture of the 1890s, *Altgeld's America* (1958), with a psalm of praise to "the vitality of this past generation that contrasts so strongly with our own confusions and lethargy. . . . When we compare the single city of Chicago a half-century ago with the entire country today, it is the country today that suffers by comparison," Ginger cried:

> In the United States today, where is the governor to rank with Altgeld? the social critic to rank with Veblen? the lawyer to rank with Darrow? the educator-philosopher to rank with Dewey? the social worker to rank with Jane Addams or a half-dozen of her associates? the novelist to rank with Dreiser? the architect to rank with Wright?

Ginger conceded Charles Dickens's common-sensical answer to all such laments for the Good Old Days, namely that at any given historical moment "It was the best of times, it was the worst of times." But the concession was only partial. "Men like Altgeld and Darrow had some ambitions that were far from noble," Ginger admitted,

> and they had more conflicts than the typical man. But in most situations they ultimately faced up to the question: What is right? The question has gone out of style. Nowadays an effort to reach a decision is likely to begin and end with the query: Am I covered? In this shift lies the collapse of a civilization, and we still do not realize exactly what has happened or how.

"Are you using such gifts as you possess for or against the people?" asked Louis Sullivan, one of those turn-of-the-century Chicagoans; a question which struck in the author of *Altgeld's America* a responsive social and, ultimately, religious chord. For activists of Ginger's political persuasion the rejuvenating answer for America—if any—lay on the Left. For a time during the later 1960s—a time Arthur Mann has aptly described as "the ungluing of America," when "policemen assigned to anti-riot duty themselves rioted in the streets" and "the nation's oldest political party nominated a President in a setting that called to mind the antics of a banana republic," it appeared—probably to more people than had come to a similar decision in the 1930s—that the center truly would not hold and that the Left had become the only politically promising direction in which one could go.

Significantly it called itself a *New* Left. The Old Left from the standpoint of insurgent youth in the 1960s seemed dusty and out-of-date; "you can always tell the guys from the C.P. [Communist Party] at one of our rallies," one young militant scornfully explained, "they're the ones who always wear jackets and ties." (So, of course, did FBI agents.) Traditional Marxism's simple grand division of modern humanity into bourgeois and proletarian—even though young activists rhetorically updated it into a similar dichotomy between "The Power Structure" and "The Movement"—just wouldn't work in this historical situation. The complex mixture of conflicts—parent versus child, man versus woman, old versus young ("don't trust anybody over/under thirty"), nonviolent marcher Martin Luther King versus armed and ready Black Panthers, "hawk" versus "dove," Barry Goldwater versus George McGovern (and, versus both of them, a massive cynicism toward *all* conventional politics), "Jesus Freak"versus proclaimer that "God is dead," John Baez versus Archie Bunker, denouncer of all "rational learning" versus Mr. Spock—challenged and, ultimately, defeated the skills of any dialectician to weave all these different strands of dissidence together. Were these many styles of protest and rejection—these "schisms in the body social," as Arnold Toynbee might have called them—symptoms of a society's death throes or of its birth pangs? The question throws a different light on the much-discussed "generation gap" of the sixties.

Unlike earlier revolutionary movements which had sought to seize control of an intact society by overturning its ruling class, many who claimed allegiance to The Movement sought to overturn *all* societal structures; true, pure radical action consisted not in seizure but in sabotage. More passively, not a few perceived the model revolutionary situation not in the storming of the Bastille or of the Winter Palace, or the stand at Concord Bridge, but in Woodstock. Turn on, tune in, drop out; the Age of Aquarius is coming; drift and let history carry you on into the "greening of America." In retrospect, the vulnerability of such a stance—if "stance" be the right word for anything so languorous—is evident; no power structure was going to give up without a struggle, and some day, while still waiting for the heavens to open, one was alas going to be thirty years old. From the apocalyptic expectations of all the diverse folk whom history had scooped together as "The Movement" it was all too easy, after that Movement collapsed, to fall into an equally comprehensive gloom toward a system which seemed both too corrupt to reform itself and too strong to overthrow. Since that system to a considerable extent had yielded a point regarding the pursuit of personal lifestyles, perhaps the wisest course was simply *sauve qui peut;* whence the sterile "self-fulfillment" quests of the seventies.

It wouldn't have occurred to most of the flower children to situate themselves in an equivalent of Rome, because most of them weren't all that interested in history; *Amerika,* imagined as a not personally remembered Nazi Germany, was as far back for historical analogy as they cared to go. Some over-thirty types who retained a foothold in the despised "square" culture, however, did speculate on the subject. The American Society of Church History, of all eminently respectable bodies, at its annual spring meeting in Chicago in 1971 devoted one entire session to the theme of "counterculture," examples of which kept turning up throughout the history of Christianity; in particular, in its early years under persecution by imperial Rome (the well-received rock opera *Jesus Christ Superstar* proceeded from somewhat similar premises). Conceivably the broad-gauged nihilism endemic in the Movement might be explicable in Arnold Toynbee's terms: after a "universal state" such as the Roman Empire develops an "internal proletariat"— which Toynbee defined not in Marxian economic class terms but rather in sociological-psychological terms, as a category of people who are "in" the society but not "of" it—the next step is spiritual secession from that society. Edward Gibbon's primary objection to the early Church was that it distracted and drained away the ablest minds in the Empire at a time when they all should have been rallying to keep that society afloat; the early Christians' answer, in effect, was: the ship is sinking; man the lifeboats. From this standpoint, Rome did not "fall" to outside attack so much as founder from its own dead weight; and perhaps *that*, politically, some pessimists proposed, was what was happening to America. A few found even the Rome parallel too fresh and modern; as technics drew civilization into the coils of a world-spanning "megamachine," Lewis Mumford argued in *The Pentagon of Power* (1970), society was reverting not to the condition of Iron Age Rome but back even further in time, to the even more absolute, slave-driving regimentation of the Bronze Age.

5. The Presidency, from Imperial to Theatrical

It would be a fundamental historical blunder, however, to go to the opposite pole from the utopianism of the sixties and contend that *nothing* permanent came out of that time of trials. If America in the 1950s had fallen into the Cold War mind-lock of rejecting whatever the socialists and communists did, the 1960s counter-culture had at least dared to be different, even if at times dumb. Long after that counterculture's demise, certain of its prophets— Peter, Paul, and Mary, for example—were still out there pitching for a better vision of the world. Moreover, American society still possessed much of its gift for inclusive incorporation. Who in 1963, for example, could have foreseen that George Wallace, who that year literally stood in a doorway at the University of Alabama symbolically barring the admission of a black student to its sovereign premises, would return to that same university one day to crown a black homecoming queen? Or that Deep South states with black voter registrations in 1960 of 3 percent or 6 percent, which Wallace carried as a presidential candidate in 1968, would be swept twenty years later on "Super Tuesday" by Jesse Jackson? In the seventies, however, with avowed segregationists being seriously proposed for seats on the Supreme Court and erstwhile liberals proposing that the nation's racial problems might best be handled by "benign neglect," it was harder to perceive such long-term and apparently irreversible historical change—especially hard for former Movement members who, before they evolved into materialistic, sold-out, self-absorbed Baby Boomers, went through a crying-into-their-beer, it's-all-over-now phase.

The structural decay and cultural stagnation pointed out by Americans who wrote Roman history, such as Kenneth White and Frank Bourne, or by less classically oriented prophets, like Arthur Ekirch and Ray Ginger—the deterioration of central cities, schools, roads, rivers, health care—continued; but the foreign adventurism that had marked the sixties, and which may have been the ultimate economic reason for all that deterioration, retreated. The U.S. did get out of Vietnam; presidents during the 1970s did negotiate *détente* with the Soviet Union and ping-pong diplomacy with China. Perhaps Americans were learning what the Romans had learned before them: that the price of administering a *pax Romana* or a *pax Britannica* or a *pax Americana* is that one's people and resources must be stretched perilously thin. Once again Rostovtzeff is instructive. "The constant movement of troops toward the theatres of war," wrote the author of *The Social and Economic History of the Roman Empire* in discussing Rome's last outward imperial surge under Trajan, "required the repair of old and the construction of new roads, the building of new ships, the mobilization of masses of draught animals and drivers, quarters in the cities for

soldiers on the march, the concentration of vast quantities of food-
stuffs at special points. . . . Only those who know from experience the difficulties presented by these problems in modern times,
despite the existence of railroads, motor-cars, and large factories,
can realize what it meant for the Roman Empire to carry on, not
a 'colonial,' but a real war for years on end." The task proved to
be too much; and the next Emperor, Hadrian, had the bitter choice
of either withdrawing from the new territories Trajan had conquered or bankruptcy. (He chose to withdraw.) Similarly, by the
end of the Lyndon Johnson administration, it was becoming doubtful
whether the American corporate economy could finance both a
comprehensive program for social betterment and, at the same time,
an effective war machine.

Nor could American political leadership expect to pay for both
by invoking what had always worked before—globe-spanning economic growth. In the short term rival national economies, "not
dependent on inefficient military spending," were selling into areas
the Americans confidently had counted upon as being theirs in per-
petuity; and in the long term the limits to growth would be
imposed—one way or another!—by the physical environment, the
fragility of the biosphere, and the finiteness of the planet itself (unless Americans took the gamble of looking for answers to these
questions in space, which in the 1970s, after the end of the Apollo
missions, they showed few signs of wishing to do). Quite aside from
Caesar's other headaches, Alan Wolfe concluded a brilliant article
in 1981, "the President cannot win. His role is reduced to one of
promising economic growth in order to be elected but then breaking his promise in order to govern."

Such was the darkening political and economic atmosphere, with
the Congress (if one may judge from its legislation) choosing butter
and the executive (if one may judge from its actions) choosing guns,
in which the Watergate crisis shook the land. In 1973, while Watergate was still unfolding before the public, Arthur Schlesinger,
Jr., produced his widely influential study of *The Imperial Presidency*. Flawed though it was by a tendency to minimize or explain
away imperial features in the author's own personal presidential
heroes (FDR, JFK), Schlesinger's book contained a frightening and
plausible interpretation of what Richard Nixon had done—and at
that moment was still doing—to the presidential office: in effect,
treating his mandate in the landslide election of 1972 as a *lex de
imperio—*

with the President accountable only once every four years, shielded in the years between elections from congressional and public harassment, empowered by his mandate to make war or to make peace, to spend or to impound, to give out information or to hold it back, superseding congressional legislation by executive order, all in the name of a majority whose choice must prevail till it made another choice four years later—unless it wished to embark on the drastic and improbable course of impeachment.

Yet it was exactly that drastic and improbable course which the guardians of America's republican institutions chose to follow; whereas Brutus, perceiving a popular master of the Roman state who "doth bestride the narrow world like a Colossus," believed he had no recourse but assassination. Conversely a Caesar, had he been pressed as hard by the Senatorial elder statesmen as Richard Nixon was, presumably would have simply purged the Forum with fire and iron—rather than meekly flying away in a helicopter.

Within a few years of that flight—not so much into exile as onto talk shows—the "malaise" Jimmy Carter thought had become the national condition washed away in a wave of national exhilaration; Ronald Reagan, who in both 1980 and 1984 said he was running against "the policies of the previous fifty years," more accurately may be said to have run against the malaise. All at once, parallels with the decline of republican or imperial Rome seemed far less convincing. In 1979, the year of the Iranian hostage crisis, Robert Heilbroner could still find "obvious . . . analogues and correspondences" between our own time period and that of the Roman Principate, even of the *late* Principate: "Then, as now, we find order giving way to disorder; self-confidence to self-doubt; moral certitude to moral disquiet." Pushing to their limit analogies bequeathed by Toynbee, Spengler, and ultimately Gibbon, Heilbroner rhetoricaly asked whether "revolutionary socialism is our Christianity; China and North Vietnam our Goths and Visigoths; the Soviet Union our Byzantium; the corporation and ministries our *latifundia*." Mere months later such prophecies sounded stale and out-of-date, as many Americans once again faced their future with a personal and national confidence unmatched since the early days of FDR.

It is true that Augustus, like Reagan, had similarly raised national morale by appealing to traditional civic and familial values—to Rome's "good old days"; but Reagan, unlike Augustus, had done so while seeming to downplay the authority of the nation-state, and implicitly of his own office. Our equivalent of the tribunician power was not assumed by the Emperor; it remained firmly in the hands of Tip O'Neill. One of the richest ironies in recent history occurred late in Reagan's first year of office when the conservative President of the United States and the Socialist President of France rounded out the American Revolution Bicentennial by observing together the two hundredth anniversary of Cornwallis's final surrender to the Americans and the French at Yorktown. One way or another, it seemed, both Revolutions had survived.

It was, however, possible that this newfound confidence of the American people was misplaced; that their rosy vision of the future resulted from a selective tunnel vision amounting at times to outright blindness. Reagan's shining "city on a hill"—a phrase borrowed without credit from Governor John Winthrop but lacking that early Puritan politician's sense of human limitation—had, like all other cities in history (to quote a Methodist social hymn) its "haunts of wretchedness and need," its "shadowed thresholds dark with fears." Nowhere was this selectivity—one is tempted to say, rationalized fantasy—more evident than in the White House itself. Guns or butter? No problem; thanks to the magic of supply-side economics we can have a balanced budget, lower taxes, an adequate "social safety net," *and* Star Wars.

But elections are not lost nor won by logic. Inflation *did* come down; so, after a savage recession, did unemployment, although much of the new employment was of a demeaning, dead-end kind. As for unfavorable trade balances and astronomical deficits, those evidently were worried about more by the kind of people who appeared on panel discussions than by such of the electorate as took the trouble to vote. The Reagan mandate continued in 1984. Then, in 1987—the same summer as the Constitution's bicentennial— came the Senate's investigation of the Iran-Contra episode, in the course of which a clean-cut young centurion named Oliver North stood up for his *imperator* (loosely translatable as Commander-in-Chief) against a dithering Senate, and Berkeley professor Franz Schurmann was moved to exclaim that the U.S. seemed more like Rome all the time.

The conservatives who had flocked around Reagan in 1980 expressed misgivings of a different kind. Frustrated budget-slasher David Stockman wrote a book on why the Reagan revolution had failed—basically, he argued, because of the Republic's "Madisonian checks and balances." The welfare state had become "the system"; if Caesar built it, as conservatives used to argue against FDR, perhaps only another Caesar could *un*build it. In foreign policy also, some "hawks" grumbled, their man was behaving like a symbolic rather than an actual Caesar; speaking at first of the USSR as an "evil empire" and then entertaining Mikhail and Raisa Gorbachev at the White House with a sing-along of "Moscow Nights" accompanied by pianist Van Cliburn. "What the president should have done" about Nicaragua, groused former Reagan speechwriter and ideologue Patrick Buchanan late in 1987, "was break relations with Managua, declare it to be U.S. policy to support the Contras until the Sandinistas are brought down and the Soviets get out, and put to Congress [the] simple question, 'Whose side are you on?'"

This prescription was a remarkable departure from what had passed for conservative doctrine during most of the twentieth century. Liberals and conservatives had in effect exchanged positions, thereby putting themselves back where they had been in the eighteenth century when the American political experiment began; when a figure as radical as Tom Paine had preached laissez-faire economics and one as anti-popular as Alexander Hamilton had called for vigorous, forceful executive action. Thus it came to be liberals and radicals who warned of Caesarism, instead of the mossback reactionaries who had so labeled Roosevelt and his New Deal; and right-wingers who bought the New Dealers' old argument for a strong presidency—including their tacit contempt toward Congress. Allan Nevins once declared that the United States was consolidated in a Hamiltonian direction by a series of reluctant Jeffersonian presidents; the rise now of a more frankly Hamiltonian elitism on behalf of "the rich, the well-born, and the able" raised the scary possibility that one day not so far off an aspirant to the purple more resolute than Nixon and less amiable than Reagan might yet prevail.

In executing this switch, both liberals and conservatives lost sight of the agenda Wendell Willkie set for the nation half a century ago. Macho conservatives now claimed that the salvation of the rest of the world depended upon its adoption of their own narrow and doctrinaire brand of "free enterprise," while liberal Democrats abandoned their party's historic commitment to international free trade in favor of a spiteful and ultimately self-destructive protectionism. At home, meanwhile, each side accused the other of controlling and manipulating the mass media to subvert the republic's ideals; rightists perceived the press and TV news people as those carping soreheads who had "lost" the war in Vietnam, while radicals saw the surge of national enthusiasm that crested in the triumph of the 1984 Olympic Games as merely a cleverly engineered Hollywood happening. If we don't all get our bread we do have our circuses, insurgent defense attorney William Kunstler, a veteran of the political apocalypse of the 1960s, told a university audience the year before Ronald Reagan came to power:

> Right now we're sitting in the Circus Maximus. In old Rome they knew that if you provided the people with enough distractions in the Colosseum, they'd pay no attention to what was going on in the Senate. We have our coliseums all over America, and if you don't want to bother going out to one, you can sit in your own home and watch the flickering tube.

But nobody was *compelling* anyone to sit there; if you seriously preferred to pay attention to what was going on in the Senate, you had only to turn the flickering tube off. The question of the American future remained open, and the best answer to determinism, Roman or other, was still Shakespeare's:

> Men at some time are masters of their fates:
> The fault, dear Brutus, is not in our stars.

6. Of Baby Teeth and the Biosphere

One of many doctrines which plagued the managers of the Roman Empire was the apocalyptic Christian prediction, notably in the Revelation of St. John, that the world might be on the verge of coming to an end. Like other traditional ideas, that one in the twentieth century became secularized. In 1896 Henri Becquerel discovered radioactivity, and in 1914 H. G. Wells, in one of his science fiction novels, *The World Set Free*, forecast an atom bomb. By the early 1920s, in quiet academic places like Cambridge and Göttingen, the theoretical work was under way which would fatefully lead to the fission in 1938 of the uranium atom.

As is evident from a 1922 pronouncement of V. I. Vernadskii, neither political ideology nor military security could ultimately bind such inquiry. "The time is drawing near when man will harness atomic energy," the Russian seer wrote. "Will man be able to utilize this force for his benefit and not for his self-destruction? Has

257

he advanced sufficiently to be able to utilize this force which science will inevitable place in his hands?" Both questions, as of the present writing, remain precariously open; to the second, Vernadskii's own homeland gave a discouragingly negative answer in 1986 at Chernobyl. But it is the first of these interrogation marks which since 1945 has hung like a pall over the earth. If an all-out thermonuclear exchange between the superpowers should result in the remains of the United States coming out of it as "a republic of insects and grass," as Jonathan Schell concluded it would in his grim appraisal *The Fate of the Earth* (1982), there could be small comfort in taking the cosmic Vernadskiian view that there probably would be little change in Earth's overall biomass.

"The scientists should not shut their eyes to the possible consequences of their scientific work," Vernadskii continued. That prophecy, at least, has come true more positively, not only in the Soviet Union but in the West also, as witness the founding of the Federation of Atomic Scientists by America's own bomb builders. Quickly they found themselves involved in other issues; for the nuclear bomb turned out to be not only an acute life-threatener, but also a chronic source of debilitating disease. It was, among other nasty things, an environmental pollutant—far more so, and far more insidiously, than (for example) cigarettes. Even to *test* these fearsome weapons in the atmosphere, as was recklessly done for nearly two decades after the initial bomb use, endangered the health of millions—not only in the U.S. and the U.S.S.R. but everywhere the winds blew. That circumstance brought biologist Barry Commoner, for one, charging out of his cloistered laboratory at Washington University in St. Louis in 1953 to set parents all over that city collecting their offspring's baby teeth for laboratory examination. It turned out that in addition to the normal element calcium those teeth contained also ominous proportions of strontium-90, one of the radioisotopes contained in the fallout from atmospheric nuclear tests—a substance which behaves chemically and physiologically much like calcium and can combine in building bones and teeth in a similar way; except that strontium-90 is highly, dangerously radioactive.

Commoner's conversion to environmental activism is particularly striking because earlier in his scientific career he had believed to a great extent in the "technological fix" for human social problems; for example, inventing new insecticides to increase crop production and thereby feed the Earth's starving millions. Serving in the Navy in World War II he had taken part in spraying Pacific islands against insect-borne diseases (e.g., malaria) with the new wonder chemical DDT, unaware as yet that indiscriminate use of such toxins was an invitation to environmental disaster—as Rachel Carson would show in her landmark work *Silent Spring* (1962). Repudiating his earlier, simplistic optimism, Commoner in the first sentence of a book published in 1966, *Science and Survival*, announced that "the age of innocent faith in science and technology may be over." A mass electric power failure all over the Northeast, the admission of children to a St. Louis hospital fifteen years after they had been exposed to radio-iodine from Nevada bomb tests, the disturbing news about DDT, and the potential menace of recombinant DNA led him to the conclusion that science, like the magic practiced by the legendary Sorcerer's Apprentice, was getting out of control.

Commoner agreed with Vernadskii that "scientists should feel responsible for the consequences of their discoveries." They could no longer simply remain at their work; they had to go out and alert the nonscientists to the problems that work was creating. "Science can reveal the depth of this crisis," *Science and Survival* concluded, "but only social action can resolve it." Social action, or at least agitation for action followed, and by 1970 *Time* Magazine was calling Barry Commoner "the Paul Revere of ecology." Commoner had not been trained professionally as an ecologist; he came to it in reaction against the dismemberment of modern science by overspecialization, such that its practitioners could not see the forest for their own narrow trees. Scientists as well as laypeople, he believed, had to be educated to the fact that in nature "everything is connected to everything else," which is the primary message of ecology.

Commoner's best-known book, *The Closing Circle* (1971), concluded that "human beings have broken out of the circle of life, driven not by biological need, but by the social organization which they have devised to 'conquer' nature. . . . We must learn how to restore to nature the wealth that we borrow from it." The political lesson to be learned from Los Angeles smog, from fertilizer-poisoned water supplies in Illinois, from algal bloom in Lake Erie, and from detergent foam everywhere, was that the older forms of both capitalism and socialism, with their emphases respectively on profit and productivity, were quite inadequate to cope with a deteriorating planet. At the same time Commoner did not want to sit back and contemplate nature with "Oriental" fatalism, or, as he called it, "inactivism." Once done, the transformations to which Vernadskii had pointed in his landmark essay of 1926 could not be undone; it was not going to be possible to let the noösphere simply fade back into the biosphere, as some of the West's more thorough-going pastoralists or preservationists seemed to advise, and trust Gaia—Mother Earth—to take care of us all. Mother has from time to time employed mass extinctions to maintain her steady-state biosphere, and she could do so again.

In the 1970s, as Richard Nixon's Congress passed laws for clean air, pure water, and the protection of the environment, warnings such as Commoner's seemed to be generating serious political and legal action because, as *Time* warned in its cover story on Commoner (February 2, 1970), "the price of pollution could be the death of man." Indeed it became quite modish to be an environmentalist—but in a scattershot, unintegrated way. Mass media tended to discuss the subject in the same way they treated other national social problems, namely on a "crisis-of-the-month" basis; and some of the crises—e.g., freezing to death in a new Ice Age to be brought on by particulate wastes in the atmosphere, versus overheating the Earth to the point of melting the polar caps and flooding Manhattan because of the industrially accelerated "greenhouse effect," were mutually exclusive dooms; a fact which easily led people into the fatally erroneous notion that the whole problem had been exaggerated and could be ignored.

In addition, as Ann Zwinger has pointed out, "the environmentalist stance is of necessity an adversary stance," and its advocates, "when clad in the armor of their own self-righteousness, can be absolutely insufferable . . . driving you against the wall, saying 'Look, you slob, what a mess you've made of this earth.'" In taking such a hard, humorless line many such friends of the Earth "have alienated the very people with whom we need to communicate. Joe Sixpack is not stupid. But he needs to be addressed in ideas that make sense to him." It is necessary to "get his attention over the rev of his engine"; to entice such persons into looking at some facet of nature, in the hope that they will get curious, appreciate it, not want to destroy it—a "low-key approach" which, Zwinger had to confess, "does not galvanize people like a good healthy panic"; but which, this naturalist-writer insisted, would do more than a finger-waving lecture to produce solid, lasting changes of heart and mind.

Despite the intrinsic obstacles in the way of communicating the ecological message, a sufficient consensus accepted it that one of the "world's fairs" which from time to time express some of the planet's material aspirations, the Spokane Expo of 1974, responded to the emerging concern and chose "the environment" as its theme. Some of the national responses were quite thought-provoking. Japan's exhibit included a film which began as if for tourist promotion, with scenes of traditional custom such as tea ceremony—and then shock-cut to a truly terrifying contrast: downtown Tokyo at rush hour. Tea ceremony, the Japanese thus acknowledged, was just not going to solve the problems of crowded, industrialized modern Japan. The Soviet Union took the environmentalist assignment very seriously and built a three-story pavilion. After getting past the inevitable Lenin icon on the facade, the visitor found inside the building a pictorial description of the environment in Vernadskiist terms. Humanity, as Vernadskii had written, is more than metaphorically born of the sun; the primordial dancing, flamelike solar prominences shown in one of the exhibition's vivid movies would after many millions of years of evolution become incarnate, as the film's poetic soundtrack told, in "the eyes of Einstein"—those same eyes that would mathematically foresee the release by man of energy like the sun's.

This Soviet exhibition did not appeal to the passive walker-through. Its ground floor amounted to a crash course in cosmology, geology, evolutionary biology, ecology, and human prehistory, and its upper floors carried the story of what was being done or planned in the environment, both internationally and in the Soviet Union. The American pavilion offered, all unawares, a painful contrast. It also showed a film, on what was billed as the tallest indoor movie screen in the world, that treated the environmental crisis as spectacle: a raging oil-field fire in Oklahoma; the dust clouds and gouged tracks of four thousand motorcycles taking off all at once across the Mojave Desert.

Interspersed with these infernos came placid closeups of an aged Native American (Hollywood's typical stereotyped "Noble Red Man") posed successively in the Florida Everglades, at the edge of the Grand Canyon, et cetera, and offering sage nature-saving proverbs prefaced by "my Dad once said to me . . . "; in short, the answer to the environmental question lay in the past. The visitor came away from that lesson into a large room behind the screen, filled with a two-story pile of, quite literally, junk; it bore a modest little sign informing people that all of this stuff could be recycled!

Was this *all* that America had to say to the world about "the environment"? One could have come away from that particular comparison of exhibits with a depressed sense that the United States was losing the Cold War in a far more subtle and fundamental way than the throw-weight of the superpowers' respective missiles or the weaponry of their respective Third World mercenaries.

"Intensive and irrational use of the resources of the biosphere . . . has shattered the myth of the infiniteness and inexhaustibility of those resources," wrote two of Vladimir Vernadskii's scientific disciples in 1970. "Numerous examples of the destructive activity of man and unfortunately rare examples of his constructive activity . . . testify to the urgency of rational management of the earth's affairs by a rational mankind . . . " Exactly so, an American reader in the early 1970s might have responded, until he or she read the rest of the passage: "which is possible only with a conversion from elementary capitalist production to the planned economy of a socialist or communist society." The foregoing quoted sentences appeared in the *Great Soviet Encyclopedia*, and seemed to pose to the reader in the West an intolerable dilemma: that there could be no middle point between unfettered overkill and regimented preservation, between slapdash "development" and soul-strangling bureaucratic "rational management."

Moreover, environmental corruption could also be promoted as the price one paid for maintaining a First World standard of living, irrational and self-defeating as such a policy must eventually be. Banking on the assumption by self-centered consumers that "to be realistic, to get things done, and to get on with one's career almost require that a person become a enemy of a free humanity and a healthy biosphere," America's corporate polluters subtly altered the terms of the debate, as Langdon Winner has shown; what had previously been described as a "danger" or a "hazard" became merely a *risk*, and risk is something macho residents in the home of the brave are supposed to accept. "In the late 1970s," Winner sums up, "the debunking of claims about environmental hazards became a major part of corporate ideology."

As for government action to deal with those hazards, after some initial years of promise, Barry Commoner for one came to believe that much of the politicians' concern with the environment and with energy conservation was a sham. He was particularly disappointed in President Jimmy Carter's national energy policy, which Commoner said was "not designed to solve the energy crisis . . . but merely to delay it." In *The Politics of Energy* (1979), Commoner called for "a national policy for the transition from the present, nonrenewable system to a renewable one"—a transition which he believed a traditional free market economy would be unable to accomplish; but "the market," as Ronald Reagan intuitively sensed in his drive for political power (or the semblance thereof), had in the meantime become one of the most sacred of American cows. Few in the land of the free paused to reflect, however, that blind, passive trust in "the market" to work things out and solve all problems is as essentially deterministic a view of the human condition as Marx's dialectics of history or Calvin's unfathomable decrees of God.

Yet all was not lost; it never is, quite. To be "realistic" *almost*, not absolutely, required that one neglect the biosphere to get on with one's career, Langdon Winner wrote, in a book that took the trouble to contest that cynical conclusion. At a symposium in the spring of 1987, John Kennedy's former Interior Secretary Stewart Udall, reflecting on historical developments since the publication in 1963 of his own pioneering environmentalist tract *The Quiet Crisis*, disputed the widely held view that the environmental movement was "fading" under the harsh klieg lights of Reaganism. In various ways it had become acceptably institutionalized. Most states had created environmental planning agencies, with legal process for enforcement; public schools for a quarter-century had been teaching environmentalism as a part of health studies; and its international linkage had become substantial—Rachel Carson's polemic *Silent Spring* by that time had been translated into 32 languages. Stewart Udall's younger brother Morris, chairman of the Interior Committee in the U.S. House of Representatives, pointed out at that same symposium that up until Reagan's time the politics of environmentalism had been fully bipartisan; even the feckless Nixon Administration had had "solid pros who knew what they were doing" working in the conservation area.

Moreover, conservation, even preservation, had been winning some unexpected political conversions. President Reagan's Surgeon-General, no less, violated his regime's anti-regulation dogma with his vehement crusade against the ill effects of tobacco in such environments as the interior of airplanes; and Barry Goldwater, summing up his 35-year career as "Mr. Conservative" in January 1987, stated that the only Senate vote he wished he could retract was his vote for the ecologically disastrous Glen Canyon Dam. If the free market economy held out little hope for the environment, the free market of ideas held out a great deal—*provided*, of course, that Americans were willing to look beyond their immediate personal concerns and do some uncharacteristically hard thinking ("What good fortune for those in power," Hitler once said, "that people do not think!")

In the meantime, while the debate over conservation, preservation, and "development" raged, human beings had gone into space. A few of them, mostly Russians, still go there from time to time; and American computer-eyes for several years have been peering at the delicate rings of Saturn and the centuries-old red storm on Jupiter, the hot, smoggy atmosphere of Venus and the sulfur-spitting volcanoes on Io. Image after image has come back from elsewhere in the Solar System, harshly barren or seductively beautiful. Aren't you disappointed that we didn't find life on Mars? somebody tauntingly asked science fiction writer Ray Bradbury after the Viking Lander settled on a not particularly scenic part of that planet in 1976 and reported back no findings of Martian princesses or bug-eyed monsters. "From this point on there *is* life on Mars," Bradbury stoutly retorted: ours—"an extension of our sensibilities." The noösphere was expanding, as the picture-taking Voyager spacecraft plunged on past Uranus toward a 1989 rendezvous with Neptune and then on into the darkness of the comet cloud. Of all those pictures relayed back to us, however, the most compelling remains that of Earth itself, deep-blue, cloud-white, by all reports from those few thus far privileged actually to see it from space incredibly lovely—and, if Vernadskii be right, the only one of those Solar System worlds that has been molded into its present form by a biosphere. That heritage is ours—Americans', Russians', everybody's—to cherish or destroy.

Afterword

Any historical account that carries its narrative up to the present runs into a formidable philosophical problem. At the bottom of the last page it becomes necessary, literally or figuratively, to write the words THE END. By accident or design, the writer thereby gives the impression that this fleeting moment—a moment which itself immediately becomes part of the past—climaxes or concludes the story, which in the nature of the case it cannot do. The historian finishes what he or she had to say, but history doesn't stop. Its *dénouement* is always further down the road.

The themes of this book qualify as unfinished business for America. I suspect that unless terminated by unspeakable catastrophe they are going to remain so for quite some time. The empty land has mostly filled up; yet along streets and shopping malls the rootless, restless inhabitants continue to face in new form the old choice between Wilderness and Paradise, barbarization and renewal. Artists, novelists, playwrights, and the makers of rock videos continue to be torn between an urge to capture the essence of their American milieu and the inward promptings of their private Muse. Science continues to strive for comprehension of the universe—and alternately to thrill us and to scare us to death with what it turns up along the way.

Two of this book's themes in particular, the long cultural-political shadows of ancient Israel and ancient Rome, tempt the writer (any writer) to some Q.E.D.'s and I-told-you-so's. The years when the book took shape saw America, "the nation with the soul of a church," acting true to form; liberals defied Federal law to give sanctuary to Central American political refugees, and conservatives denounced them for doing so—both on religious grounds. Debates over Supreme Court nominations turned as much on moral as on political qualifications. Clergymen—a Pat Robertson, a Jesse

265

Jackson—made serious runs for the highest office in the land. It did not appear that this kind of rationale for political action, despite the fears of some religionists and the hopes of some "secular humanists," would soon cease. So with the Rome theme; if science and faith have been having at each other since the time of Lucretius, so have freedom and order.

At the moment this manuscript reached its final page, the nation was midway through a presidential election year; neither major party had definitively chosen its candidates. We were in the midst of events whose outcome we could not know. Pollsters, professors, and anchorpeople get paid for pronouncing authoritatively what an election "means"; but not all of the returns come in on Election Day. Some—in particular, whether a given election moves the Republic closer to a Principate, or further away from it, or in another direction altogether—may not be known for generations.

By the time I returned the edited version of the manuscript to Columbia University Press to be set in type, the results of that election were known. The loser until the last minute had forsworn ideological commitment, just as the social-science pundits of the 1950s had urged one should do—with disastrous results. The winner had previously prepped for the position by holding a series of Washington-insider jobs (ambassador to the UN, chairman of his party's National Committee, head of the CIA), not unlike the *cursus honorum* through which young Roman patricians in the late Republic had moved—successively holding office as *aedile, censor, quaestor, praetor*—on their way toward the supreme magistracy. Neither candidate looked very prepossessing from the standpoint of Grover Cleveland just one hundred years before, urging that "it is better to be defeated battling for an honest principle than to win by a cowardly subterfuge." Indeed, the consensus in one university class in American history, asked in an essay exam to compare and contrast the presidential elections of 1888 and 1988, found that the earlier contest—theretofore usually considered one of America's most forgettable elections—came off, if anything, rather better than the recent one; it had decided a substantive issue about which people passionately cared. To the extent that voters in 1988 decided anything, it seemed to be for "more of the same"—which, in a world as convulsively changing as that of the late twentieth century, was literally to ask for the impossible.

On that same date when these pages were written, the United States and its favorite adversary for the previous forty years were in the act of exchanging ratifications of a treaty that curtailed the use of certain categories of nuclear weapons—accompanied by a blizzard of pro-and-con commentary on the meaning of that act. Was it truly a move toward world peace? or only a truce of the kind Rome and Carthage observed from time to time while consolidating their respective empires? Or in terms of another of the concerns of this book, is the political resolution of incompatible—capitalist and socialist—economic systems as unachievable as the political resolution of the issue between freedom and slavery in the United States turned out to be, so that the question becomes resolvable only by violence? Or may we find ground for hope in the fact that both capitalism and socialism, in their modern forms, derive theoretically from an eighteenth-century faith in the capacity of human beings to organize society rationally? One year before Reagan and Gorbachev exchanged those documents of ratification, a high school senior meditating on that modern 18-year-old male American's rite of passage, the decision whether to sign up with Selective Service, burst out in fury against the fatalist view that the U.S. was "due" for a major war, a view he encountered among many in his age group: "No, we aren't 'due.' There's no deadline for going to war. . . . I'm not saying that eternal peace is probable, only that it's possible. It really depends on whether we approach the problem with hope or with despair; whether we run from that which we fear or confront it." That young American, at least, carried on the tradition of revolt against destiny; nor did he exemplify the then much-talked-of "closing of the American mind."

Faced with unfinished history, the historian may be tempted to play scientist; to plot a curve that he or she hopes will intersect with some future happening, in the way chemists classically could deduce the properties of a not-yet-found element from its position in the Periodic Table, or astronomers from orbital perturbations known to them could determine where to look for an undiscovered planet. However, historical trends just don't seem to work that way. Again and again, in American history—and in other histories as well—the most honest reaction is one that breaks the chain of logic: "But whoever would have expected *that?*" History, John Dewey wisely observed eighty years ago, does not *settle* controverted questions; it changes the subject and takes up something else.

Another temptation in a moment of flux is to prophesy, in accordance with the historian's own heart's desire or deepest fears. One of the most distinguished of all U.S. historians, Charles Beard, proposed engaging in "written history as an act of faith," gambling that the historian's personal *confessio fidei*, entering the stream of public discourse, would at least modestly influence the future course of history in a direction in accordance with that faith. Less modestly Lewis Mumford, in book after book from *The Story of Utopias* in 1922 to *The Pentagon of Power* in 1970, regularly concluded a sweeping account of human history by telling the world in no uncertain terms what it ought to do.

Here, such advice would be logically inappropriate because out of character with the rest of the book. "The American past," one highly perceptive reader of this manuscript pointed out, "is really a dialogue between different versions of what the future should be, with the dialogue carried now by Washington and Napoleon, Jefferson and Adams, and again by Jackson and Calhoun, Douglas and Lincoln;" or, in later chapters, by Powell and Grant, Dewey and Bryan, FDR and Reagan. Moreover, the same critic continues, "The whole structure and method of the book is counterpoint and contradiction." Written history as an act of faith in Charles Beard's sense would then come down paradoxically to an act of faith that Americans will continue to dissent from one another; to differ strongly as to whether the human will is bound or free; to revolt against what others declare to be their destiny—and a hope against hope that they will learn to temper their revolt with respect for the physical limitations of the Earth, and that they will contrive to escape the "simplification of all the functions of political, social, economic, and intellectual life" that has characterized the decline of other civilizations—words Michael Rostovtzeff wrote even before the advent of TV.

However, I owe it to my professional colleagues to relate this book more explicitly to those in the same broadly synoptic genre which have preceded mine. That same astute critic of the manuscript suggests a parallel with Merle Curti's *American Paradox*; a suggestion I take as a compliment, for although that parallel had not occurred to me I have long admired Curti's work. But the earliest influence upon the present study, in terms of my own reading, has to be Vernon Parrington's *Main Currents in American Thought*, one of those rare academically produced works which find a good many readers outside the academy. I first saw a copy of it lying on a table in a tin quonset-hut library on a muddy Navy base in Gulfport, Mississippi; opened it, turned to the section on the South where I was then stationed, and instantly became hooked.

In graduate school in the 1950s I learned that Parrington had in the meantime come under severe criticism, from Perry Miller and many other scholars, and I dutifully entered their criticisms in the margins of my own battered copy of *Main Currents.* In the classroom, however, as a teacher, I began to find that the discrete parts of Parrington's analysis often fared better than his admittedly simplistic whole.

Moreover, his own enthusiasms led him into a tantalizing contradiction, unresolved because the work was interrupted by its author's death; a contradiction between the theme of his second volume, "The Romantic Revolution in America," and his third, "The Beginnings of Critical Realism in America." Nineteenth-century American Romanticism was something for which Parrington clearly felt affinity—but so was "critical realism." And Romanticism was something intellectuals of Parrington's generation weren't supposed to approve of. I was helped out of this dilemma by Jacques Barzun's civilized account of the European historical movement which constituted American Romanticism's context; originally called *Romanticism and the Modern Ego,* but more recently retitled *Classic, Romantic, and Modern.*

In the meantime, between that Navy quonset hut and graduate school, I had discovered (and written an Honors thesis on) Arnold Toynbee, and Toynbee in turn led me to Rostovtzeff. My wife, who was studying Roman history during the 1970s, turned up several of those classical journal essays on Rome and America which gave shape and point to my concluding chapter. This Roman theme distinguishes my book from the one with which it will most probably be compared, Louis Hartz's *The Liberal Tradition in America.* We set ourselves much the same task, and the structure of the two books is almost parallel. Hartz, however, finds the essence of the liberal tradition in the presence of free land and the absence of a feudal past; I find it in the willed selection of republican government, imagined metaphorically as Roman. The reader will have seen that I do note the importance of the empty New World; Turner's "frontier" did mean something. But "free land" can be filled with anything; rather than the yeoman-farmer culture upheld by Jefferson there could just as logically have arisen an authoritarian "baronial" way of life that would have been just as rural.

In regions lacking the Roman republican ideology—*e.g.,* the Spanish North American borderlands—that is exactly what happened. Nor would I say, with Hartz, that a Jacksonian Democrat was simply a small-propertied Whig, nor a Populist merely petty-bourgeois, nor the New Deal a statist, capitalism-rescuing sham. I share Hartz's (and William Appleman Williams's) concern, however, lest America cease to see the relevance of its own Revolution to a competitively revolutionary world.

I share also in what Henry F. May has called "the recovery of American religious history," and here the decisive influence has been the work of Sidney E. Mead, abetted by Reinhold Niebuhr's *The Irony of American History.* Here occurs my own most explicit dissent from Parrington; I perceive religion in history as an independent—and dynamic—variable, not simply as a strategy of rationalization. Here I am not so far from my Marxist colleagues as might be supposed; some of them in recent years have labored in the same scholarly-critical vineyard. I remain aware, however, of the intellectual force and moral power of Parrington's grim description of "the darkening skies of letters," and not of letters alone; darkening under the inescapable imperatives of a scientific world view.

As to the science itself, I remain convinced that the "two cultures" can only demean themselves and each other by putting each other down. Wistfully, I wish more scientists I know had read Parrington, and that more of my humanities colleagues had heard of Vernadskii (as distinguished from his son the historian). To fulfill an undergraduate science requirement I elected geology, which not by coincidence is of all the natural or "hard" sciences the most historical. It merely hitches the span of the historian's subject matter onto a broader sweep of time.

This book has been in the making for quite some while, and it has accumulated many unrepayable debts. Mentors, some dating from high school years, others from college and graduate school, still others from outside the academic realm altogether; colleagues in the dozen institutions where I have taught; and especially my long-suffering students who had drafts of the early chapters and rough notes for others thrown at them as captive audiences—all have contributed. So have the libraries I have drawn upon, particularly those of the Universities of Montana and Arizona. Books of this kind always owe much to other books, and my debts of that kind are detailed in the bibliographic essay that follows. Portions of chapters 6 and 7 are taken from two essays I wrote for the Tucson Public Library/Arizona Historical Society project "Writers of the Purple Sage" in 1983; three sections of chapter 7 appeared as an article in the *Antioch Review* in 1985. I gratefully acknowledge permission of both publishers to reprint the material here.

My wife, Julie K. Carter, years ago challenged me to break out of a nonwriting mode and begin to get my thoughts on paper instead of letting them echo away into the air. Although the book took shape after we had moved away from DeKalb, Illinois in 1973, my friends and peers in the lively history department there at Northern Illinois University helped to form this work, more than most of them know; particularly Mary Furner, who always knew, and kindly but insistently said, that I ought to write an opus of this kind. The influence of Arizona and the Southwest, especially on the later chapters, is pervasive and subtle. Paul Martin, of the University of Arizona's Desert Laboratory, had a decisive impact on the ecology chapter, and Roger DeLaix, Roman historian at UA, helped with my Latin.

All writers, whether they admit it or not, experience "dry spells;" Nikki Matz, who painstakingly typed and gently criticized the first half of this manuscript during one such spell, never lost faith in the outcome for a moment, and knows how much I owe her for that faith. Mary Sue Passe-Smith promptly and cheerfully typed the other half, and gave freely of her feisty iconoclasm, to the manuscript's betterment.

Kate Wittenberg, editor extraordinaire at Columbia University Press, saw the potential in this work even in its very early stages when most remained unwritten—and as later chapters crossed her desk she spoke out candidly at points where they flagged in clarity. Leslie Bialler, who capably and joyously copyedited *four* previous book manuscripts of mine for Columbia University Press, was on board again for this one, and I am grateful for the continuity.

Tucson, Arizona
December 5, 1988

Where This Book Came From:
A Bibliographical Essay

1. The Dream of the West

Loren Baritz's erudite, richly textured essay "The Idea of the West," *American Historical Review* 66 (April 1961), has had a profound influence upon this opening chapter. Convergent with the Baritz article's thesis is an essay by George Huntston Williams, "The Wilderness and Paradise in the History of the Church," *Church History* 28 (March 1959). From a similar perspective came the striking reinterpretation of *The Saga of Eric the Red* which I have quoted from Sydney E. Ahlstrom, *A Religious History of the American People* (New Haven: Yale University Press, 1972).

Lancelot Hogben clearly described and pictured how Eratosthenes of Alexandria measured the earth in *Science for the Citizen* (Garden City, NY: Garden City Publishing Co., 1943). George Sarton's monumental work, *A History of Science: Hellenistic Science and Culture in the Last Three Centuries B.C.* (Cambridge: Mass.: Harvard University Press, 1959) makes that earth-measuring experiment's social context clear. Vincent H. Cassidy, *The Sea Around Them: The Atlantic Ocean, A.D. 1250* (Baton Rouge: Louisiana State University Press, 1968) contains the quotation from St. Augustine concerning "the nonsense about there being *antipodae*"; the full passage is in Augustine, *City of God*, Book XVI, Chapter 9, as translated by Gerald G. Walsh et al. (Garden City: Image Books, 1958)—a translation which avoids the sermonic pomp that creeps into most modern renderings of Augustine, and lets us see his wit and urbanity. For Hesiod's *Theogony* I used the translation by Norman O. Brown (New York: Liberal Arts Press, 1953); for Homer's *Odyssey*, the translation by E. V. Rieu (Baltimore: Penguin Books, 1946); for Dante's *Divine Comedy*, the Carlyle-Wicksteed translation (New York: Modern Library, 1932).

Samuel Eliot Morison, *Admiral of the Ocean Sea: A Life of Christopher Columbus* (Boston: Little, Brown, 1942) despite its Proper Bostonian archaisms and macho sailor talk, remains a model of graceful, well-founded historical writing. The fanciful travel literature that was generated in Europe by the discovery of America receives its due in Howard Mumford Jones, *O Strange New World* (New York: Viking Press, 1967), chaps. 1 and 2. The horrendous early image of America in a 1579 atlas is pictured and described by Benjamin Keen in his wondrously learned and lively work, *The Aztec Image in Western Thought* (New Brunswick, N.J.: Rutgers University Press, 1971). The challenging thesis that Shakespeare's *Tempest* is really a play about America is set forth in the second chapter of Leo Marx, *The Machine in the Garden: Technology and the Pastoral Ideal in America* (New York: Oxford University Press, 1964).

Glimpses of the New World's reality, scarcely less vivid than its literary and artistic representations, appear in Thomas Haricot, *A Brief and True Report of the New Found Land of Virginia*, edited by Randolph G. Adams (New York: History Book Club, 1951, reproducing in facsimile the 1588 edition) and in William Bradford, *Of Plymouth Plantation*, edited by Harvey Wish (New York: Capricorn Books, 1962). The excerpt from Richard Hakluyt's promotional pitch, "A Discourse on Western Planting" (1584), was included by Ray Billington, Bert Loewenberg, and Samuel Brockunier in their fine documents collection *The Making of American Democracy* (New York: Rinehart, 1950). Richard Hofstadter, *America at 1750* (New York: Knopf, 1971) is all that exists of what would have been a major synoptic work on American history, tragically cut off by its author's death.

Frederick Jackson Turner, "The Significance of the Frontier in American History," exists in many editions. Thorstein Veblen's observation that the culture which received Turner's great essay was "peculiarly matter-of-fact" if not "opaque" is in Veblen, "The Place of Science in Modern Civilization," also available in several editions. I first encountered it in Perry Miller's excellent anthology *American Thought: Civil War to World War I* (New York: Rinehart, 1954). An important modification of Turner's agrarian thesis occurs in David Potter, *People of Plenty: Economic Abundance and the American Character* (Chicago: University of Chicago Press, 1954). From a paper by Karen Anderson, my colleague in the University of Arizona History Department, prepared for the Tucson Public Library's thoughtfully conceived project on "Writers of the Purple Sage" (1983), I got the characterization of pioneering women as "draftees in a male enterprise"; from Henry David Thoreau's *Walking,* first published in the *Atlantic Monthly* (June 1862), came the lines about walking toward Oregon rather than toward Europe. I used the version that appears in Oscar Cargill, editor, *Henry D. Thoreau: Selected Writings on Nature and Liberty* (New York: Liberal Arts Press, 1952).

The aphorism by John Locke, "In the beginning all the world was America," occurs in Locke, *Second Treatise on Civil Government,* 5:49; I used the version edited by Sir Ernest Barker, *Social Contract: Essays by Locke, Hume, and Rousseau* (New York: Oxford University Press, 1948). A daring elaboration from the germ of Locke's idea, by way of F. J. Turner, is Walter Prescott Webb, *The Great Frontier* (Austin: University of Texas Press, 1964).

Franklin Roosevelt's—or his speechwriters'—rather pessimistic version of the Turner thesis was aired in an address delivered at the Commonwealth Club in San Francisco during the 1932 presidential campaign; I used the text as printed in Basil Rauch, editor, *Franklin D. Roosevelt: Selected Speeches, Messages, Press Conferences, and Letters* (New York: Rinehart, 1957). An imaginative, well-argued explanation of events leading up to the election of 1980, whose winner vowed to reverse the half-century of history since the initial victory of FDR, is Theodore H. White, *America in Search of Itself: The Making of the President, 1956–1980* (New York: Harper and Row, 1982). The quotations from Ronald Reagan and Edward Kennedy at their parties' respective 1980 nominating conventions, statements which taken together constitute a reprise on this chapter's themes, were taken from accounts in the *New York Times,* July 18 and August 13, 1980.

2. Caesar's Ghost in America

A special tribute is in order here to a high school Latin teacher, Mamie R. Capellen, who convinced several generations of teenagers in Blackfoot, Idaho, that the Latin language and Roman culture were inescapably part of the language they themselves used and the culture they lived in. To read the *Gallic Wars* in one of her classes—learning that it was among other things a coolly composed campaign document for Julius Caesar's methodical march to supreme power—was to be initiated into the same Rome-oriented issues, fears, and hopes that haunted this nation's founders two hundred years ago. On those founders' familiarity with Rome— "the very vocabulary of government was Roman"—see Henry Steele Commager, *The Empire of Reason* (New York: Oxford University Press [paperback] 1982; copyright, 1977), p. 63 and especially the bibliographic mini-essay on p. 268, n. 59.

In quoting Scripture, here and in other chapters, I *always* use the sonorous, swinging King James Version in preference to more modern translations, whose occasional (but not invariable) gains in accuracy of meaning are more than offset by the banality— sometimes to the point of "dumbing down"—of their prose. In citing the translations of ancient Rome's foremost historian by D. R. Dudley, *The Annals of Tacitus* (New York: New American Library, 1966), Book I, Chapter 1, and George Gilbert Ramsey, *The Histories of Tacitus* (London: John Murray, 1915), Book I, Chapter 1, I consulted with my colleague in Roman history at the University of Arizona, Roger De Laix, to make certain that the English given for one crucial passage—*postquam bellatum apud Actium atque omnem potentiam ad unum conferri pacis interfuit*—actually means what the translator reported Tacitus as having said.

The quip by Mary McCarthy to the effect that the Florentines invented the modern world is in McCarthy, *The Stones of Florence* (New York: Harcourt, Brace, 1963). The excursions of Thomas Jefferson and John Adams into Roman history—and much, much else!—can be found in Lester J. Cappon, ed., *The Adams-Jefferson Letters* (Chapel Hill: University of North Carolina Press, 2 vols., 1959), a carefully edited, handsomely printed work which is a browser's delight. A crucial letter from Jefferson to James Madison was conveniently included in Adrienne Koch, ed., *The American Enlightenment* (New York: George Braziller, 1965). Other Jefferson letters cited in this chapter were excerpted in Edward Dumbauld, ed., *The Political Writings of Thomas Jefferson* (Indianapolis: Bobbs-Merrill, 1955).

The thesis that revolutions follow a deterministic cycle from reform, through extremism, to reaction—borrowed, with updating, from Aristotle—is set forth in Crane Brinton, *The Anatomy of Revolution* (New York: Alfred Knopf, 1938). I found Alexander Hamilton's warnings to Lafayette that just such a cycle could be expected for France in Gertrude Atherton, ed., *A Few of Hamilton's Letters* (New York: Macmillan, 1903). George Canning's gleeful High

Tory "I-told-you-so" reaction to the failure of French revolutionary democracy was found and quoted by the industrious and ever-watchful Henry Adams in his *History of the United States of America during the Second Administration of Thomas Jefferson* (New York: Scribner's, 1909 [copyright 1890]), 2:59.

The Napoleonic coup that created what could be termed a French Principate is graphically narrated in H. A. L. Fisher, *Napoleon* (London: Oxford University Press, 1962 [copyright 1912]). Its near equivalent in America, the soldiers' protest and demonstration at Philadelphia in 1783, is definitively described in Edmund Cody Burnett, *The Continental Congress* (New York: Macmillan, 1941; paper, W. W. Norton, 1964). The complaint by the *Petersburg* (Va.) *Intelligencer* that after such a blow to its revolutionary hopes France would be better off under Louis XVIII is reported in Joseph D. Shuler, *The Old Dominion and Napoleon Bonaparte: A Study in American Opinion* [Columbia University Studies in the Social Sciences, 572] (New York: AMS Press, 1968). Bonaparte's rationalization that political dissent of the kind indulged in by Americans or Britons was not practicable in his version of "Revolutionary" France is quoted in J. Christopher Herold, *The Age of Napoleon* (New York: American Heritage/Harper and Row, 1963).

The quotations from John Locke and from Jean-Jacques Rousseau are as printed in Sir Ernest Barker, ed., *Social Contract: Essays by Locke, Hume, and Rousseau*, previously cited in chapter 1. (Incidentally, no reader of that collection should overlook Barker's brilliant Introduction, itself an important contribution to political theory.) The pioneering American social contract essay by John Wise, *Government of New England Churches Vindicated* (1717), is excerpted in Perry Miller, ed., *The American Puritans: Their Prose and Poetry* (New York: Columbia University Press, 1982 [first copyright 1956]). Thomas Paine's *Common Sense* is frequently reprinted; I used it as found in Richard Hofstadter, ed., *Great Issues in American History* (New York: Vintage, 1958). Paine's acute critique of the whole notion of social contract is in Paine, *The Rights of Man*, Part II, excerpts as printed in Edwin H. Cady, ed., *Literature of the Early Republic*, 2nd edition (San Francisco: Rinehart Press, 1969). Paine's truly eighteenth-century portrayal of God as an "Almighty Lecturer" is in Paine, *The Age of Reason*, Part I (1794); I cite the version edited by Alburey Castell (Indianapolis: Bobbs-Merrill, 1957).

Voltaire's warning against "the insane idea of becoming wholly reasonable" is noted in a luminous book by Charles Frankel, *The*

Faith of Reason: The Idea of Progress in the French Enlightenment (New York: King's Crown Press, 1948). Further elaboration on the irrationality of rationalism occurs in that classic defense of conservatism by Edmund Burke, *Reflections on the Revolution in France*, available in many editions; I used the one published in New York by Rinehart, 1959. Thomas Craven tied this issue of political rationality in the French Revolution back to Greco-Roman values as an aside to his chapter on the French Revolutionary and Napoleonic painter Jacques Louis David, in Craven, *Men of Art* (New York: Simon and Schuster, 1940).

I have used, and made some of my students read, Clinton Rossiter's spendid edition of Alexander Hamilton, James Madison, and John Jay, *The Federalist Papers* (New York: New American Library, 1961). An acute comment on *The Federalist* from a perhaps unexpected quarter is Jeane Kirkpatrick, "Sources of Stability in the American Tradition," in Kirkpatrick, *Dictatorships and Double Standards: Rationalism and Reason in Politics* (New York: Simon and Schuster, 1982). Also helpful for interpreting *The Federalist* was a biography by John C. Miller, *Alexander Hamilton: Portrait in Paradox* (New York: Harper, 1959).

Charles A. Beard's classic *An Economic Interpretation of the Constitution* (1913) is discussed, with full attention to its subsequent historiography, in Richard Hofstadter, *The Progressive Historians: Turner, Parrington, Beard* (New York: Vintage Books, 1970). Charles Warren, *The Making of the Constitution* (Boston: Little, Brown, 1928, 1937), throws further light on the motives of the Framers, as does an essay by Henry Steele Commager, "The Economic Interpretation of the Constitution Reconsidered," in Commager, *The Search for a Usable Past* (New York: Alfred Knopf, 1967). Charles Pinckney's rejection of a Greco-Roman model for the political situation in American occurs in a speech Pinckney delivered to the Federal Convention in Philadelphia, June 25, 1787, as recorded in Max Farrand, ed., *The Records of the Federal Convention of 1787* (New Haven: Yale University Press, 1911), 1:397ff.

Richard Hofstadter, *The Idea of a Party System* (Berkeley and Los Angeles: University of California Press, 1969), treats its subject with its author's characteristic quiet irony. It is well complemented by Roy F. Nichols, *The Invention of the American Political Parties* (New York: Macmillan, 1967). Light is thrown on the foreign policy dimension of this question in Harry Ammon, "The Genet Mission and the Development of American Political Parties,"

Journal of American History 52 (March 1966). The text of George Washington's Farewell Address, with its warnings against "factionalism," may be read in James D. Richardson, ed., *Messages and Papers of the Presidents* ([Washington, D.C.] Bureau of National Literature, 1911), 1:205–216. A recent, well argued "counter-revisionist" essay on this subject—in effect returning to Washington and rejecting Madison!—is Ralph E. Ketcham, *Presidents Above Party: The First American Presidency, 1789–1829* (Chapel Hill: University of North Carolina Press, 1984).

3. *How Shall We Sing the Lord's Song in a Strange Land*

The grim little poem in which a child in a "burying place" contemplates "graves shorter there than I" can be found in the *New England Primer*, which I used in a twentieth-century reprint made in facsimile "from an original published, as nearly as can be determined, between the years 1785 and 1790" (Boston: Ginn and Company, n.d.). The wrath-filled verse which follows, by Isaac Watts, was quoted in Frank Luther Mott, *Golden Multitudes: The Story of Best Sellers in the United States* (New York: Macmillan, 1947).

Marcus Cunliffe's excellent brief work, *George Washington: Man and Monument* (New York: New American Library, 1960), is not so much a biography as it is an assessment of Washington's public role. It quotes both the incoming President's letter (to Henry Knox) confessing his misgivings about that role and the sharply observant journal entry by Senator William Maclay on the delivery of the inaugural address. The text of the First Inaugural itself is in James D. Richardson, editor, *Messages and Papers of the Presidents*, previously cited in chapter 2. See also my discussion of "The Pastoral Office of the President," *Theology Today* 25 (April 1968).

Luther Martin's complaint to the Maryland legislature about the Federal Constitution's lack of religious orthodoxy, and the letter from Jonas Phillips complaining against the excessive orthodoxy in the state constitution of Pennsylvania, are both in Max Farrand, editor, *The Records of the Federal Convention of 1787* (previously cited in chapter 2), vol. 3, at pp. 227 and 78, respectively. Edmund Burke's defense of Britain's Established Church is in his *Reflections on the Revolution in France*, as cited in chapter 2; Nathaniel Ward's defense of religious intolerance, "The Simple Cobbler of Aggawam," is in Perry Miller, editor, *The American Puritans*, also as cited in chapter 2. Texts of the Maryland Toleration Act, the Virginia Statute of Religious Freedom, and the Memorial of the Hanover Presbytery may be found in H. Shelton Smith, Robert T. Handy, and Lefferts A. Loetscher, editors, *American Christianity: An Historical Interpretation with Representative Documents* (New York: Scribner's, 1960), vol. 1. (Hereafter cited as *American Christianity*.)

Sidney E. Mead—whose ways of thinking have powerfully influenced my own work—quotes the lines from Hector St. John de Crèvecoeur and from Lyman Beecher, respectively, in *The Lively Experiment: The Shaping of Christianity in America* (New York: Harper and Row, 1963) and in *The Old Religion in the Brave New World: Reflections on the Relation Between Christendom and the Republic* (Berkeley: University of California Press, 1977). The line from Isaac Backus on religious voluntarism is quoted in William G. McLoughlin's fine study, *Isaac Backus and the American Pietistic Tradition* (Boston: Little, Brown, 1967).

Thomas Paine's cry that "my own mind is my own church" is in *The Age of Reason*, previously cited in chapter 2. The furious sermon by Timothy Dwight, which identifies the humane heterodoxy of Paine and Jefferson with the wildest excesses of the French Revolution, is in *American Christianity*. Ezra Stiles Ely's vitriolic address on "The Duty of Christian Freemen to Elect Christian Rulers" (1828) was reprinted in Joseph L. Blau, editor, *American Philosophic Addresses* (New York: Columbia University Press, 1947). The further evolution of church-state separation, American-style, is discussed in a lucid, civilized book by Mark De Wolfe Howe, *The Garden and the Wilderness: Religion and Government in American Constitutional History* (Chicago: University of Chicago Press, 1965).

Jonathan Edwards, *A Treatise Concerning Religious Affections* (1746), has had the benefit of the scholarly editing—in this case by John E. Smith—and of the republication that has been undertaken in modern times at Edwards's alma mater (New Haven: Yale University Press, 1959). A partial text of the Cambridge Platform is in *American Christianity*. John Winthrop's *Speech to the General Court* is in Perry Miller, *The American Puritans*, previously cited, as is the quotation in this chapter from John Wise. Thomas Jefferson's First Inaugural Address is in the *Messages and Papers*. The argument that Calvinism's dim view of human nature is not intrinsically inconsistent with representative government—"Democracy is not a method which is effective only with virtuous men"—may be found in Harry N. Davis and Robert C. Wood,

Reinhold Niebuhr on Politics (New York: Scribner, 1960), p. 184 [citing Niebuhr, *The Self and the Dramas of History*, 1959].

The anti-theological Biblicism so characteristic of nineteenth-century American evangelicals is manifest in "The Last Will and Testament of Springfield Presbytery" and in Thomas Campbell, "Declaration and Address," both as printed in *American Christianity*. Isaac Hecker's comment on "the withering, soul-destroying horrors of Calvinism" occurs in an editorial, "The Roots of Our Present Evils," *Catholic World* 23 (May, 1876); see my discussion on this point in *The Spiritual Crisis of the Gilded Age* (De Kalb: Northern Illinois University Press, 1971), chapter 3. "The Deacon's Masterpiece," that satiric allegory on the downfall of New England theology, can be found in some poetry anthologies, and, of course, the sulphurous Calvinist sermon Mark Twain reports as having been unwillingly endured by Tom Sawyer exists in many editions.

G. K. Chesterton's striking description of the United States as "a nation with the soul of a church" became the point of departure for another provocative book by Sidney E. Mead, *The Nation With the Soul of a Church* (New York: Harper and Row, 1975). The process of "nationalization"—breaking Old World ties and establishing New World organization—for American churches is clearly and concretely described in William Warren Sweet, *Religion in the Development of American Culture* (New York: Scribner's, 1952). Light is thrown on the same subject from another angle in Nathan Glazer, *American Judaism* (Chicago; University of Chicago Press, 1952); see also Israel Knox, *Rabbi in America: The Story of Isaac Mayer Wise* (Boston: Little, Brown, 1957). The Lutheran organizational statement by Henry Muhlenberg in 1761, the Catholic Revolutionary War sermon of 1779, and John Carroll's remonstrance with Rome in 1785 concerning the special needs of Catholics in America, with much other material of the same kind, are in *American Christianity*.

All the high drama of the dying John C. Calhoun's last Senate speech is well captured by Margaret L. Coit in *John C. Calhoun: American Portrait* (Boston: Houghton Mifflin, 1950). The speech itself, with its acute analysis of how the bond of religious organizations had eroded in the slavery controversy, is in the old but still useful documents collection edited by Edwin C. Rozwenc, *The Compromise of 1850* (Boston: D. C. Heath, 1957). On the Methodist schism, see the bibliographic discussion in my essay "The Negro and Methodist Union," *Church History* 21 (March 1952). A more recent study is Donald G. Matthews, *Slavery and Methodism: A*

Chapter in American Mortality, 1780–1845 (Princeton, N.J.: Princeton University Press, 1965).

Text of the report by James Henley Thornwell on "The Church and Slavery" is in Robert T. Handy, editor, *Religion in the American Experience* (New York: Harper and Row, 1972). Sharp exception to Thornwell's dictum that the church had no business pronouncing judgment on such questions as slavery was taken by the fictional protagonist of *The Minister's Wooing* by Harriet Beecher Stowe in chapters 10 and 15 (New York: Hurst & Company, n.d.). Quotations attributed to Abraham Lincoln and John Brown occur in Carl Sandburg, *Abraham Lincoln: The Prairie Years* (New York: Harcourt, Brace, 1926), 2:192, 406. On Lincoln, I owe much to a trenchant essay, "Abraham Lincoln and the Self-Made Myth," in Richard Hofstadter, *The American Political Tradition* (New York: Knopf, 1948), and to the chapter titled "Abraham Lincoln's 'Last, Best Hope of Earth'" in Sidney E. Mead, *The Lively Experiment*, previously cited.

4. It Nearly Didn't Work

Willliam Allen White's genial quip that Americans would have had a hard time at the barricades occurs in *The Autobiography of William Allen White* (New York: Macmillan, 1946)—a book whose political wit and wisdom I have plundered in the classroom again and again. Washington's Farewell Address is as cited in chapters 2 and 3. On the elections of 1796 and 1800, I have again used Roy F. Nichols, *The Invention of the American Political Parties*, as cited in chapter 2, and in addition the excellent essay on those elections by Noble Cunningham in Arthur M. Schlesinger, Jr. and Fred L. Israel, eds., *History of American Presidential Elections* (New York: Chelsea House/ McGraw-Hill, 1971).

Linda Kerber, *Federalists in Dissent* (Ithaca: Cornell University Press, 1971) was highly useful for this chapter. Henry Adams, *History of the United States During the Administrations of Thomas Jefferson and James Madison* was again helpful, especially volume 2, chapter 4; volume 7, p. 68; and volume 8, chapter 8. The 1804 quotation from Timothy Dwight on secession appears in Margaret Coit, *John C. Calhoun*, cited in chapter 3. Paul Goodman described the Jeffersonian inroads into Massachusetts, that supposedly die-hard Federalist stronghold, in *The Democratic-Republicans of Massachusetts* (Cambridge: Harvard Univeristy Press, 1964).

Both Henry Clay's fire-eating "war hawk" speech urging the conquest of Canada, and John C. Calhoun's admonition to Congress that the greatest of calamities is disunion—as well as Calhoun's later statement on slavery as the basis for a high civilization—were reprinted in the excellent documents collection by Ray Billington, Bert Lowenberg, and S. H. Brockunier, *The Making of American Democracy*, cited also in chapter 1. Richard Leopold and Arthur Link, in their anthology *Problems in American History* (Englewood Cliffs: Prentice-Hall, 1957), included John Randolph's warning in 1812 that if Americans declared war on Britain they would thereby "become the virtual allies of Bonaparte." The letter from Vermont Chief Justice Royall Tyler is reproduced as an Appendix in Roger H. Brown, *The Republic in Peril: 1812* (New York: W. W. Norton, 1971). Brown's book, a thoroughly revisionist treatment of the War of 1812, must be set alongside older studies such as Julius W. Pratt, *Expansionists of 1812* (New York: Macmillan, 1925); and especially the monumental work of Henry Adams, still the starting point for all serious discussion of that war.

Thomas Jefferson's letter to John Adams on the downfall of Napoleon, and Adams's reply, are in Lester Cappon, editor, *The Adams-Jefferson Letters*, cited in chapter 2, as are their musings on the post-Waterloo international situation. The iconography of Napoleon's tomb is described, with engravings, in Colonel Pol Payard, *The Tomb of Napoleon* (Paris: Editions Albert Morance, n.d.); a bronze statuary group subsequently added in the tomb, depicting sorrowful World War I *poilus* as they bear Marshall Foch off to eternity, extends this militaristic mystique into the twentieth century. Emerson's rather tacky essay "Napoleon; or The Man of the World," originally in *Representative Men*, was reprinted in Ralph Waldo Emerson, *Complete Writings* (New York: William H. Wise, 1929).

Jefferson's famous "fire-bell in the night" line may be found in Merrill D. Peterson, editor, *The Portable Thomas Jefferson* (New York: Penguin Books, 1977). Allan Nevins, editor, *The Diary of John Quincy Adams* (New York: Scribner's, 1951), records the spirited exchanges between the younger Adams and John C. Calhoun on the Missouri crisis of 1820. Andrew Jackson's proclamation to the people of South Carolina in 1832 is in the *Messages and Papers of the*

Presidents (as cited in chapter 2), 2:1203–1219. See also James C. Curtis, *Andrew Jackson and the Search for Vindication* (Boston: Little, Brown, 1976), a psychologically perceptive study of Jackson.

Leonard Baker, *John Marshall: A Life in Law* (New York: Macmillan, 1974), not only contains the cited letters from the Chief Justice, but also describes the valiant stand of his son, Thomas, against slavery in the legislature of their native state, Virginia. Fletcher M. Green describes the paradox of widening white enfranchisement simultaneously with black disfranchisement in "Cycles of American Democracy," *Mississippi Valley Historical Review* 48 (June 1961). The description of the slave-burdened South by Charles Dickens appears in *Pictures from Italy and American Notes for General Circulation* (Boston: Houghton Mifflin, 1877).

The 1847 statement by Abraham Lincoln on useful vs. useless labor—downright socialist sounding if taken apart from its Whig-protectionist context—appears in Carl Sandburg, *The Prairie Years* (as cited in chapter 3), 1:348–350. The evolution of that general thesis about the rights of labor into an explicitly antislavery argument becomes clear from careful reading of Paul M. Angle, editor, *Created Equal? The Complete Lincoln-Douglas Debates of 1858* (Chicago: University of Chicago Press, 1958). Jefferson Davis's threat to tear Mississippi's star from the flag should Lincoln's doctrines be carried into the White House is quoted in Allan Nevins, *The Emergence of Lincoln* (New York: Scribner's 1950), 1:414.

South Carolina's *Declaration of the Causes of Secession* and Davis's Message to the Confederate Congress justifying the action both appear in Richard Hofstadter, editor, *Great Issues in American History*, cited also in chapter 2. The speech by Alexander Stephens on black inequality as the cornerstone of the Confederacy was reprinted in the Billington-Lowenberg-Brockunier documents anthology, previously cited. Lincoln's rationale for the Civil War as a "people's contest," together with his classic statement of the "fatal contradiction" in all republican government, appears in his Special Message to Congress, July 4, 1861, in *Messages and Papers* (previously cited), 5:3221–3232.

Emory Thomas took a fresh look at the short-lived Southern nation in *The Confederacy as a Revolutionary Experience* (Englewood Cliffs: Prentice-Hall, 1971), a book given its new insight by the then-recent experience of the 1960s, even though the longer-term political consequences of that turbulent decade have thus far been less than revolutionary. Henry Steele Commager succinctly summed up his oft-stated thesis that the South perished because of its own states' rights doctrines in a Civil War Centennial essay, "How the Lost Cause Was Lost," *New York Times* August 4, 1963; reprinted in Commager, *The Search for a Usable Past,* cited also in chapter 2.

Vernon L. Parrington's lament at the loss of the option of localist Jeffersonian liberalism as a result of that principle's involvement with slavery occurs in a thoughtful essay on Alexander H. Stephens in Parrington, *Main Currents in American Thought* (New York: Harcourt, Brace, 1930), 2:83–93. Parrington is also perceptive, and still fresh, in discussing the "Greek democracy" ideal which seduced the slave-owning generation of John C. Calhoun. George H. Dennison draws the somber conclusion that the old republic died in giving birth to empire in his judicious, carefully reasoned study *The Dorr War: Republicanism on Trial, 1831–1861* (Lexington: University of Kentucky Press, 1970). Details of Robert E. Lee's pilgrimage from Washington, as a Union officer, to Richmond, and his destiny with the Army of Northern Virginia, are chronicled in Douglas Southall Freeman, *R. E. Lee: A Biography* (New York: Scribner's, 1934), 1:436–447.

5. *Growing Up, or Running Away?*

To revise is not necessarily to improve. What happened to Philip Freneau's poetical Muse in this regard can be judged by comparing the initial appearance of his "Account of the Island of Santa Cruz: Containing an Original Poem on the Beauties of that Island" in the *United States Magazine* for February 1779 with the extended and reworked 1786 draft as reprinted in Fred Lewis Pattee, editor, *The Poems of Philip Freneau, Poet of the American Revolution* (Princeton: University Library, 1902). Editor Pattee carefully annotated the latter version, showing exactly what Freneau had changed. Lewis Leary, editor of *The Last Poems of Philip Freneau* (New Brunswick: Rutgers University Press, 1945) attributes first publication of "The City Poet" to *The True American* for October 6, 1821—but notes that the poem appears in virtually the same form as an autograph on the flyleaf of Freneau's copy of Benjamin Rush, *Addresses to the Inhabitants of the British Settlements in America upon Slave-Keeping* (Philadelphia, 1773). Biographical data on Freneau may be found in Jacob Axelrod, *Philip Freneau, Champion of Democracy* (Austin: University of Texas Press, 1967). Do not overlook Vernon Louis

Parrington's essay "Philip Freneau: Poet of Two Revolutions"—partisan, but shrewd nonetheless—in Parrington, *Main Currents in American Thought* (previously cited in chapter 4), 1:368–381.

The text of the opinion by Justice Royall Tyler in *Selectmen* v. *Jacob*, 1802, is in Marius Péladeau, editor, *The Prose of Royall Tyler* (Montpelier: Vermont Historical Society; Rutland and Tokyo: Charles E. Tuttle Co., 1972), pp. 392–394. Tyler's charge to the jury in *State of Vermont* v. *Cyrus B. Dean*, 1808, is in *ibid.*, pp. 407–411. The circumstances leading up to these two cases are discussed at pp. 360–365. The work by Tyler commonly considered to have been the earliest American novel, *The Algerine Captive*, has been edited for modern readers by Don L. Cook (New Haven: College and University Press, 1970).

Partly on account of its special status as the first American play produced after the Revolution by an American company, Royall Tyler's *The Contrast* may be found in many American Literature anthologies. I used one edited by Edwin H. Cady, *Literature of the Early Republic*, second edition (as cited in chapter 2), which contains also six chapters from the *Knickerbocker History of New York* by Washington Irving, discussed further on in this chapter. The letter from Thomas Jefferson to John Banister, Jr., detailing the moral peril to Americans in a European education may be found in Merrill Peterson, editor, *The Portable Thomas Jefferson*, previously cited in chapter 4.

The British put-down of U.S. culture in *The Courier* (1813) is quoted by Henry Adams in his *History of the United States During the Administrations of Thomas Jefferson and James Madison* (previously cited in chapters 2 and 4), 7:359. The elitist essay by Matthew Arnold, "America Is Not Interesting," excerpted from Arnold's *Civilization in the United States* (1888), may be found in Henry Steele Commager, editor, *America in Perspective: The United States through Foreign Eyes* (New York: New American Library, 1948).

Ralph Waldo Emerson's essay "The American Scholar" is available in many editions. I used it as printed in Joseph L. Blau, editor, *American Philosophic Addresses*, previously cited in chapter 3, a book which conveniently includes the musings of several other nineteenth-century writers—notably George Bancroft and Wendell Phillips—on the proper role of the intellectual under democratic government. I have also quoted from the essays "Self-Reliance" and "Society and Solitude," as anthologized by the distinguished

Emerson scholar Stephen E. Whicher in *Selections from Ralph Waldo Emerson* (Boston: Houghton Mifflin, 1957).

Washington Irving's *Sketch Book of Geoffrey Crayon, Gent.*, is available in William P. Kelly, editor, *Selected Writings of Washington Irving* (New York: Modern Library, 1984). Philip Freneau's anti-Irving jibe, "To a New-England Poet," is in Lewis Leary, editor, *Last Poems of Philip Freneau*, cited above. Still fresh and to the point after nearly six decades is the essay on Irving in Vernon L. Parrington, *Main Currents in American Thought* (cited above), 2:203–212.

The long-winded *Memoirs* of Lorenzo da Ponte, Mozart's librettist and a sometime Columbia professor, have been made available in a modern edition (New York: Dover Publications, 1967). Paralleling for the visual arts what Parrington accomplished for literature is Oliver Larkin, *Art and Life in America*, revised edition (New York: Holt, Rinehart, and Winston, 1960). A different kind of critical sensibility from Larkin's is evident in Lillian Miller, "Painting, Sculpture, and the National Character, 1815–1860," *Journal of American History*, 53 (March 1967).

A useful study, but with a thesis that is all too easy to oversimplify, is Ann Douglas, *The Feminization of American Culture* (New York: Knopf, 1977). The flip side of Douglas' argument, in a sense, is Leslie Fiedler, *Love and Death in the American Novel* (Cleveland: World Publishing Company, 1962). But see also Fiedler, *What Was Literature? Class, Culture and Mass Society* (New York: Simon and Schuster, 1982), in which the author candidly revises, and even rebuts, some of the views set forth in *Love and Death*.

The critical essay by Edgar Allan Poe on "Longfellow's Ballads," which appeared originally in the *Gentleman's Magazine* (1842), is available in F. C. Prescott, editor, *Selections from the Critical Writings of Edgar Allan Poe* (New York: Henry Holt, 1909; new edition, New York: Gordian Press, 1981). The short story "The Man of the Crowd" is in most editions of Poe's tales.

Henry Nash Smith, *Virgin Land* (New York: Vintage Books, 1957), which bears also upon the themes of chapter 1 above, contains a discussion of Fenimore Cooper, "Leatherstocking and the Problem of Social Order," that was helpful for the present chapter. Henry David Thoreau's great essay *Walking* is cited as in chapter 1; his essay *Ktaadn* (or *Katahdin*, to use the spelling which appears in the Appalachian Mountain Club's trail guide to that mountain) is in *The Writings of Henry David Thoreau*, III: *The Maine Woods* (Boston:

Houghton Mifflin, 1892 [copyright 1864 by Ticknor and Fields]). Leo Marx, both in *The Machine in the Garden* previously cited in chapter 1, and in the more tightly focused essay from which that book derives, "The Machine in the Garden," *New England Quarterly*, 29 (March 1956), shows how the raucous clangor of a new industrial civilization jangled against the shrinking ear of Nathaniel Hawthorne.

The Scarlet Letter, Hawthorne's acknowledged magnum opus, exists in many editions; I used one edited by Harry Levin (Boston: Houghton Mifflin, 1961). Annette Kolodny, in her Introduction to Nathaniel Hawthorne, *The Blithedale Romance* (New York: Penguin Books, 1983), challenges the conventional scholars' consensus that "Blithedale" was a disguised version of Brook Farm; the novel, she argues, was just what Hawthorne called it, a "romance." My own view of the novelistic character Zenobia, as compared to the real Margaret Fuller, splits the difference. After having been long out of print, Fuller's classic *Woman in the Nineteenth Century* reappeared after the modern movement for the liberation of women had begun to raise the consciousness of at least a few men (New York: W. W. Norton, 1971). I have benefited from an unpublished colloquium paper by Adelaide Elm, "The Liberation of Margaret Fuller" (University of Arizona, 1986).

Frank Luther Mott's humanely democratic study *Golden Multitudes*, previously cited in chapter 3, is highly germane to this chapter also. Mott avoided the trap, into which many subsequent investigators in this field have fallen, of assuming that if "popular" culture is to rise in esteem, "high" culture must fall.

Harriet Beecher Stowe, *The Minister's Wooing*, first published in 1859, has had the benefit of a modern paperback reissue (Hartford: Stowe-Day Foundation, 1978), with a helpful scholarly introduction by Sandra Duguid which deciphers for modern readers the real-life originals of Stowe's principal characters.

There are many, many editions of Herman Melville's *Moby-Dick, or the White Whale*, some with elaborate scholarly apparatus, but in the classroom I like to use one published by Dodd, Mead in 1922, with colorful illustrations by Mead Schaeffer. Such paintings of romantically imagined seagoing life remind us that before the literary analysts got hold of it this was generally perceived as an adventure story for not-quite-grown boys.

Of the flood of books published for the Civil War centennial, perhaps the very best is Edmund Wilson, *Patriotic Gore* (New York:

Oxford, 1962; republished in paper with corrections, 1966). Stephen Kern, *The Culture of Time and Space* (Cambridge: Harvard University Press, 1983) is an ambitious synthesis of all the forces, from the fiction of Proust, Mann, and Joyce to the theories of Einstein and Freud, from the Eiffel Tower to the telephone, from Nietzsche to Gertrude Stein, that have made modern culture truly modern. It will have to be reckoned with by all future students of Euro-American cultural history.

Henry F. May described "the innocent rebellion" in America before World War I in *The End of American Innocence* (New York: Knopf, 1959). Siegfried Giedion set American architectural achievements into a wider international and historical context in *Space, Time, and Architecture,* 5th rev. ed. (Cambridge: Harvard University Press, 1967). The reverse impact of American upon European literature can be illustrated by comparing intercut narrative passages in John Dos Passos, *Manhattan Transfer* (Boston: Houghton Mifflin, 1963; first published in 1925) with the same literary device as employed in Jean-Paul Sartre, *The Reprieve,* translated by Eric Sutton (New York: Modern Library, 1967; first published in 1947).

6. *The Age of the Dinosaurs*

The text of interlude V, and also the opening paragraphs of this chapter, first appeared in my essay *Out West: The Literature of Action,* edited by Karen J. Dahood and published by the Tucson Public Library/Arizona Historical Society (Tucson, 1983), although I have taken the argument in a somewhat different direction this time. I gratefully acknowledge permission to reprint them here. Physical detail for my description of Green River, Wyoming, in 1869 was taken from William Culp Darrah, *Powell of the Colorado* (Princeton, N.J.: Princeton University Press, 1969 [copyright, 1951]). My quotations from John Wesley Powell, *Canyons of the Colorado,* are taken from the handsome edition published by Chautauquan-Century Press (Meadville, Pa., 1895); it contains steel engravings, many of them made from Grand Canyon photographs by Thomas Moran, which convey (far better than *Arizona Highways* superchromes!) the way the Grand Canyon seemed to the late nineteenth-century imagination.

Joseph Wood Krutch, *Grand Canyon: Today and all Its Yesterdays*

(New York: William Sloane, 1958) is the work of a transplanted Easterner whose intellectual interest in and concern for the environment long preceded his discovery of Arizona; he was the author also of an outstanding biography of Thoreau. A work that should be better known is Stephen J. Pyne, *Dutton's Point: An Intellectual History of the Grand Canyon* (Grand Canyon, Ariz.: Grand Canyon Natural History Association, 1982). George Gaylord Simpson's essay "Historical Science," originally in *The Fabric of Geology*, edited by C. A. Albretton (1963), was reprinted in Frank H. T. Rhodes and Richard O. Stone, editors, *Language of the Earth* (New York: Pergamon Press, 1981).

My description of the Grand Canyon fossil record, bottom to top, is collated from Powell, *Canyons of the Colorado*, and Krutch, *Grand Canyon*, as cited above; Edwin D. McKee, *Ancient Landscapes of the Grand Canyon Region* (1931) as reprinted in Bruce Babbitt, editor, *Grand Canyon: An Anthology* (Flagstaff: Northland Press, 1978); and an excellent manual by Halka Chronic, up to date factually and conceptually as of 1983 but written in language accessible to non-geoscientists, *Roadside Geology of Arizona* (Missoula, Montana: Mountain Press, 1986).

The quotation from the Rev. Clement Moore (better known as the author of "A Visit from St. Nicholas") may be found in Linda K. Kerber, *Federalists in Dissent*, as cited in chapter 4. George McCready Price's put-down of John Wesley Powell's work on the Colorado appears in Price, *The Fundamentals of Geology* (Mountain View, Cal.: Pacific Press, 1913). Willard Gatewood has carefully traced the continuing importance of Price's ideas for subsequent generations of special creationists, right down to the 1980s, in "From Scopes to Creation Science: The Decline and Revival of the Evolution Controversy," *South Atlantic Quarterly* 83 (1984); that article was reprinted in Leonard Dinnerstein and Kenneth T. Jackson, editors, *American Vistas*, 5th edition (New York: Oxford, 1987). The present judicial status of that controversy may be inferred from the 1987 Supreme Court decision striking down a Louisiana "creation science" law, *Edwards* v. *Aguillard* (96 L Ed 2d 510); do not overlook Justice Scalia's probing dissent.

The remark by Samuel Sewall about Cotton Mather's having preached a heliocentric solar system in 1714 is in Sewall's *Diary*, excerpts as reprinted in Perry Miller, editor, *The American Puritans*, previously cited in chapters 2 and 3. On science in America prior to the nineteenth century see Brooke Hindle, *The Pursuit of Science in Revolutionary America* (Chapel Hill: University of North Carolina Press, 1956) and, in microcosm, Carl and Jessica Bridenbaugh, *Rebels and Gentlemen: Philadelphia in the Age of Franklin* (New York: Oxford, 1962 [first copyright 1942]), especially chapters 8 and 9. Ralph Waldo Emerson's important transitional essay "Fate" appears in Stephen E. Whicher, editor, *Selections from Ralph Waldo Emerson*, as cited in chapter 5.

Edwin H. Colbert, himself one of America's foremost paleontologists, has written a highly readable account of his predecessors' work, *Men and Dinosaurs: The Search in Field and Laboratory* (New York: Dutton, 1968). Howard S. Miller, "Fossils and Free Enterprisers," originally in Miller, *Dollars for Research* (1970), appears in Rhodes and Stone, *Language of the Earth*, as cited above. Fernando Savater, professor of philosophy in the University of Madrid, probes the literary significance of the dinosaur in *Childhood Regained: The Art of the Storyteller* (New York: Columbia University Press, 1982). A gallery of artistic renderings of the dinosaur from the Victorian era to more modern and scientifically corrected interpretations—reflecting two exhibitions that opened in Washington in 1987 and then went on tour, one titled "Dinosaurs Past and Present," and the other a retrospective of the work of dinosaur artist Charles R. Knight—appeared with an article by John P. Wiley, Jr., "Dinosaurs Shake the Ground in Paint and Sculpture," *Smithsonian* 18 (June 1987).

Edward Drinker Cope wrote "On the Geology and Paleontology of the Cretaceous Strata of Kansas" in a lively style one would certainly not expect to find in a similarly titled monograph today; it appears in F. V. Hayden, *Preliminary Report of the United States Geological Survey of Montana and Portions of Adjacent Territories* (Washington: Government Printing Office, 1872). A similarly Romantic essay on "The Ancient Lakes of Western America" by J. S. Newberry, concluding with some philosophical reflections on Western America's prehuman inhabitants and on future human prospects, was published in Hayden's *Preliminary Report of the United States Geological Survey of Wyoming* (Washington: Government Printing Office, 1872). Biographies of Newberry and of astronomer Simon Newcomb fortuitously adjoin each other in Charles Coulston Gillispie, editor, *Dictionary of Scientific Biography* 10 (New York: Scribner's, 1974).

The landmark work on the attempt to apply evolutionary theory to human society is still Richard Hofstadter, *Social Darwinism in American Thought* (Boston: Beacon Press, 1955; first published in 1944), although the reader should also take note of cautionary comments on that subject by Edward Kirkland in his gracefully written *Dream and Thought in the Business Community* (Chicago: Quadrangle Books, 1964; first published in 1956). The views of William Graham Sumner, Lester F. Ward, and other participants in this debate may be found—in completely reprinted articles, not anthology snippets—in R.J. Wilson, editor, *Darwinism and the American Intellectual* (Chicago: Dorsey Press, 2nd ed., 1989), and in Perry Miller, *American Thought: Civil War to World War I*, cited also in chapter 1. Darwin's and Thomas Huxley's own views are illuminatingly discussed by William Irvine in his quite delightful *Apes, Angels, and Victorians* (Cleveland: World Publishing Company, 1955). For the European context, see the references to Darwinism in Carleton J. H. Hayes, *A Generation of Materialism, 1871–1900* (New York: Harper, 1941)—an old-fashioned textbook, but one of the very best of its kind.

Lewis Henry Morgan's heroic attempt at an evolutionary overview of the whole of human history, published in 1877 and long out of print, has again become readily available, with a new preface by one of Morgan's own former students, Elisabeth Tooker; Morgan, *Ancient Society* (Tucson: University of Arizona Press, 1985). Thorstein Veblen, *The Theory of the Leisure Class*, exists in many editions; I used that of the Modern Library (New York: Random House, 1934). *White Fang*, by Jack London, typifies the Darwinist, struggle-for-existence theme in turn-of-the-century fiction; my copy had been published by Scholastic Book Services (New York, n.d.) —indicating that the education establishment considers at least some forms of Darwinism suitable for youthful minds.

John Quincy Adams's striking proposal and rationale for government-sponsored scientific development occurs toward the end of his First Annual Message to Congress, December 6, 1825, in James D. Richardson, editor, *Messages and Papers of the Presidents*, previously cited in chapters 2, 3, and 4. Lewis Mumford has a pungent essay on the U.S. national capital, "The Lessons of Washington," in his monumental survey, *The City in History* (New York: Harcourt, Brace, and World, 1961). From Allan Nevins, *Hamilton Fish: The Inner History of the Grant Administration* (New York: Dodd, Mead,

1936)—a book somewhat dated conceptually but still the starting point for studying the political and diplomatic history of the Grant era—came, among other things, the line about diamond-laden carriages stuck in mudholes.

A. Hunter Dupree, *Science in the Federal Government* (Cambridge, Mass: Belknap Press, 1957), was indispensable for this chapter. Helpful also was Curtis M. Hinsley, Jr., *Savages and Scientists: The Smithsonian Institution and the Development of American Anthropology* (Washington, D.C.: Smithsonian Institution Press, 1981), a thoughtful study whose concerns and implications go far beyond its seemingly narrow institutional theme. Paul F. Boller's splendid essay "New Men and New Ideas: Science and the American Mind" appeared in H. Wayne Morgan, editor, *The Gilded Age: A Reappraisal* (Syracuse, N.Y.: Syracuse University Press, 1963), a collection of revisionist essays which has revolutionized our understanding of that much-misunderstood period in American history. Boller elaborated on the same theme in *American Thought in Transition: The Impact of Evolutionary Naturalism* (Chicago: Rand McNally, 1969), an excellent work.

J. Kirkpatrick Flack, *Desideratum in Washington* (Cambridge, Mass.: Schenkman, 1975), gives an account of the intellectual community in the nation's capital from 1870 to 1900—a period during which we stereotypically do not think of that city as having abounded in intellectuals. Dupree and Darrah, cited above, throw light on the founding of the United States Geological Survey. A subtle, sociologically sophisticated account of the emergence of scientific research in the Department of Agriculture occurs in Charles E. Rosenberg, *No Other Gods: On Science and American Social Thought* (Baltimore: Johns Hopkins, 1976), chapter 9. Robert Wiebe, *The Search For Order* (New York: Hill and Wang, 1967), describes acutely the wider institutional-historical context for such professional evolution. Mary O. Furner, in *Advocacy and Objectivity* (Lexington: University Press of Kentucky, 1975) describes the parallel process among the social as distinguished from the natural sciences, a process demonstrating that there are few gains in the progress of ideas without some corresponding loss. Jack Remington, in "Beyond Big Science in America: The Binding of Inquiry," *Social Studies of Science* 18 (1988), dissects and details some of that loss in the American way of "doing" science in recent years, and proposes a modest remedy.

7. *World Wreckers or Planetary Custodians?*

Descriptive data for Interlude VI were gleaned from A.P. Coleman, *The Last Million Years* (Toronto: University of Toronto Press, 1941). A cautious, qualified statement of an extinction hypothesis anticipating that of Paul S. Martin may be found in a standard—and rather dry—geology textbook by Richard Foster Flint, *Glacial and Pleistocene Geology* (New York: John Wiley and Sons, 1957). Professor Martin, with savage irony, titled his theory of the extermination of Ice Age megafauna by the first humans to cross the Bering Strait "The Discovery of America," *Science*, 179 (March 9, 1973). He presented his "overkill" hypothesis even more forcefully as a guest lecturer to an undergraduate class in glacial geology (Geosciences 254, University of Arizona) on May 3, 1978, from which I took notes, citing in particular Lewis F. Richardson, *Statistics of Deadly Quarrels* (Pittsburgh: Boxwood Press, 1960), a work all the more devastating for its studiously mathematical tone.

A spirited rebuttal to that hypothesis is Calvin Martin, *Keeper of the Game* (Berkeley: University of California Press, 1978), especially pp. 168–172. A more recent symposium, summing up the pros and cons of the "overkill" thesis and generalizing it to the planet as a whole, is Paul S. Martin and Richard G. Klein, editors, *Quaternary Extinctions: A Prehistoric Revolution* (Tucson: University of Arizona Press, 1984). Also relevant to that debate is Paul Chrisler Phillips, *The Fur Trade* (Norman: University of Oklahoma Press, 1961), especially chapter 1.

Willy Ley, in *The Lungfish and the Unicorn* (New York: Modern Age Books, 1941) detailed the melancholy fate of the European bison in chapter 7. James Fenimore Cooper in *The Pioneers* (Albany: State University of New York Press, 1980 [first published in 1823]) fictionally recaptured early Americans' take-no-thought-for-the-morrow attitude toward the passenger pigeon, while Emerson Hough imaginatively re-created the wild prairie onto which those pioneers marched after Cooper's time in *The Covered Wagon* (New York: Grosset & Dunlap, 1922).

George Perkins Marsh addressed the whole subject of planet-wide human despoiling of the natural environment a century and a quarter ago in *Man and Nature* (Cambridge, Mass.: Belknap Press, 1965; first published in 1864). Forty years ago William Vogt wrote a hard-hitting tract to the same point, *Road to Survival* (New York:

William Sloane, 1948). Both books should—but won't—abate the belief by trend-hopping but historically unaware activists that concepts like "conservation," "ecology," or "environmentalism" came into existence only the day before yesterday. The comment by Wallace Stegner on how the devastation of the landscape got worse as people moved farther west occurs in Richard W. Etulain, editor, *Conversations with Wallace Stegner on Western History and Literature* (Salt Lake City, Utah: University of Utah Press, 1983).

The essay I wrote for the Tucson Public Library/Arizona Historical Society's intelligently conceived project "Writers of the Purple Sage," *Out West: The Literature of Action*, from which I drew the opening for chapter 6, above, furnished a few additional lines here also. I have taken from a similar article, *Golden West: The Literature of Comprehension*, edited by Karen J. Dahood (Tucson: Tucson Public Library/Arizona Historical Society, 1983), the material dealing with the planetary astronomer Percival Lowell's work as symbolic of a growing national concern with a natural resource shortage (water); again I am grateful to both sponsoring organizations for permission to reprint those paragraphs here. That essay in turn owes much to a thoughtfully conceived monograph by the late William Hoyt, *Lowell and Mars* (Tucson: University of Arizona Press, 1976). The thesis that Lowell may have been, in a sense, right after all about the Martians is set forth in Richard C. Hoagland, *The Monuments of Mars* (Berkeley: North Atlantic Books, 1987). The controversy over that thesis has been extreme, with stridency on one side and refusal even to consider the matter on the other—I suspect because profound philosophic issues turn upon the answer, rendering impossible any truly dispassionate consideration of the evidence. Lowell's own hypotheses, although scientifically long outdated, still make absorbing reading; see Percival Lowell, *Mars and its Canals* (New York: Macmillan, 1906); *Mars as the Abode of Life* (New York: MacMillan, 1908); and especially "Mars and the Future of the Earth," *Century Magazine* 75 (April 1908). (Sources for other quotations in Section 3 of the present chapter are annotated in my *Golden West* essay, p. 16.)

John Van Dyke, *The Desert* (Tucson: Arizona Historical Society, 1976), first published in 1901, is a translation of the issues and values Thoreau had described in the language of the humid East in works like *Ktaadn* (cited in chapter 5) into the terms of the arid Southwest; compare Joseph Wood Krutch, *Henry David Thoreau* (New York: William Sloane, 1948). See also Lawrence Clark Powell, "The Desert Odyssey of John C. Van Dyke," *Arizona Highways* 58 (October, 1952)—a journal, by the way, whose often sophisticated articles and essays are not just filler inserted between its blazing Kodachromes. Another classic work from Van Dyke's period, reprinted for modern readers, is John Muir, *The Mountains of California* (Berkeley: Ten Speed Press, 1977; first published in 1894). A sketch of Muir's life by a later sharer in his environmentalist values is Supreme Court Justice William O. Douglas, *Muir of the Mountains* (Boston: Houghton Mifflin, 1961). The useful typological disjunction between "preservationism" and "conservationism" comes from Donald Fleming, "Roots of the New Conservation Movement," in *Perspectives in American History* 6 (Cambridge, Mass.: Center for Studies in American History, 1972). Treating this subject more broadly as intellectual/literary history is Roderick Nash, *Wilderness and the American Mind* (New Haven: Yale University Press, 1967). For other examples of literary environmentalism, see Aldo Leopold, *A Sand County Almanac* (New York: Oxford, 1966; first published in 1949), a book which has been subtly but pervasively influential on the later environmental movement; and Rachel Carson, *The Sea Around Us* (New York: Oxford, 1951), a work with a global outlook resembling that of Vernadskii, cited below. Carson's best-known work is, of course, *Silent Spring* (Boston: Houghton Mifflin, 1962), a grim forecast of the consequences of indiscriminate use of pesticides.

The passages on forest conservation in Theodore Roosevelt's first annual message to Congress, December 3, 1901, are as printed in *Messages and Papers of the Presidents* (previously cited in chapters 2, 4, 5, and 6), 9:6653-6655. The quotation from Senator Henry Teller is taken from Judy Margolis, "Saving Forests Didn't Come Naturally, in the U.S.," *Arizona Daily Star*, February 6, 1984, in that newspaper's excellent and historically well-researched series "National Forests: The West's Treasure." The passage in this chapter from William James is from his typically provocative "On A Certain Blindness in Human Beings," first published in 1899; available as Chapter 9 in James, *Essays on Faith and Morals* (Cleveland: World Publishing Co., 1962).

Pare Lorenz's great thirty-minute motion picture *The River*, and its companion piece *The Plow that Broke the Plains*—prints of which I was fortunate enough to have available for screening from the University of Arizona's well-stocked film archive—convey more vividly than thousands of words the distinctive conservationist ideology of the New Deal. Broadus Mitchell's warmly favorable portrayal of the Tennessee Valley Authority in his economic history of the *Depression Decade* (New York: Rinehart, 1947), no doubt is colored by the experience—as Mitchell himself acknowledges—of one "who was born within hailing distance of the scene, and whose family all but surrendered there before surviving to witness the miracle"; nevertheless his account of the TVA as a striking and healthy departure from some other New Deal activities—"here abundance was not expected somehow to profit from induced scarcity"—is cogent and persuasive. *Depression Decade*, by the way, holds up remarkably well after forty years; its critique of the New Deal anticipated much that has appeared on that subject more recently and it is written with unheard-of felicity for a work dealing with economics. It remains indispensable for any reader who is more than casually interested in the history of the New Deal.

In addition to the lecture by Paul S. Martin cited above, two statements quoted in this chapter were heard first-hand. Amiya Chakravarty, formerly a leader in India's independence movement and subsequently a professor of comparative religion, movingly addressed a Quaker-sponsored International Student Seminar in which I was a participant at Woodstock, Vermont in July of 1952. The unreconstructed Republican, unknown to me by name, who commented on the TVA and otherwise regaled me with his conservative political philosophy in compensation for having picked me up as a hitchhiker in my less-than-affluent student years, never foresaw, I suppose, how his epigram woudl one day be used. My apologies; one takes wisdom wherever one can find it.

This chapter benefited from a doctoral dissertation by Douglas R. Weiner which I was privileged to read in manuscript prior to publication, *Models of Nature: Conservation, Ecology, and Cultural Revolution in Soviet Russia* (Bloomington: Indiana University Press, 1988). Dr. Weiner kindly shared his ideas and findings thus far toward his next project, which will be a study of conservation history in the U.S.S.R. since World War II, in a History Department colloquium at the University of Arizona, February 2, 1988. The observation that socialist and capitalist countries have had comparably bad records of environmental destruction occurs in the 1984–85 Gifford Lectures by Jürgen Moltmann, a German theologian who writes in his nation's tradition of academic discourse: ponderous but profound. Moltmann, *God in Creation* (London: SCM Press, 1985), chapter 2.

All quotations from academician Vladimir Vernadskii is this chapter are from *La Biosphère* (Paris: Librairie Félix Alcan, 1929), for which Vernadskii evidently made his own translation from the Russian original (*Biosfera*, 1926). The subsequent translations from the French into English are my labored own. *The Biosphere* had been long out of print in the West, and I am pleased that at least an 82-page abridgement, also based on the 1929 French edition, has been published in America (Oracle, Arizona: Synergetic Press, 1986), beginning at last to give this pioneering thinker his due. Now we need a full-dress biography—one is forthcoming, I am told— free from both the worshipful tone and the chivvying efforts to peg him within the confines of Soviet-style Marxist dialectics that mar the otherwise quite useful study by R. K. Balandin, *Vladimir Vernadsky* (Moscow: Mir Publishers, 1982, translated into English by Alexander Repyev and revised from a 1979 version in Russian). Balandin does, however, acknowledge the curious cross-tie between Vernadskii and that very un-Marxist Jesuit evolutionary scientist Pierre Teilhard de Chardin; see also the cryptic mention of Vernadskii in Claude Cuénot, *Teilhard de Chardin* (Baltimore: Helicon, 1965, translated from a 1958 original in French).

8. *The Majority Has Always Been Moral*

In any discussion of the history of science it is necessary to update one's data; compare what is said about "Neanderthal Man" in the *Encyclopaedia Britannica* (Chicago: William Benton, 1959), vol. 22, with what appears on that subject in the *New Encyclopaedia Britannica* 15th edition (Chicago: Helen Hemingway Benton, 1975), *Macropaedia*, vol. 12. I first became aware of Rudolf Virchow's "expert" debunking of the Neanderthal find in a popular science account by Willy Ley, *The Days of Creation* (New York: Modern Age Books, 1941). Ley described Virchow's rejection of the fossil evidence as "a masterpiece of senile resistance to new ideas," which is rather unfair to a distinguished nineteenth-century scientist and, at least by Imperial German standards, humane and socially conscious politician; see the authoritative article in C. C. Gillispie, editor, *Dictionary of Scientific Biography* (previously cited in chapter 6).

The text of the Populist party platform of 1892 may be found in Richard Hofstadter, editor, *Great Issues in American History* (previously cited in chapters 2 and 4), vol. 2; here also may be found

William Jennings Bryan's "Cross of Gold" oration. Hofstadter discussed Populism rather unsympathetically in *The Age of Reform* (New York: Knopf, 1955); John D. Hicks treated it with more approval in *The Populist Revolt* (Minneapolis: University of Minnesota Press, 1931)—a book that should not be condescended to merely on the ground that it is older. The continuing controversy concerning Populism, over which a great deal of historians' ink has been spilled, is candidly and pungently described by Ray Ginger in the superb bibliographical essay which accompanies Ginger's *Age of Excess: The United States from 1877 to 1914* (New York: Macmillan, 1965).

Populism's only presidential candidate, James B. Weaver, wrote for the 1892 campaign a book, thoughtful enought to merit the modern reader's attention, titled *A Call to Action;* it has been reprinted in a series edited by Kenneth Carpenter, *Gold: Historical and Economic Aspects* (New York: Arno Press, 1974). The definition of business leaders as "Christian men," etc., by George F. Baer is quoted by Ray Ginger is his definitive biography of perennial Socialist presidential candidate Eugene V. Debs, *The Bending Cross* (New Brunswick: Rutgers University Press, 1949)—a book which also notes in passing Debs's lifelong love-hate relationship with Christianity. The remarkable oration by Roscoe Conkling Simmons, implicitly comparing Hoover to Christ, appears in *Text-Book of the Republican Party* (Chicago: Republican National Committee, 1932). FDR's first inaugural address may be found in Basil Rauch, editor, *Franklin D. Rossevelt: Selected Speeches, Messages, Press Conferences, and Letters* (previously cited in chapter 1); my own Biblical annotations of that address were checked with a standard concordance to the King James Version.

William James's classic study *The Varieties of Religious Experience*—a work "too psychological to have shaped most religious inquiry and too religious to have influenced much psychological research," Martin Marty ironically notes, but nonetheless widely read for the past eighty years by "amateurs and experts on both sides of the psychology/religion fence"—has been reissued (New York: Penguin Books, 1982) with a provocative introduction by Marty. The quotation in this chapter from William McLoughlin leads off McLoughlin's essay on "Revivalism" in Edwin S. Gaustad, editor, *The Rise of Adventism: Religion and Society in Mid-Nineteenth Century America* (New York: Harper and Row, 1974). My own comment on the resemblance between the rhetoric of revivalism and that of militant political activism in the 1960s is based in part upon personal observation of, and participation in, political rallies triggered by the invasion of Cambodia in 1970 and the like. I have discussed the paradox of George McGovern's presidential candidacy in an essay "Of Towns and Roads, Three Novelists, and George McGovern," *Columbia Forum* 2 (Spring 1973), later reworked as the opening chapter in *Another Part of the Twenties* (New York: Columbia University Press, 1977).

The quotations from Henry Clay, William H. Seward, and John C. Calhoun on the legitimacy, or not, of political compromise may be found in Edwin C. Rozwenc, editor, *The Compromise of 1850*, as cited in chapter 3. Wendell Phillips made adroit use of James Russell Lowell's poem "The Present Crisis" in *The Scholar in a Republic* (1881); text available in Joseph L. Blau, editor, *American Philosophic Addresses*, as cited in chapters 3 and 5. For a different kind of use of the Lowell poem see *The Methodist Hymnal* (Nashville: Methodist Publishing House, 1966), no. 242. The Blau anthology contains also the address—shocking to traditional religionists—which the elder Oliver Wendell Holmes delivered to Harvard's Phi Beta Kappa society in 1870, "Mechanism in Thought and Morals."

The *Pensées* of Pascal—that "Gallic Faust," as a perceptive lecturer once called him—is cited here in the elegant translation by W. F. Trotter (New York: Modern Library, 1941). Vernon Louis Parrington's *Main Currents in American Thought*, which is cited also in chapters 1, 4, and 5, is a literary unfinished symphony. Truncated by its author's death but pieced out by his publishers with essays on then-contemporary novels, classroom lecture notes, and other such fragments, the third volume—though tantalizing in its incompleteness—remains fresh and deeply rewarding to the modern reader; and nowhere more so than in the few pages titled "The Darkening Skies of Letters," with which the actual manuscript ends. The bleak essay by Joseph Wood Krutch, "Love, or the Life and Death of a Value" in the *Atlantic Monthly* 142 (August 1928)—which Parrington may well have read—appeared as chapter 4 in Krutch, *The Modern Temper* (New York: Harcourt Brace, 1956 [first published in 1929)]—a book which I have found still speaks to the students' condition, even though Krutch himself in a new preface retreated from his former position ("I still describe but no longer accept") and despite all the torrents of historical and cultural change since 1929.

The disconcerting judgment that the simple magnet is no different in principle from the profound philosopher was included in John Trowbridge, "Notes by the Editor, on the Progress of Science in the Year 1869," *Annual of Scientific Discovery, or Year-Book of Facts in Science and Art* (Boston: Gould and Lincoln, 1870); excerpts reprinted in John C. Burnham, editor, *Science in America: Historical Selections* (New York: Holt, Rinehart, and Winston, 1971). The devastating lengths to which it is possible to go from that initial reductionist premise are illustrated in Patricia Smith Churchland, *Neurophilosophy: Toward a Unified Science of the Mind/ Brain* (Cambridge: MIT Press, 1986)—an important book which challenges anyone whose philosophy, psychology, theology, or scientific perspective is not out-and-out materialist. The argument is answerable, but it takes work. Churchland has read the history of philosophy since Descartes very selectively, picking out those strands which point toward her position in the present (as, sadly, do many professional philosophers themselves these days), and discarding everything else. Unless one sees this loading of the dice, however, her carefully, logically argued conclusions—reinforced by recent experimental work in the neurological laboratory—seem inescapable.

Emerson's essay *Fate* is in Stephen E. Whicher, editor, *Selections from Ralph Waldo Emerson*, also cited in chapters 5 and 6. Whicher is right, I believe, in considering this essay a crucial turning point in Emerson's life and thought, and also in arguing that *Fate* throws light on *all* of Emerson's much-misunderstood work; see Whicher, *Freedom and Fate* (Philadelphia: University of Pennsylvania Press, 1953). The quotation in this chapter from Harriet Beecher Stowe is from her regionalist novel *Oldtown Folks* (Boston: Fields, Osgood, and Co., 1869). On the transition between religious predestination and scientific determinism see further my discussion in *The Spiritual Crisis of the Gilded Age* (previously cited above in chapter 3), chapter 3. Chapter 2 in the same work cites the 1892 address by Rudolph Virchow that attacked Darwin's "missing link" between ape and man as "a phantom"; text of that lecture appeared in *Popular Science Monthly* 42 (January 1893), in translation from *Revue Scientifique*.

The essay by William James on "The Dilemma of Determinism," first delivered as an address in 1884, was selected by Ralph Barton Perry in 1942 for inclusion in James, *Essays on Faith and Morals*, previously cited in chapter 7. The same anthology also contains an essay by James that daringly bridges the gap between psychology and theology, "Reflex Action and Theism." Diary excerpts depicting James's personal existential crisis of 1870 are included in a judicious essay on William James by John J. McDermott in John J. Stuhr, editor, *Classical American Philosophy* (New York: Oxford University Press, 1987). James's *Pragmatism*, since its first publication in 1907, has been reprinted again and again; I used a paperback edition published in New York by Meridian Books (1955).

Two excellent biographies of scientists whose work would help to undermine the determinism that had given James such anxiety are Lynde Phelps Wheeler, *Josiah Willard Gibbs* (New Haven: Yale University Press, 1951) and Bernard Jaffe, *Michelson and the Speed of Light* (Garden City: Doubleday, 1960). Wheeler's book makes a valiant effort to bridge the "two cultures" gulf and explain to the layperson the mathematics that underlie physical chemistry. The continuing determinism in the social sciences after the natural sciences had begun to abandon it is well illustrated by William Graham Sumner's classic *Folkways* (Boston: Ginn and Company, 1906; I used a facsimile reprint, New York: Dover Publications, 1959). Stow Persons briefly but perceptively discussed the "nature-nurture" controversy in his excellent, now somewhat neglected, *American Minds* (New York: Henry Holt, 1958), chapter 14. That sharp high school student who succinctly summed up the issue between evolution and pragmatism was quoted in an article by Jane Erikson, "Committee seeks end to University High racial imbalance," *Arizona Daily Star*, April 1, 1987.

The statement that a value-free social science seemed to render impossible any moral justification for democracy appears in William Graebner, *The Engineering of Consent* (Madison: University of Wisconsin Press, 1987). Graebner's argument follows in large part from that of Edward A. Purcell, *The Crisis of Democratic Theory* (Lexington: University Press of Kentucky, 1973), but Graebner's conclusions are far more pessimistic than Purcell's. A fresh appraisal of John Dewey as a social philosopher occurs in Thomas Bender, *New York Intellect* (New York: Knopf, 1987), an appreciative but critical account of intellectual life in Gotham since 1750. George Dykhuizen, *The Life and Mind of John Dewey* (Carbondale: Southern Illinois University Press, 1973), although embarrassingly hagiographic at at times, reports the successive stages of Dewey's intellectual life with painstaking accuracy. Thoughtful commentary on John Dewey appears also in Martin E. Marty, *Modern American*

Religion, Volume 1, *The Irony Of It All* (Chicago: University of Chicago Press, 1986).

Timothy L. Smith, *Revivalism and Social Reform* (Nashville: Abingdon, 1957), is important for understanding the long-term historical context of William Jennings Bryan's religious politics. Also insightful in that connection is George Marsden, *Fundamentalism and American Culture* (New York: Oxford, 1980); and see also the chapter titled "The Protestant Majority as a Lost Generation" in R. Laurence Moore, *Religious Outsiders and the Making of Americans* (New York: Oxford, 1986). I have addressed some of these issues in "The Fundamentalist Defense of the Faith," a chapter in John Braeman et al, editors, *Change and Continuity in Twentieth-Century America: The 1920s* [Columbus:] Ohio State University Press, 1968.

William Jennings Bryan's Jeffersonian portrayal of the two perennial parties in every country, one of them trusting the people and the other mistrusting them, occurs in a rather striking setting: his book *In His Image* (New York: Fleming H. Revell, 1922), the primary purpose of which was to attack the evolutionary explanation of human origins and defend the literal Biblical account. Bryan's use of the term "moral majority," apropos of the Democratic Party's defeat in 1920, is quoted in Lawrence W. Levine, *Defender of the Faith* (New York: Oxford, 1965), a thorough study of Bryan's last ten years of life. Levine's judicious monograph ought to have—but has not—laid to rest the caricature of Bryan that had characterized both scholarly and popular writing about him ever since H. L. Mencken's spiteful obituary immediately following the Scopes Trial in 1925—a widely reprinted hatchet job which should only be read in the context of a far more fair-minded contemporary appraisal by "secular humanist" John Dewey, "The American Intellectual Frontier," *New Republic*, May 10, 1922. See also Robert A. Garson, "Political Fundamentalism and Popular Democracy in the 1920s," *South Atlantic Quarterly* 76 (Spring 1977).

Justice Scalia's dissenting opinion in *Edwards* v. *Aguillard*, a case cited also in chapter 6, may serve as a reprise, at a far higher intellectual level, on the issues raised by Bryan and Clarence Darrow in *Tennessee* v. *John Thomas Scopes*. A useful compendium of those issues, with generous excerpts from the trial transcript itself, is Sheldon N. Grebstein, editor, *Monkey Trial* (Boston: Houghton Mifflin, 1960). The liberal Protestant "social gospel" position on secular sociopolitical issues, with which (one must stress) Bryan was in total agreement, is authoritatively if somewhat minimally stated in the *Social Creed of the Churches* (1912); text is included in H. Shelton Smith, Robert T. Handy, and Leffers A. Loetscher, eds., *American Christianity* (as cited in chapter 3), vol. 2, Document 158. I have discussed the subsequent revision and updating of that statement in a more government-interventionist direction in *The Decline and Revival of the Social Gospel* (Ithaca: Cornell University Press, 1956), chapter 11.

An acute, highly perceptive essay on Jerry Falwell is Frances Fitzgerald, "A Disciplined, Changing Army," *New Yorker*, May 18, 1981; I drew upon its insights when writing an essay on Falwell for the *New Encyclopedia of World Biography* (New York: McGraw-Hill, 1987). Falwell—like Bryan!—has always worn his political heart on his sleeve, and his books, such as *America Can Be Saved* (Murfreesboro, Tennessee: Sword Of The Lord Publishers, 1979), and especially *Listen, America!* (Garden City: Doubleday, 1980) are frank and self-revelatory. A more philosophical objection than Falwell's to what has come to be termed "secular humanism" is Will Herberg, "What Is The Moral Crisis Of Our Age?", *Intercollegiate Review*, Fall 1986; see also the typically complacent *Time* essay, "A Letter to the Year 2086," *Time*, December 29, 1986. A forceful argument for a position diametrically the opposite of Falwell's is Adolph Grünbaum, "The Place of Secular Humanism in Current American Political Culture," *Vital Speeches*, 54 (November 1, 1987); "all too often," Grünbaum regretfully comments, "the level of public discourse in our country on philosophical issues of national importance is unjustifiably and painfully low."

The quickening of political concern and action among previously apolitical Fundamentalists is detailed in Robert Booth Fowler, *A New Engagement: Evangelical Political Thought, 1966–1976* (Grand Rapids: Erdmans, 1982); see also Martin E. Marty, *The Public Church* (New York: Crossroad, 1981). The testament of an evangelical activist who vigorously dissented from the political conservatism preached by people like Falwell, charging that they "actively promote the culture's worst values," is Jim Wallis, *The Call to Conversion* (San Francisco: Harper and Row, 1981). Senator George Mitchell's observation that "God does not take side in American politics" occurred during one of the 1987 Iran-Contra hearings telecasts, from which I took notes. I was personally present at the concert in Tucson, Arizona in 1985 at which Joan Baez played her Jerry Falwell card—a gesture which should not have surprised anyone familiar with Baez's Pentecostal church singing background, or with her knack for sensing what an audience was prepared to hear.

9. Imperial Rome and Progressive America

The quotation that opens the chapter is from the Introduction to H. Bruce Franklin, *Future Perfect* (New York: Oxford, 1978). America's move toward overseas involvement during the ostensibly isolationist Gilded Age received definitive treatment in Walter LaFeber, *The New Empire* (Ithaca: Cornell University Press, 1963); see especially chapter 2. Grover Cleveland's stinging rebuke to the Senate over the proposed Hawaii treaty of 1893 may be found in *Messages and Papers of the Presidents* (previously cited in Chapters 2, 4, 5, and 6) 8: 5892-5904; a document in striking contrast, in its candor, clarity, and bluntness, to more recent presidents' accounts of U.S. foreign policy actions.

The poem by Rudyard Kipling, "The White Man's Burden," is in most collections of Kipling's writings. The statement by Henry Watterson is quoted in David Noble's rather somber account of *The Progressive Mind*, rev. ed. (Minneapolis: Burgess Publishing Co., 1981); for context, see the biographical sketch of Watterson by Arthur Krock in *Dictionary of American Biography* (New York: Scribner's, 1935). Finley Peter Dunne's sarcastic "Mr. Dooley on the Pacification of the Philippines," which could have been taken as a rejoinder to Kipling, originally a newspaper column, was included in Dunne, *Observations by Mr. Dooley* (New York: Scribner's, 1902).

Dorr v. *United States*, 195 U.S. 138, is one of many landmark decisions reprinted in Noel Dowling, *Cases on Constitutional Law*, 5th ed. (Brooklyn: Foundation Press, 1954). William Graham Sumner's biting essay "The Conquest of the United States by Spain," originally written as an immediate reaction to the Spanish-American War, was reprinted in *The Conquest of the United States by Spain and Other Essays* (Chicago: Regnery, 1965). C. F. Adams's reply to Carl Schurz, that "our emperor is here now and we call him 'boss,'" was quoted in Robert L. Beisner, *Twelve Against Empire* (New York: McGraw-Hill, 1968). Richard Croker's rejoinder that bossism performed the service of engrafting new citizens upon the Republic was quoted in Arthur Mann, "When Tammany Was Supreme," a new introduction to William L. Riordon, ed., *Plunkitt of Tammany*

Hall (New York: Dutton, 1963; originally published in 1905). The friendly inscription from Kaiser Wilhelm II to his supposed American opposite number was reported in Henry F. Pringle, *Theodore Roosevelt* (New York: Harcourt, Brace, 1956 [1931]).

Guglielmo Ferrero's Lowell Lectures of 1908 were published as *Characters and Events of Roman History from Caesar to Nero* (New York: G. Putnam, 1909). See also the Preface to the American edition of Ferrero's multi-volume *Greatness and Decline of Rome* (New York: Putnam, 1907–9), and his evaluation of America in *Europe's Fateful Hour* (New York: Dodd, Mead, 1918). Ferrero's interpretation of a passage from Horace as showing anti-technological bias may not be accurate; the poet could have been *praising* the impious ships that cross the god-forbidden ocean, *Star Trek* style. See the standard Loeb Classics edition, *Horace: The Odes and Epodes*, tr. by C. E. Bennett (London: William Heinemann, 1960), Book I, Ode III. H. G. Wells reported his colloquy with Theodore Roosevelt in *The Future in America* (New York: Arno Press, 1974; first published in 1906 by Harper's). Richard Hofstadter's quip about Roosevelt occurs in *The Age of Reform*, previously cited in chapter 8. The Rossevelt chants at the 1912 Progressive national convention, and TR's reaction to them, are described in George E. Mowry, *Theodore Roosevelt and the Progressive Movement* (Madison: University of Wisconsin Press, 1946), citing reports in the *Chicago Tribune* and *New York Times*. Herbert Hadley, who had been the respected floor leader for the Roosevelt forces at the 1912 Republican national convention, updated Ferrero's argument in a noteworthy comparative study, *Rome and the World Today* (New York: Putnam, 1922).

The first Roosevelt's own conception of the nature of presidential leadership emerges clearly and eloquently from his address to the Progressive nominating convention on August 6, 1912, as quoted in the essay by George Mowry in Arthur M. Schlesinger, Jr. and Fred L. Israel, editors, *History of American Presidential Elections*, previously cited in chapter 4. This may be compared and contrasted with the Woodrow Wilson quotations in Ralph E. Ketcham, *Presidents Above Party* (previously cited in chapter 2), Chapter 11.

Stephen Kern, *The Culture of Time and Space*, previously cited in chapter 5, winds up its general argument with a specific application to World War I, in a chapter Kern titled "The Cubist War." For H. G. Wells's *Outline of History* I used the third American edition (New York: Macmillan; published for the Review of Reviews, 1921). The other Wells quotations in this section are from *The Shape of Things to Come* (New York: Macmillan, 1933), an extrapolative history of the *next* two hundred years. At times solemnly parodying the style of historical texts of the kind actually assigned to students in Wells's day (and, alas, in ours), Wells in retrospect clearly missed the mark in many of his specific prophecies; nevertheless it is quite astonishing how often his forecasts went straight to their target. Information on the Taiping Rebellion, or as the Chinese now prefer to call it, the Taiping *Revolution*, may be found in Tung Chi-Ming, *An Outline History of China* (Beijing: Foreign Languages Press, 1959)—making due allowances for the political emphases of any book published in China at that time.

John Dewey's rueful comment on how and why the comfortable middle classes failed to foresee the coming disaster of World War I, and his caution against America's becoming involved in World War II, may be found in George Dykhuizen, *The Life and Mind of John Dewey*, previously cited in chapter 8. H. Stuart Hughes has written a brief, thoughtful critique of *Oswald Spengler* (New York: Scribner's, 1952). The quotations from Brooks Adams, *The New Empire* (1902) and *The Theory of Social Revolutions* (1913), may be found in Perry Miller, ed., *American Thought: Civil War to World War I*, previously cited in chapters 1 and 6.

Frank Frost Abbott, *Roman Politics* (Boston: Marshall Jones, 1923), a still useful study, contains several references to Benito Mussolini's then-recent march on Rome. Far more reckless is an article of the "he should have known better" variety, W. Y. Elliott, "Mussolini, Prophet of the Pragmatic Era in Politics," *Political Science Quarterly* 41 (June 1926). More critical, but still respectful, is F. H. Simonds, "Benito Africanus," *Atlantic Monthly* 56 (November 1935). John Buchan's fine biography *Augustus* (Boston: Houghton Mifflin, 1937) was written, as its closing pages make pointedly clear, in full consciousness of the painful contrast between Octavian and his two-millennia-displaced self-proclaimed heir. Even more biting in its assessment of Mussolini, comparing his imperial war in Africa to the action of "a bankrupt businessman who takes his last resources and plays them on a number in Monte Carlo," is George Seldes, *Sawdust Caesar* (New York: Harper, 1935).

Dated somewhat by subsequent scholarship and by its emigre author's anti-Marxist elitism, Michael Rostovtzeff's *Social and Economic History of the Roman Empire* (Oxford: at the Clarendon

Press, 1926)—written with a clarity and grace quite unusual in the ponderous realm of classical scholarship—must still be reckoned with. Aiming at a wider, nonacademic audience, Will and Ariel Durant in *Caesar and Christ*, Volume 3 of their encyclopedic *Story of Civilization* (New York: Simon and Schuster, 1935) reflect many of Rostovtzeff's concerns. I am indebted to Professor Sidney E. Mead for reminding me how much the Durants in that widely read book implicitly accepted "the idea of inevitable, inexorable movement through democracy, oligarchy, dictatorship, monarchy, etc." (Mead to this writer, May 30, 1985).

Anne Morrow Lindbergh, *The Wave of the Future* (New York: Harcourt, Brace, 1940), is representative of the widespread pessimism about the prospective fate of the Western democracies which made Hitler's task much easier at the outset. Franklin Roosevelt's First Inaugural Address is as quoted in chapter 8. H. P. Lovecraft's arch comparison of FDR with Octavian—"ol' Gus"!—occurs in a letter of August, 1936 to Catherine L. Moore, with whom Lovecraft platonically but passionately argued politics during his last months of life; in August Derleth and James Turner, editors, *H. P. Lovecraft: Selected Letters 1934–1937* (Sauk City, Wisconsin: Arkham House, 1976).

Henry A. Wallace, *New Frontiers* (New York: Reynal & Hitchcock, 1934) is an eloquent apologia for the New Deal; would that Roosevelt's and Wallace's lightweight political epigoni in 1988 could have put their cases so articulately and to the point! H. J. Haskell, *The New Deal in Old Rome* (New York: Knopf, 2nd rev. ed., 1947), details some suggestive parallels. The scare headline "Willkie Predicts Dictatorship Here" appeared in the *New York Times*, September 17, 1940; the speech was—perhaps appropriately—delivered in Coffeyville, Kansas. The sad abdication of France's constitutional government in 1940 is chronicled in William L. Shirer, *The Collapse of the Third Republic* (New York: Simon & Schuster, 1969)—a significantly better book historically, by the way, than Shirer's far more widely read *Rise and Fall of the Third Reich*.

Charles Beard's double judgment on the Roosevelt Administration—admiration for its transvaluation of American values, from "rugged" individualism to what he termed "humanistic democracy," coupled with misgivings about its drive toward what he thought of as international adventurism—can be assessed from Charles A. Beard and Mary R. Beard, *America in Midpassage* (Gloucester, Mass.: Peter Smith, 1966 [first published in 1939]), chapters 17 and 10. *America in Midpassage* is one of those "forgotten classics" of American historical writing; the kind people haven't time to read. They ought to; its 949 pages are no more than many an ephemeral best-seller blockbuster contains, and they are a good deal more interesting.

10. *World Revolution/Empire/Community*

I became conscious of the continuing germaneness of Wendell Willkie's long out-of-print *One World* (New York: Simon & Schuster, 1943) when using it in the classroom during the sixties; it spoke loud and clear to the condition of the era's radicalized students— more so in the long run, I venture to say, than their then-voguish *Sayings of Chairman Mao.* Of the New Left historiography produced in that same turbulent time, the most lasting has been the revolution in the study and teaching of diplomatic history; since the work of William Appleman Williams and three successive generations (of his graduate students, their students, and their students' students) it has simply become impossible for us to look at the history of American foreign policy in the old way again. Williams's *The Tragedy of American Diplomacy* (New York: Dell, 2nd rev. ed., 1972) is an outstanding example of this New Left scholarship, together with Walter LaFeber, *The New Empire*, previously cited in chapter 9. The sort of thing Williams and LaFeber—and, for that matter, Wendell Willkie—were complaining about in American attitudes toward "foreigners" is exemplified in Carl Crow, *Four Hundred Million Customers* (New York: Harper, 10th ed., 1937). I have discussed Adlai Stevenson's reprise on Willkie—go around the world and write a book about it—in *Another Part of the Fifties* (New York: Columbia University Press, 1983). The Godkin lectures, which were Stevenson's equivalent, more or less, of *One World*, were published as *A Call to Greatness* (New York: Harper, 1954).

Daniel Boorstin, *The Lost World of Thomas Jefferson* (Boston: Beacon Press, 1948; New York: Holt, 1948) throws light on the intellectual dilemma described by Edward Purcell in *The Crisis of Democratic Theory* (previously cited in chapter 8)—namely, the loss through the relativizing tendency of the social sciences of any axiomatic or moral rationale for democracy. Boorstin's work also exemplifies the solution which many intellectuals found to resolve that dilemma—namely, to state that the nonideological nature of democracy *is* its ideology. That this solution did not get them all the way out of the woods in shown by the fact that Boorstin later on became a prime mover in the historiographic tendency among American historians—admired in the 1950s, reviled in the 1960s —usually known, not quite accurately, as the "consensus school."

Jeanine Basinger, *The World War II Combat Film* (New York: Columbia University Press, 1986; paperback reprint, 1988) has the rare virtue of being both lively and analytical, and it utterly eschews the pretension that has lately crept into film criticism (always "film," in the singular, never "movies"). John Dewey's Columbia University lecture of 1908, "Intelligence and Morals," epitomizes much that is perennial in Dewey's social thought; it and another major Dewey essay, "The Influence of Darwinism on Philosophy," are included in Perry Miller, ed., *American Thought: Civil War to World War I*, previously cited in chapters 1 and 6. Reinhold Niebuhr, *The Irony of American History* (New York: Scribner's, 1952), and other works by this leading theologian-activist are discussed and quoted in Edward Purcell's *Crisis of Democratic Theory*, cited above. It is worth pointing out here that although Niebuhr in some of his writings espoused *Jamesian* pragmatism, he quite explicitly rejected Dewey; see Niebuhr, *Moral Man and Immoral Society* (New York: Scribner's, paper, 1960; first published in 1932), especially the introduction. A powerful, reasoned polemic underscoring one of Dewey's main points, that philosophical absolutism logically implies political absolutism—particularly with reference to Plato's much over-admired *Republic!*— is Karl S. Popper, *The Open Society and its Enemies* (London: Routledge, 1947), especially chapters 6 and 10.

A brief, still useful account of the origins of America's "Open Door" policy toward China is in George Kennan, *American Diplomacy* (New York: New American Library, 1952), chapters 2 and 3; its conclusions on that point are not so inconsistent with those of "New Left" historians, such as Williams, previously cited, as one might expect. (Surely rational leftists and non-leftists can agree with Kennan's epigram: "A nation which excuses its own failures by the sacred untouchableness of its own habits can excuse itself into complete disaster.")

Margaret Truman reports her father's imminent expectation of war in 1948 in her book *Harry S. Truman* (New York: William Morrow, 1973)—needless to say a highly uncritical source, but also one which reveals a side of Truman worth remembering: his absolute frankness and candor with his daughter in discussing politics and world affairs, treating her even in early-teen years the way one would a respected and trusted adult. An early, still useful account of the origins of the "military-industrial complex" is Bruce Catton's first book, *The War Lords of Washington* (New York: Harcourt, Brace, 1948). A discussion of the changing status of the military in American life from a sociologist's point of view is C. Wright Mills, *The Power Elite* (New York: Oxford, 1956), chapters 8 and 9. Lincoln's prophetic warning of the power of a president "to make war at pleasure" is quoted in Carl Sandburg, *Abraham Lincoln: The Prairie Years*, (previously cited in chapters 3 and 4), 1:371.

Arnold Toynbee's comment on the Marshall Plan and related initiatives is in *Civilization on Trial* (New York: Oxford University Press, 1948); his warning against taking Greco-Roman history as a "horoscope" for our own is in *The World and the West* (New York: Oxford, 1953). The classical historians, who officially viewed the Principate of Augustus as a triumphant march onward and upward forever, were embarrassed to say the least by the rout of the Roman legions in Germany's Teutoburg Forest under P. Quintilius Varo in 9 A.D.; Tacitus (*Annales* I, 60), may be the best of several biased accounts. A vivid modern description of the disaster is in John Buchan, *Augustus*, previously cited in chapter 9. Arthur Ekirch, in *The Decline of American Liberalism* (New York: Longmans, Green, 1955) quoted effectively from the Roman historian Chester G. Starr, "The Perfect Democracy of the Roman Empire," *American Historical Review* 58 (October 1952). Other Romanists who commented on contemporary affairs from the context of antiquity, and vice versa, included Kenneth D. White, "Roman Economic Problems and Current Issues," *Classical Journal* 53 (March 1958), and Frank C. Bourne, "Reflections on Rome's Urban Problems," *Classical World* 62 (February 1969).

I have discussed the literature of social criticism during the 1950s in *Another Part of the Fifties*, as cited above, especially chapter 6. An example of this criticism is the concluding chapter in Ray Ginger, *Altgeld's America* (New York: Funk & Wagnalls, 1958), which uses the Chicago of the 1890s as a microcosm for the Republic as a whole—a refreshing choice, in contrast to the usual New York/New England focus of such inquiries. That book followed by a decade Ginger's definitive biography of Eugene Debs, *The Bending*

Cross, previously cited in chapter 8, the implications of which seem to me far more optimistic than the Altgeld book's hortatory conclusion. I have studiously avoided quoting from the mostly ephemeral gurus of the 1960s; for a devastating analysis of one of them, see the essay by Lewis Mumford in *The Pentagon of Power* (New York: Harcourt Brace Jovanovich, 1970), chapter 10, part 6: "Electronic Entropy."

A wise, sensible essay on the subject usually stereotyped as "ethnicity" is Arthur Mann, *The One and the Many* (Chicago: University of Chicago Press, 1979). Professor Mann shares with some top-notch athletes the gift of "making it look easy," so don't be put off by the book's brevity or by its clear, eloquent prose; its scholarship is profound. The lively 1971 spring meeting of the American Society of Church History, which I attended with several of my students, produced a discussion of "counterculture" in early phases of religious history that was exciting and provocative, even if it violated the former unbreakable axiom in graduate history programs that one must avoid at all costs being "present-minded." In this case, for example, it was most illuminating to think of that vehement early church father Tertullian not simply as the old reactionary modern scholars usually picture him to have been, but also as a counterculturalist against all the traits that secular Roman culture had considered virtues. By the time that session took place Arnold Toynbee's *A Study of History*, with its discussion of the secession of the "internal proletariat" from a society which has lost their allegiance, had been around for quite some while; volumes 1–3 since 1933, volumes 4–6 since 1939, a widely read abridgement since 1947, volumes 7–10 since 1954 (all from Oxford University Press)—but the events of the 1960s in America and in the rest of the Western world gave new plausibility to such Toynbeean concepts as "Schism in the Body Social" and "Schism in the Soul."

Arthur Schlesinger, Jr., *The Imperial Presidency* (Boston: Houghton Mifflin, 1973), may have been outdated for its own immediate purpose by the resignation of Richard Nixon, but its wit and erudition, ranging back to the Washington Administration for examples of its point, make it of lasting historical value. Robert Heilbroner, *An Inquiry Into the Human Prospect, Undated and Reconsidered for the 1980s* (New York: Norton, 1980) invites comparison with an earlier version of the same work, published in 1974. A savage essay written as the first of the "baby boom" generation turned 40, by a writer who had just turned 21, is Julie Phillips, "Get Real, Boomers," *Tucson Weekly* 4 (November 25, 1987). Evidently generation gaps are self-replicating: "It's not the baby boom that's going to fight the next war," Phillips writes; "it's more likely that the baby boom will start it."

Alan Wolfe, "Presidential Power and the Crisis of Modernization," *democracy* 1 (April 1981), is the best of several articles in that same issue of this lively journal assessing "Democracy's State" as the Reagan era opened. David Stockman's *The Triumph of Politics: Why the Reagan Revolution Failed* (New York: Harper and Row, 1986), making due allowance for its author's biases, both personal and ideological, is insightful and highly informative. Another disillusioned ideologue's philippic is Patrick J. Buchanan, "The Decline of Ronald Reagan," originally distributed through [Chicago] Tribune News Services, which I found the *Arizona Daily Star*, November 15, 1987. The *Star* also picked up Franz Schurmann's Constitution Bicentennial Lament, "U.S. is more like Rome all the time": *ibid.*, October 8, 1987. The passage beginning "Right now we're sitting in the Circus Maximus" occurred in a public lecture delivered by William Kunstler, who had been legal counsel to the "Chicago Seven" and champion of other radical causes in the sixties, at the University of Montana, Missoula, October 24, 1979.

Robert Jungk has written engagingly of the early, peaceful, internationally cooperative years of nuclear research in *Brighter Than A Thousand Suns* (New York: Harcourt, Brace, 1956), chapters 1 and 2. The atom-bomb quote from Vernadskii ocurs in a brief biographical sketch by A. P. Vinogradov, "The Scientific Legacy of V. I. Vernadskii." This essay introduced a two-volume *festschrift* honoring the centenary of Vernadskii's birth, *Chemistry of the Earth's Crust* (Jerusalem: Israel Program for Scientific Translations, 1966; translated from a Russian-language edition published by the Academy of Sciences of the USSR [Moscow, 1963]). The monographs which follow that introduction are replete with openers on the order of "The vast scientific legacy left to us by V. I. Vernadskii," "V. I. Vernadskii constantly stressed," "V. I. Vernadskii's profound scientific intuition," "Vernadskii . . . showed great foresight in indicating the fields calling for the closest attention," etc. It is hard to imagine any scientist in the West, even Einstein, getting quite that treatment; there is a problem here in the history and sociology of science that would be well worth exploring. The article titled "Biosphere," by V. A. Kovda and A. N. Tiuriukanin, *Great So-*

viet Encyclopedia (New York: Macmillan, 1973; translated from the third edition of *Bol'shaia Sovetskaia Entskilopediia,* Moscow, 1970), indicates how far Vernadskii's hypotheses have come to be accepted as official doctrine in that country.

I have written on Barry Commoner for the *New Encyclopedia of World Biography,* previously cited in chapter 8. Anne Chisholm discusses Commoner, together with other outstanding figures in the modern environmental movement—among them René Dubos, Lewis Mumford, F. Fraser Darling, and Paul Ehrlich—in an informative account, *Philosophers of the Earth* (New York: Dutton, 1972). Commoner's own books include *Science and Survival* (New York: Viking, 1966), *The Closing Circle* (New York: Knopf, 1971), and *The Politics of Energy* (New York: Knopf, 1979). An approach to the biosphere which sharply departs from Vernadskii's and to some extent from Commoner's prescriptive political conclusions is J. E. Lovelock, *Gaia: A New Look At Life on Earth* (New York: Oxford, 1979). My comments on the contrast between the American and Soviet exhibits at the Spokane Expo of 1974 are based on personal attendance. Ann Zwinger's warning lest environmentalists alienate the people they most need to convert—"Joe Sixpack is not stupid"— occurs in her delightful essay "Writers of the Purple Figwort," which she delivered with verve at a conference on Southwestern writing held in Tucson, November 14–17, 1985. My notes captured a few ad libs which did not get recorded in the formal conference proceedings: *Old Southwest/New Southwest,* Judy Lensink, editor (Tucson: Tucson Public Library, 1987).

Jonathan Schell, *The Fate of the Earth* (New York: Knopf, 1982), although somewhat overdrawn—he jumped to conclusions about "nuclear winter," for example, which have not checked out—is "must" reading for its unflinching exploration of the metaphysical meaning of total annihilation; prolonged public consciousness of that prospect without hope of abatement by disarmament, Schell argued, could be nearly as psychologically and socially destructive as nuclear war itself. A thoughtful, deceptively quiet study of certain other issues pertinent to this chapter is Langdon Winner, *The Whale and the Reactor* (Chicago: University of Chicago Press, 1986); particularly chapter 7, "The State of Nature Revisited," which details what happened to the ecological movement when it began to confuse prescription with description in the same logically entrapped way as did the social scientists whose dilemma Edward Purcell detailed in *The Crisis of Democratic Theory* (chapter 9).

Stewart Udall, *The Quiet Crisis* (New York: Holt-Rinehart-Winston, 1963) was reconsidered by its author and his Congressman brother Morris at a National Resources Policy Forum held at the University of Arizona on April 13, 1987. My comment on that symposium is based upon my own notes, which caught a few things the subsequent newspaper account missed; but see Keith Bagwell, "Udalls prod environmentalists to tackle growth, water issues," *Arizona Daily Star*, April 14, 1987. Hitler's epigram that it is fortunate for those in power that people do not think was quoted in Carl Sagan, "The Common Enemy," *Parade*, February 7, 1988. The remark by Ray Bradbury about our life now being on Mars was reported in *Time*, August 2, 1976. The false forced choice some publicists proclaim, that one may have environmental protection OR a space program but not both, I have explored somewhat in *The Creation of Tomorrow* (New York: Columbia University Press, 1977), especially in the concluding chapter; science fiction also, consciously and unconsciously, involves an issue as between surrender to and revolt against destiny.

Afterword

The protest against a notion that the U.S. is somehow "due" for a major war occurs in an eloquent editorial by Robert Carter, "Newly-registered teen hopes war fear will make peace last," *Tucson Citizen*, December 2, 1986. I used a paperback edition of Jacques Barzun's essay *Classic, Romantic, and Modern* (Garden City: Doubleday, 1961).

INDEX